VR Programming with Unity and Oculus

Maxwell Vector

Contents

1 Foundations of VR Software Architecture in Unity 18

Architectural Paradigms in Virtual Reality Applications 18

Component-Based Design in Unity 18

Modularity in Immersive Environments 19

The Runtime Environment and
Event-Driven Messaging 19

Real-Time Constraints and Performance Considerations 20

C# Code Snippet 20

2 Unity VR Workflow: Exploring the Editor for Immersive Development 25

Project Navigation and Asset Management 25

Scene Organization and Hierarchical Structuring . . 26

Tool Utilization in the Unity Editor 26

C# Code Snippet 27

3 Organizing VR Scenes: Scene Hierarchy and Asset Management 31

Fundamental Principles of Scene Graph Construction 31

Asset Management Paradigms in Virtual Environments 32

Integration of Scene Hierarchy and Asset Management 32

Considerations for Scalability and Maintainability . 33

C# Code Snippet 34

4 Implementing VR GameObjects and Components 39

Conceptual Framework of VR GameObjects 39

Component-Based Architecture and Modular Design 40

1

Management of Interactivity and Dynamic Behavior   40

Architectural Considerations and Performance Optimization 41

C# Code Snippet 41

5   Scripting Fundamentals for VR Interactions in Unity   47

Preliminary Overview of the Scripting Environment   47

Core Programming Constructs and Control Structures   47

Event-Driven Programming and Interaction Handling   48

Architectural Patterns for Modularity and Reusability   48

Timing, Optimization, and Real-Time Considerations   49

Integration and Coordination of Multi-Component Systems 49

C# Code Snippet 50

6   Utilizing the Oculus Integration Package   54

Architectural Overview of the Oculus Integration Package 54

Examination of Oculus-Specific Libraries and Interfaces 54

Leveraging Asset Integration and Utility Tools   . . .   55

Dynamic Integration of Hardware-Specific Capabilities   55

Methodological Considerations in Oculus Integration   56

C# Code Snippet 56

7   Configuring the VR Camera Rig in Unity   60

Architectural Overview of the VR Camera Rig   . . .   60

Stereo Rendering and Projection Matrix Configuration   60

Ensuring Proper Alignment for Head Tracking   . . .   61

Rig Calibration and Integration with
Unity's Rendering Pipeline   62

C# Code Snippet 62

8   Implementing Head Tracking and Player Orientation   66

Foundations of Head Tracking in Immersive Systems   66

Coordinate Transformations and Spatial Alignment .   67

Quaternion-Based Orientation Representation   67

Sensor Fusion and Noise Mitigation   68

Mapping Head Movements to Virtual Camera Dynamics 68

C# Code Snippet 68

9 VR Controller Input Mapping with Oculus   **72**

    Oculus Controller Input Architecture 72

    Unity Input System Abstractions 73

    Integrating Oculus APIs for Input Acquisition 73

    Mapping Controller Signals to In-Game Actions . . . 74

    C# Code Snippet 74

10 Processing Hand Gesture Inputs for VR   **79**

    Sensor Modalities for Hand Gesture Capture 79

    Preprocessing and Feature Extraction 79

    1   Temporal Signal Filtering and Noise Reduction 80

    2   Spatial Feature Extraction and Kinematic Modeling 80

    Gesture Segmentation and Classification 80

    1   Temporal Segmentation and Feature Vector Assembly 81

    2   Classification Algorithms and Decision Boundaries 81

    Mapping Gesture Inputs to Virtual Interactions . . . 81

    C# Code Snippet 82

11 Creating Interactive VR Objects Using Physics   **88**

    Foundations of Physics Simulation in VR Environments 88

    1   Discrete Time Integration and Rigid Body Dynamics 89

    Physical Material Properties and Dynamics 89

    1   Material Coefficients and Frictional Interfaces 89

    Collision Detection and Contact Mechanics 90

    1   Bounding Volumes and Contact Resolution . 90

    Environmental Forces and Interactive Dynamics . . 90

    1   Superposition of Forces and Impulse Applications 91

    Integration of Physics with User-Driven Interactions 91

    1   Impulse Forces and Kinematic Constraints . . 91

    C# Code Snippet 92

12 Designing Immersive Environments with Spatial Layouts   **96**

    Foundations of Spatial Perception and Environmental Coherence 96

    Hierarchical Organization of Environmental Elements 97

Integration of Scale, Proportion, and Depth 97
Contextual Cues and Zonal Delineation 97
Mathematical Modelling of Spatial Layouts 98
C# Code Snippet 98

13 Techniques for Natural User Interfaces in VR   103
Foundations of Natural Interface Design 103
Integration of Multimodal Interaction and Sensor
Fusion 104
Spatial Embedding and Context-Aware Interface Com-
ponents 104
Dynamic Adaptation and Real-Time
Feedback Mechanisms 105
Quantitative Metrics and Evaluative
Methodologies 105
C# Code Snippet 106

14 Building 3D User Interfaces for Virtual Reality   109
Foundational Concepts in
Three-Dimensional Interface Design 109
Spatial Embedding and Geometric Transformations . 110
Contextual Coherence and Usability Considerations   110
Cognitive and Perceptual Dimensions of 3D User In-
terfaces 111
Advanced Interaction Models and Spatial Mapping
Techniques 111
C# Code Snippet 112

15 Implementing VR Menus and HUD Elements   116
Design Rationale and Aesthetic Considerations . . . 116
Architectural Integration in Virtual Reality Appli-
cations 117
Visual Clarity and Cognitive Load Minimization . . 117
Spatial Placement and Dynamic Interaction Models   118
C# Code Snippet 119

**16 Scripting 3D Interactions: Raycasting and Object
Selection   122**
Raycasting Fundamentals in
Three-Dimensional Environments 122
Geometric Intersection and Analytical Approaches . 123

4

Selection Mechanics for Interactive Object Manipulation 123
Performance and Responsiveness in Raycasting Operations 124
C# Code Snippet 124

17 Implementing Grab-and-Release Mechanics in VR 129
Modeling Interaction Forces and
Constraints 129
Designing the Object State Machine for Interaction . 130
Implementation of Natural Object Manipulation in
Virtual Environments 130
Handling Release Dynamics and Residual Motion . . 131
C# Code Snippet 131

18 Designing Teleportation Locomotion for VR   135
Foundations and Theoretical Rationale 135
1   Physical and Cognitive Constraints in VR
        Locomotion 135
2   Biomechanical Considerations and Spatial Orientation 136
Mathematical and Algorithmic Modeling of Teleportation 137
1   Mathematical Representation of Discrete Spatial Transitions 137
2   Algorithmic Strategies for Teleportation Point
        Selection 137
Design Practices to Mitigate Motion Sickness 138
1   Visual Transition Techniques and Perceptual
        Continuity 138
2   Spatial Orientation and Feedback Mechanisms 139
3   Parameter Tuning and Safety Criteria 139
C# Code Snippet 139

19 Scripting Smooth Locomotion in Virtual Space   144
Theoretical Foundations of Continuous Motion . . . 144
Mathematical Modeling of Trajectory
Smoothness 144
Algorithmic Implementation of Interpolated Movement 145
Ergonomic Considerations and Real-Time Filtering . 146
C# Code Snippet 146

20 Implementing VR Snap Turning Mechanics   151
    Conceptual Framework of Snap Turning 151
    Mathematical Modeling of Discrete Rotations 151
    Architectural Considerations in Snap Turning Implementation 152
    Ergonomic and Usability Analysis of Discrete Turning 153
    C# Code Snippet 153

21 Using VR Input Event Systems for Interaction   156
    Architectural Foundations of Event-Driven Interaction 156
    Event Propagation and Handling in Virtual Reality . 156
    Integration of the Event System with Interactive Components 157
    Temporal Dynamics and Synchronization of Input Events 157
    Enhancing Responsiveness through Event Prioritization 158
    C# Code Snippet 159

22 Scripting Object Manipulation and Transformation 164
    Mathematical Foundations of Object Transformations 164
    Translation 165
    Rotation 165
    Scaling 165
    Composite Transformations and Their Order 166
    Dynamic Object Manipulation in Virtual Reality . . 166
    C# Code Snippet 167

23 Adding Physics-Based Interactions to VR Objects 171
    Newtonian Dynamics and Equations of Motion . . . 171
    1   Newtonian Mechanics in Virtual Environments 172
    2   Impulse and Momentum Conservation 172
    Collision Detection and Response Mechanisms 172
    1   Geometric Collision Detection 173
    2   Collision Response and Restitution Models . 173
    Force Fields, Constraints, and Energy Dissipation . . 173
    1   Force Field Modeling and Constraints 174
    2   Energy Dissipation and Stability Considerations 174
    Numerical Integration and Stabilization Techniques . 174
    1   Temporal Discretization Methods 175
    2   Adaptive Integration and Error Control . . . 175

C# Code Snippet 175

24 Implementing Collision Detection in VR Scenes   180
Mathematical Foundations of Collision Detection . . 180
Spatial Partitioning and Hierarchical Techniques . . 181
Temporal Coherence and Robustness in Dynamic
Environments 182
C# Code Snippet 183

25 Integrating Audio Spatialization in VR   187
Foundations of Audio Spatialization 187
Mathematical Modeling of Sound Propagation 187
Spatial Audio Implementation in Unity 188
Layered Dynamic Sound Environments 189
C# Code Snippet 189

26 Creating Immersive Spatial Soundscapes   193
Theoretical Foundations of Spatial Audio 193
Directional Sound Design 193
Ambient Sound Formation in Virtual Environments 194
Integration Strategies and Spatial Cohesion 194
C# Code Snippet 195

27 Scripting Environmental Sound Triggers for VR   198
Acoustic and Computational Foundations 198
Event Detection and Classification in Virtual Envi-
ronments 199
Real-Time Audio Feedback Mechanisms 199
Temporal and Spatial Considerations in Sound Trig-
gering 200
C# Code Snippet 200

28 Implementing 3D Positional Audio with Oculus   204
Architectural Foundations and Integration Strategy . 204
Mathematical Modeling of Spatial Audio Cues . . . 205
Signal Processing and Positional Audio Rendering . 205
Performance Optimization and System Synchroniza-
tion 206
C# Code Snippet 206

29 Creating Realistic Lighting in VR Environments 210

    Directional Lighting Techniques 210

    Point Lighting Configurations 211

    Ambient Illumination Considerations 211

    C# Code Snippet 212

30 Working with Lightmapping for VR 216

    Theoretical Underpinnings of Lightmapping 216

    Techniques for UV Unwrapping and

    Lightmap Baking 217

    Baked Lighting Integration in VR Rendering Pipelines217

    Performance Optimization and Visual Fidelity in Lightmap-

    ping 218

    C# Code Snippet 218

31 Optimizing Scene Lighting for Immersion 222

    Challenges in VR Lighting Optimization 222

    Techniques for Enhanced Visual Fidelity 222

    Optimization Strategies in Rendering Architectures . 223

    Balancing Computational Load through Hybrid Light-

    ing Schemes 223

    C# Code Snippet 224

32 Implementing Shadow Effects in Virtual Reality 229

    Mathematical Foundations of Shadow Computation

    in VR 229

    Dynamic Shadow Generation Techniques 230

    Enhancing Depth Perception Through

    Shadow Cues 230

    Optimization Strategies and Performance Consider-

    ations 231

    C# Code Snippet 232

33 Creating Custom Shaders for VR Immersion 236

    Fundamentals of Shader Development in Unity . . . 236

    Mathematical Foundations of Shader Computations 237

    Physically Based Material Representation and Light

    Interaction 237

    Integration of Custom Shaders in the VR Rendering

    Pipeline 238

    Performance Considerations in Custom

    Shader Implementation 238

C# Code Snippet 239

34 Scripting Post-Processing Effects for VR   **243**
    Bloom: Dynamic Luminance Enhancement 243
    Depth of Field: Simulating Optical Focus 244
    Color Grading: Tonal Harmonization in VR 244
    Mathematical Modeling of Post-Processing Effects . 245
    Optimization Strategies for VR
    Post-Processing 245
    C# Code Snippet 246
    Summary 249

35 Integrating Particle Systems in VR Scenes   **250**
    Theoretical Framework of Particle Systems 250
    Architectural Integration in Virtual Reality Envi-
    ronments 251
    Mathematical Modeling and Simulation Dynamics . 251
    Visual and Atmospheric Enhancement
    Techniques 252
    Performance Optimizations and Computational Con-
    straints 252
    C# Code Snippet 253

36 Scripting Environmental Effects: Fog, Rain, and Fire   **258**
    Fog Simulation: Physical and Optical Considerations 258
    Rain Dynamics and Simulation 259
    Fire Simulation: Combustion Dynamics and Visual
    Effects 260
    Synthesis and Integration of Atmospheric Effects . . 260
    C# Code Snippet 261

37 Animating VR Characters and Objects   **267**
    Overview of VR Animation Systems 267
    Skeletal Animation Techniques for Avatars 267
    Procedural Animation for Inanimate Objects 268
    Animation Blending and Transitioning 269
    Inverse Kinematics for Realistic Motion 269
    C# Code Snippet 270

38 Developing Dynamic Animation Controllers for VR 276

    Architectural Foundations of Dynamic Controllers . 276

    Integration of Player Interaction Data 277

    Interpolation and Transition Dynamics 277

    Context-Sensitive State Management 278

    Mathematical Modeling and Controller Calibration . 278

    C# Code Snippet 279

39 Scripting Physics-Based Animations in Unity VR 285

    Foundational Concepts in Physics-Driven Animation 285

    Integration of Physics Simulation with Animation

    Systems 286

    1   Modeling Reactive Dynamics 286

    2   Temporal Coherence and Numerical Stability 287

    Physical Constraints and Energy Minimization in

    Animation Blending 287

    Empirical Calibration of Physics-Driven Animations 288

    C# Code Snippet 288

40 Implementing IK Systems for VR Avatars 292

    Foundations of Inverse Kinematics in Virtual Reality 292

    Mathematical Formulation of Inverse Kinematics . . 293

    Constraint Optimization in Inverse Kinematics . . . 293

    Dynamic Integration and Temporal Continuity . . . 294

    Enhanced User Representation through Inverse Kine-

    matics 294

    C# Code Snippet 295

41 Handling Object Interactions with Inverse Kinemat-

  ics   **299**

    Theoretical Underpinnings of Object Interaction via

    IK 299

    Mathematical Formulation and Constraint Integration 300

    Integration of Object Interaction

    Constraints 300

    Dynamic Considerations and Temporal

    Continuity 301

    Optimization of Joint Trajectories for Precise Ma-

    nipulation 301

    C# Code Snippet 302

42 Creating Realistic Avatar Movements in Oculus VR 309
Motion Capture and Sensor Fusion Techniques . . . 309
Temporal Alignment and Interpolation
Mechanisms 310
Kinematic Consistency and Constraint Enforcement 310
Adaptive Kinematics and Dynamic Adjustment . . . 311
Representation Fidelity and Accuracy Assessment . 311
C# Code Snippet 312

**43 Optimizing VR Performance: Rendering Pipeline
Basics 321**
Overview of Unity's Rendering Pipeline 321
Geometry Processing and Spatial Partitioning Tech-
niques 322
Advanced Culling Mechanisms and Their Computa-
tional Impact 322
Shader and Material Optimization 323
Batching, Draw Call Reduction, and Resource Man-
agement 323
Optimization of Post-Processing Effects and Over-
head Mitigation 324
C# Code Snippet 324

44 Implementing Occlusion Culling in VR Scenes 331
Fundamental Concepts of Occlusion Culling 331
Mathematical Formulation and Algorithmic Approaches 332
1   Geometric Representations and Bounding Volumes 332
2   Spatial Data Structures and Visibility Coherence 332
Architectural Integration within VR Rendering Pipelines 333
Computational Analysis and Performance Considerations 333
C# Code Snippet 334

45 Managing Level of Detail for Immersive VR 340
Fundamental Concepts of Level-of-Detail Strategies . 340
Geometric Simplification and Hierarchical Represen-
tations 341
Adaptive LOD Selection and Evaluation Metrics . . 341
Integration of LOD Strategies in Immersive VR Ren-
dering 342

C# Code Snippet 342

46 Implementing VR-Friendly Material Systems   347
Material Abstraction and Representation in Virtual
Reality 347
Optimization Techniques for Shader Design 348
Texture Management and Compression Strategies . . 348
Adaptive Parameterization and Material State Man-
agement 349
Integration of Material Systems with Rendering Pipelines349
C# Code Snippet 350

47 Scripting Interactive Environment Triggers   355
Event Detection and Classification 355
Architectural Design of Interactive Trigger Systems . 356
Mathematical Modeling of Trigger Conditions 356
Dynamic Response and Adaptive Scene Modification 357
C# Code Snippet 357

48 Integrating Particle Collision Systems   362
Particle Representations and Collision
Primitives 362
Spatial Partitioning and Optimization
Strategies 362
Collision Detection Algorithms and Theoretical Con-
siderations 363
Integration of Collision Responses with Interactive
Visual Effects 364
Real-Time Considerations and Interaction Dynamics 364
C# Code Snippet 365

49 Scripting Real-Time Environmental Reactions   372
Overview of Real-Time Reaction Mechanisms 372
Event-Driven Architectures in Virtual Environments 373
Modeling Environmental Dynamics and State Tran-
sitions 373
Temporal Synchronization and Coherent Update Cy-
cles 374
Adaptive Control of Visual and Auditory Feedback . 374
C# Code Snippet 375

50 Implementing Dynamic Object Spawning in VR   380

Theoretical Underpinnings and Architectural Considerations 380
Event-Driven Object Instantiation Mechanisms . . . 381
Resource Allocation, Object Pooling, and Optimization Constraints 381
Spatial Modeling and Contextual Criteria for Spawning 382
Temporal Dynamics and Feedback Integration 382
C# Code Snippet 383

51 Scripting Procedural Environment Modifications   387

Theoretical Foundations of Procedural Generation . 387
Mathematical Models and State Transformations in Virtual Environments 388
Algorithmic Strategies for Procedural Modifications   388
Parameterization and Randomization Techniques . . 389
Dynamic Integration and Real-Time Evolution . . . 389
C# Code Snippet 390

52 Managing Object States in VR Scenes   393

Formal Representation and Modelling of Object States 393
Mechanisms of State Transition and Tracking 394
Patterns and Paradigms for State Management in VR 394
Consistency and Responsiveness in Dynamic Environments 395
Temporal Integration and Real-Time Constraints . . 395
C# Code Snippet 396

53 Implementing Save and Load Systems for VR Worlds 401

Formalization of Persistent VR States 401
Serialization Methodologies and Data Fidelity Preservation 401
Atomicity and Consistency Constraints in State Persistence 402
Reloading Mechanisms and Reconstruction of VR Scenes 402
Performance, Scalability, and Real-time Constraints in Save/Load Operations 403
C# Code Snippet 403

54 Scripting Contextual Object Interactions   **408**

    Formal Framework for Contextual Interactions . . . 408

    Proximity-Based Interaction Paradigms 409

    Modeling User State for Adaptive Interactions 409

    Synthesis of Contextual Dynamics 410

    Environmental Semantics in Contextual Modeling . . 410

    C# Code Snippet 411

55 Designing VR Puzzle and Interaction Mechanics   **414**

    Theoretical Foundations in Interactive Puzzle Design 414

    Architectural Considerations for VR Puzzle Mechanics 415

    Spatial-Temporal Dynamics in Puzzle Environments 415

    Enhancing Engagement through Intuitive Interaction Mechanics 416

    Multi-Modal Interactions and Adaptive Puzzle Dynamics 416

    C# Code Snippet 417

56 Scripting Interactive Narratives in Immersive Environments   **423**

    Theoretical Foundations of Interactive Narratives . . 423

    Architectural Paradigms for Narrative Integration . 424

    Stateful Narrative Modeling and Dynamic Scripting 424

    Temporal-Spatial Narrative Synchronization 425

    User Engagement and Adaptive Narrative Evolution 425

    C# Code Snippet 426

57 Implementing Physics-Based Puzzles for VR   **431**

    Modeling Physical Interactions in Immersive Puzzles 431

    Integration of Rigid Body Dynamics with Puzzle Elements 432

    Designing Interactive Mechanisms and Logical Puzzle Constraints 432

    Constraint-Based Modeling in Environmental Puzzle Layouts 433

    Analysis of Dynamic Puzzle Responses and Logical Progression 433

    C# Code Snippet 434

58 Scripting Object-Based Storytelling in VR   **438**

    Object-Centric Narrative Constructs 438

    Environmental Cue Integration 438

Mechanisms of Dynamic Narrative Propagation . . . 439
Formal Modeling of Narrative Dynamics 439
Interaction Semantics and Contextual Modifiers . . . 440
C# Code Snippet 441

**59 Creating Interactive Tutorials within VR Environ-
ments   446**
Architectural Constructs for In-VR Tutorials 446
Mechanisms of Engagement in Tutorial Interactions 447
Contextual Prompting and Adaptive Cue Integration 447
Dynamic State Transitions in Tutorial Flow 448
Quantitative Analysis and Theoretical Modeling of
Tutorial Dynamics 448
C# Code Snippet 449

60 Scripting Gesture-Based Commands and Shortcuts 454
Foundational Concepts in Gesture Recognition Sys-
tems 454
Mathematical Formulation and Signal Preprocessing 455
Feature Extraction and Temporal Analysis 455
Classification Algorithms and Command Binding . . 456
System Integration and Interaction Latency Opti-
mization 456
Robustness and Adaptability in Gesture-Based In-
teraction 456
C# Code Snippet 457

61 Implementing VR Spatial Awareness Systems   462
Theoretical Foundations of Spatial Awareness in Vir-
tual Environments 462
Visual Cue Integration for Enhanced Perception . . 462
Auditory Signal Processing for Spatial Localization . 463
Sensor Fusion and Calibration Methodologies 464
Evaluation of Spatial Awareness Metrics 464
C# Code Snippet 465

62 Scripting Environment-Based Feedback Mechanisms 469
Theoretical Foundations of Environmental Feedback 469
Visual Feedback Mechanisms 470
Auditory Feedback Mechanisms 470
Temporal Dynamics and Adaptive Calibration 471

Quantitative Metrics and Evaluation of Feedback
Systems 471
C# Code Snippet 472

63 Integrating Real-Time Data into VR Scenes   **476**
Overview of Real-Time Data Streams in Virtual Re-
ality 476
Data Acquisition and Preprocessing 476
Dynamic Scene Updating and Data-Driven Interac-
tions 477
Architectural Considerations for
Data-Driven VR Systems 477
Synchronization and Latency Management 478
Mathematical Models for Adaptive Data Integration 478
C# Code Snippet 479

64 Scripting Adaptive User Interfaces in VR   **483**
Theoretical Foundations of Adaptive User Interfaces 483
User Behavior and Contextual Modeling 484
1   Behavioral Dynamics in Immersive Environments 484
2   Contextual Cues and Environmental Dynamics 484
Algorithmic Frameworks for Adaptive UI Scripting . 484
1   Mathematical Formalization of Adaptive Mappings 484
2   Optimization Strategies and Adaptive Algorithmic Design 485
Architectural Integration and Modular Design Considerations 485
1   Component-Based Architecture for Dynamic
UI Elements 485
2   Data Flow Pipelines and Interface Update
Mechanisms 486
Performance Considerations in Adaptive User Interfaces 486
1   Temporal Responsiveness and Latency Minimization 486
2   Scalability and Resource Optimization in Adaptive Systems 487
C# Code Snippet 487

65 Implementing Custom VR Animation Transitions 491

Fundamental Principles in Custom VR Animation
Transitions 491

Mathematical Formalization of Transition Mappings 492

Temporal Interpolation Techniques and Easing Functions 492

Context-Sensitive Modulation of Animation Transitions 493

Integrative Approaches to Visual Fluidity and Naturalism 493

C# Code Snippet 494

66 Integrating Core Systems to Build Immersive VR Environments 500

Architectural Integration Framework 500

Temporal and Spatial Synchronization
Mechanisms 501

Dynamic Adaptation of Scripted Systems and Contextual Modulation 501

Interoperability of Multimedia and Interaction Subsystems 502

Optimization and Scalability in
Multi-Modal System Integration 502

C# Code Snippet 503

Chapter 1

Foundations of VR Software Architecture in Unity

Architectural Paradigms in Virtual Reality Applications

The design of virtual reality software architectures is rigorously underpinned by established software engineering principles that prioritize abstraction and decoupling. In the context of immersive environments, the necessity for rapid, deterministic interaction loops is interwoven with the demands for dynamic scene management and accurate spatial representation. The prevailing paradigms advocate a decomposition of overall system functionality into discrete, loosely coupled components. Such a strategy enables the independent evolution of subsystems without adverse impacts on holistic system behavior. The analysis of interactive workflows and state transitions within this architectural framework reveals that encapsulation of functionality not only mitigates complexity but also reinforces system robustness under stringent real-time constraints.

Component-Based Design in Unity

Unity inherently adopts a component-based design philosophy, which serves as a foundational cornerstone for constructing complex virtual reality applications. In this design paradigm, entities are treated as containers that aggregate a plethora of components, each responsible for discrete computational or visual tasks. This decomposition facilitates a fine-grained allocation of responsibilities; for instance, rendering, physics simulation, and input processing are segregated into dedicated modular units. Such a design minimizes interdependencies by enabling each component to operate autonomously with clearly defined interfaces. The architecture thereby ensures that the addition or modification of a component affects only its immediate operational context while preserving the integrity of the overall system. The intrinsic modularity permits iterative refinement and fosters enhanced maintainability in environments demanding rapid prototyping and scalability.

Modularity in Immersive Environments

A modular system architecture is imperative in the realm of immersive virtual reality due to the inherently multifaceted nature of spatial simulations. Each module is entrusted with a specific domain, such as environment rendering, audio spatialization, or user interaction tracking. The independence of these modules is formalized by the definition of precise interfaces that mitigate inter-module coupling. Consider a set of modules denoted by $M_1, M_2, \ldots, M_n$, where each M_i encapsulates functionality that can be individually enhanced or substituted. Such an arrangement not only supports parallel development but also simplifies integration testing, as inter-module interactions are governed by rigorously specified contracts. The quantitative assessment of modularity—through metrics such as cohesion and coupling—corroborates the central thesis that a system structured in this fashion is optimally suited for the dynamic, iterative nature of immersive environment development.

The Runtime Environment and Event-Driven Messaging

The operational dynamics of Unity-based VR applications are defined by an event-driven runtime environment that orchestrates the myriad subsystems involved in real-time simulation. A continuous cycle of state updates, executed through methods commonly referenced as $Update()$ and $FixedUpdate()$, underpins the synchronized operation of interactive elements, rendering routines, and physical simulations. Within this framework, an internal messaging system disseminates events across components, thereby enabling reactive adaptations to changes in user input and environmental conditions. This design facilitates a decentralized propagation of state changes that is critical for maintaining temporal consistency. The precise coordination ensured by this event-driven architecture plays a pivotal role in aligning system responses with the user's perceptual experience, thereby safeguarding the immersive quality of the virtual environment through minimal latency and coherent state transitions.

Real-Time Constraints and Performance Considerations

Meeting the rigorous performance requirements of immersive virtual reality invariably necessitates a detailed examination of real-time constraints and computational resource management. Paramount among these constraints is the imperative to minimize latency, denoted by L, which must be rigorously maintained below a critical threshold ϵ in order to sustain perceptual fidelity and prevent adverse physiological effects. The architecture is meticulously structured to distribute computational loads across multiple processing units, embracing techniques such as asynchronous task scheduling and parallel execution to optimize throughput. The deterministic nature of update cycles, when combined with a responsive and event-driven messaging system, establishes a robust framework for managing stochastic real-time events. Such a synthesis of performance considerations ensures that the architecture not only meets the stringent demands of immersive interaction but also facilitates sustained high-fidelity simulation across diverse deployment contexts.

C# Code Snippet

```
using System;
using System.Collections.Generic;
using System.Diagnostics;
using System.Threading.Tasks;
```

```
namespace VRSimulation
{
    // Interface defining the modular structure for VR subsystems.
    public interface IModule
    {
        // Initialize the module.
        void Initialize();
        // Per-frame update, analogous to Unity's Update() method.
        void Update(float deltaTime);
        // Fixed timestep update, analogous to Unity's FixedUpdate()
        ↪ method.
        void FixedUpdate(float fixedDeltaTime);
    }

    // Base class for modules implementing IModule.
    public abstract class Module : IModule
    {
        public virtual void Initialize() { }
        public virtual void Update(float deltaTime) { }
        public virtual void FixedUpdate(float fixedDeltaTime) { }
    }

    // Event-driven messaging system to decouple module
    ↪ interactions.
    public static class EventManager
    {
        // Delegate for VR message handling.
        public delegate void VRMessageHandler(string message, object
        ↪ data);
        public static event VRMessageHandler OnVRMessage;

        // Dispatch a message to subscribed modules.
        public static void SendMessage(string message, object data)
        {
            OnVRMessage?.Invoke(message, data);
        }
    }

    // Module handling rendering; simulates visual update
    ↪ responsibilities.
    public class RenderingModule : Module
    {
        public override void Initialize()
        {
            Console.WriteLine("Rendering Module Initialized.");
        }

        public override void Update(float deltaTime)
        {
            // Simulating rendering computations.
            // Equation: Frame Update Calculation -> R =
            ↪ f(deltaTime)
```

```csharp
            Console.WriteLine($"[Rendering] Update - Delta Time:
            ↪  {deltaTime:F3} sec");
    }
}

// Module handling physics simulation; encapsulating collision
↪  and movement.
public class PhysicsModule : Module
{
    public override void Initialize()
    {
        Console.WriteLine("Physics Module Initialized.");
    }

    public override void FixedUpdate(float fixedDeltaTime)
    {
        // Simulate physics update using fixed timestep.
        // This can be related to the modular equation:  M_i
        ↪  (M_i: physics) update.
        Console.WriteLine($"[Physics] FixedUpdate - Fixed Delta
        ↪  Time: {fixedDeltaTime:F3} sec");
    }
}

// Module handling input capture and event reception.
public class InputModule : Module
{
    public override void Initialize()
    {
        Console.WriteLine("Input Module Initialized.");
        // Subscribe to global VR events.
        EventManager.OnVRMessage += HandleVRMessage;
    }

    public override void Update(float deltaTime)
    {
        // Poll for inputs; can be extended to process gesture
        ↪  or controller data.
        Console.WriteLine($"[Input] Update - Delta Time:
        ↪  {deltaTime:F3} sec");
    }

    // Event handler responding to VR messages.
    private void HandleVRMessage(string message, object data)
    {
        Console.WriteLine($"[Input] Received Message: {message}
        ↪  with data: {data}");
    }
}

// Central manager simulating Unity's runtime cycle and
↪  integration of modules.
public class VRManager
```

```csharp
{
    private List<IModule> modules = new List<IModule>();
    private Stopwatch stopwatch = new Stopwatch();

    // Real-time performance constraint:
    // Latency L must be maintained below a threshold
    ↪   (epsilon).
    // In this simulation, epsilon is set to 0.016 seconds
    ↪   (16ms), a common VR frame budget.
    private const float epsilon = 0.016f;

    public VRManager()
    {
        // Register modules representing discrete components
        ↪   (M1, M2, ..., Mn).
        modules.Add(new RenderingModule());
        modules.Add(new PhysicsModule());
        modules.Add(new InputModule());
    }

    public void Initialize()
    {
        foreach (var module in modules)
        {
            module.Initialize();
        }
    }

    // Simulate the main loop including Update and FixedUpdate
    ↪   cycles.
    public async Task RunSimulation(int frameCount)
    {
        float fixedDeltaTime = 0.02f; // Simulated fixed
        ↪   timestep (20ms)
        int fixedUpdateCounter = 0;

        Console.WriteLine("Starting simulation loop...");

        for (int i = 0; i < frameCount; i++)
        {
            stopwatch.Restart();

            // In a real system, deltaTime would be dynamic.
            float deltaTime = fixedDeltaTime;

            // Invoke Update for each module.
            foreach (var module in modules)
            {
                module.Update(deltaTime);
            }

            // Dispatch a VR event for this frame.
            EventManager.SendMessage("FrameUpdate", i);
```

```csharp
            // Periodically invoke FixedUpdate (e.g., every 2
            ↪  frames).
            if (fixedUpdateCounter % 2 == 0)
            {
                foreach (var module in modules)
                {
                    module.FixedUpdate(fixedDeltaTime);
                }
            }
            fixedUpdateCounter++;

            // Simulate workload and frame delay.
            await Task.Delay(10);

            stopwatch.Stop();
            float frameLatency =
            ↪  (float)stopwatch.Elapsed.TotalSeconds;
            Console.WriteLine($"Frame {i + 1} Duration:
            ↪  {frameLatency:F4} sec");

            // Verify that the latency L satisfies L < .
            if (frameLatency >= epsilon)
            {
                Console.WriteLine($"Warning: Frame latency
                ↪  {frameLatency:F4} sec exceeds threshold
                ↪  {epsilon:F4} sec");
            }
        }
    }
}

// Program entry simulating the VR application start-up.
public class Program
{
    public static async Task Main(string[] args)
    {
        VRManager vrManager = new VRManager();
        vrManager.Initialize();
        Console.WriteLine("VR Simulation is running...");
        await vrManager.RunSimulation(5);
        Console.WriteLine("VR Simulation has ended.");
    }
}
}
```

24

Chapter 2

Unity VR Workflow: Exploring the Editor for Immersive Development

Project Navigation and Asset Management

Within the Unity Editor, the structural organization of a project is governed by a rigorous taxonomy that facilitates both scalability and rapid discovery of resources. The asset management system is underpinned by a hierarchical directory structure that categorizes assets according to type, purpose, and interdependencies. This structural paradigm supports dynamic project evolution by enabling efficient retrieval and modification of resources. The Project panel serves as the central repository, where assets are indexed and organized in a manner akin to a search tree. Quantitative analyses of retrieval efficiency typically denote that the underlying search algorithms operate in an average time complexity of $O(n)$, thereby ensuring that even expansive projects maintain navigational responsiveness. Furthermore, the metadata associated with each asset is systematically maintained, reinforcing consistency across the development workflow and aiding in the prevention of inadvertent discrepancies that may manifest in immersive environments.

Scene Organization and Hierarchical Structuring

The orchestration of scene organization within the Unity Editor is critical when developing immersive virtual reality experiences. The scene itself is conceived as a collection of interrelated entities, each represented as a node within a hierarchical structure. Mathematically, the scene graph can be represented as a directed acyclic graph $G = (V, E)$, where each vertex $v \in V$ delineates an individual game object and each edge $e \in E$ encapsulates parent-child relationships that define spatial and logical hierarchies. This formalism not only supports the systematic layering of interactive elements but also ensures that spatial relationships are preserved with high fidelity. The precision with which objects are arranged, both in terms of global positioning and relative orientation, directly influences the perceptual realism of the virtual environment. Consequently, maintaining an optimal balance between hierarchical depth and breadth is essential in reducing computational overhead while facilitating rapid scene iteration during development. The integration of collated scene data also permits dynamic loading and unloading procedures, which are critical for sustaining performance in expansive environments with significant resource demands.

Tool Utilization in the Unity Editor

The suite of tools available within the Unity Editor is designed to provide an extensive array of functionalities that streamline the development of immersive virtual reality applications. The Editor integrates multiple panels—such as the Scene view, Inspector, Hierarchy, and Console—that collectively facilitate a comprehensive understanding of the virtual environment's state. The Scene view offers an interactive three-dimensional workspace where transformations, spatial alignments, and visual feedback occur with a granularity that often approaches sub-millimeter precision, for example, 10^{-3} meters. The Inspector panel, on the other hand, elucidates the parameters and properties of selected objects, thereby enabling fine-tuned control over rendering, physics, and interactivity attributes. A deliberate configuration of these tools within the workflow allows for iterative refinement of both visual and functional aspects of the immersive environment. The robust integration of these utilities permits a seamless transition between high-level scene manipulations and granular component adjustments, thus establishing an environment where iterative design and systematic testing coexist harmoniously. This cohesive toolset not only enhances the fidelity of the immersive experience but also supports experimental modifications that can be rapidly evaluated within the context of realistic simulation parameters.

C# Code Snippet

```csharp
using System;
using System.Collections.Generic;

namespace VRWorkflow
{
    // Represents an asset in the project with associated metadata.
    public class Asset
    {
        public string Name { get; set; }
        public string Type { get; set; }
        public Dictionary<string, string> Metadata { get; set; }

        public Asset(string name, string type)
        {
            Name = name;
            Type = type;
            Metadata = new Dictionary<string, string>();
        }
    }

    // Manages a collection of assets and provides search
    ↪    functionality.
    public class AssetManager
    {
        // Underlying collection of assets.
        private List<Asset> assets = new List<Asset>();

        // Adds a new asset to the project.
        public void AddAsset(Asset asset)
        {
            assets.Add(asset);
        }

        // Searches for an asset by name using a linear search
        ↪    algorithm (O(n)).
        public Asset FindAssetByName(string name)
        {
            foreach (Asset asset in assets)
            {
```

```csharp
            if (asset.Name.Equals(name,
            ↪   StringComparison.OrdinalIgnoreCase))
            {
                return asset;
            }
        }
        return null;
    }
}

// Minimal representation of a 3D vector structure.
public struct Vector3
{
    public float x, y, z;

    public Vector3(float x, float y, float z)
    {
        this.x = x;
        this.y = y;
        this.z = z;
    }

    public override string ToString()
    {
        return string.Format("({0}, {1}, {2})", x, y, z);
    }
}

// Represents a node in the scene graph. The scene is modeled as
↪   a directed acyclic graph G = (V, E).
public class SceneNode
{
    public string Name { get; set; }
    public Vector3 Position { get; set; }
    public SceneNode Parent { get; private set; }
    public List<SceneNode> Children { get; private set; }

    public SceneNode(string name, Vector3 position)
    {
        Name = name;
        Position = position;
        Children = new List<SceneNode>();
    }

    // Establishes a parent-child relationship.
    public void AddChild(SceneNode child)
    {
        child.Parent = this;
        Children.Add(child);
    }
}
```

```csharp
// Encapsulates the scene hierarchy and provides methods for
// traversal.
public class SceneGraph
{
    public SceneNode Root { get; private set; }

    public SceneGraph(SceneNode root)
    {
        Root = root;
    }

    // Depth-first traversal (DFS) of the scene graph to
    // visualize hierarchical structure.
    public void Traverse(SceneNode node, int depth = 0)
    {
        if (node == null)
            return;

        // Indent output based on the hierarchy level.
        Console.WriteLine(new string('-', depth * 2) + node.Name
            + " at " + node.Position.ToString());
        foreach (SceneNode child in node.Children)
        {
            Traverse(child, depth + 1);
        }
    }
}

// Main program to demonstrate asset management and scene
// organization in the Unity Editor context.
public class Program
{
    public static void Main(string[] args)
    {
        // Demonstrate the asset management system.
        AssetManager assetManager = new AssetManager();
        assetManager.AddAsset(new Asset("Terrain",
            "Environment"));
        assetManager.AddAsset(new Asset("Player", "Character"));
        assetManager.AddAsset(new Asset("Enemy", "NPC"));

        Console.WriteLine("Searching for asset 'Player'...");
        Asset foundAsset =
            assetManager.FindAssetByName("Player");
        if (foundAsset != null)
            Console.WriteLine("Found asset: " + foundAsset.Name
                + ", Type: " + foundAsset.Type);
        else
            Console.WriteLine("Asset not found.");

        // Construct the scene graph.
```

```csharp
// The scene graph is modeled as a directed acyclic
↪   graph G = (V, E), where each node represents a game
↪   object.
SceneNode root = new SceneNode("RootScene", new
↪   Vector3(0f, 0f, 0f));
SceneNode environmentNode = new SceneNode("Environment",
↪   new Vector3(0.001f, 0f, 0f)); // Precision example:
↪   10^{-3} meters.
SceneNode lightingNode = new SceneNode("Lighting", new
↪   Vector3(0f, 0.001f, 0f));
SceneNode interactiveNode = new
↪   SceneNode("InteractiveObjects", new Vector3(0f, 0f,
↪   0.001f));

// Building the hierarchical structure.
root.AddChild(environmentNode);
root.AddChild(lightingNode);
environmentNode.AddChild(interactiveNode);

// Create the scene graph and traverse it.
SceneGraph sceneGraph = new SceneGraph(root);
Console.WriteLine("\nScene Graph Hierarchy:");
sceneGraph.Traverse(sceneGraph.Root);
        }
    }
}
```

Summary: This comprehensive C# code snippet demonstrates
key algorithms and formulas discussed in the chapter. It implements an asset management system using a linear search with $O(n)$
complexity and models a scene graph as a directed acyclic graph (G
= (V, E)). The depth-first traversal of the scene graph illustrates
hierarchical structuring essential for immersive VR development
workflows.

Chapter 3

Organizing VR Scenes: Scene Hierarchy and Asset Management

Fundamental Principles of Scene Graph Construction

Virtual reality scenes are fundamentally structured around the concept of a scene graph, a formal representation model in which individual entities are organized in a hierarchical manner. In this framework, each scene element is represented as a node within a directed acyclic graph $G = (V, E)$, where V denotes the set of vertices corresponding to discrete game objects or spatial elements, and E represents the set of ordered pairs that define parent-child relationships. This structure not only promotes spatial coherence but also enforces a logical dependency that underpins the operations of transformation, rendering, and collision detection. The rigorous application of graph-theoretic principles facilitates efficient traversal algorithms, thereby ensuring that hierarchical queries and updates propagate in a controlled manner across the entire scene.

The meticulous construction of a scene graph is predicated on the careful delineation of node responsibilities and interdependencies. Each node is instantiated with a set of properties, including but not limited to spatial coordinates, orientation vectors, and transformation matrices. Such systematic organization allows for the precise orchestration of scene elements, as well as rapid identification and isolation of subtrees for purposes such as frustum culling and dynamic level of detail adjustments. The formalism inherent in this approach minimizes computational overhead when navigating complex scenes, thereby preserving the performance characteristics necessary for immersive virtual environments.

Asset Management Paradigms in Virtual Environments

The management of digital assets in virtual reality applications extends beyond mere storage paradigms, encompassing a comprehensive system of metadata tagging, categorization, and indexing that supports both scalability and maintainability. Assets are typically organized within a hierarchical directory structure that reflects inherent relationships based on type, functional role, and interdependency with other assets. Conceptually, the asset repository may be viewed as a mapping function $A : T \to R$, where T denotes categories of asset types and R signifies the corresponding resource sets. This formulation ensures that the retrieval, modification, and replacement of individual assets occur with unambiguous consistency and minimal latency.

A systematic asset management strategy incorporates rigorous naming conventions, version control metadata, and dependency tracking. These measures serve to enforce consistency across the development lifecycle, thereby reducing the probability of resource conflicts or redundancies. The integration of metadata indexing also permits the use of advanced search algorithms which, even under worst-case scenarios, operate with a time complexity of $O(n)$, where n is the number of managed assets. Through such considerations, the asset management subsystem functions as both a repository and an operational backbone for scene assembly and real-time modifications.

Integration of Scene Hierarchy and Asset Management

The efficacy of virtual reality scene organization is enhanced through the seamless integration of the scene graph framework with robust asset management methodologies. In practice, each node within the scene graph is not only a spatial representation but also a reference to a suite of digital assets that define its appearance, behavior, and interactivity. This confluence is achieved by ensuring that identifiers and metadata associated with assets are synchronized with corresponding nodes in the scene graph. Such an integrated approach facilitates the dynamic instantiation and replacement of scene elements without compromising the logical consistency or visual continuity of the environment.

The unification of these subsystems supports a bidirectional flow of information. On one hand, the scene graph provides a contextual framework that informs the appropriate categorization and usage of assets; on the other hand, the asset management system supplies a repository of validated resources that can be dynamically mapped to scene nodes. This reciprocity is essential for accommodating iterative modifications and experimental adjustments during the development cycle, as it allows for rapid reconfiguration of both the scene architecture and the underlying resource database while maintaining a high degree of coherence.

Considerations for Scalability and Maintainability

Scalability and maintainability represent critical parameters in the design of complex virtual reality environments. As scenes grow in size and intricacy, the underlying data structures and management protocols must be engineered to support an expanding number of nodes and assets without a concomitant degradation in performance. The balanced construction of the scene graph, with a careful trade-off between hierarchical depth and breadth, ensures that traversal operations remain efficient, typically exhibiting a linear time complexity $O(|V|)$ where $|V|$ is the number of nodes. This balance is further augmented by the implementation of caching strategies and dynamic loading protocols that mitigate the computational costs associated with managing extensive virtual spaces.

On the asset management front, scalability is achieved through modular organization, where assets are compartmentalized into discrete, logically related clusters. This modularization not only simplifies the process of asset retrieval but also facilitates the adoption of distributed version control systems, which can efficiently manage concurrent modifications and large-scale integration tasks. Together, these practices contribute to a development framework that prioritizes both system robustness and ease of future maintenance, ensuring that immersive virtual environments can evolve organically without incurring prohibitive overheads related to resource management or scene reorganization.

C# Code Snippet

```csharp
using System;
using System.Collections.Generic;
using System.Numerics;

namespace VRSceneGraph
{
    // Class representing a digital asset in the VR environment.
    public class Asset
    {
        public string Id { get; set; }
        public string Name { get; set; }
        public string Type { get; set; }   // Example types:
        ↪  "Model", "Texture", "Audio", etc.
        public string FilePath { get; set; }

        public Asset(string id, string name, string type, string
        ↪  filePath)
        {
            Id = id;
            Name = name;
            Type = type;
            FilePath = filePath;
        }

        public override string ToString()
        {
            return $"Asset: [ID: {Id}, Name: {Name}, Type: {Type},
            ↪  File: {FilePath}]";
        }
    }

    // Asset Manager implements a mapping A: T -> R, where T is the
    ↪  asset type and R is the collection of assets.
    public class AssetManager
    {
        private Dictionary<string, List<Asset>> assetDictionary;

        public AssetManager()
        {
            assetDictionary = new Dictionary<string, List<Asset>>();
        }

        // Adds an asset to the asset repository.
```

```csharp
public void AddAsset(Asset asset)
{
    if (!assetDictionary.ContainsKey(asset.Type))
    {
        assetDictionary[asset.Type] = new List<Asset>();
    }
    assetDictionary[asset.Type].Add(asset);
}

// Retrieves all assets of a given type.
public List<Asset> GetAssetsByType(string type)
{
    if (assetDictionary.ContainsKey(type))
    {
        return assetDictionary[type];
    }
    return new List<Asset>();
}

// Searches for an asset by its ID within all asset
//   categories. Worst-case time complexity is O(n).
public Asset FindAssetById(string id)
{
    foreach (var assetList in assetDictionary.Values)
    {
        foreach (var asset in assetList)
        {
            if (asset.Id == id)
            {
                return asset;
            }
        }
    }
    return null;
}
}

// SceneNode represents a node in the scene graph.
// The scene graph is modeled as a directed acyclic graph G =
//   (V, E),
// where V are scene nodes and E are the parent-child
//   relationships.
public class SceneNode
{
    public string Name { get; set; }
    public Matrix4x4 LocalTransform { get; set; }  // Local
    //   transformation matrix.
    public Matrix4x4 WorldTransform { get; set; }  // Global
    //   transformation computed recursively.
    public List<SceneNode> Children { get; set; }
    public SceneNode Parent { get; set; }
    public Asset AssociatedAsset { get; set; }    // Digital
    //   asset linked to this node.
```

35

```csharp
public SceneNode(string name, Matrix4x4 localTransform)
{
    Name = name;
    LocalTransform = localTransform;
    WorldTransform = localTransform; // With no parent,
    ↪ world transform equals local transform.
    Children = new List<SceneNode>();
    Parent = null;
    AssociatedAsset = null;
}

// Adds a child node and sets its Parent reference.
public void AddChild(SceneNode child)
{
    child.Parent = this;
    Children.Add(child);
}

// Recursively updates the world transformation using the
↪ parent's transformation.
// Uses a depth-first traversal (complexity O(|V|), with |V|
↪ being the number of nodes).
public void UpdateWorldTransform(Matrix4x4
↪ parentWorldTransform)
{
    WorldTransform = LocalTransform * parentWorldTransform;
    foreach (var child in Children)
    {
        child.UpdateWorldTransform(WorldTransform);
    }
}

// Recursively prints the scene graph structure along with
↪ associated asset information.
public void PrintNodeHierarchy(string indent = "")
{
    Console.WriteLine($"{indent}Node: {Name}");
    if (AssociatedAsset != null)
    {
        Console.WriteLine($"{indent}  Associated Asset:
        ↪ {AssociatedAsset.Name}");
    }
    foreach (var child in Children)
    {
        child.PrintNodeHierarchy(indent + "  ");
    }
}
}

// Main program to demonstrate integration of scene graph and
↪ asset management.
class Program
```

```csharp
{
    static void Main(string[] args)
    {
        // Initialize the Asset Manager and add assets with
        ↪   metadata.
        AssetManager assetManager = new AssetManager();
        Asset asset1 = new Asset("A001", "MainCharacterModel",
        ↪   "Model", "Assets/Models/MainCharacter.fbx");
        Asset asset2 = new Asset("A002", "EnvironmentTexture",
        ↪   "Texture", "Assets/Textures/Env.jpg");
        Asset asset3 = new Asset("A003", "BackgroundMusic",
        ↪   "Audio", "Assets/Audio/BGM.mp3");
        assetManager.AddAsset(asset1);
        assetManager.AddAsset(asset2);
        assetManager.AddAsset(asset3);

        // Create the root of the scene graph.
        SceneNode rootNode = new SceneNode("Root",
        ↪   Matrix4x4.Identity);

        // Create a child node for the main character and
        ↪   associate its asset.
        SceneNode characterNode = new SceneNode("Character",
        ↪   Matrix4x4.CreateTranslation(new Vector3(0, 0, 5)));
        characterNode.AssociatedAsset =
        ↪   assetManager.FindAssetById("A001");
        rootNode.AddChild(characterNode);

        // Create a child node for the environment and associate
        ↪   the relevant asset.
        SceneNode environmentNode = new SceneNode("Environment",
        ↪   Matrix4x4.CreateTranslation(new Vector3(10, 0, 0)));
        environmentNode.AssociatedAsset =
        ↪   assetManager.FindAssetById("A002");
        rootNode.AddChild(environmentNode);

        // Add a subnode to represent a dynamically spawned
        ↪   object.
        SceneNode dynamicObjectNode = new
        ↪   SceneNode("DynamicObject",
        ↪   Matrix4x4.CreateTranslation(new Vector3(2, 0, 2)));
        environmentNode.AddChild(dynamicObjectNode);

        // Update world transformations for the entire scene
        ↪   graph.
        rootNode.UpdateWorldTransform(Matrix4x4.Identity);

        // Print the hierarchical structure of the scene graph.
        Console.WriteLine("Scene Graph Hierarchy:");
        rootNode.PrintNodeHierarchy();

        // Demonstrate asset retrieval by type.
```

```
        Console.WriteLine("\nRetrieving Assets by Type
        ↪  'Audio':");
        List<Asset> audioAssets =
        ↪  assetManager.GetAssetsByType("Audio");
        foreach (var asset in audioAssets)
        {
            Console.WriteLine(asset.ToString());
        }

        // End of simulation.
        Console.WriteLine("\nVR Scene Graph and Asset Management
        ↪  simulation complete.");
        }
    }
}
```

Summary: This comprehensive C# code snippet demonstrates an integrated approach to organizing VR scenes using a scene graph and asset management system. It models the scene graph as a directed acyclic graph $(G = (V, E))$ with nodes that maintain local and world transformation matrices, and it employs a depth-first traversal algorithm $(O(|V|))$ to update these transforms. The AssetManager class implements the mapping A: $T \rightarrow R$ to manage assets by type, ensuring scalability and efficient metadata handling. The code illustrates how digital assets are associated with scene nodes, thereby providing a robust foundation for building and maintaining immersive virtual environments.

Chapter 4

Implementing VR GameObjects and Components

Conceptual Framework of VR GameObjects

Within the Unity engine, a GameObject is not a monolithic entity but a container designed to aggregate a variety of discrete behavioral and visual elements. Each GameObject functions as an abstraction that encapsulates both spatial properties and dynamic behaviors, with its state defined by a collection of attached components. In immersive virtual reality applications, these objects are instrumental in representing not only static entities but also interactive elements that respond to user inputs and environmental dynamics. The design paradigm embraces modularity, where a GameObject operates as an aggregation node in a larger hierarchical structure, and its overall functionality emerges from the composite behavior of its constituent components.

Component-Based Architecture and Modular Design

The underlying philosophy of Unity's object model is rooted in a component-based architecture. Each component contributes a distinct, encapsulated feature—ranging from physics simulation to visual rendering and interactive logic. The architecture permits developers to extend the capabilities of a GameObject by appending new components, thereby segregating responsibilities in a manner that promotes code reusability and system maintainability. Interaction logic, collision detection, and audio feedback are examples of discrete properties that are realized as separate components. The resulting composite architecture not only simplifies the evolution of complex behaviors but also ensures that overlapping concerns remain isolated. For instance, the transformation of a GameObject is mathematically formalized as a compositional product of local transformation matrices. If T_{local} represents the intrinsic transformation of a component and T_{parent} denotes its parent's global transformation, then the effective world transformation is computed as

$$T_{world} = T_{local} \times T_{parent}.$$

Management of Interactivity and Dynamic Behavior

The creation of interactive elements in a virtual reality environment hinges upon the dynamic interplay of multiple components. Each interactive GameObject is equipped with components responsible for monitoring and handling real-time signals such as user input events, collision states, and physics updates. This interactivity is orchestrated through a well-defined event propagation infrastructure within Unity that mimics aspects of the observer design pattern. As the state of one component changes—owing to external stimuli or internal logic—notification messages are directed through the system, thereby initiating corresponding behavioral adjustments in others. Such a decoupled scheme not only mitigates the computational overhead associated with centralized processing but also enhances the responsiveness required for immersive applications.

Architectural Considerations and Performance Optimization

In the construction of interactive VR environments, the integration of GameObjects with diverse components mandates careful attention to both architectural design and performance considerations. The isolation of behaviors into distinct components supports parallel processing and refined debugging, contributing to overall system robustness. The careful balancing of real-time update loops with graphical rendering pipelines necessitates that each component be optimized to minimize computational redundancy. In scenarios where numerous GameObjects are present, the decomposition of responsibilities into hierarchical layers allows for traversal and update operations to occur with efficiency generally bounded by linear time complexity $O(|V|)$, where $|V|$ denotes the number of active nodes. Moreover, the modular nature of component-based design facilitates the adaptation of the system to evolving requirements, as intervening components can be independently enhanced or replaced without inducing systemic disruptions.

C# Code Snippet

```csharp
using System;
using System.Collections.Generic;

namespace VRGameObjects
{
    // A basic 4x4 matrix structure to represent transformation
    //    data.
    public struct Matrix4x4
    {
        public float[,] m;

        public Matrix4x4(float[,] matrix)
        {
            m = matrix;
        }

        // Returns the identity matrix.
        public static Matrix4x4 Identity()
        {
            return new Matrix4x4(new float[4, 4] {
                {1, 0, 0, 0},
                {0, 1, 0, 0},
                {0, 0, 1, 0},
```

```
                {0, 0, 0, 1}
        });
    }


    // Multiplies two 4x4 matrices.
    // Implements the formula: T_world = T_local * T_parent.
    public static Matrix4x4 Multiply(Matrix4x4 a, Matrix4x4 b)
    {
        float[,] result = new float[4, 4];
        for (int i = 0; i < 4; i++)
        {
            for (int j = 0; j < 4; j++)
            {
                result[i, j] = 0;
                for (int k = 0; k < 4; k++)
                {
                    result[i, j] += a.m[i, k] * b.m[k, j];
                }
            }
        }
        return new Matrix4x4(result);
    }
}


// Transform class encapsulates the local and global (world)
↪   transformation matrices.
public class Transform
{
    // Local transformation matrix (T_local).
    public Matrix4x4 LocalMatrix { get; set; }
    // World transformation matrix (T_world).
    public Matrix4x4 WorldMatrix { get; private set; }
    // Reference to the parent's transform, if any.
    public Transform Parent { get; set; }

    public Transform()
    {
        LocalMatrix = Matrix4x4.Identity();
        WorldMatrix = Matrix4x4.Identity();
        Parent = null;
    }

    // Updates the world transformation matrix using the
    ↪   formula:
    // T_world = T_local * T_parent.
    public void UpdateWorldMatrix()
    {
        if (Parent != null)
        {
            WorldMatrix = Matrix4x4.Multiply(LocalMatrix,
            ↪   Parent.WorldMatrix);
        }
        else
```

```
        {
            WorldMatrix = LocalMatrix;
        }
    }
}

// The base Component class represents discrete behaviors that
↪  can be attached to a GameObject.
public abstract class Component
{
    public GameObject gameObject { get; set; }
    public virtual void Update() { }
}

// An example component that processes user interaction events.
public class InteractiveComponent : Component
{
    public override void Update()
    {
        // Simulate handling user input and propagating events.
        Console.WriteLine("InteractiveComponent: Processing user
        ↪  input events...");
    }
}

// The GameObject acts as a container for multiple components
↪  and holds spatial data.
public class GameObject
{
    public string Name { get; set; }
    public Transform transform { get; set; }
    private List<Component> components;

    public GameObject(string name)
    {
        Name = name;
        transform = new Transform();
        components = new List<Component>();
    }

    // Adds a new component to the GameObject.
    public void AddComponent(Component comp)
    {
        comp.gameObject = this;
        components.Add(comp);
    }

    // Retrieves a component of type T if it exists.
    public T GetComponent<T>() where T : Component
    {
        foreach (var comp in components)
        {
            if (comp is T)
```

```
            {
                return (T)comp;
            }
        }
        return null;
    }

    // Updates the GameObject by refreshing its transformation
    ↪  and delegating update calls to its components.
    public void Update()
    {
        transform.UpdateWorldMatrix();
        foreach (var comp in components)
        {
            comp.Update();
        }
    }
}

// Scene class to manage a collection of GameObjects and
↪  propagate update events.
public class Scene
{
    private List<GameObject> gameObjects;

    public Scene()
    {
        gameObjects = new List<GameObject>();
    }

    public void AddGameObject(GameObject obj)
    {
        gameObjects.Add(obj);
    }

    // Updates all GameObjects in the scene.
    // The traversal operates with linear time complexity O(n),
    ↪  where n is the number of objects.
    public void UpdateScene()
    {
        foreach (var obj in gameObjects)
        {
            obj.Update();
        }
    }
}

// The main program demonstrating the component-based
↪  architecture through a simple VR scene simulation.
public class Program
{
    public static void Main(string[] args)
    {
```

```
// Create a parent GameObject and set its local
↪   transformation.
GameObject parentObj = new GameObject("ParentObject");
parentObj.transform.LocalMatrix = new Matrix4x4(new
↪   float[4, 4] {
    {1, 0, 0, 5},
    {0, 1, 0, 0},
    {0, 0, 1, 0},
    {0, 0, 0, 1}
});

// Create a child GameObject and define its
↪   transformation relative to its parent.
GameObject childObj = new GameObject("ChildObject");
childObj.transform.Parent = parentObj.transform;
childObj.transform.LocalMatrix = new Matrix4x4(new
↪   float[4, 4] {
    {1, 0, 0, 2},
    {0, 1, 0, 3},
    {0, 0, 1, 4},
    {0, 0, 0, 1}
});

// Attach an interactive component to the child to
↪   handle user interactions.
childObj.AddComponent(new InteractiveComponent());

// Create a scene and add the GameObjects.
Scene scene = new Scene();
scene.AddGameObject(parentObj);
scene.AddGameObject(childObj);

// Update the scene: this refreshes transformations and
↪   propagates update events.
scene.UpdateScene();

// Display the computed world transformation matrix of
↪   the child GameObject.
Console.WriteLine("Child's World Transformation
↪   Matrix:");
PrintMatrix(childObj.transform.WorldMatrix);
}

// Helper method to print a 4x4 matrix in a readable format.
public static void PrintMatrix(Matrix4x4 matrix)
{
    for (int i = 0; i < 4; i++)
    {
        for (int j = 0; j < 4; j++)
        {
            Console.Write(matrix.m[i, j].ToString("F2") +
            ↪   "\t");
        }
```

```
            Console.WriteLine();
        }
      }
    }
}
```

Chapter 5

Scripting Fundamentals for VR Interactions in Unity

Preliminary Overview of the Scripting Environment

The Unity engine provides an extensive C# scripting environment designed to articulate the dynamic behaviors and interactions inherent to virtual reality. The scripting framework establishes a rigorous paradigm in which modules are developed to respond to both user input and the evolving state of the virtual scene. In this framework, mechanisms of object-oriented programming are employed to encapsulate functionality into discrete components, each responsible for facets of behavior and state management. The synchronization of event handling with real-time updates is afforded by Unity's tightly controlled execution cycles, enabling reactive adjustments to both computational and perceptual stimuli.

Core Programming Constructs and Control Structures

At the foundation of the scripting discipline in Unity lie the fundamental constructs of C#, including data types, control flow structures, and object-oriented design principles. The language's statically-typed nature ensures that variables and methods adhere to strict definitions, promoting robustness in the face of complex interaction models. Conditional statements, iterative loops, and logical operators provide the necessary control over execution flow. The object-oriented model further supports inheritance, polymorphism, and encapsulation, features that are critical for partitioning functionalities and ensuring that behavior modifications remain isolated to their intended modules. These constructs are integrated within Unity's deterministic execution order, such that the execution of routines like the *Update*(), *FixedUpdate*(), and *LateUpdate*() methods contributes to a coherent and predictable behavioral framework.

Event-Driven Programming and Interaction Handling

A central tenet of scripting in VR is the adoption of an event-driven programming model, whereby discrete events generated by user interactions and environmental triggers are captured and processed. The Unity engine implements a sophisticated event propagation mechanism that ensures the rapid dissemination of these events to the appropriate handlers. Delegates and event listeners are employed internally, allowing a decoupling of event sources and processors; this decoupling minimizes the likelihood of latency and enhances script responsiveness. The asynchronous nature of these events requires that the scripting architecture remain both rigorous and adaptable: the management of input events, collision responses, and temporal triggers must be executed with precision, thereby allowing the VR experience to maintain a fluid and immersive quality.

Architectural Patterns for Modularity and Reusability

The design of C# scripts within Unity adheres to well-established architectural patterns that promote modularity and reusability. The observer pattern, for example, is extensively exploited to enable indirect communication between independent components. In this configuration, changes in one module are broadcast to observing entities, thus facilitating dynamic yet loosely coupled interactions. This method of compartmentalization is consistent with Unity's component-based architecture, wherein GameObjects act as composite entities whose overall functionality emerges from the synergy of attached behavior-specific components. Each module is designed to operate autonomously while simultaneously integrating into a larger system, with interdependencies minimized via clear interface definitions and strict encapsulation. Mathematical abstractions, such as the computation of the world transformation through the relationship $T_{world} = T_{local} \times T_{parent}$, serve as illustrative examples of the precision and structured methodology underpinning these design principles.

Timing, Optimization, and Real-Time Considerations

Real-time execution demands an acute awareness of timing and performance within the scripting environment of Unity. The deterministic scheduling of update cycles is imperative to synchronizing script execution with the real-time constraints of virtual reality. Each invocation of scripting routines must be optimized to balance computational efficiency with the necessity for rapid responsiveness. Strategies for optimization include the elimination of redundant processing steps and the minimization of expensive memory allocations that might provoke increased garbage collection activity. Profiling and fine-tuning of execution pathways are thus integral to preserving the high performance required for sustained immersion. The systematic reduction of computational overhead ensures that both the visual rendering and the interactive behavioral layers proceed harmoniously, a necessary condition for maintaining the seamless quality of VR experiences.

Integration and Coordination of Multi-Component Systems

The orchestration of diverse script components undergirds the complex interactivity present in VR systems. Each component, though designed to perform a distinct function, must operate in coordination with its peers, contributing collectively to a coherent behavioral model. The integration is achieved through synchronized update cycles and well-defined communication channels that facilitate the propagation of state changes. This modular coordination allows disparate components—ranging from physics simulations to collision detectors and user input processors—to interact seamlessly within the rigid temporal confines of Unity's execution loop. The dynamic state of the VR simulation is maintained through rigorous state management protocols and efficient inter-component messaging that keep the system responsive to incremental changes. Such an integrated approach to multi-component coordination exemplifies the high degree of sophistication required to model and control VR interactions in a real-time environment.

C# Code Snippet

```csharp
using UnityEngine;
using System;

// Delegate definition for VR interaction events.
public delegate void VRInteractionEvent(VRObject obj);

// This class represents a VR object with a custom transform that
// computes its world transformation based on its local transform
↪   and parent's transform.
public class VRObject : MonoBehaviour
{
    // Local transformation matrix (for demonstration purposes,
    ↪   using Unity's Matrix4x4)
    public Matrix4x4 localTransform = Matrix4x4.identity;

    // Reference to a parent VRObject to simulate hierarchical
    ↪   transformations.
    public VRObject parentObject = null;

    // Computes the world transformation using the formula: T_world
    ↪   = T_local * T_parent
    public Matrix4x4 ComputeWorldTransform()
    {
        if (parentObject != null)
        {
            // Recursively compute the parent's world transformation
            ↪   and then multiply.
            return localTransform *
            ↪   parentObject.ComputeWorldTransform();
        }
        return localTransform;
    }
```

```csharp
    // Start is called before the first frame update.
    void Start()
    {
        // Log the computed world transformation for debugging
        ↪ purposes.
        Debug.Log("World Transform of " + gameObject.name + ": " +
        ↪ ComputeWorldTransform());
    }
}

// This manager class demonstrates event-driven programming and
↪ real-time interaction handling.
// It listens for input, performs raycasts for object interaction,
↪ and raises events accordingly.
public class VRInteractionManager : MonoBehaviour
{
    // Event that is fired when a VR object is grabbed.
    public event VRInteractionEvent OnObjectGrabbed;

    // Update is called once per frame.
    void Update()
    {
        // Check for a simulated grab input (e.g., pressing the 'G'
        ↪ key).
        if (Input.GetKeyDown(KeyCode.G))
        {
            VRObject grabbedObject = GetGrabbedObject();
            if (grabbedObject != null)
            {
                Debug.Log("Grabbed: " +
                ↪ grabbedObject.gameObject.name);
                // Trigger the grab event if any listeners are
                ↪ registered.
                OnObjectGrabbed?.Invoke(grabbedObject);
            }
        }

        // Additional real-time interaction handling can be
        ↪ performed here.
        HandleEnvironmentalEvents();
    }

    // Simulates the grabbing mechanism through a simple raycast.
    VRObject GetGrabbedObject()
    {
        Ray ray = new Ray(transform.position, transform.forward);
        RaycastHit hit;
        if (Physics.Raycast(ray, out hit, 10f))
        {
            // Attempt to retrieve the VRObject component from the
            ↪ hit collider.
            VRObject vrObj = hit.collider.GetComponent<VRObject>();
            return vrObj;
```

```
        }
        return null;
    }

    // Placeholder method to handle other interactive or
    ↪  environmental events.
    void HandleEnvironmentalEvents()
    {
        // Example: Check for collision triggers or invoke
        ↪  sound/visual feedback.
    }
}


// An observer class that listens for VR interaction events.
// Implements the observer pattern to decouple event generation from
↪  processing.
public class VRInteractionListener : MonoBehaviour
{
    // Reference to the VRInteractionManager that raises events.
    public VRInteractionManager interactionManager;

    // Register to the event when this listener is enabled.
    void OnEnable()
    {
        if (interactionManager != null)
        {
            interactionManager.OnObjectGrabbed += OnGrabbed;
        }
    }

    // Unregister from the event when this listener is disabled.
    void OnDisable()
    {
        if (interactionManager != null)
        {
            interactionManager.OnObjectGrabbed -= OnGrabbed;
        }
    }

    // Callback method invoked when a VR object is grabbed.
    void OnGrabbed(VRObject vrObj)
    {
        Debug.Log("VRInteractionListener: Detected grabbed object -
        ↪  " + vrObj.gameObject.name);
        // Example action: Change the object's color to indicate a
        ↪  successful interaction.
        Renderer renderer = vrObj.GetComponent<Renderer>();
        if (renderer != null)
        {
            renderer.material.color = Color.green;
        }
    }
```

```
}
```

Summary: The code snippet above integrates core principles discussed in the chapter, including the computation of world transformations using the formula T_world = T_local * T_parent, event-driven interaction handling via delegates and events, and modular component coordination through Unity's update cycle and observer pattern. This comprehensive example illustrates how VR interactions can be efficiently scripted in Unity using C#.

Chapter 6

Utilizing the Oculus Integration Package

Architectural Overview of the Oculus Integration Package

The Oculus Integration Package is engineered as a modular repository of libraries and assets specifically tailored to interface with the Oculus hardware ecosystem. This framework is designed to integrate seamlessly with established game engines, particularly Unity, by encapsulating discrete functionalities into independent, yet intercommunicating, modules. The overall architecture adheres to object-oriented design principles, ensuring that each subsystem maintains a well-defined operational context while communicating through rigorously specified interfaces. Components responsible for handling head tracking, spatial input, and rendering synchronizations coexist with modules that perform environmental interaction and haptic feedback processing, thereby forming a cohesive structure that underpins immersive virtual reality applications.

Examination of Oculus-Specific Libraries and Interfaces

A fundamental aspect of the package is the curated suite of Oculus-specific libraries that abstract the intricacies of low-level hardware interactions. These libraries are constructed to deliver robust and real-time access to multisensory data streams, including positional tracking, orientation data, and gesture recognition. The interfaces exposed by these libraries conform to strict API contracts that enforce strong typing and consistency, thereby mitigating errors in critical real-time operations. In addition, these APIs support an event-driven architecture wherein sensor inputs and user interactions are processed through asynchronous mechanisms. Such design rigor enables the precise synchronization of hardware events with the graphical and interactive subsystems, ensuring high fidelity in virtual reality experiences.

Leveraging Asset Integration and Utility Tools

Complementing the core libraries, the integration package offers a comprehensive set of preconfigured assets and utility tools. These assets include prefabricated GameObjects, optimized shaders, and environment templates that are inherently designed for the Oculus platform. The utility tools provided are instrumental in streamlining the development process; they offer diagnostic capabilities, performance profiling, and calibration utilities that facilitate systematic optimization. Asset integration is driven by a strategy that minimizes initial configuration overhead, allowing for swift assembly of immersive environments. The validation processes embedded within these tools ensure that graphical fidelity and interactive responsiveness are dynamically maintained, even under varying computational loads.

Dynamic Integration of Hardware-Specific Capabilities

The package encapsulates a layered approach to the integration of hardware-specific functionalities. At the lower levels, precise sensor inputs—such as those obtained from inertial measurement units—are processed and abstracted into higher-level interaction events. This abstraction layer isolates application logic from direct hardware dependencies and enables a unified programming model that is both robust and scalable. Key capabilities include advanced haptic feedback, real-time spatial tracking, and adaptive display adjustments that cater to variable latency constraints. The system harnesses asynchronous processing and rapid state updates, ensuring that dynamic interactions are executed with minimal delay. Such an approach is vital to preserving the immersive quality of virtual reality, where responsiveness and precision are of paramount importance.

Methodological Considerations in Oculus Integration

The integration of Oculus-specific functionalities within sophisticated virtual reality systems demands a methodical approach that emphasizes iterative performance benchmarking and modular design. Each component of the Oculus Integration Package is subject to rigorous profiling to evaluate parameters such as the update cycle duration, denoted by τ_{update}, and the sensor sampling frequency, represented by f_s. These quantitative metrics form the basis for tuning subsystem interactions and ensuring that system-wide latencies remain within acceptable limits. The design methodology mandates strict adherence to encapsulated interface contracts, which not only allow for the decomposition of complex systems into manageable submodules but also ensure predictable performance and scalability over time. This systematic framework enables the effective incorporation of Oculus-specific capabilities into virtual reality applications without compromising on rendering performance or interactive responsiveness.

C# Code Snippet

```csharp
using System;
using System.Collections;
using System.Threading.Tasks;
using UnityEngine;

public class OculusIntegrationExample : MonoBehaviour
{
    // Update cycle duration (_update) in seconds
    private float updateCycleDuration = 0f;
    // Sensor sampling frequency (f_s) in Hertz
    private float sensorSamplingFrequency = 0f;

    // Variables to simulate sensor data
    private Vector3 simulatedSensorPosition;
    private Quaternion simulatedSensorRotation;
```

```csharp
// Time tracker for update cycle calculation
private float lastUpdateTime = 0f;

// Start is called before the first frame update
void Start()
{
    Debug.Log("Oculus Integration Example started.");
    lastUpdateTime = Time.time;
    // Begin asynchronous sensor simulation at approximately
    ↪  60Hz
    StartCoroutine(SimulateSensorUpdates());
}

// Coroutine to simulate sensor updates and process
↪  Oculus-specific interactions
IEnumerator SimulateSensorUpdates()
{
    while (true)
    {
        // Wait for a fixed interval (simulate ~60Hz sensor
        ↪  update rate)
        yield return new WaitForSeconds(1.0f / 60.0f);

        // Calculate the update cycle duration (_update)
        float currentTime = Time.time;
        updateCycleDuration = currentTime - lastUpdateTime;
        lastUpdateTime = currentTime;

        // Calculate sensor sampling frequency (f_s = 1 /
        ↪  _update)
        sensorSamplingFrequency = (updateCycleDuration > 0f) ?
        ↪  1f / updateCycleDuration : 0f;

        // Simulate sensor data (position and rotation) using
        ↪  mathematical functions
        simulatedSensorPosition = new Vector3(
            Mathf.Sin(currentTime),
            Mathf.Cos(currentTime),
            Mathf.Sin(currentTime * 0.5f)
        );
        simulatedSensorRotation = Quaternion.Euler(
            Mathf.Sin(currentTime) * 30f,
            Mathf.Cos(currentTime) * 45f,
            Mathf.Sin(currentTime * 0.5f) * 60f
        );

        // Log computed timing and sensor values
        Debug.Log(string.Format("Update Duration (_update):
        ↪  {0:F4} sec, Sensor Frequency (f_s): {1:F2} Hz",
                    updateCycleDuration,
                    ↪  sensorSamplingFrequency));
```

```csharp
        Debug.Log(string.Format("Sensor Position: {0}, Sensor
        ↪   Rotation: {1}",
                    simulatedSensorPosition,
                    ↪   simulatedSensorRotation));

        // Conditional check to simulate haptic feedback trigger
        ↪   based on sensor magnitude
        if (simulatedSensorPosition.magnitude > 0.9f)
        {
            TriggerHapticFeedback();
        }

        // Synchronize the in-game camera with simulated Oculus
        ↪   sensor data
        SyncCameraWithSensor(simulatedSensorPosition,
        ↪   simulatedSensorRotation);
    }
}

// Asynchronous method to simulate a haptic feedback event
↪   triggered by sensor conditions
async void TriggerHapticFeedback()
{
    Debug.Log("Triggering haptic feedback...");
    await Task.Delay(50); // Simulate a 50ms delay for haptic
    ↪   response
    Debug.Log("Haptic feedback executed.");
}

// Method to align the main camera's transform with the sensor's
↪   position and orientation
void SyncCameraWithSensor(Vector3 position, Quaternion rotation)
{
    if (Camera.main != null)
    {
        Camera.main.transform.position = position;
        Camera.main.transform.rotation = rotation;
    }
}

// Simulates the initialization of Oculus-specific sensors and
↪   API integrations
void InitializeOculusSensors()
{
    Debug.Log("Initializing Oculus sensors and APIs...");
    // Here, actual Oculus Integration Package initialization
    ↪   routines would be invoked.
    // This method demonstrates the modular initialization
    ↪   approach.
}

// Update is called once per frame
void Update()
```

```
{
    // For demonstration purposes, pressing the Spacebar
    ↪   triggers Oculus sensor initialization.
    if (Input.GetKeyDown(KeyCode.Space))
    {
        InitializeOculusSensors();
    }
}
}
```

Summary: The above C# code snippet demonstrates a comprehensive implementation of key components outlined in the chapter. It simulates sensor data updates at approximately 60Hz and computes both the update cycle duration (_update) and sensor sampling frequency (f_s) in real time using the relation f_s = 1 / _update. The snippet also integrates asynchronous haptic feedback via Task-based delays, synchronizes camera transforms with simulated sensor inputs, and includes a modular initialization routine for Oculus-specific APIs. This structured approach encapsulates the performance and modular design strategies critical for developing immersive VR applications using the Oculus Integration Package.

Chapter 7

Configuring the VR Camera Rig in Unity

Architectural Overview of the VR Camera Rig

The VR camera rig in Unity serves as the foundational construct representing the user's viewpoint in an immersive virtual environment. This rig is established as a hierarchical assembly of transforms, wherein a primary parent node aggregates real-time head tracking data, and subordinate nodes—typically two in number—correspond to the left and right eyes. Each camera node is spatially arranged with an offset defined by the inter-pupillary distance, denoted as d_{IPD}, to reproduce a realistic stereo disparity. The design adheres strictly to rigid-body transformation principles, ensuring that the rig's overall configuration is invariant under the application of translation and rotation operations. This modular structure not only emulates the natural physical movements of the user but also forms the basis for subsequent integration with stereo rendering techniques and sensor-based calibration processes.

Stereo Rendering and Projection Matrix Configuration

Stereo rendering in Unity is achieved through the simultaneous operation of dual camera streams, each configured to produce a perspective view that, when combined, yields a stereoscopic image. The projection matrix of each camera is a central element in this process and is derived from fundamental principles of perspective mathematics. Specifically, the projection matrix is formulated using a modified pinhole camera model, represented as

$$
P = \begin{pmatrix}
\frac{2n}{r-l} & 0 & \frac{r+l}{r-l} & 0 \\
0 & \frac{2n}{t-b} & \frac{t+b}{t-b} & 0 \\
0 & 0 & -\frac{f+n}{f-n} & -\frac{2fn}{f-n} \\
0 & 0 & -1 & 0
\end{pmatrix},
$$

where n and f denote the near and far clipping planes, and l, r, b, and t represent the extents of the viewing frustum. Each eye's camera is assigned a distinct projection matrix that accounts for its eccentric position relative to the rig's central axis. The careful computation of these matrices ensures that the parallax effect—central to producing depth perception—remains consistent across various viewing angles. By modulating parameters such as the field of view and asymmetrical frustum boundaries, Unity facilitates the creation of two coherent, yet distinct, images that merge seamlessly in the user's visual field.

Ensuring Proper Alignment for Head Tracking

The fidelity of head tracking is critical to maintaining the immersive quality of virtual reality, and it directly influences the operational efficacy of the VR camera rig. Sensor data extracted from head-mounted displays (HMDs) must be accurately mapped onto the virtual camera's transform to replicate the user's physical movements. This mapping is accomplished through a continuous update strategy where the rig's position and orientation are recalculated in real time. The transformation is expressed as

$$
T_{\text{rig}} = T_{\text{position}} \cdot R_{\text{orientation}},
$$

where T_{position} denotes the translational component and $R_{\text{orientation}}$ is a rotation represented by a unit quaternion $q \in \mathbb{S}^3$. The adoption of quaternions is particularly significant due to their advantage in facilitating smooth and unambiguous interpolation, thereby avoiding the pitfalls of gimbal lock commonly associated with Euler angles. Moreover, precise calibration routines ensure that systematic deviations between the physical sensor outputs and the virtual rig's coordinate system are minimized. This exactitude is essential not only to preserve spatial congruence but also to mitigate motion-induced discomfort that can arise from even minute misalignments.

Rig Calibration and Integration with Unity's Rendering Pipeline

The calibration of the VR camera rig constitutes a meticulous process that reconciles the raw sensor data from the HMD with the intricate demands of Unity's rendering pipeline. Calibration parameters, including the field of view, lens distortion corrections, and aspect ratio adjustments, are finely tuned to ensure that the projected imagery aligns with the preconfigured coordinate frames of the rig. Special attention is devoted to harmonizing the rig's spatial configuration with the sequential stages of Unity's rendering workflow. This synchronization is achieved by aligning the calibration routines with the camera's update cycle, thereby ensuring that the stereo images are produced with optimal geometric accuracy and visual coherence. The integration of calibration data into the rendering pipeline not only supports high-fidelity visual output but also reinforces the overall stability of the virtual environment under dynamic conditions.

C# Code Snippet

```csharp
using UnityEngine;
using UnityEngine.XR;

public class VRCameraRig : MonoBehaviour
{
    // Public references for the left and right eye cameras
    public Camera leftEyeCamera;
    public Camera rightEyeCamera;

    // Calibration parameters
    public float interPupillaryDistance = 0.064f; // Typical IPD, in
    ↪    meters (e.g., ~64 mm)
    public float fieldOfView = 90f;               // Field of view
    ↪    in degrees
```

```csharp
public float nearClipPlane = 0.1f;
public float farClipPlane = 1000f;

// Private frustum boundaries computed from the FOV and aspect
↪   ratio
private float leftBoundary;
private float rightBoundary;
private float topBoundary;
private float bottomBoundary;

void Start()
{
    // Validate that both cameras have been assigned.
    if (leftEyeCamera == null || rightEyeCamera == null)
    {
        Debug.LogError("Both left and right eye cameras must be
        ↪   assigned in the Inspector.");
        return;
    }

    // Setup the camera rig with proper local positions and
    ↪   initial projection settings.
    SetupCameraPositions();
    CalculateFrustumBoundaries();
    UpdateProjectionMatrices();
}

void Update()
{
    // Continuously update head tracking data to ensure proper
    ↪   alignment.
    UpdateRigTransform();
}

// Sets the local positions of the left and right eye cameras
↪   based on the IPD.
void SetupCameraPositions()
{
    leftEyeCamera.transform.localPosition = new
    ↪   Vector3(-interPupillaryDistance / 2f, 0f, 0f);
    rightEyeCamera.transform.localPosition = new
    ↪   Vector3(interPupillaryDistance / 2f, 0f, 0f);

    // Initialize camera parameters.
    leftEyeCamera.fieldOfView = fieldOfView;
    rightEyeCamera.fieldOfView = fieldOfView;
    leftEyeCamera.nearClipPlane = nearClipPlane;
    rightEyeCamera.nearClipPlane = nearClipPlane;
    leftEyeCamera.farClipPlane = farClipPlane;
    rightEyeCamera.farClipPlane = farClipPlane;
}
```

```
// Computes the frustum boundaries for the near clipping plane
↪  using the FOV and camera aspect ratio.
void CalculateFrustumBoundaries()
{
    float aspect = leftEyeCamera.aspect; // Assuming both
    ↪  cameras share the same aspect ratio.
    float halfFovRad = Mathf.Deg2Rad * (fieldOfView / 2f);
    float tanHalfFov = Mathf.Tan(halfFovRad);

    float height = nearClipPlane * tanHalfFov;
    float width = height * aspect;

    leftBoundary = -width;
    rightBoundary = width;
    bottomBoundary = -height;
    topBoundary = height;
}

// Computes the asymmetric perspective projection matrix for an
↪  eye camera.
Matrix4x4 ComputeProjectionMatrix(float eyeOffset)
{
    // Modify the horizontal boundaries to account for the eye's
    ↪  offset.
    float l = leftBoundary + eyeOffset;
    float r = rightBoundary + eyeOffset;
    float b = bottomBoundary;
    float t = topBoundary;

    float n = nearClipPlane;
    float f = farClipPlane;

    Matrix4x4 projection = new Matrix4x4();
    projection[0, 0] = (2.0f * n) / (r - l);
    projection[0, 1] = 0f;
    projection[0, 2] = (r + l) / (r - l);
    projection[0, 3] = 0f;

    projection[1, 0] = 0f;
    projection[1, 1] = (2.0f * n) / (t - b);
    projection[1, 2] = (t + b) / (t - b);
    projection[1, 3] = 0f;

    projection[2, 0] = 0f;
    projection[2, 1] = 0f;
    projection[2, 2] = -(f + n) / (f - n);
    projection[2, 3] = -(2.0f * f * n) / (f - n);

    projection[3, 0] = 0f;
    projection[3, 1] = 0f;
    projection[3, 2] = -1f;
    projection[3, 3] = 0f;
```

```
        return projection;
    }

    // Updates the projection matrices for both left and right
    ↪   cameras.
    void UpdateProjectionMatrices()
    {
        // Calculate eye offsets: left eye gets negative half IPD;
        ↪   right eye gets positive half IPD.
        float leftOffset = -interPupillaryDistance / 2f;
        float rightOffset = interPupillaryDistance / 2f;

        leftEyeCamera.projectionMatrix =
        ↪   ComputeProjectionMatrix(leftOffset);
        rightEyeCamera.projectionMatrix =
        ↪   ComputeProjectionMatrix(rightOffset);
    }

    // Updates the overall rig's transform according to head
    ↪   tracking data.
    void UpdateRigTransform()
    {
        // Obtain head tracking data from the XR device. In real
        ↪   applications, this is provided by the HMD's sensors.
        Vector3 headPosition =
        ↪   InputTracking.GetLocalPosition(XRNode.Head);
        Quaternion headRotation =
        ↪   InputTracking.GetLocalRotation(XRNode.Head);

        // Update the rig's transformation matrix: T_rig =
        ↪   T_position * R_orientation.
        transform.localPosition = headPosition;
        transform.localRotation = headRotation;
    }
}
```

Summary

This C# code snippet demonstrates the implementation of a VR camera rig in Unity. It establishes the camera hierarchy with left and right eye cameras positioned using the inter-pupillary distance, computes asymmetrical projection matrices based on a modified pinhole camera model, and seamlessly integrates head tracking data to update the rig's transform in real time. These elements collectively ensure accurate stereo rendering and maintain high immersion in VR applications.

Chapter 8

Implementing Head Tracking and Player Orientation

Foundations of Head Tracking in Immersive Systems

The acquisition and processing of head tracking data constitute a fundamental component in correlating real-world movements with their virtual counterparts. In state-of-the-art head-mounted displays, sensor arrays encompassing inertial measurement units, accelerometers, gyroscopes, and magnetometers generate continuous streams of data that capture both angular velocities and linear accelerations. These data streams are mathematically processed to yield a robust estimation of the device's orientation and position. The most prevalent representation of three-dimensional orientation leverages unit quaternions, denoted by $q \in \mathbb{S}^3$, which encapsulate rotations in a compact and numerically stable form, thereby circumventing the limitations associated with Euler angle representations.

Coordinate Transformations and Spatial Alignment

The translation of head tracking measurements to the virtual world necessitates precise coordinate transformations. Within the context of a VR application, the mapping is achieved by aligning the sensor-derived data with the virtual camera rig's transformation hierarchy. This process involves the application of rigid-body transformations, where each update can be represented as a composition of a translational shift and a rotational adjustment. Mathematically, the overall rig transformation is expressed as

$$T_{\text{rig}} = T_{\text{position}} \cdot R_{\text{orientation}},$$

where T_{position} describes the translation vector in three-dimensional space and $R_{\text{orientation}}$ represents the rotation matrix derived from the orientation estimation. Such transformations ensure that the spatial configuration of the in-game camera remains consistent with the physical movements experienced by the user.

Quaternion-Based Orientation Representation

Quaternions are central to the computational paradigm underlying head tracking due to their capacity to represent orientations without incurring singularities. A quaternion, given as

$$q = w + xi + yj + zk,$$

enables the smooth interpolation of rotations through spherical linear interpolation (slerp), which is pivotal for achieving natural and continuous motion of the virtual camera. The avoidance of gimbal lock, a common pitfall in Euler angle systems, affords quaternions a distinct advantage when dealing with rapid and multidirectional head movements. The inherent efficiency in combining successive rotational updates using quaternion multiplication further underscores their suitability for real-time applications within immersive environments.

Sensor Fusion and Noise Mitigation

The reliability of head tracking is contingent upon the refinement of raw sensor data through sophisticated sensor fusion techniques. Multiple sensor modalities, each with its unique noise characteristics and error profiles, are integrated using statistical filtering methods such as the Kalman filter or complementary filtering approaches. These algorithms dynamically combine measurements, weighing each sensor's contribution to produce an optimized estimate of the head's position and orientation. The result is a reduction in sensor noise and drift, yielding a more stable and accurate representation of motion. This refined data forms the basis for the transformation computations that align the in-game camera with the user's real-world movements.

Mapping Head Movements to Virtual Camera Dynamics

The final phase in the implementation involves the meticulous mapping of the processed head tracking data to the configuration of the virtual camera rig. Calibration procedures ensure that systematic offsets between the physical sensor outputs and the virtual coordinate frames are identified and corrected. This calibration covers critical parameters such as axis alignment, scale factors, and latencies inherent in sensor data acquisition. The integration process adjusts the in-game camera's orientation and position in real time, thereby mirroring every nuance of the user's head movement. The composite transformation not only preserves the immersion of the virtual environment but also ensures that the dynamic response of the camera remains robust under varying conditions of motion, thereby enhancing the overall fidelity of the VR experience.

C# Code Snippet

```
using UnityEngine;

public class HeadTrackingController : MonoBehaviour
{
    // Complementary filter factor (close to 1 gives more weight to
    ↪  gyro data)
    public float complementaryFilterFactor = 0.98f;
```

```csharp
// The current orientation of the head or camera rig.
private Quaternion currentOrienFation = Quaternion.identity;
// The current position of the rig; in a complete system, this
↪    could be updated with positional tracking.
private Vector3 currentPosition = Vector3.zero;

void Start()
{
    // Initialize current orientation and position based on the
    ↪    object's transform.
    currentOrientation = transform.rotation;
    currentPosition = transform.position;
}

void Update()
{
    // Compute the time step.
    float dt = Time.deltaTime;

    // Retrieve simulated sensor data.
    Vector3 gyroReading = SimulateGyro();    // angular velocity
    ↪    in radians per second.
    Vector3 accelReading = SimulateAccel();    // acceleration in
    ↪    m/s^2 (typically dominated by gravity).

    // -- Gyroscope Integration (Equation: q_dot = 0.5*q*omega)
    ↪    --
    // Convert gyro readings to a delta quaternion.
    Quaternion gyroDelta = GyroToQuaternion(gyroReading, dt);
    // Predict the new orientation by integrating the gyroscope
    ↪    data.
    Quaternion predictedOrientation = currentOrientation *
    ↪    gyroDelta;
    predictedOrientation.Normalize();

    // -- Accelerometer-Based Orientation Estimation --
    // Estimate orientation from accelerometer data (assuming
    ↪    static gravity).
    Quaternion accelOrientation =
    ↪    EstimateOrientationFromAccel(accelReading);

    // -- Sensor Fusion using Complementary Filter --
    // Fuse the gyro and accelerometer estimates.
    Quaternion fusedOrientation = Quaternion.Slerp(
        predictedOrientation,
        accelOrientation,
        1 - complementaryFilterFactor
    );

    // Optional smoothing: blend the fused result with the
    ↪    previous orientation.
```

```
    currentOrientation = Quaternion.Slerp(currentOrientation,
    ↪   fusedOrientation, 0.5f);

    // -- Mapping to Virtual Camera Dynamics --
    // Apply the fused orientation to the transform.
    // The overall transformation of the head rig is defined as:
    // T_rig = T_position * R_orientation
    transform.rotation = currentOrientation;
    transform.position = currentPosition;
}

// Converts angular velocity from the gyroscope into a delta
↪   rotation quaternion.
private Quaternion GyroToQuaternion(Vector3 gyro, float dt)
{
    // Calculate the rotation angle (in radians) over the time
    ↪   step.
    float angle = gyro.magnitude * dt;
    if (angle < 1e-6f)
        return Quaternion.identity;

    // Determine the rotation axis.
    Vector3 axis = gyro.normalized;
    // Convert the angle from radians to degrees for Unity's
    ↪   AngleAxis.
    return Quaternion.AngleAxis(angle * Mathf.Rad2Deg, axis);
}

// Estimates orientation from accelerometer data by interpreting
↪   gravity direction.
private Quaternion EstimateOrientationFromAccel(Vector3 accel)
{
    // Normalize the accelerometer vector to isolate the gravity
    ↪   direction.
    Vector3 gravity = accel.normalized;
    // Compute approximated pitch and roll angles.
    float pitch = Mathf.Asin(-gravity.x); // Approximation for
    ↪   pitch.
    float roll = Mathf.Asin(gravity.z);      // Approximation for
    ↪   roll.
    // Yaw cannot be derived from accelerometer data alone.
    return Quaternion.Euler(pitch * Mathf.Rad2Deg, 0f, roll *
    ↪   Mathf.Rad2Deg);
}

// Simulates gyroscope sensor data.
private Vector3 SimulateGyro()
{
    // For demonstration purposes, simulate a slow rotation
    ↪   around the Y-axis (10° per second).
    return new Vector3(0f, Mathf.Deg2Rad * 10f, 0f);
}
```

```
// Simulates accelerometer sensor data.
private Vector3 SimulateAccel()
{
    // Under static conditions, the accelerometer senses
    ↪   gravity: (0, -9.81, 0) m/s^2.
    return new Vector3(0f, -9.81f, 0f);
}
}
```

This comprehensive code snippet demonstrates the implementation of key head tracking algorithms in a VR system. It integrates gyroscope-based rotation using quaternion mathematics, estimates device inclination from accelerometer readings, and applies sensor fusion via a complementary filter. The resulting orientation is then mapped to the virtual camera rig through the combined transformation Trig = Tposition · Rorientation, ensuring that real-world head movements are faithfully reproduced in the immersive environment.

Chapter 9

VR Controller Input Mapping with Oculus

Oculus Controller Input Architecture

The Oculus controllers are engineered with a comprehensive array of input modalities including multi-axis analog sensors, digital buttons, capacitive touch interfaces, and trigger mechanisms. Each of these components emits data at a high resolution that is subsequently subjected to normalization and calibration processes. The sensor outputs can be represented as a time-dependent vector function, $s(t) \in \mathbb{R}^n$, where n denotes the total number of discrete sensor channels available on the controller. Such a representation facilitates analysis of the fidelity and temporal dynamics inherent in the input signals, ensuring that the granularity of the digital readings accurately reflects the subtle variations in user-operated stimuli.

The design of these controllers emphasizes both sensitivity and reliability. Integral to their operation is the mechanism for signal conditioning, which mitigates the detrimental effects of noise and sensor drift. The output from each sensor channel is subject to filtering algorithms, thereby generating a set of refined measurements that serve as the foundation for subsequent mapping procedures within the virtual environment.

Unity Input System Abstractions

The Unity Input System provides a robust abstraction layer that encapsulates numerous hardware devices under a unifying framework. This system processes raw data streams and translates them into structured input events $e \in \mathcal{E}$, where each event corresponds to a specific type of user interaction. The event-driven architecture permits precise handling of diverse input modalities such as digital button activations, analog axis movements, and gesture-based interactions.

Within this framework, the transformation of the raw sensor vector $s(t)$ into higher-level phenomena is achieved by mapping the individual sensor readings to predefined in-game actions. This mapping is accomplished through an internal state machine that interprets the continuous and discrete aspects of the input data. The abstraction provided by Unity not only simplifies the integration of third-party hardware devices like the Oculus controllers but also ensures that input perturbations are reconciled in a predictable manner, thereby retaining consistency in the user experience.

Integrating Oculus APIs for Input Acquisition

The seamless integration of Oculus-specific APIs with Unity's Input System introduces a layered approach to input acquisition. The Oculus SDK exposes a suite of API calls that permit direct interrogation of the controller states, allowing for real-time access to sensor readings corresponding to touch, pressure, and positional data. These API functions, denoted as mappings $f_i : \mathbb{R} \rightarrow \Omega_i$, where Ω_i represents the value domain specific to the ith sensor, furnish a systematic method for extracting meaningful data from the raw sensor outputs.

This integration is further refined by the application of calibrated scaling factors and dead zone definitions that are crucial in isolating intentional user inputs from inadvertent signals. The theoretical foundation for this calibration involves the implementation of threshold functions and normalization routines, which convert the physical sensor outputs from the controllers into a standardized range. Consequently, the refined signals are then relayed through Unity's input event channels, allowing for immediate mapping into the virtual domain. This multi-stage acquisition and pre-processing pipeline ensures that the in-game responsiveness is both accurate and temporally coherent.

Mapping Controller Signals to In-Game Actions

The translation of processed controller signals into in-game actions hinges upon a deterministic mapping function, $\Phi : \mathbb{R}^n \to \mathcal{A}$, where $\mathcal{A}$ denotes the set of all possible actions within the virtual space. This mapping function is meticulously decomposed into sub-functions, each tailored to handle specific categories of input. Continuous inputs, such as those emanating from thumbsticks or variable trigger pressures, are subjected to scaling and interpolation techniques. This yields analog values that can be smoothly integrated into movement or orientation systems within the game engine. Discrete inputs, by contrast, are processed through a thresholding mechanism that delineates between signal noise and deliberate actuation.

Mathematical constructs such as linear and non-linear scaling functions are employed to ensure that the transformation from sensor readings to in-game magnitudes preserves both sensitivity and precision. The implementation of these functions is informed by rigorous calibration procedures which adjust for systemic offsets, sensor variability, and latency considerations. In effect, the mapping function Φ provides a cohesive framework that bridges the physical dynamics of the controller with the abstract representations of in-game entities. The resulting system is characterized by its capacity to generate responsive and reliable interactions, thereby underpinning a high-fidelity virtual reality experience without the introduction of perceptible processing delays.

C# Code Snippet

```csharp
using UnityEngine;
using System.Collections;

// Enum representing all possible in-game actions
public enum VRAction
{
    None,
    MoveForward,
```

```
    MoveBackward,
    TurnLeft,
    TurnRight,
    GrabObject,
    ReleaseObject
}

public class VRControllerInputMapper : MonoBehaviour
{
    // Calibration parameters for sensor normalization and signal
    ↪   conditioning
    public float deadZone = 0.1f;        // Minimum magnitude to
    ↪   overcome sensor noise
    public float smoothing = 0.1f;       // Smoothing factor for
    ↪   low-pass filtering
    public float sensitivity = 1.0f;     // Scaling factor for input
    ↪   responsiveness

    // Variables to hold raw sensor readings from the Oculus
    ↪   controller
    private Vector2 rawThumbstick;
    private float rawTrigger;

    // Variables to hold filtered (low-pass) sensor values
    private Vector2 filteredThumbstick;
    private float filteredTrigger;

    // Initialization: set initial filtered values to zero
    void Start()
    {
        filteredThumbstick = Vector2.zero;
        filteredTrigger = 0f;
    }

    // Update is called once per frame
    void Update()
    {
        // Step 1: Acquire raw sensor data (s(t)  )
        AcquireInput();

        // Step 2: Calibrate and normalize raw sensor data using
        ↪   dead zone and scaling
        Vector2 calibratedThumb =
        ↪   CalibrateThumbstick(rawThumbstick);
        float calibratedTrig = CalibrateTrigger(rawTrigger);

        // Step 3: Apply low-pass filtering to smooth the sensor
        ↪   inputs
        filteredThumbstick =
        ↪   LowPassFilterThumbstick(calibratedThumb,
        ↪   filteredThumbstick, smoothing);
        filteredTrigger = LowPassFilterTrigger(calibratedTrig,
        ↪   filteredTrigger, smoothing);
```

```csharp
    // Step 4: Map the filtered sensor signals to in-game
    ↪   actions using mapping function :  ↩
    VRAction action = MapInputToAction(filteredThumbstick,
    ↪   filteredTrigger);

    // Step 5: Execute the mapped in-game action
    ExecuteAction(action);
}

// Simulate acquisition of raw input data from the Oculus
↪   controllers using Unity Input APIs
void AcquireInput()
{
    // Retrieve thumbstick axis values and trigger pressure
    rawThumbstick = new
    ↪   Vector2(Input.GetAxis("Oculus_Left_ThumbstickX"),
        Input.GetAxis("Oculus_Left_ThumbstickY"));
    rawTrigger = Input.GetAxis("Oculus_Right_Trigger");
}

// Calibrate and normalize thumbstick input:
// Implements: if |s| < deadZone then s = 0, else normalized s =
↪   (|s| - deadZone)/(1 - deadZone)
Vector2 CalibrateThumbstick(Vector2 raw)
{
    if (raw.magnitude < deadZone)
        return Vector2.zero;

    float scale = (raw.magnitude - deadZone) / (1f - deadZone);
    return raw.normalized * scale * sensitivity;
}

// Calibrate trigger input with dead zone handling and scaling.
float CalibrateTrigger(float raw)
{
    if (raw < deadZone)
        return 0f;
    return ((raw - deadZone) / (1f - deadZone)) * sensitivity;
}

// Apply a simple low-pass filter to smooth thumbstick input:
// filteredValue = previous + smoothing * (current - previous)
Vector2 LowPassFilterThumbstick(Vector2 current, Vector2
↪   previous, float smoothingFactor)
{
    return Vector2.Lerp(previous, current, smoothingFactor);
}

// Similar low-pass filter for trigger input
float LowPassFilterTrigger(float current, float previous, float
↪   smoothingFactor)
{
```

```
        return Mathf.Lerp(previous, current, smoothingFactor);
}

// Mapping function  :  ↪  transforms sensor signals into
↪    discrete in-game actions.
// Continuous inputs from the thumbstick and discrete inputs
↪    from the trigger are merged here.
VRAction MapInputToAction(Vector2 thumb, float trigger)
{
    // Process discrete input: if trigger exceeds high
    ↪    threshold, trigger grab action.
    if (trigger > 0.8f)
    {
        return VRAction.GrabObject;
    }
    // A low trigger value (but non-zero) maps to a release
    ↪    action.
    else if (trigger > 0.0f && trigger < 0.2f)
    {
        return VRAction.ReleaseObject;
    }

    // Process continuous input from thumbstick:
    // If magnitude is significant, determine movement direction
    ↪    based on angle.
    if (thumb.magnitude > 0.5f)
    {
        // Calculate angle (in degrees) between the thumb vector
        ↪    and the upward direction.
        float angle = Vector2.SignedAngle(Vector2.up, thumb);
        if (angle >= -45f && angle <= 45f)
            return VRAction.MoveForward;
        else if (angle > 45f && angle < 135f)
            return VRAction.TurnLeft;
        else if (angle < -45f && angle > -135f)
            return VRAction.TurnRight;
        else
            return VRAction.MoveBackward;
    }
    return VRAction.None;
}

// Execute the action resulting from the mapping:
// This method links the abstract VRAction to actual game
↪    behaviour.
void ExecuteAction(VRAction action)
{
    switch (action)
    {
        case VRAction.MoveForward:
            Debug.Log("Action: Move Forward");
            // Insert movement code here
            break;
```

```
    case VRAction.MoveBackward:
        Debug.Log("Action: Move Backward");
        // Insert movement code here
        break;
    case VRAction.TurnLeft:
        Debug.Log("Action: Turn Left");
        // Insert rotation code here
        break;
    case VRAction.TurnRight:
        Debug.Log("Action: Turn Right");
        // Insert rotation code here
        break;
    case VRAction.GrabObject:
        Debug.Log("Action: Grab Object");
        // Insert grabbing code here
        break;
    case VRAction.ReleaseObject:
        Debug.Log("Action: Release Object");
        // Insert releasing code here
        break;
    case VRAction.None:
    default:
        // No action mapped - idle state.
        break;
    }
  }
}
```

Summary: This comprehensive C# code snippet demonstrates a full pipeline—from acquiring raw sensor data (s(t)) from Oculus controllers, through calibration (using dead zone and scaling), low-pass filtering for signal smoothing, to applying the mapping function that translates these inputs into actionable commands () within the virtual environment. The code integrates continuous and discrete input handling, ensuring high-fidelity, responsive VR interactions that align with the theoretical algorithms and equations discussed in the chapter.

Chapter 10

Processing Hand Gesture Inputs for VR

Sensor Modalities for Hand Gesture Capture

The acquisition of hand gesture inputs is predicated upon sensor systems that capture the complex spatio-temporal dynamics of human hand movements. Sensors such as depth cameras, inertial measurement units, and infrared trackers provide multidimensional data streams. These data streams can be modeled as a time-dependent vector function, $g(t) \in \mathbb{R}^m$, where the dimensionality m reflects the number of discrete sensor channels—encompassing joint positions, orientations, and acceleration vectors. Such a representation is crucial for characterizing fingertip trajectories, inter-finger spacing, and the subtle variances that distinguish one gesture from another. The inherent noise, calibration inconsistencies, and sensor drift are mitigated by sensor fusion techniques and signal conditioning methodologies that ensure a robust foundation for subsequent processing stages.

Preprocessing and Feature Extraction

After initial acquisition, the raw sensor output $g(t)$ undergoes preprocessing to enhance its fidelity and extract relevant features. These preprocessing stages serve to reduce noise and amplify discriminative characteristics that are essential for accurate gesture interpretation.

1 Temporal Signal Filtering and Noise Reduction

Temporal filtering is employed to alleviate high-frequency noise artifacts and sensor jitter. A standard approach involves the application of a recursive low-pass filter defined by

$$g_f(t) = \alpha \, g(t) + (1 - \alpha) \, g_f(t - \Delta t),$$

where $g_f(t)$ denotes the filtered signal at time t, $\alpha \in (0,1)$ is the filter constant, and Δt is the sampling interval. This filtering operation not only smooths the transient fluctuations but also retains the essential dynamics necessary for capturing the evolution of hand postures over time.

2 Spatial Feature Extraction and Kinematic Modeling

Spatial processing of the sensor data entails the extraction of features that encapsulate the geometric configuration of the hand. Each hand can be viewed as a kinematic chain with multiple degrees of freedom; joint positions are denoted by $p_i(t)$, with the inter-joint distances computed as

$$d_{ij}(t) = \|p_i(t) - p_j(t)\|,$$

where i and j index the distinct hand joints. These distances, coupled with angular measurements between adjacent segments, form a set of descriptors that define the hand's pose. Such descriptors are often aggregated into feature vectors that serve as effective proxies for the underlying gesture state. Advanced techniques in manifold learning and dimensionality reduction may also be applied to these feature spaces, thereby isolating the intrinsic parameters of gesture variability.

Gesture Segmentation and Classification

The transition from continuous sensor signals to discrete gesture commands necessitates a rigorous segmentation and classification framework. The segmentation process identifies temporal windows within which the hand's motion is relatively homogeneous, while the classification step assigns semantic labels to these segmented gestures based on their feature representations.

1 Temporal Segmentation and Feature Vector Assembly

Temporal segmentation is typically realized using sliding window techniques that partition the filtered signal $g_f(t)$ into segments $W = [t - \Delta, t]$, where Δ denotes the window duration. Within each window, a feature vector $\mathbf{x} \in \mathbb{R}^k$ is computed to summarize the key characteristics of the motion. These feature vectors may encapsulate statistical measures such as mean, variance, and higher-order moments, as well as dynamic features derived from time derivatives. This assembly of feature vectors systematically converts the continuous sensor output into discrete, analyzable data points that are amenable to classification.

2 Classification Algorithms and Decision Boundaries

Once feature vectors have been extracted, a mapping function $\Psi : \mathbb{R}^k \rightarrow \mathcal{G}$ is employed to associate each vector with a corresponding gesture class $g_i \in \mathcal{G}$. The classifier is typically trained on a dataset that spans a variety of gesture instances, ensuring robustness against inter-user variability and environmental inconsistencies. Techniques ranging from statistical models and support vector machines to hidden Markov models and neural networks are utilized to delineate decision boundaries within the feature space. The classifier's performance is mathematically characterized by metrics such as accuracy, precision, and recall, and it operates under the assumption that distinct gestures occupy separable regions within the transformed feature space.

Mapping Gesture Inputs to Virtual Interactions

The final stage in the gesture processing pipeline involves the translation of recognized hand gestures into actions within a virtual environment. A mapping function

$$\Phi : \mathcal{G} \to \mathcal{A}$$

associates the gesture class space $\mathcal{G}$ with a set of virtual actions $\mathcal{A}$ designed for interactive engagement. This function is designed to ensure that the latency between gesture capture and action execution remains imperceptibly low, thereby preserving the temporal coherence of the virtual experience.

The mapping function Φ is derived by minimizing an error metric that quantifies the discrepancy between the intended and achieved virtual behaviors. Formally, an optimization problem is framed such that

$$\min_{\Phi} \|\Phi(\Psi(\mathbf{x})) - a\|, \quad a \in \mathcal{A},$$

where the objective is to closely align the virtual feedback a with the detected gesture. The transformation must account for the continuous nature of the gesture recognition process while accommodating the inherent indeterminacies introduced by sensor noise and variances in hand morphology.

This mapping is further refined through iterative calibration and adaptive learning algorithms, which adjust the parameters of Φ based on real-time performance measures and user-specific input patterns. The confluence of precise sensor modeling, robust segmentation, and sophisticated classification culminates in a gesture recognition system that enables natural and immersive interaction within complex virtual environments.

C# Code Snippet

```
using System;
using System.Collections.Generic;
using System.Linq;
using System.Numerics;

namespace VRGestureProcessing
{
    // Class representing a single sensor reading of the hand at a
    ↪ given timestamp.
    // Each reading contains a list of joint positions.
    public class HandData
    {
        public double Timestamp { get; set; }
```

```csharp
    public List<Vector3> JointPositions { get; set; }

    public HandData(double timestamp, List<Vector3>
    ↪  jointPositions)
    {
        Timestamp = timestamp;
        JointPositions = jointPositions;
    }
}

// Class representing a feature vector extracted from a segment
↪  of sensor data.
// For simplicity, we use the average inter-joint distance as a
↪  key feature.
public class FeatureVector
{
    public double AverageInterJointDistance { get; set; }
    // Additional features (mean, variance, derivatives, etc.)
    ↪   could be added here.
}

// The GestureProcessor encapsulates filtering, segmentation,
↪  feature extraction,
// gesture classification, and mapping of gestures to virtual
↪  actions.
public class GestureProcessor
{
    private double alpha;
    private int windowSize;
    private Dictionary<string, string> gestureActionMapping;

    public GestureProcessor(double alpha, int windowSize)
    {
        this.alpha = alpha;      // Filter constant in (0,1)
        this.windowSize = windowSize; // Number of samples per
        ↪   sliding window

        // Initialize the mapping function :   → .
        // For example, "OpenHand" maps to the action "Select
        ↪   Object" and
        // "ClosedHand" maps to "Grab Object".
        gestureActionMapping = new Dictionary<string, string>()
        {
            { "OpenHand", "Select Object" },
            { "ClosedHand", "Grab Object" }
        };
    }

    // Applies a recursive low-pass filter to a list of HandData
    ↪   readings.
    // Implements the equation:
    //     g_f(t) =  * g(t) + (1 -  ) * g_f(t -  t)
```

```csharp
public List<HandData> ApplyLowPassFilter(List<HandData>
↪    rawData)
{
    List<HandData> filteredData = new List<HandData>();

    if (rawData == null || rawData.Count == 0)
        return filteredData;

    // Initialize with the first reading (no previous
    ↪    filtered value available).
    filteredData.Add(rawData[0]);

    for (int i = 1; i < rawData.Count; i++)
    {
        var previousFiltered = filteredData[i - 1];
        var currentRaw = rawData[i];
        List<Vector3> filteredJoints = new List<Vector3>();

        // Apply filtering to each joint position.
        for (int j = 0; j < currentRaw.JointPositions.Count;
        ↪    j++)
        {
            Vector3 filteredPosition = alpha *
            ↪    currentRaw.JointPositions[j] +
                (1 - alpha) *
                ↪    previousFiltered.JointPositions[j];
            filteredJoints.Add(filteredPosition);
        }

        filteredData.Add(new HandData(currentRaw.Timestamp,
        ↪    filteredJoints));
    }

    return filteredData;
}

// Computes the average inter-joint distance for a single
↪    HandData reading.
// Implements the equation:
//      d_{ij}(t) = ||p_i(t) - p_j(t)||
public double ComputeAverageInterJointDistance(HandData
↪    data)
{
    double sumDistances = 0.0;
    int count = 0;

    for (int i = 0; i < data.JointPositions.Count; i++)
    {
        for (int j = i + 1; j < data.JointPositions.Count;
        ↪    j++)
        {
```

```
            sumDistances +=
            ↪   Vector3.Distance(data.JointPositions[i],
            ↪   data.JointPositions[j]);
            count++;
        }
    }

    return (count > 0 ? sumDistances / count : 0.0);
}

// Segments the filtered sensor data using a sliding window.
// For each window, it assembles a feature vector (e.g.,
↪   average inter-joint distance).
public List<FeatureVector>
↪   SegmentAndExtractFeatures(List<HandData> filteredData)
{
    List<FeatureVector> featuresList = new
    ↪   List<FeatureVector>();

    // Apply a sliding window of length 'windowSize' across
    ↪   the data.
    for (int start = 0; start <= filteredData.Count -
    ↪   windowSize; start++)
    {
        List<HandData> windowData =
        ↪   filteredData.GetRange(start, windowSize);
        double avgDistance = windowData.Average(data =>
        ↪   ComputeAverageInterJointDistance(data));

        FeatureVector vector = new FeatureVector
        {
            AverageInterJointDistance = avgDistance
        };

        featuresList.Add(vector);
    }

    return featuresList;
}

// Classifies a feature vector into a gesture class.
// Simulates the mapping : ~k →  where decision boundaries
↪   are established based on thresholds.
public string ClassifyGesture(FeatureVector feature)
{
    // Determine a threshold value that distinguishes
    ↪   between gestures.
    double threshold = 0.1;
    if (feature.AverageInterJointDistance > threshold)
    {
        return "OpenHand";
    }
    else
```

```csharp
        {
            return "ClosedHand";
        }
    }

    // Maps the recognized gesture class to a virtual action.
    // Implements the mapping function: :  ↵
    public string MapGestureToAction(string gesture)
    {
        if (gestureActionMapping.ContainsKey(gesture))
        {
            return gestureActionMapping[gesture];
        }
        else
        {
            return "No Action";
        }
    }
}

public class Program
{
    // Generates sample sensor data for demonstration purposes.
    // Each HandData contains simulated joint positions for a
    ↵  hand.
    public static List<HandData> GenerateSampleData(int
    ↵  numSamples, int numJoints)
    {
        Random rand = new Random();
        List<HandData> samples = new List<HandData>();
        double timestamp = 0.0;
        double deltaTime = 0.033; // Approximate time interval
        ↵  (~30 FPS)

        for (int i = 0; i < numSamples; i++)
        {
            List<Vector3> joints = new List<Vector3>();
            for (int j = 0; j < numJoints; j++)
            {
                // Simulate joint positions with random values.
                float x = (float)rand.NextDouble();
                float y = (float)rand.NextDouble();
                float z = (float)rand.NextDouble();
                joints.Add(new Vector3(x, y, z));
            }

            samples.Add(new HandData(timestamp, joints));
            timestamp += deltaTime;
        }

        return samples;
    }
```

```csharp
public static void Main(string[] args)
{
    // Step 0: Generate sample raw sensor data (e.g., 50
    ↪   samples with 5 joints each).
    List<HandData> rawData = GenerateSampleData(50, 5);

    // Initialize the processor with filter constant  and a
    ↪   window size for segmentation.
    GestureProcessor processor = new GestureProcessor(alpha:
    ↪   0.5, windowSize: 5);

    // Step 1: Preprocess - Apply the low-pass filter to
    ↪   reduce noise.
    List<HandData> filteredData =
    ↪   processor.ApplyLowPassFilter(rawData);

    // Step 2: Feature Extraction - Segment the filtered
    ↪   data into sliding windows and extract features.
    List<FeatureVector> features =
    ↪   processor.SegmentAndExtractFeatures(filteredData);

    // Step 3: Gesture Segmentation and Classification.
    // For each feature vector, classify the gesture and map
    ↪   it to a corresponding virtual action.
    foreach (var feature in features)
    {
        string gesture = processor.ClassifyGesture(feature);
        string action =
        ↪   processor.MapGestureToAction(gesture);
        Console.WriteLine($"Computed Avg Distance:
        ↪   {feature.AverageInterJointDistance:F3} ->
        ↪   Gesture: {gesture}, Action: {action}");
    }

    // The above pipeline integrates:
    // - Sensor data acquisition and low-pass filtering
    ↪   (using the recursive filter formula).
    // - Spatial feature extraction via inter-joint distance
    ↪   computations.
    // - Temporal segmentation using sliding window
    ↪   techniques.
    // - Gesture classification based on feature thresholds.
    // - Mapping of gestures to virtual actions via an
    ↪   optimized function .
    }
  }
}
```

Chapter 11

Creating Interactive VR Objects Using Physics

Foundations of Physics Simulation in VR Environments

The simulation of interactive objects in virtual reality hinges on the rigorous application of physical principles within a discrete computational framework. Rigid body dynamics are at the core of this simulation, where each object is modeled by its mass, inertia, and the net forces acting upon it. The underlying physics engine employs discrete time integration methods, such as the explicit Euler scheme, in which the update equations take the form

$$v_{t+\Delta t} = v_t + a_t\,\Delta t \quad \text{and} \quad x_{t+\Delta t} = x_t + v_t\,\Delta t,$$

where v_t and x_t denote the object velocity and position at time t, a_t represents the acceleration derived from the applied force, and Δt is the fixed time step. This mathematical formulation encapsulates the continuous evolution of object dynamics in a stepwise manner, ensuring that the simulation remains computationally tractable while preserving a high degree of physical veracity.

1 Discrete Time Integration and Rigid Body Dynamics

Within the simulation framework, the integration of force vectors with respect to time results in the dynamic evolution of object states. Each object is treated as a rigid body subject to Newtonian mechanics, where the governing equation

$$F = m \cdot a$$

relates the net force F to the acceleration a through the mass m of the object. The discretization inherent in the simulation process necessitates a careful balance between numerical stability and fidelity. The engine's solver, which iteratively updates velocities and positions, must resolve the instantaneous effects of both constant environmental forces and transient user inputs.

Physical Material Properties and Dynamics

Realistic object behavior is achieved through the precise adjustment of physical material properties. Key parameters such as mass, friction, drag, and restitution are assigned to each object to emulate the empirical characteristics observed in real-world materials. The dynamic friction coefficient, denoted by μ, directly influences the resistance encountered when objects are in contact, while the restitution coefficient e regulates the elasticity of collisions, thereby dictating the energy retained after impact.

1 Material Coefficients and Frictional Interfaces

The formulation of inter-object interactions involves the implementation of frictional interfaces where forces opposing motion are proportional to the normal force at the point of contact. The drag force is modeled in accordance with the equation

$$F_d = -c_d\, v,$$

in which c_d is the drag constant and v represents the instantaneous velocity of the object. In addition, the parameters governing friction and restitution are embedded within the collision resolution algorithms, ensuring that impact responses are computed based on both the geometric and material properties of the interacting bodies.

Collision Detection and Contact Mechanics

The fidelity of interactive simulations is critically dependent on robust collision detection algorithms and accurate contact mechanics. The physics engine utilizes a hierarchical approach to collision detection, initially employing simplified bounding volumes before engaging in more detailed mesh-based intersection tests. This multilevel strategy not only improves computational efficiency but also ensures that collisions are identified with high precision.

1 Bounding Volumes and Contact Resolution

Bounding volumes, such as spheres, boxes, and capsules, are used as primary filters for potential collisions. Once an overlap is detected between the bounding volumes of two objects, the engine refines the analysis by calculating the exact contact points and normals. The impulse generated during collisions is computed through the application of the formula

$$J = \frac{(1+e)\,\Delta v}{\frac{1}{m_1} + \frac{1}{m_2}},$$

where J represents the collision impulse, Δv is the relative velocity at the point of contact, and m_1 and m_2 denote the masses of the colliding objects. These calculations ensure that momentum and energy are conserved according to the foundational principles of collision mechanics.

Environmental Forces and Interactive Dynamics

The realistic behavior of VR objects is further enriched by the simultaneous application of multiple forces, both environmental and user-induced. Gravity, modeled as a constant acceleration vector g, serves as a pervasive influence that affects all objects. Moreover, environmental forces such as wind or pressure differentials can be superimposed upon the gravitational field, resulting in a net force

$$F_{\text{net}} = F_{\text{gravity}} + F_{\text{external}}.$$

The resultant acceleration, computed as

$$a = \frac{F_{\text{net}}}{m},$$

dictates the translational motion of the object. In addition, rotational dynamics are captured by applying torques that generate angular acceleration α, with the relationship

$$\tau = I\,\alpha,$$

where τ is the torque and I is the moment of inertia. The interplay between these forces facilitates a rich simulation of motion that mirrors the complexities inherent in physical systems.

1 Superposition of Forces and Impulse Applications

The mathematical principle of superposition permits the concurrent application of multiple force vectors. In an interactive virtual environment, objects are subject to continuous gravitational pull as well as discrete impulse forces resulting from user interactions. These impulse forces are characterized by their magnitude and duration, and their incorporation into the simulation is governed by the cumulative effect on object momentum. The resulting dynamic response is a composite of internal material properties and externally applied forces, which together define the trajectory and orientation changes of the object in real time.

Integration of Physics with User-Driven Interactions

The realistic simulation of VR objects is greatly enhanced by the seamless integration of user-driven interactions. In these scenarios, direct manipulations—often generated by hand gestures or input devices—are converted into physical impulses that act upon objects in the virtual space. The physics engine treats these inputs as additional force vectors, allowing them to modify the state of an object in a manner consistent with the laws of mechanics.

1 Impulse Forces and Kinematic Constraints

When an external input is received, the corresponding impulse is applied to the object at a specific location, resulting in both linear and angular momentum changes. These interactions are bounded by kinematic constraints that preserve the continuity and stability of the simulation. By incorporating instantaneous impulses into the overall force calculations, the engine ensures that the objects respond to user commands in a natural and physically coherent fashion. The resulting modifications to velocity and angular momentum are governed by equations that maintain the conservation of momentum, ultimately leading to interactions that are both predictable and visually consistent with real-world behavior.

C# Code Snippet

```csharp
using System;
using System.Numerics;

// This class represents a physics-enabled object in the VR
↪    environment.
// It encapsulates properties like mass, position, velocity, and
↪    material characteristics.
public class PhysicsObject {
    public float Mass { get; set; }
    public float InverseMass { get; private set; }
    public Vector3 Position { get; set; }
    public Vector3 Velocity { get; set; }
    public Vector3 AccumulatedForces { get; set; }
    public float Restitution { get; set; }        // Coefficient of
↪    restitution (e)
    public float FrictionCoefficient { get; set; }   // Dynamic
↪    friction coefficient ()
    public float DragCoefficient { get; set; }       // Drag
↪    constant (c_d)

    public PhysicsObject(float mass, Vector3 position, Vector3
↪    velocity, float restitution, float friction, float drag) {
        Mass = mass;
        InverseMass = (mass > 0) ? 1.0f / mass : 0.0f;
        Position = position;
        Velocity = velocity;
        AccumulatedForces = Vector3.Zero;
        Restitution = restitution;
        FrictionCoefficient = friction;
        DragCoefficient = drag;
    }

    // Apply additional forces (e.g., user interactions) to the
↪    object.
    public void ApplyForce(Vector3 force) {
        AccumulatedForces += force;
```

```csharp
    }

    // Update the physics state of the object using explicit Euler
    ↪    integration.
    // Equations:
    //    v_{t+t} = v_t + a_t * t
    //    x_{t+t} = x_t + v_t * t
    public void Update(float deltaTime) {
        // Apply gravity force (g = 9.81 m/s² downward).
        Vector3 gravity = new Vector3(0, -9.81f, 0);
        ApplyForce(gravity * Mass);

        // Apply drag: F_d = -c_d * v.
        Vector3 dragForce = -DragCoefficient * Velocity;
        ApplyForce(dragForce);

        // Calculate acceleration from net force: a = F_net / m.
        Vector3 acceleration = AccumulatedForces * InverseMass;

        // Update velocity: v = v + a * t.
        Velocity += acceleration * deltaTime;

        // Update position: x = x + v * t.
        Position += Velocity * deltaTime;

        // Reset accumulated forces for the next time step.
        AccumulatedForces = Vector3.Zero;
    }
}

// A helper class for collision detection and resolution.
public static class CollisionHelper {
    // Calculates the collision impulse using:
    //    J = (1 + e) * v / (1/m1 + 1/m2)
    // where v is the relative velocity along the contact normal.
    public static Vector3 ComputeImpulse(PhysicsObject obj1,
    ↪    PhysicsObject obj2, Vector3 contactNormal, Vector3
    ↪    relativeVelocity) {
        float restitution = MathF.Min(obj1.Restitution,
        ↪    obj2.Restitution);
        float inverseMassSum = obj1.InverseMass + obj2.InverseMass;

        // Compute relative velocity along the normal: v =
        ↪    relativeVelocity · contactNormal.
        float velAlongNormal = Vector3.Dot(relativeVelocity,
        ↪    contactNormal);

        // Do not resolve if objects are separating.
        if (velAlongNormal > 0)
            return Vector3.Zero;

        float jScalar = (1.0f + restitution) * (-velAlongNormal) /
        ↪    inverseMassSum;
```

```
        return jScalar * contactNormal;
    }

    // Resolves collision by applying computed impulse to both
    ↪  objects.
    public static void ResolveCollision(PhysicsObject obj1,
    ↪  PhysicsObject obj2, Vector3 contactNormal, Vector3
    ↪  contactPoint) {
        Vector3 relativeVelocity = obj2.Velocity - obj1.Velocity;
        Vector3 impulse = ComputeImpulse(obj1, obj2, contactNormal,
        ↪  relativeVelocity);

        // Update velocities based on the impulse: v = impulse / m.
        obj1.Velocity -= impulse * obj1.InverseMass;
        obj2.Velocity += impulse * obj2.InverseMass;
    }
}

// The Simulation class runs a simple simulation step, updating
↪  objects and handling collisions.
public class Simulation {
    public PhysicsObject Object1 { get; set; }
    public PhysicsObject Object2 { get; set; }
    public float DeltaTime { get; set; }

    public Simulation(PhysicsObject obj1, PhysicsObject obj2, float
    ↪  deltaTime) {
        Object1 = obj1;
        Object2 = obj2;
        DeltaTime = deltaTime;
    }

    // Executes a single simulation step.
    public void Step() {
        // Update the physical state of each object.
        Object1.Update(DeltaTime);
        Object2.Update(DeltaTime);

        // Simple collision detection using bounding spheres
        ↪  (assumed radius = 1.0f).
        float radius = 1.0f;
        Vector3 delta = Object2.Position - Object1.Position;
        if (delta.Length() < 2 * radius) {
            // Determine contact normal and point.
            Vector3 contactNormal = Vector3.Normalize(delta);
            Vector3 contactPoint = Object1.Position + contactNormal
            ↪  * radius;
            // Resolve collision between the two objects.
            CollisionHelper.ResolveCollision(Object1, Object2,
            ↪  contactNormal, contactPoint);
        }
    }
}
```

```csharp
// Main program demonstrating the physics simulation.
public class Program {
    public static void Main(string[] args) {
        // Initialize two physics objects (e.g., VR objects) with
        ↪   mass, initial position, and velocity.
        PhysicsObject ball1 = new PhysicsObject(
            mass: 2.0f,
            position: new Vector3(0, 5, 0),
            velocity: new Vector3(1, 0, 0),
            restitution: 0.8f,   // Elasticity factor.
            friction: 0.5f,      // Friction coefficient.
            drag: 0.1f           // Drag constant.
        );

        PhysicsObject ball2 = new PhysicsObject(
            mass: 3.0f,
            position: new Vector3(0, 3, 0),
            velocity: new Vector3(-1, 0, 0),
            restitution: 0.8f,
            friction: 0.5f,
            drag: 0.1f
        );

        // Create a simulation instance with a fixed time step
        ↪   (approx. 60 FPS => 0.016 sec).
        Simulation simulation = new Simulation(ball1, ball2,
        ↪   deltaTime: 0.016f);

        // Run the simulation for 100 steps.
        for (int i = 0; i < 100; i++) {
            simulation.Step();
            Console.WriteLine($"Step {i}:");
            Console.WriteLine($"  Ball1 Position: {ball1.Position},
            ↪   Velocity: {ball1.Velocity}");
            Console.WriteLine($"  Ball2 Position: {ball2.Position},
            ↪   Velocity: {ball2.Velocity}");
        }
    }
}
```

Chapter 12

Designing Immersive Environments with Spatial Layouts

Foundations of Spatial Perception and Environmental Coherence

The construction of immersive virtual environments requires an intricate understanding of how spatial cues are perceived and interpreted. The efficacy of such environments is rooted in the ability to simulate a coherent three-dimensional space, in which geometric relationships are preserved and enhanced by perceptual cues. An immersive space must exhibit continuity that supports a natural mapping between the virtual and real domains. In formal terms, the spatial layout is defined over a metric space $M = (X, d)$, where X represents the set of points in the simulated environment and d is the distance function, ensuring that the Euclidean properties expected of physical space are maintained. The deliberate orchestration of depth, perspective, and positional context is integral to achieving a level of verisimilitude that underpins both user comfort and perceptual reliability.

Hierarchical Organization of Environmental Elements

A rigorous approach to environmental composition involves the establishment of a hierarchical structure that governs the placement and interrelation of visual elements. This organization is implemented by categorizing objects and spatial regions according to their functional and aesthetic significance. A well-structured scene relies on a series of nested groupings, where primary elements act as anchors and secondary elements are arranged relative to these landmarks. By constructing a scene graph that encapsulates not only the spatial coordinates but also the relational dependencies among objects, a designer can ensure that the overall layout is both coherent and scalable. Such an approach allows for the application of transformational hierarchies, where local spatial adjustments propagate through the hierarchy in a controlled manner, maintaining the integrity of the overall design.

Integration of Scale, Proportion, and Depth

The interplay between scale, proportion, and depth is a cornerstone in the design of virtual realities that appear both convincing and comfortable. Immersive environments demand that virtual objects are scaled relative to one another and to the viewpoint, following mathematical ratios that often mirror the proportions found in the natural world. The optimal relationship among dimensions is frequently expressed through ratios such as $r = \frac{w}{h}$, where w and h denote width and height respectively, or through principles akin to the golden ratio. Moreover, the simulation of depth is enhanced by techniques that dynamically adjust the apparent size and occlusion of objects, thereby reinforcing depth cues. The accurate rendering of these spatial relationships is fundamental to avoiding perceptual dissonance, which could otherwise lead to discomfort or disorientation when interacting within the virtual domain.

Contextual Cues and Zonal Delineation

Environmental composition in VR extends beyond the mere arrangement of objects; it also encompasses the strategic deployment of contextual cues that signal functional and thematic zones within the virtual space. The deliberate segmentation of the environment into distinct regions is accomplished through variations in lighting, texture gradients, and structural framing. These design strategies evoke contextual associations that guide user navigation implicitly. For instance, subtle changes in ambient illumination may mark the boundary between zones of interaction and reflective spaces, while discrete alterations in architectural motifs serve as markers of spatial transitions. The encoding of such contextual information often adheres to principles derived from perceptual psychology, ensuring that the delineation between functional areas is both intuitive and aesthetically integrated within the overall design.

Mathematical Modelling of Spatial Layouts

The rigorous analysis and synthesis of spatial layouts can be formalized via mathematical models that leverage both geometric and topological constructs. The process begins by mapping the virtual environment to a coordinate system in which each element is assigned a position vector $\mathbf{x} \in \mathbb{R}^3$. Relationships among these elements are subsequently quantified through distance metrics, angular relationships, and volumetric occupancies. The spatial configuration may further be modeled by employing transformation matrices that encapsulate rotations, translations, and scaling operations. In particular, the homogeneous transformation matrix

$$T = \begin{bmatrix} R & \mathbf{t} \\ \mathbf{0}^T & 1 \end{bmatrix}$$

serves to concisely represent the linear and translational displacements applied to an object, where R is the rotation matrix and $\mathbf{t}$ is the translation vector. Such formalisms provide a robust framework that supports simulation fidelity by ensuring that spatial modifications adhere precisely to the established physical and perceptual constraints.

C# Code Snippet

```csharp
using System;
using System.Collections.Generic;
using UnityEngine;
```

```csharp
namespace VREnvironments
{
    // Utility class for mathematical operations in VR spatial
    ↪   layouts.
    public static class MathUtilities
    {
        // Computes the Euclidean distance between two points in 3D
        ↪   space.
        public static float EuclideanDistance(Vector3 pointA,
        ↪   Vector3 pointB)
        {
            float dx = pointA.x - pointB.x;
            float dy = pointA.y - pointB.y;
            float dz = pointA.z - pointB.z;
            return Mathf.Sqrt(dx * dx + dy * dy + dz * dz);
        }

        // Computes the aspect ratio using the formula r = width /
        ↪   height.
        public static float ComputeAspectRatio(float width, float
        ↪   height)
        {
            if (Mathf.Approximately(height, 0.0f))
            {
                throw new DivideByZeroException("Height cannot be
                ↪   zero when computing aspect ratio.");
            }
            return width / height;
        }

        // Creates a homogeneous transformation matrix T = [R, t;
        ↪   0^T, 1] given a rotation and translation.
        public static Matrix4x4
        ↪   CreateTransformationMatrix(Quaternion rotation, Vector3
        ↪   translation)
        {
            // Unity's TRS method constructs a matrix from
            ↪   Translation, Rotation, and Scale.
            Matrix4x4 matrix = Matrix4x4.TRS(translation, rotation,
            ↪   Vector3.one);
            return matrix;
        }
    }

    // Represents a node in a hierarchical scene graph used for
    ↪   organizing VR environments.
    public class SceneNode
    {
        public string Name { get; private set; }
        public Vector3 Position { get; set; }
        public Quaternion Rotation { get; set; }
        public Vector3 Scale { get; set; }
```

```csharp
public SceneNode Parent { get; private set; }
public List<SceneNode> Children { get; private set; }

public SceneNode(string name, Vector3 position, Quaternion
↪  rotation, Vector3 scale)
{
    Name = name;
    Position = position;
    Rotation = rotation;
    Scale = scale;
    Children = new List<SceneNode>();
}

// Adds a child node under this node, establishing a
↪  hierarchical relationship.
public void AddChild(SceneNode child)
{
    child.Parent = this;
    Children.Add(child);
}

// Computes the local transformation matrix for the current
↪  node.
public Matrix4x4 GetLocalTransformation()
{
    return Matrix4x4.TRS(Position, Rotation, Scale);
}

// Recursively computes the global transformation matrix by
↪  combining parent's transformation.
public Matrix4x4 GetGlobalTransformation()
{
    if (Parent != null)
    {
        return Parent.GetGlobalTransformation() *
        ↪  GetLocalTransformation();
    }
    return GetLocalTransformation();
}

// Updates the node's scale based on depth to help maintain
↪  environmental proportions.
public void UpdateNode(float depthScaleFactor)
{
    // Using the distance from the origin as a simple depth
    ↪  measure.
    float depth = Vector3.Distance(Vector3.zero, Position);
    float scaleAdjustment = 1.0f + depth * depthScaleFactor;
    Scale = new Vector3(scaleAdjustment, scaleAdjustment,
    ↪  scaleAdjustment);
}
}
```

100

```csharp
// Manages the scene graph and applies spatial updates across
↪    the hierarchy.
public class SpatialLayoutManager
{
    public SceneNode RootNode { get; private set; }

    public SpatialLayoutManager(SceneNode root)
    {
        RootNode = root;
    }

    // Recursively updates each node in the scene graph.
    public void UpdateSceneGraph(SceneNode node, float
    ↪    depthScaleFactor)
    {
        if (node == null)
            return;

        node.UpdateNode(depthScaleFactor);
        foreach (SceneNode child in node.Children)
        {
            UpdateSceneGraph(child, depthScaleFactor);
        }
    }

    // Demonstrates the updated transformations by logging
    ↪    global matrices.
    public void DemoSceneGraphUpdate()
    {
        Debug.Log("Root Global Transformation: " +
        ↪    RootNode.GetGlobalTransformation());
        foreach (SceneNode child in RootNode.Children)
        {
            Debug.Log(child.Name + " Global Transformation: " +
            ↪    child.GetGlobalTransformation());
        }
    }
}

// A demonstration class incorporating spatial layout algorithms
↪    and formulas.
public class DemoSpatialLayout
{
    // Main entry point for the demo.
    // In a Unity project, this could be invoked in a
    ↪    MonoBehaviour's Start() method.
    public static void Main()
    {
        // Create a root node and child nodes to form a
        ↪    hierarchical scene graph.
        SceneNode root = new SceneNode("Root", Vector3.zero,
        ↪    Quaternion.identity, Vector3.one);
```

```
SceneNode child1 = new SceneNode("Child1", new
↪    Vector3(2.0f, 0.0f, 0.0f), Quaternion.Euler(0, 30,
↪    0), Vector3.one);
SceneNode child2 = new SceneNode("Child2", new
↪    Vector3(0.0f, 3.0f, 0.0f), Quaternion.Euler(0, 45,
↪    0), Vector3.one);

// Build the hierarchical structure.
root.AddChild(child1);
root.AddChild(child2);

// Instantiate the layout manager and update the scene
↪    graph with a specified depth scale factor.
SpatialLayoutManager layoutManager = new
↪    SpatialLayoutManager(root);
layoutManager.UpdateSceneGraph(root, 0.05f);
layoutManager.DemoSceneGraphUpdate();

// Demonstrate creating a transformation matrix using
↪    rotation (90° about the Y-axis) and translation.
Matrix4x4 transformationMatrix =
↪    MathUtilities.CreateTransformationMatrix(Quaternion.
Euler(0, 90, 0), new Vector3(5.0f, 0.0f, 0.0f));
Debug.Log("Transformation Matrix: " +
↪    transformationMatrix);

// Compute and display the aspect ratio using the
↪    formula r = width / height.
float aspectRatio =
↪    MathUtilities.ComputeAspectRatio(1920.0f, 1080.0f);
Debug.Log("Aspect Ratio (r = w/h): " +
↪    aspectRatio.ToString("F2"));

// Compute and display the Euclidean distance between
↪    two distinct points.
float distance = MathUtilities.EuclideanDistance(new
↪    Vector3(1.0f, 2.0f, 3.0f), new Vector3(4.0f, 5.0f,
↪    6.0f));
Debug.Log("Euclidean Distance between points: " +
↪    distance.ToString("F2"));
    }
  }
}
```

Chapter 13

Techniques for Natural User Interfaces in VR

Foundations of Natural Interface Design

The formulation of natural user interfaces (NUIs) within virtual reality (VR) environments is predicated upon an interdisciplinary synthesis of cognitive science, perceptual psychology, and advanced interaction paradigms. In this context, the term "natural" signifies an interface that minimizes the cognitive distance between user intention and system response, thereby approximating the immediacy and fluidity of real-world interactions. The design process is underpinned by rigorous empirical studies and formal models which quantify the mapping between sensory input and motor output. This relationship is often conceptualized through transformation functions $f : \mathbb{R}^n \to \mathbb{R}^m$, where the goal is to ensure that a user's gestural or vocal input is translated with minimal distortion into virtual actions. The theoretical framework thus developed reinforces the imperative for interfaces to exhibit properties of transparency and directness, reducing reliance on extraneous intermediary steps.

Integration of Multimodal Interaction and Sensor Fusion

The deployment of NUIs in VR necessitates the concerted integration of multiple sensory modalities. Input signals drawn from gesture recognition, speech processing, and eye tracking converge through sophisticated sensor fusion algorithms. Each modality contributes a unique dimension of data, and their simultaneous consideration enhances the precision and responsiveness of the interaction model. Mathematical techniques ranging from statistical estimation to Bayesian inference are employed to interpret the raw sensor data. The resulting integrated signal, denoted here as $\mathbf{I} \in \mathbb{R}^k$, serves as the primary input for subsequent processing pipelines. This multimodal convergence facilitates a more robust interpretation of the user's intent, thereby enabling a seamless and natural interface that operates effectively even amid noisy or ambiguous inputs.

Spatial Embedding and Context-Aware Interface Components

A central design strategy in VR user interfaces involves the spatial embedding of interactive elements within the virtual environment. The placement of controls, menus, and feedback mechanisms in three-dimensional space is orchestrated such that these elements align with the user's natural perceptual and motor repertoires. Spatial embedding leverages transformation matrices, typically expressed in the form

$$T = \begin{bmatrix} R & \mathbf{t} \\ \mathbf{0}^T & 1 \end{bmatrix},$$

where R represents the rotation matrix and $\mathbf{t}$ the translation vector, to accurately position interface components. This method ensures that interface elements are contextually congruent, thereby reducing the cognitive effort required for spatial reinterpretation. Moreover, the incorporation of contextual cues—such as variations in lighting, depth-of-field, and haptic feedback—serves to delineate interactive zones and reinforce the natural mapping between virtual controls and their real-world analogs.

Dynamic Adaptation and Real-Time Feedback Mechanisms

The dynamism inherent in VR environments calls for interfaces that are capable of real-time adaptation in response to continuously evolving user interactions. Real-time feedback loops are established to monitor parameters such as movement velocity, acceleration, and directional changes. These metrics are integrated into a temporal response function $g(t)$, which governs the adaptive behavior of interface elements. Through the use of adaptive control theory, interface components modulate their properties in direct response to changes in user input and environmental context. This dynamic interplay ensures that the interface remains perpetually in sync with the user's actions, thereby maintaining a high degree of responsiveness and reducing latency. In effect, the system's adaptability is achieved through the iterative calibration of interaction parameters, fostering a level of immersion that is both sustained and inherently natural.

Quantitative Metrics and Evaluative Methodologies

The optimization of natural user interfaces in VR is contingent upon the establishment of quantitative metrics that rigorously assess usability and immersion. A suite of evaluative methodologies is employed to measure response time, precision, and perceptual fidelity. Let $U : \mathbb{R}^n \to \mathbb{R}$ denote a usability function that encapsulates metrics such as error rate, task completion time, and subjective comfort levels. Experimental designs typically involve controlled user studies wherein variables are systematically manipulated and their impacts on interface performance are recorded. Statistical analyses, including variance analysis and regression modeling, are subsequently applied to ascertain the strength and significance of observed correlations. These evaluative frameworks provide a robust basis for iterative refinement and enhancement of UI designs, ensuring that the resultant interface achieves a harmonious balance between intuitive operation and technological sophistication.

C# Code Snippet

```csharp
using System;
using System.Numerics;

namespace VRNUI
{
    public class NaturalUserInterface
    {
        // Applies the transformation function f: ^n -> ^m using a
        //   homogeneous transformation matrix.
        public Vector3 TransformInput(Vector3 input, Matrix4x4
        →   transformation)
        {
            // Convert the 3D vector into a 4D homogeneous
            //   coordinate.
            Vector4 homogeneousInput = new Vector4(input, 1.0f);
            // Transform the vector using the provided matrix.
            Vector4 transformed =
            →   Vector4.Transform(homogeneousInput, transformation);
            // Return the 3D vector part of the result.
            return new Vector3(transformed.X, transformed.Y,
            →   transformed.Z);
        }

        // Fuses sensor data from gesture, speech, and eye tracking
        //   into a single input vector.
        public Vector3 FuseSensorData(Vector3 gestureData, Vector3
        →   speechData, Vector3 eyeTrackingData)
        {
            // For demonstration, use a simple average for fusion.
            return (gestureData + speechData + eyeTrackingData) /
            →   3.0f;
        }

        // Computes the temporal response function g(t) using
        //   exponential smoothing.
        // newValue = alpha * currentInput + (1 - alpha) *
        //   previousOutput.
        public float ComputeAdaptiveResponse(float previousOutput,
        →   float currentInput, float alpha)
        {
            return alpha * currentInput + (1.0f - alpha) *
            →   previousOutput;
        }

        // Calculates a usability metric U based on error rate, task
        //   completion time, and subjective comfort level.
        // A higher returned value indicates better usability.
        public float CalculateUsability(float errorRate, float
        →   completionTime, float comfortLevel)
        {
```

```
        // The formula balances minimal error and quick task
        ↪   completion against the comfort level.
        return comfortLevel / (errorRate * completionTime +
        ↪   1.0f);
    }

    // Creates a transformation matrix T = [R | t] based on
    ↪   rotation (using axis-angle) and translation inputs.
    public Matrix4x4 CreateTransformationMatrix(Vector3
    ↪   rotationAxis, float angle, Vector3 translation)
    {
        // Generate a rotation matrix from the given axis and
        ↪   angle.
        Matrix4x4 rotationMatrix =
        ↪   Matrix4x4.CreateFromAxisAngle(
        Vector3.Normalize(rotationAxis), angle);
        // Generate a translation matrix from the translation
        ↪   vector.
        Matrix4x4 translationMatrix =
        ↪   Matrix4x4.CreateTranslation(translation);
        // Combine both matrices: rotation is applied first,
        ↪   then translation.
        return rotationMatrix * translationMatrix;
    }
}

public class Program
{
    public static void Main(string[] args)
    {
        NaturalUserInterface nui = new NaturalUserInterface();

        // Example: Transforming an input vector using a defined
        ↪   transformation matrix.
        Vector3 inputVector = new Vector3(1.0f, 2.0f, 3.0f);
        // Create a transformation matrix: 45° rotation around
        ↪   Y-axis and a translation of (5, 0, 0).
        Matrix4x4 transformation =
        ↪   nui.CreateTransformationMatrix(new Vector3(0, 1, 0),
        ↪   (float)(Math.PI / 4), new Vector3(5.0f, 0, 0));
        Vector3 transformedVector =
        ↪   nui.TransformInput(inputVector, transformation);
        Console.WriteLine("Transformed Vector: " +
        ↪   transformedVector);

        // Example: Fusing sensor data from gesture, speech, and
        ↪   eye tracking modalities.
        Vector3 gestureData     = new Vector3(0.5f, 1.0f, 1.5f);
        Vector3 speechData      = new Vector3(1.0f, 0.5f, 1.0f);
        Vector3 eyeTrackingData = new Vector3(0.8f, 1.2f, 1.0f);
        Vector3 fusedSensorData =
        ↪   nui.FuseSensorData(gestureData, speechData,
        ↪   eyeTrackingData);
```

```
Console.WriteLine("Fused Sensor Data: " +
↪    fusedSensorData);

// Example: Calculating an adaptive response using an
↪    exponential smoothing approach.
float previousResponse = 0.0f;
float currentInput = 2.0f;
float alpha = 0.2f; // Smoothing factor
float adaptiveResponse =
↪    nui.ComputeAdaptiveResponse(previousResponse,
↪    currentInput, alpha);
Console.WriteLine("Adaptive Response: " +
↪    adaptiveResponse);

// Example: Calculating a usability metric given error
↪    rate, completion time, and comfort level.
float errorRate = 0.05f;        // 5% error rate
float completionTime = 30.0f; // 30 seconds task
↪    duration
float comfortLevel = 8.0f;      // Subjective comfort
↪    score
float usabilityScore = nui.CalculateUsability(errorRate,
↪    completionTime, comfortLevel);
Console.WriteLine("Usability Score: " + usabilityScore);
    }
  }
}
```

Summary: This comprehensive C# code snippet demonstrates key algorithms and mathematical formulations for natural user interfaces in VR. It integrates transformation functions using homogeneous matrices, multimodal sensor fusion, adaptive response computation via exponential smoothing, and quantitative usability evaluation, thereby reflecting the theoretical and practical underpinnings of natural interface design.

Chapter 14

Building 3D User Interfaces for Virtual Reality

Foundational Concepts in Three-Dimensional Interface Design

The development of three-dimensional user interfaces (3D UIs) in the context of virtual reality necessitates the synthesis of several theoretical domains, including human-computer interaction, spatial cognition, and computational geometry. This paradigm integrates principles from cognitive science and perceptual psychology with advanced computational models to establish interfaces that not only respond to user input but also adhere to the inherent spatial structure of the virtual environment. The conceptual framework is built upon the premise that a 3D UI must reduce the cognitive overhead associated with deciphering abstract interface elements by leveraging natural mapping between user actions and system responses. In this setting, interface elements are designed to embody properties of dimensional consistency and contextual relevance, thereby ensuring that their behavior within the virtual world is both predictable and mutable in response to the dynamic spatial context.

Spatial Embedding and Geometric Transformations

Embedding user interface components into a three-dimensional space requires rigorous attention to the mathematical principles governing spatial transformations. At the heart of this process is the proper handling of coordinate systems and transformation matrices, which enable the precise placement and orientation of UI elements relative to the user's viewpoint. A fundamental transformation can be expressed as

$$T = \begin{bmatrix} R & \mathbf{t} \\ \mathbf{0}^\top & 1 \end{bmatrix},$$

where R is a rotation matrix and $\mathbf{t}$ is a translation vector. This representation facilitates the composition of multiple transformations, such as scaling, rotation, and translation, ensuring that the resultant spatial configuration maintains consistency with both the virtual scene geometry and the user's perceptual frame of reference. The mathematical rigor underpinning these transformations is essential for achieving a seamless transition between the abstract representations of interface controls and their tangible manifestations within the virtual environment.

Contextual Coherence and Usability Considerations

The integration of 3D UI elements into virtual reality environments mandates that these components communicate a coherent spatial narrative. The design process involves embedding interactive elements within the environment in a manner that is both contextually intuitive and functionally robust. This demands an exploration of spatial hierarchies and layout strategies that align with the physical affordances and perceptual tendencies of users. In practice, elements such as menus, control panels, and feedback indicators are distributed throughout the three-dimensional workspace so that their placement minimizes the need for excessive head or body movement, aligning their spatial distribution with natural user interactions. The interplay between the virtual spatial context and the usability of the interface is governed by a set of design constraints that balance aesthetic coherence with performance metrics, ensuring that the system responds fluidly to rapid shifts in user attention and orientation.

Cognitive and Perceptual Dimensions of 3D User Interfaces

An in-depth understanding of the cognitive and perceptual processes involved in interacting with 3D UIs is paramount to the design of interfaces that are both immersive and effective. In virtual reality, the user's sensory input is multidimensional, combining depth perception, motion parallax, and stereoscopic vision to form a cohesive mental model of the environment. Effective interface design leverages these perceptual cues to reduce ambiguity and enhance the intuitiveness of interaction. By aligning virtual controls with the user's natural visual and motor habits, the interface promotes a reduction in mental load, thereby allowing users to focus on the task at hand rather than on deciphering the mechanics of the interface. The challenge lies in accurately mapping raw sensor data to discernible UI actions, a process that benefits from the integration of probabilistic models and statistical inference techniques to account for uncertainties in human behavior and sensory noise.

Advanced Interaction Models and Spatial Mapping Techniques

The design of advanced interaction models for 3D UIs extends beyond static placement and involves dynamic spatial mapping techniques that account for both user movement and environmental variability. This approach incorporates adaptive algorithms that refine the position, scale, and orientation of interface elements in real time, based on continuous feedback drawn from user interactions and sensor inputs. Mathematical models, such as transformation functions $f : \mathbb{R}^n \to \mathbb{R}^m$, are deployed to encapsulate the varying degrees of freedom inherent in three-dimensional space and to ensure that interactions remain responsive and contextually appropriate. Furthermore, techniques from differential geometry and topology are applied to analyze the curvature and connectivity of virtual surfaces, thereby informing the design of interfaces that can gracefully accommodate non-linear spatial deformations. The result of these integrated approaches is an immersive user interface that not only adapts to the intricacies of the virtual scene but also enhances the overall fidelity and usability of the virtual reality experience.

C# Code Snippet

```csharp
using UnityEngine;

namespace VRUIExample
{
    // Utility class demonstrating the core transformation equation:
    // T = [ R | t ]
    //     [ 0 | 1 ]
    // This class provides methods for creating a transformation
    ↪  matrix,
    // applying it to a 3D point, and even manually constructing the
    ↪  matrix.
    public static class TransformationUtility
    {
        // Creates a transformation matrix using translation,
        ↪  rotation, and scale.
        // This internally uses Unity's Matrix4x4.TRS method.
        public static Matrix4x4 CreateTransformationMatrix(Vector3
        ↪  translation, Quaternion rotation, Vector3 scale)
        {
            // Constructs the homogeneous transformation matrix:
            // T = Translation * Rotation * Scale
            return Matrix4x4.TRS(translation, rotation, scale);
        }

        // Alternative method to manually create a transformation
        ↪  matrix based on the equation:
        // T = [ R | t ]
        //     [ 0 | 1 ]
        // This method explicitly sets the rotation and translation
        ↪  components.
        public static Matrix4x4
        ↪  ManualCreateTransformationMatrix(Vector3 translation,
        ↪  Quaternion rotation)
        {
            Matrix4x4 matrix = Matrix4x4.Rotate(rotation);
            // Set the translation part in the last column.
            matrix.SetColumn(3, new Vector4(translation.x,
            ↪  translation.y, translation.z, 1));
            return matrix;
        }

        // Applies a given transformation matrix to a 3D point using
        ↪  homogeneous coordinates.
        // This function encapsulates the mapping f: ˉ3 → ˉ3.
```

```csharp
    public static Vector3 TransformPoint(Matrix4x4 matrix,
    ↪   Vector3 point)
    {
        Vector4 homogeneousPoint = new Vector4(point.x, point.y,
        ↪   point.z, 1);
        Vector4 transformed = matrix * homogeneousPoint;
        return new Vector3(transformed.x, transformed.y,
        ↪   transformed.z);
    }
}

// Represents a 3D UI element within a VR environment.
// This component updates its transformation based on simulated
↪   sensor input.
public class VRUIElement : MonoBehaviour
{
    public Vector3 initialPosition = new Vector3(0, 1, 2);
    public Quaternion initialRotation = Quaternion.identity;
    public Vector3 initialScale = Vector3.one;

    private Matrix4x4 transformationMatrix;

    void Start()
    {
        // Initialize the transformation matrix with initial
        ↪   parameters.
        transformationMatrix = TransformationUtility.
        CreateTransformationMatrix(initialPosition,
        ↪   initialRotation, initialScale);
    }

    void Update()
    {
        // Simulate dynamic input (e.g., head tracking) by
        ↪   oscillating the rotation angle.
        float dynamicAngle = Mathf.Sin(Time.time) * 30f;
        Quaternion dynamicRotation = Quaternion.Euler(0,
        ↪   dynamicAngle, 0);

        // Recalculate the transformation matrix with the
        ↪   updated rotation.
        transformationMatrix = TransformationUtility.
        CreateTransformationMatrix(initialPosition,
        ↪   dynamicRotation, initialScale);

        // Update the object's world position using the
        ↪   translation component (fourth column).
        transform.position = transformationMatrix.GetColumn(3);

        // Extract the forward and upward directions from the
        ↪   matrix and update the rotation.
        Vector3 forward = transformationMatrix.GetColumn(2);
        Vector3 upwards = transformationMatrix.GetColumn(1);
```

```csharp
        transform.rotation = Quaternion.LookRotation(forward,
        ↪   upwards);
    }

    // Demonstrates the mapping of a local UI control point to
    ↪   world space.
    public Vector3 MapUIControlPoint(Vector3 controlPoint)
    {
        return
        ↪   TransformationUtility.TransformPoint(transformationMatrix,
        ↪   controlPoint);
    }
}

// Manager class that dynamically adjusts multiple VR UI
↪   elements based on simulated spatial mapping.
// For instance, it rotates UI elements to face the user's
↪   current head position.
public class VRUIManager : MonoBehaviour
{
    public VRUIElement[] uiElements;

    void Update()
    {
        // Simulate a user head position moving along a
        ↪   sinusoidal path.
        Vector3 simulatedHeadPosition = new
        ↪   Vector3(Mathf.Sin(Time.time), 1.6f,
        ↪   Mathf.Cos(Time.time));

        // For each UI element, compute the direction toward the
        ↪   head position and adjust its rotation.
        foreach (VRUIElement element in uiElements)
        {
            Vector3 directionToHead = (simulatedHeadPosition -
            ↪   element.transform.position).normalized;
            Quaternion desiredRotation =
            ↪   Quaternion.LookRotation(directionToHead);
            // Smoothly interpolate to the new rotation to
            ↪   ensure fluid transitions.
            element.transform.rotation =
            ↪   Quaternion.Slerp(element.transform.rotation,
            ↪   desiredRotation, Time.deltaTime * 2f);
        }
    }
}
```

Summary: This comprehensive C# code snippet demonstrates key algorithms and formulas central to the chapter. It illustrates creating transformation matrices using translation, rotation, and scaling (expressed by $T = [\,R\mid t;\,0\mid 1\,]$), applying these transformations to map 3D points, and dynamically adjusting VR UI elements in response to simulated sensor data. The snippet integrates concepts from spatial embedding, geometric transformations, and adaptive interaction models, providing a practical implementation for building immersive 3D user interfaces in virtual reality.

Chapter 15

Implementing VR Menus and HUD Elements

Design Rationale and Aesthetic Considerations

The integration of immersive menus and heads-up displays within virtual reality applications necessitates a design paradigm that reconciles rigorous computational models with refined aesthetic judgment. The formulation of these interface components is grounded in the synthesis of principles from human–computer interaction, spatial cognition, and computational geometry. The interface elements are conceived so as to embody intrinsic spatial consistency and to facilitate an intuitive mapping between user intent and system response, thereby reducing extraneous cognitive effort. Aesthetic considerations are addressed through a deliberate calibration of visual weight, contrast, and typographic clarity, ensuring that textual and graphical elements yield an unambiguous visual hierarchy.

An emphasis on visual fidelity compels the designer to systematically integrate theories of perceptual organization and color dynamics. The adoption of geometric constructs within the design process enables the partitioning of the display space into discrete, yet harmoniously related, zones in which individual elements maintain both autonomy and contextual relevance. This framework not only exploits established principles of Euclidean layout but also accommodates curvilinear spatial arrangements demanded by VR's immersive properties.

Architectural Integration in Virtual Reality Applications

The architectural underpinnings of VR menus and HUD elements are defined by the seamless amalgamation of software design patterns and runtime rendering strategies. The pervasive use of layered rendering pipelines, in conjunction with precise coordinate transformations, is central to the construction of these interfaces. Central to this integration is the mathematical formalism of transformation matrices, such as

$$T = \begin{bmatrix} R & \mathbf{t} \\ \mathbf{0}^\top & 1 \end{bmatrix},$$

which enables the systematic combination of rotation and translation operations essential for situating interface components within a dynamic three-dimensional coordinate space. The abstraction of these operations into a layered architectural framework further aids in the compartmentalization of rendering complexity from user interaction logic.

Intrinsic to this architectural model is the recognition that performance constraints in virtual reality are intimately tied to rendering fidelity and system responsiveness. The design mandates that transformation routines and spatial computations operate within stringent temporal bounds, ensuring that the visual output conforms to the high refresh rate and low latency requirements typical of immersive systems. Such modularity in system design provides a robust platform on which adaptive interface elements can be instantiated, thereby preserving both computational efficiency and visual consistency.

Visual Clarity and Cognitive Load Minimization

A primary objective in the design of VR menus and HUD elements is the attainment of visual clarity that minimizes cognitive load while conveying critical data in an accessible format. The visual clarity of interface components is largely determined by the proportional balance between textual and graphical representations, the judicious use of high contrast color schemes, and the scalable resolution of interface elements. In environments where rapid shifts in user perspective are inevitable, these design imperatives attain further significance, necessitating the attenuation of visual noise and the enhancement of salient cues.

The interface is architectured to facilitate an unobstructed perceptual field, wherein each HUD element is meticulously positioned to avoid visual occlusion and to promote an immediate comprehension of its operational semantics. Considerations of legibility, particularly under conditions of varying illumination and dynamic motion, give rise to robust design strategies that draw upon principles of psychovisual ergonomics. Such strategies include the optimization of font metrics, iconography scaling, and the temporal modulation of transparency—all of which converge to yield a system that dynamically adjusts to the viewer's instantaneous perceptual context.

Spatial Placement and Dynamic Interaction Models

Spatial anchoring of VR menus and HUD elements is achieved through a rigorous application of coordinate mapping techniques that adaptively realign interface components relative to the user's position and field of view. The interaction model is predicated on transformation functions of the form

$$f \colon \mathbb{R}^3 \to \mathbb{R}^3,$$

which encapsulate the transition from local object coordinates to a globally consistent framework that accommodates head tracking and scene motion. This dynamic realignment is executed via continuous recalibration processes that leverage sensor fusion data to determine the optimal placement of interface elements.

The dynamic interaction model accommodates both static anchoring, where elements remain fixed within a virtual frame of reference, and dynamic repositioning, in which the elements exhibit smooth, responsive transitions in tandem with user movements. The spatial placement algorithms are underpinned by differential geometric principles and manifold theory, allowing for the graceful accommodation of non-linear spatial deformations inherent in immersive environments. This ensures that the interface not only maintains an invariant level of visual clarity but also adapts to the changing spatial context in a manner that upholds the integrity of user–system interactions.

C# Code Snippet

```csharp
using System.Collections;
using UnityEngine;

public class VRMenuHUD : MonoBehaviour
{
    // The HUD element (menu or heads-up display) to be dynamically
    //   positioned in VR.
    public Transform hudElement;
    // Reference to the user's head or camera transform.
    public Transform headTransform;
    // Desired distance from the head for the HUD.
    public float distanceFromHead = 2.0f;
    // Smoothing coefficient for position and rotation transitions.
    public float smoothingSpeed = 5.0f;
    // Optional offset to fine-tune HUD placement relative to the
    //   head's forward direction.
    public Vector3 hudOffset = new Vector3(0, -0.3f, 0);

    void Update()
    {
        // Continuously update the spatial placement and orientation
        //   of the HUD element.
        UpdateHUDPosition();

        // For demonstration: Uncomment the next line to test
        //   transformation mapping each frame.
        // ExampleTransformation();
    }

    // Dynamically repositions and rotates the HUD element so that
    //   it always faces the user.
    void UpdateHUDPosition()
    {
        // Calculate the target position using the head's position,
        //   forward direction,
        // defined distance, and additional offset.
        Vector3 targetPosition = headTransform.position +
            headTransform.forward * distanceFromHead + hudOffset;
```

```csharp
    // Smoothly interpolate the current HUD position towards the
    ↪   target position.
    hudElement.position = Vector3.Lerp(hudElement.position,
    ↪   targetPosition, Time.deltaTime * smoothingSpeed);

    // Determine the rotation required for the HUD to face the
    ↪   user.
    Quaternion targetRotation =
    ↪   Quaternion.LookRotation(hudElement.position -
    ↪   headTransform.position);

    // Smoothly interpolate the current HUD rotation towards the
    ↪   target rotation.
    hudElement.rotation = Quaternion.Lerp(hudElement.rotation,
    ↪   targetRotation, Time.deltaTime * smoothingSpeed);
}


// ComputeTransformationMatrix:
// This method computes a transformation matrix T (4x4) for a
↪   given rotation and translation.
// The matrix is defined as:
//     T = [ R    t ]
//         [ 0^T  1 ]
// where R is a 3x3 rotation matrix and t is a 3x1 translation
↪   vector.
Matrix4x4 ComputeTransformationMatrix(Quaternion rotation,
↪   Vector3 translation)
{
    // Using Unity's TRS (Translation-Rotation-Scale) to
    ↪   construct the matrix.
    return Matrix4x4.TRS(translation, rotation, Vector3.one);
}


// MapLocalToWorld:
// Transforms a point from local coordinates to world
↪   coordinates using the provided transformation matrix.
// This function embodies the mapping: f: ~3 → ~3.
Vector3 MapLocalToWorld(Vector3 localPosition, Matrix4x4
↪   transformationMatrix)
{
    return transformationMatrix.MultiplyPoint3x4(localPosition);
}


// ExampleTransformation demonstrates how to use the computed
↪   transformation matrix
// to map a point from a local coordinate system to the world
↪   coordinate system.
void ExampleTransformation()
{
    // Define a sample local coordinate.
    Vector3 localPoint = new Vector3(1, 1, 1);
```

```csharp
        // Compute the transformation matrix using the current HUD
        //   element's orientation and position.
        Matrix4x4 transformation =
        //   ComputeTransformationMatrix(hudElement.rotation,
        //   hudElement.position);

        // Map the local point to world coordinates.
        Vector3 worldPoint = MapLocalToWorld(localPoint,
        //   transformation);

        // Output the computed world point to the console with
        //   three-decimal precision.
        Debug.Log("World Point: " + worldPoint.ToString("F3"));
    }

    // Optional: SmoothReposition demonstrates a coroutine for
    //   smoothly repositioning and reorienting an object.
    // This can be used for dynamic transitions when the HUD or menu
    //   elements need to animate between placements.
    IEnumerator SmoothReposition(Transform targetTransform, Vector3
    //   newPosition, Quaternion newRotation, float duration)
    {
        Vector3 initialPosition = targetTransform.position;
        Quaternion initialRotation = targetTransform.rotation;
        float elapsed = 0f;

        while (elapsed < duration)
        {
            elapsed += Time.deltaTime;
            float t = Mathf.Clamp01(elapsed / duration);
            // Interpolate position and rotation over the specified
            //   duration.
            targetTransform.position = Vector3.Lerp(initialPosition,
            //   newPosition, t);
            targetTransform.rotation =
            //   Quaternion.Slerp(initialRotation, newRotation, t);
            yield return null;
        }

        // Ensure final position and rotation are set.
        targetTransform.position = newPosition;
        targetTransform.rotation = newRotation;
    }
}
```

Chapter 16

Scripting 3D Interactions: Raycasting and Object Selection

Raycasting Fundamentals in Three-Dimensional Environments

In three-dimensional virtual environments, raycasting serves as a foundational technique for determining intersections between directional queries and objects within the scene. A ray is mathematically represented by the parametric equation

$$P(t) = P_0 + t\,d,$$

where P_0 denotes the origin of the ray, d is a normalized direction vector, and $t \geq 0$ is a scalar parameter corresponding to the distance traversed along the ray. This compact formulation captures the linear trajectory of the ray and establishes the basis for evaluating spatial relationships in a virtual space. Such evaluations are critical in scenarios involving interactive object manipulation, precise visual feedback, and sensor-based environmental analysis in virtual reality systems.

Geometric Intersection and Analytical Approaches

The determination of intersection points between a ray and various geometric entities requires a meticulous application of principles from linear algebra and computational geometry. For example, consider a sphere defined by its center C and radius r. The intersection condition is derived from the implicit equation

$$\|P(t) - C\|^2 = r^2,$$

which, when combined with the parametric representation of the ray, results in a quadratic equation in t. Solutions to this equation indicate potential points of contact subject to the constraint of $t \geq 0$. Similarly, intersections with planar surfaces are evaluated using the plane equation

$$n \cdot (P(t) - P_{\text{plane}}) = 0,$$

where n is the unit normal to the plane and P_{plane} is a known point on the plane. The systematic resolution of these equations underlies the analytical approach to geometric intersection testing and demands careful attention to numerical stability and precision, particularly in real-time applications.

Selection Mechanics for Interactive Object Manipulation

Building upon the precise calculation of intersection points, the next critical component entails the mapping of these data into selection mechanics that govern object interaction in a three-dimensional context. Typically, when multiple intersections are computed, the selection algorithm prioritizes the object with the smallest positive t value, thereby designating the nearest intersection point along the ray. This methodology ensures that the object closest to an interaction query is identified accurately. Furthermore, selection mechanisms often incorporate collision hierarchies and heuristic filters to manage complex scenarios such as overlapping objects or interactions with semi-transparent surfaces. The interleaving of spatial intersection data with such refined selection criteria enables the design of systems that provide accurate, responsive, and contextually appropriate interactions within immersive environments.

Performance and Responsiveness in Raycasting Operations

The computational efficiency of raycasting operations has direct implications for the performance and responsiveness of a virtual reality system. Given the necessity for high frame rates in immersive applications, optimizations in the implementation of raycasting are paramount. Techniques to reduce computational overhead include the use of hierarchical spatial data structures such as bounding volume hierarchies, octrees, or k-d trees. These structures serve to constrain the set of candidate objects for detailed intersection testing, thereby reducing the average computational complexity associated with each raycast. Additionally, careful management of numerical precision and the minimization of redundant calculations across successive frames contribute to sustaining the desired responsiveness. The synthesis of these performance enhancement strategies ensures that the system maintains a delicate balance between computational rigor and the stringent temporal constraints imposed by real-time interactive environments.

C# Code Snippet

```csharp
using UnityEngine;
using System.Collections.Generic;

public class CustomRaycaster : MonoBehaviour
{
    // Class representing a sphere in the scene
    public class Sphere
    {
        public Vector3 center;
        public float radius;

        public Sphere(Vector3 center, float radius)
        {
            this.center = center;
            this.radius = radius;
        }
    }

    // Class representing a plane in the scene (defined by a point
    ↪   and a normal)
    public class PlaneEntity
    {
        public Vector3 point;    // Any point on the plane
```

```
    public Vector3 normal;    // Should be normalized

    public PlaneEntity(Vector3 point, Vector3 normal)
    {
        this.point = point;
        this.normal = normal.normalized;
    }
}

// Structure to store the result of an intersection test
public struct IntersectionResult
{
    public bool hit;
    public float t;            // Parameter along the ray P(t) =
    ↪   origin + t * direction
    public Vector3 point;      // The computed intersection point

    public IntersectionResult(bool hit, float t, Vector3 point)
    {
        this.hit = hit;
        this.t = t;
        this.point = point;
    }
}

// Computes the intersection of a ray with a sphere.
// The ray is given by: P(t) = origin + t*d, where t >= 0.
// The sphere is defined by: ||(P(t) - center)||^2 = radius^2.
// This expands to a quadratic equation in t which is solved
↪   using the quadratic formula.
public IntersectionResult IntersectRaySphere(Vector3 origin,
↪   Vector3 direction, Sphere sphere)
{
    Vector3 oc = origin - sphere.center;
    float a = Vector3.Dot(direction, direction); // Should be 1
    ↪   if direction is normalized.
    float b = 2.0f * Vector3.Dot(oc, direction);
    float c = Vector3.Dot(oc, oc) - sphere.radius *
    ↪   sphere.radius;
    float discriminant = b * b - 4 * a * c;

    if (discriminant < 0)
    {
        return new IntersectionResult(false, float.MaxValue,
        ↪   Vector3.zero);
    }
    else
    {
        float sqrtDisc = Mathf.Sqrt(discriminant);
        // Find the smallest positive t value
        float t1 = (-b - sqrtDisc) / (2.0f * a);
        float t2 = (-b + sqrtDisc) / (2.0f * a);
        float t = float.MaxValue;
```

```
            if (t1 > 0 && t1 < t)
                t = t1;
            if (t2 > 0 && t2 < t)
                t = t2;

            if (t == float.MaxValue)
                return new IntersectionResult(false, t,
                ↪   Vector3.zero);

            Vector3 hitPoint = origin + t * direction;
            return new IntersectionResult(true, t, hitPoint);
        }
    }

    // Computes the intersection of a ray with a plane.
    // The plane is defined by a point on the plane and a normal.
    // Using the equation: n · (P(t) - P_plane) = 0, we find t = n ·
    ↪   (P_plane - origin) / n · d.
    public IntersectionResult IntersectRayPlane(Vector3 origin,
    ↪   Vector3 direction, PlaneEntity plane)
    {
        float denom = Vector3.Dot(plane.normal, direction);
        // If denom is near zero, the ray is parallel to the plane.
        if (Mathf.Abs(denom) < 1e-6f)
        {
            return new IntersectionResult(false, float.MaxValue,
            ↪   Vector3.zero);
        }

        float t = Vector3.Dot(plane.point - origin, plane.normal) /
        ↪   denom;
        if (t < 0)
        {
            // The intersection occurs behind the ray's origin.
            return new IntersectionResult(false, t, Vector3.zero);
        }

        Vector3 hitPoint = origin + t * direction;
        return new IntersectionResult(true, t, hitPoint);
    }

    // Casts a ray and checks for intersections with provided
    ↪   spheres and planes.
    // Returns the closest intersection (smallest positive t) from
    ↪   the ray's origin.
    public IntersectionResult CastRay(Vector3 origin, Vector3
    ↪   direction, List<Sphere> spheres, List<PlaneEntity> planes)
    {
        IntersectionResult closestResult = new
        ↪   IntersectionResult(false, float.MaxValue, Vector3.zero);

        // Test intersection with each sphere
        foreach (Sphere sphere in spheres)
```

```csharp
    {
        IntersectionResult result = IntersectRaySphere(origin,
        ↪   direction, sphere);
        if (result.hit && result.t < closestResult.t)
        {
            closestResult = result;
        }
    }

    // Test intersection with each plane
    foreach (PlaneEntity plane in planes)
    {
        IntersectionResult result = IntersectRayPlane(origin,
        ↪   direction, plane);
        if (result.hit && result.t < closestResult.t)
        {
            closestResult = result;
        }
    }

    return closestResult;
}

// Demo initialization to illustrate raycasting in the scene.
void Start()
{
    // Define the ray starting at the object's position and
    ↪   pointing forward.
    Vector3 rayOrigin = transform.position;
    Vector3 rayDirection = transform.forward.normalized;

    // Create a list of spheres in the scene.
    List<Sphere> spheres = new List<Sphere>
    {
        new Sphere(new Vector3(0, 0, 10), 2.0f),
        new Sphere(new Vector3(2, 1, 15), 1.5f)
    };

    // Create a list of planes in the scene.
    List<PlaneEntity> planes = new List<PlaneEntity>
    {
        new PlaneEntity(new Vector3(0, -1, 0), Vector3.up) // A
        ↪   horizontal plane below the origin.
    };

    // Cast the ray and determine the closest intersection.
    IntersectionResult result = CastRay(rayOrigin, rayDirection,
    ↪   spheres, planes);
    if (result.hit)
    {
        Debug.Log("Ray hit an object at: " + result.point + "
        ↪   with distance t = " + result.t);
    }
```

```
        else
        {
            Debug.Log("Ray did not hit any objects.");
        }
    }
}
```

Summary: The code above implements essential raycasting algorithms as discussed in this chapter. It covers the mathematical ray equation $P(t) = P + t \cdot d$, computes intersections with a sphere using a quadratic formula, and calculates intersections with a plane using the dot product method. The CastRay method aggregates these tests to select the nearest intersected object, thereby demonstrating the foundational techniques for interactive object selection in three-dimensional virtual environments.

Chapter 17

Implementing Grab-and-Release Mechanics in VR

Modeling Interaction Forces and Constraints

Realistic grab-and-release interactions necessitate a detailed mathematical framework to model the forces and constraints that govern object manipulation in a virtual environment. The process begins by defining the spatial relationship between the virtual hand, represented as a point or volume, and the object being manipulated. This spatial correspondence is established through transformation matrices that convert local object coordinates to the coordinate system of the user's input device. To accurately simulate grasping, the applied forces must follow Newtonian mechanics, wherein $F = m\,a$ serves as the foundational principle determining acceleration based on mass m and applied force F. The simulation further requires the insertion of constraint conditions that prevent unnatural displacements or rotations during the interaction. A system of equations is employed to ensure that the relative position and orientation between the user's controller and the object remain consistent throughout the duration of the grab.

Designing the Object State Machine for Interaction

The temporal evolution of an interactive object's properties is best encapsulated through the formulation of a state machine. In this construction, states are delineated as *idle, grabbed,* and *released,* with each state governing a unique subset of physical behaviors and permissible transitions. When an object transitions from the idle to the grabbed state, the virtual environment imposes binding constraints that effectively attach the object to the user's input mechanism. This transition is mathematically characterized by updating the object's transformation matrix with an offset that reflects the relative pose of the user's controller. On release, the state machine dictates that the object's dynamics revert to a simulation governed solely by the environment's physical laws. Consequently, integration methods are applied to update the object's velocity and rotation; in particular, the conservation of momentum is preserved where $p = m\,v$, with momentum p, mass m, and velocity v, ensuring physical realism upon release.

Implementation of Natural Object Manipulation in Virtual Environments

A comprehensive formulation of natural object manipulation requires the seamless synthesis of coordinate transformation, collision detection, and continuous physical simulation. The spatial alignment during a grab is often achieved by computing the relative offset vector $d = P_{\text{hand}} - P_{\text{object}}$, where P_{hand} represents the position of the user's controller and P_{object} denotes the object's origin. This offset is maintained dynamically through subsequent updates, ensuring that the object's position P'_{object} satisfies the relationship

$$P'_{\text{object}} = P_{\text{hand}} - d.$$

Rotational alignment is similarly maintained by decomposing the rotational transformation into Euler angles or quaternions, thus preserving the object's intrinsic orientation during manipulation. The interplay between user input and object state is continuously monitored, and collision detection algorithms are invoked to preemptively mitigate interpenetration with other scene elements. In this manner, the system enforces physical plausibility while delivering an interaction that is both intuitive and congruent with environmental physics.

Handling Release Dynamics and Residual Motion

When the grab action is terminated, the object is released into the surrounding virtual space under the influence of gravitational and inertial forces. At the moment of release, the virtual environment computes the residual velocity v_{res} based on the instantaneous state of the object and its interaction history. This velocity may be represented as

$$v_{\text{res}} = v_{\text{current}} + \delta v,$$

where δv accounts for any corrective adjustments due to constraint removal and physical damping. The object subsequently adheres to a differential equation of motion of the form

$$\frac{d^2 P}{dt^2} = g,$$

where g denotes the gravitational acceleration vector. Additionally, the implementation must account for frictional forces and potential impacts with other objects, thereby necessitating the continuous integration of collision responses. Through detailed analysis of contact normals, restitution coefficients, and damping factors, the virtual system ensures that the released object exhibits behavior that convincingly mimics that of a tangible, physical object in the real world.

C# Code Snippet

```
using UnityEngine;

// Enum representing the state of the interactive object.
public enum InteractionState
{
    Idle,
    Grabbed,
    Released
}
```

```
// This class implements grab-and-release mechanics for VR,
// incorporating the following key physical principles and
↪    equations:
// - Newton's Second Law: F = m * a
// - Momentum: p = m * v
// - Object alignment: d = P_hand - P_object, updated as P_object' =
↪    P_hand - d
// - Differential motion during release: d²P/dt² = g
//
// It utilizes a state machine (Idle, Grabbed, Released) to update
↪    object behavior
// and manual Euler integration to simulate release dynamics.
public class VRGrabReleaseMechanics : MonoBehaviour
{
    // Public variables exposed in the Unity Inspector.
    public InteractionState currentState = InteractionState.Idle;
    public Transform handTransform; // VR controller or hand
    ↪    transform.
    public float damping = 0.98f; // Damping factor to simulate
    ↪    friction.
    public Vector3 gravity = new Vector3(0, -9.81f, 0); //
    ↪    Gravitational acceleration.

    // Private variables for physics simulation.
    private Rigidbody rb;
    private Vector3 grabOffset;        // Offset vector d between
    ↪    hand and object upon grabbing.
    private Vector3 customVelocity;    // Custom velocity used for
    ↪    manual integration.
    private float mass;                // Mass of the object.

    // Initialization.
    void Start()
    {
        rb = GetComponent<Rigidbody>();
        if (rb != null)
        {
            mass = rb.mass;
            customVelocity = rb.velocity;
        }
        else
        {
            mass = 1.0f; // Default mass if Rigidbody is not
            ↪    assigned.
            customVelocity = Vector3.zero;
        }
    }

    // Update is called once per frame.
    void Update()
    {
        if (currentState == InteractionState.Grabbed)
        {
```

132

```
        // Modeling Interaction Forces and Constraints.
        // Compute the relative offset: d = P_hand - P_object.
        grabOffset = handTransform.position -
        ↪    transform.position;
        // Update object's position to follow the hand:
        ↪    P_object' = P_hand - d.
        transform.position = handTransform.position -
        ↪    grabOffset;

        // For rotational alignment, a similar approach using
        ↪    quaternions can be applied.
    }
    else if (currentState == InteractionState.Released)
    {
        // Handling Release Dynamics and Residual Motion.
        // Calculate acceleration (a = g), since by F = m * a we
        ↪    have a = g.
        Vector3 acceleration = gravity;

        // Update velocity using Euler integration: v =
        ↪    v_current + a * dt.
        customVelocity = rb.velocity;
        customVelocity += acceleration * Time.deltaTime;
        // Apply damping to simulate friction: v = v * damping.
        customVelocity *= damping;

        // Compute momentum for reference: p = m * v.
        Vector3 momentum = mass * customVelocity;

        // Update object's position: P = P_current + v * dt.
        transform.position += customVelocity * Time.deltaTime;

        // Update the Rigidbody's velocity.
        rb.velocity = customVelocity;
    }
}

// Method to initiate the grab action.
public void GrabObject()
{
    if (currentState != InteractionState.Idle)
        return;

    currentState = InteractionState.Grabbed;
    // Compute and store the offset between the hand and the
    ↪    object.
    grabOffset = handTransform.position - transform.position;
    // Freeze physics simulation while the object is grabbed.
    if (rb != null)
        rb.isKinematic = true;
}

// Method to release the object.
```

```csharp
public void ReleaseObject()
{
    if (currentState != InteractionState.Grabbed)
        return;

    currentState = InteractionState.Released;
    // Re-enable physics simulation.
    if (rb != null)
        rb.isKinematic = false;

    // Compute residual velocity upon release.
    // v_res = v_current + delta_v, where delta_v comes from the
    // ↪ hand's movement.
    Vector3 vCurrent = customVelocity;
    Vector3 deltaV = Vector3.zero;
    Rigidbody handRb = handTransform.GetComponent<Rigidbody>();
    if (handRb != null)
    {
        deltaV = handRb.velocity;
    }
    Vector3 residualVelocity = vCurrent + deltaV;
    if (rb != null)
        rb.velocity = residualVelocity;
}

// FixedUpdate is used for consistent physics updates.
void FixedUpdate()
{
    if (currentState == InteractionState.Released && rb != null)
    {
        // Apply gravitational acceleration consistently
        // ↪ (d²P/dt² = g).
        Vector3 acceleration = gravity;
        rb.velocity += acceleration * Time.fixedDeltaTime;
    }
}
}
```

Chapter 18

Designing Teleportation Locomotion for VR

Foundations and Theoretical Rationale

Teleportation locomotion represents a discrete spatial transition technique, implemented to circumvent the sensory discrepancies that emerge during continuous virtual movement. The method relies on instantaneous relocation events designed to mitigate the vestibular-visual mismatches responsible for user discomfort. The theoretical underpinnings of this approach are rooted in an understanding of the physiological and cognitive constraints intrinsic to virtual reality (VR) immersion. Continuous locomotion in VR often generates conflicting signals between the user's visual perception and vestibular feedback. Teleportation, by replacing continuous motion with a series of discrete positional updates, obviates the need for sustained optic flow, thereby reducing the incidence of motion sickness.

1 Physical and Cognitive Constraints in VR Locomotion

Central to the adoption of teleportation locomotion is the observation that human motion perception is highly dependent on the congruence between visual and vestibular stimuli. Conventional movement models involve a continuous transformation of the user's perspective, which is typically expressed as a function $P(t)$ mapping time t to spatial position. In contrast, teleportation implements a discontinuous mapping

$$T: P_{\text{current}} \mapsto P_{\text{target}},$$

where P_{current} represents the user's current position and P_{target} denotes a destination determined by user input. This abrupt positional change eliminates the continuous acceleration profile that would otherwise be approximated by an equation of the form

$$\frac{d^2 P}{dt^2} = a,$$

with constant acceleration a. By circumventing the need for such acceleration profiles, teleportation minimizes the potential for cognitive dissonance between sensed and simulated motion.

2 Biomechanical Considerations and Spatial Orientation

The biomechanical interpretation of teleportation solutions emphasizes the retention of spatial orientation while eliminating proprioceptive disturbances inherent to continuous locomotion. The instantaneous nature of teleportation necessitates that the virtual environment provide sufficient visual and auditory cues to anchor the user's sense of spatial continuity. In this framework, the transformation function

$$\mathbf{T}(P_{\text{current}}, R) = P_{\text{target}},$$

where $R \subset \mathbb{R}^3$ represents a set of candidate relocation regions subject to environmental constraints, ensures that the computed target position maintains relative consistency with the user's intended directional input. The orthogonal decomposition of the environment's coordinate system into a forward vector and an up vector, corresponding respectively to the user's heading and the gravitational norm, is fundamental in preserving orientation during and after the teleportation event.

Mathematical and Algorithmic Modeling of Teleportation

The algorithmic implementation of teleportation locomotion requires a detailed mathematical model that encapsulates both the discrete nature of spatial transitions and the constraints imposed by VR environments. A robust model integrates coordinate transformation, spatial eligibility constraints, and user feedback mechanisms in a coherent framework.

1 Mathematical Representation of Discrete Spatial Transitions

Teleportation is formally modeled as a mapping from a current position $P_{\text{current}} \in \mathbb{R}^3$ to a target position $P_{\text{target}} \in \mathbb{R}^3$, subject to a feasibility condition

$$P_{\text{target}} \in \mathcal{R},$$

where $\mathcal{R}$ is defined as the set of all spatial locations that satisfy environmental boundaries and collision constraints. The transition is effected instantaneously through an operator $\mathcal{T}$, such that

$$P_{\text{target}} = \mathcal{T}(P_{\text{current}}, \boldsymbol{\theta}),$$

where $\boldsymbol{\theta}$ encapsulates the directional input and orientation preferences of the user. The operator $\mathcal{T}$ ensures consistency with pre-defined safety criteria by invoking spatial sampling techniques and applying raycasting methods to interrogate the environmental model.

2 Algorithmic Strategies for Teleportation Point Selection

The selection of an appropriate teleportation destination involves the resolution of an optimization problem defined in the spatial domain. Given a query ray emerging from the user's input device, the teleportation system calculates intersections with the virtual environment. Let the query be expressed as

$$\mathbf{q}(t) = P_{\text{hand}} + t \cdot \mathbf{d},$$

with $\mathbf{d}$ as the directional unit vector and $t \geq 0$ representing the distance parameter. The intersection point with a suitable surface is computed, and candidate locations are further filtered by ensuring that landing zones possess valid terrain characteristics and are free from occlusions. These candidate positions are then evaluated based on a cost function $C(P)$, which is defined to incorporate parameters such as angular deviation from the user's current heading and proximity to environmental hazards. The optimal teleportation target is selected as the position where

$$C(P_{\text{target}}) = \min_{P \in \mathcal{R}} C(P).$$

Design Practices to Mitigate Motion Sickness

A critical design aspect of teleportation locomotion is the attenuation of motion sickness through careful manipulation of visual transitions and environmental cues. By introducing perceptual modulations during and after teleportation events, the system can significantly reduce user discomfort.

1 Visual Transition Techniques and Perceptual Continuity

The discrete nature of teleportation necessitates the incorporation of visual transition techniques that maintain perceptual continuity. Fading effects, image blurring, or strategically timed transitional blackouts are employed to mask the absence of intermediate spatial states. Mathematically, these techniques can be described by time-dependent visibility functions $V(t)$, which modulate the opacity of rendered frames such that

$$V(t) = \begin{cases} 1, & t < t_0 \text{ or } t > t_1, \\ f(t), & t_0 \leq t \leq t_1, \end{cases}$$

where $f(t)$ is a smooth function that interpolates between full visibility and complete blackout over the interval $\Delta t = t_1 - t_0$. Through this mechanism, the abrupt change in spatial position is rendered less jarring, thereby attenuating the triggers of motion-induced discomfort.

2 Spatial Orientation and Feedback Mechanisms

Preservation of spatial orientation during teleportation is achieved through the consistent retention of an environmental frame of reference. The design ensures that post-teleportation orientation O_{target} aligns with contextual ambient cues, such as the gravitational vector and landmark configurations. This alignment is critical, as dissonance between the user's perceived orientation and the virtual environment can exacerbate discomfort. Feedback mechanisms, both visual and auditory, serve to reinforce the coherence of spatial orientation. The maintenance of a persistent horizon line and subtle auditory cues derived from the new location are examples of such mechanisms, and they are modeled to provide continuous reinforcement of the spatial context.

3 Parameter Tuning and Safety Criteria

Implementing an effective teleportation locomotion system requires comprehensive parameter tuning to align with ergonomic standards and reduce the incidence of adverse effects. Parameters such as maximum teleportation range, angular thresholds for target acceptance, and the duration of transitional effects are iteratively optimized. In a formal sense, let Λ denote the vector of tunable parameters, and let $S(\Lambda)$ be a scalar metric reflecting the system's performance in terms of user comfort and navigational efficacy. Then, the optimal parameter vector Λ^* is obtained by solving the optimization problem

$$\Lambda^* = \arg\min_{\Lambda} S(\Lambda),$$

subject to the constraints defined by environmental layout and user interface design. The resulting values of Λ^* determine the precise operational characteristics of the teleportation mechanism, ensuring both effectiveness in navigation and minimization of motion sickness.

C# Code Snippet

```
using UnityEngine;
using System.Collections;
using System.Collections.Generic;

namespace VRTeleportation
```

```csharp
{
    public class TeleportationController : MonoBehaviour
    {
        // Tunable parameters representing the parameter vector .
        [Header("Teleportation Parameters")]
        [Tooltip("Maximum allowable teleport distance.")]
        public float maxTeleportDistance = 10.0f;

        [Tooltip("Duration for fade in/out effects during
        ↪   teleportation.")]
        public float teleportFadeDuration = 0.5f;

        [Tooltip("Layer mask defining valid teleportable
        ↪   surfaces.")]
        public LayerMask teleportLayerMask;

        [Tooltip("List of hazard objects to avoid during
        ↪   teleportation.")]
        public List<Transform> hazardZones = new List<Transform>();

        [Header("Fade Effect Reference")]
        [Tooltip("Canvas group used to perform fade transitions.")]
        public CanvasGroup fadeCanvasGroup;

        // Computes the teleportation target using a transformation
        ↪   operator:
        // P_target = T(P_current, )
        public Vector3 CalculateTeleportTarget(Vector3
        ↪   currentPosition, Vector3 handPosition, Vector3
        ↪   direction)
        {
            // Cast a ray from the hand position along the input
            ↪   direction.
            Ray ray = new Ray(handPosition, direction.normalized);
            RaycastHit hit;
            Vector3 candidatePoint = currentPosition;

            // Use raycasting to determine candidate teleport
            ↪   position within maxDistance.
            if (Physics.Raycast(ray, out hit, maxTeleportDistance,
            ↪   teleportLayerMask))
            {
                candidatePoint = hit.point;
            }
            return candidatePoint;
        }

        // Cost function C(P) evaluating candidate teleport
        ↪   positions.
        // Lower cost is assigned to targets that minimize angular
        ↪   deviation and avoid hazards.
        public float ComputeCost(Vector3 target, Vector3
        ↪   currentForward)
```

```
{
    // Compute the angular deviation cost.
    Vector3 movementDirection = (target -
    ↪    transform.position).normalized;
    float angleCost = Vector3.Angle(currentForward,
    ↪    movementDirection);

    // Compute hazard proximity cost by summing the inverse
    ↪    distances to each hazard.
    float hazardCost = 0f;
    foreach (Transform hazard in hazardZones)
    {
        float distance = Vector3.Distance(target,
        ↪    hazard.position);
        // Prevent division by zero.
        if (distance < 0.001f)
            distance = 0.001f;
        hazardCost += 1.0f / distance;
    }
    return angleCost + hazardCost;
}


// Currently, we assume one candidate point from the
↪    raycast.
// This method can be extended to evaluate multiple
↪    candidates.
public Vector3 SelectOptimalTeleportTarget(Vector3
↪    candidatePoint, Vector3 currentForward)
{
    // In a comprehensive implementation, multiple candidate
    ↪    points would be evaluated.
    return candidatePoint;
}


// Implements a visual fade effect based on a time-dependent
↪    opacity function V(t).
// V(t) transitions smoothly between full visibility and
↪    blackout.
IEnumerator FadeTeleportation(float duration)
{
    float t = 0f;
    // Fade out (increasing opacity).
    while (t < duration)
    {
        t += Time.deltaTime;
        // Interpolate opacity from 0 (fully visible) to 1
        ↪    (blackout).
        float alpha = Mathf.Lerp(0f, 1f, t / duration);
        if (fadeCanvasGroup != null)
        {
            fadeCanvasGroup.alpha = alpha;
        }
        yield return null;
```

```csharp
    }

    // Optional: brief pause at full fade.
    yield return new WaitForSeconds(0.1f);

    t = 0f;
    // Fade in (decreasing opacity).
    while (t < duration)
    {
        t += Time.deltaTime;
        float alpha = Mathf.Lerp(1f, 0f, t / duration);
        if (fadeCanvasGroup != null)
        {
            fadeCanvasGroup.alpha = alpha;
        }
        yield return null;
    }
}

// Public method to initiate teleportation.
// It integrates spatial sampling, cost evaluation, and
↪   visual transitions.
public void Teleport(Vector3 handPosition, Vector3
↪   inputDirection)
{
    // Step 1: Calculate candidate teleport target using the
    ↪   transformation operator.
    Vector3 candidateTarget =
    ↪   CalculateTeleportTarget(transform.position,
    ↪   handPosition, inputDirection);

    // Step 2: Evaluate candidate target using the cost
    ↪   function C(P).
    Vector3 optimalTarget =
    ↪   SelectOptimalTeleportTarget(candidateTarget,
    ↪   transform.forward);
    float cost = ComputeCost(optimalTarget,
    ↪   transform.forward);
    Debug.Log("Optimal Teleport Target: " + optimalTarget +
    ↪   " | Cost: " + cost.ToString("F2"));

    // Step 3: Initiate visual transition before performing
    ↪   the instantaneous teleportation.
    StartCoroutine(TeleportRoutine(optimalTarget));
}

// Teleport routine that manages the fade effect and
↪   instantaneous positional update.
IEnumerator TeleportRoutine(Vector3 targetPosition)
{
    // Apply fade-out effect.
    yield return
    ↪   StartCoroutine(FadeTeleportation(teleportFadeDuration));
```

142

```
            // Instantaneous relocation: P_target = T(P_current, ).
            transform.position = targetPosition;

            // Fade-in effect is integrated within the
            ↪  FadeTeleportation coroutine.
            yield break;
        }
    }
}
```

Summary: This comprehensive C# code snippet models the
teleportation locomotion mechanism described in the chapter. It
encapsulates key equations and algorithmic processes—such as the
discontinuous mapping T(P_current,) for target selection, the
evaluation of candidate positions via a cost function incorporating
angular deviation and hazard proximity, and a visual transition effect modeled by the time-dependent opacity function $V(t)$—within
a Unity framework using C. The code integrates raycasting for environmental queries, safety parameter tuning, and fade transitions
to ensure a smooth and comfortable user experience during teleportation.

Chapter 19

Scripting Smooth Locomotion in Virtual Space

Theoretical Foundations of Continuous Motion

In immersive virtual environments, the representation of user movement necessitates the formulation of a continuous trajectory function, denoted by $P(t)$, where t represents time and $P(t) \in \mathbb{R}^3$ describes the user's position in three-dimensional space. The function $P(t)$ is required to be at least twice continuously differentiable, i.e., $P(t) \in C^2(I)$ for an interval I, in order to guarantee continuity in both velocity, $P'(t)$, and acceleration, $P''(t)$. Such smoothness is critical to minimize abrupt kinematic changes that may induce perceptual dissonance or user discomfort during navigation within expansive virtual spaces.

Mathematical Modeling of Trajectory Smoothness

The generation of a smooth locomotion trajectory is accomplished by interpolating discrete control points derived from user inputs. Consider a set of sampled positions $\{P_i\}$ recorded at corresponding time stamps $\{t_i\}$. The objective is to construct an interpolating function $P(t)$ satisfying the constraints $P(t_i) = P_i$ for all indices i. Techniques such as cubic spline interpolation are often employed to ensure that the second derivative is continuous at the knot points. In a general form, the trajectory may be expressed as

$$P(t) = \sum_{i=0}^{n} P_i\, B_i(t),$$

where $B_i(t)$ are the basis functions with properties that enforce C^2 continuity. This formulation guarantees that the velocity and acceleration profiles transition smoothly between successive control points, thereby reducing transient dynamic effects.

Algorithmic Implementation of Interpolated Movement

Algorithmic implementation of smooth locomotion involves blending real-time user inputs with continuous filtering methods to update the positional state. Raw control signals, represented by a function $u(t)$, are often subject to high-frequency variations that must be attenuated. Application of a low-pass filter is a common approach, mathematically represented by the convolution

$$v(t) = \int_{-\infty}^{t} K(t - \tau)\, u(\tau)\, d\tau,$$

where $K(t)$ is a smoothing kernel designed to suppress abrupt fluctuations, and $v(t)$ represents the smoothed velocity. The updated position is then obtained by integrating the smoothed velocity:

$$P(t) = P(t_0) + \int_{t_0}^{t} v(\tau)\, d\tau.$$

In practical implementations, it is essential that the filtered trajectory remain confined within a feasible region $\Omega \subset \mathbb{R}^3$, which may represent navigable space free from collisions or other environmental constraints. This projection onto Ω ensures that the continuous motion adheres to the spatial limitations of the virtual domain.

Ergonomic Considerations and Real-Time Filtering

Ensuring the comfort of the user during locomotion is a paramount consideration in the design of continuous movement systems. The sensitivity of human perceptual systems to sudden variations in acceleration—quantified by the jerk, defined as

$$j(t) = \frac{d^3 P}{dt^3},$$

—necessitates that the magnitude of $j(t)$ remain bounded within acceptable limits. This requirement can be cast as an optimization problem, where the objective is to minimize the cost function

$$J(P) = \int_{t_0}^{t_f} \|j(t)\|^2 \, dt,$$

over a specified time interval $[t_0, t_f]$. Real-time filtering techniques and adaptive control schemes are employed to adjust the smoothing parameters dynamically, thereby ensuring that the synthesized locomotion remains responsive to immediate user inputs while maintaining a continuous and comfortable motion profile. These methods allow the movement system to compensate for perturbations and rapidly changing navigational commands without sacrificing the smoothness required for immersive VR experiences.

C# Code Snippet

```
using System;
using System.Collections.Generic;
using UnityEngine;

// This class implements trajectory smoothing by interpolating
↪    discrete control points
// using Catmull-Rom splines. It also provides methods for low-pass
↪    filtering raw velocity
// signals and integrating velocity to update position. These
↪    methods embody the key equations:
//     - Spline interpolation: P(t) = P_i * B_i(t)
//     - Low-pass filtering: v(t)  Lerp(previousFiltered,
↪    rawVelocity, smoothingFactor)
//     - Euler integration: P(t) = P(t0) +  v() d
//     - Finite-difference estimation for jerk: j(t)
↪    (a(t)-a(t-dt))/dt
```

```csharp
public class TrajectorySmoother
{
    // List of control points representing user-sampled positions in
    ↪   space.
    public List<Vector3> controlPoints;
    // Corresponding time stamps for each control point.
    public List<float> timeStamps;
    // Smoothing factor for the low-pass filter (value between 0 and
    ↪   1).
    public float smoothingFactor;

    public TrajectorySmoother(List<Vector3> points, List<float>
    ↪   times, float smoothingFactor = 0.1f)
    {
        this.controlPoints = points;
        this.timeStamps = times;
        this.smoothingFactor = smoothingFactor;
    }

    // Evaluates the interpolated position P(t) at a given time t.
    // Uses Catmull-Rom spline interpolation to ensure C2
    ↪   continuity.
    public Vector3 EvaluateSpline(float t)
    {
        int segment = 0;
        // Locate the appropriate segment for time t.
        while (segment < timeStamps.Count - 1 && t >
        ↪   timeStamps[segment + 1])
        {
            segment++;
        }

        // Define indices for control points with clamping.
        int i0 = Math.Max(segment - 1, 0);
        int i1 = segment;
        int i2 = Math.Min(segment + 1, controlPoints.Count - 1);
        int i3 = Math.Min(segment + 2, controlPoints.Count - 1);

        float t0 = timeStamps[i1];
        float t1 = timeStamps[i2];

        // Remap t to a local parameter in [0, 1].
        float localT = (t - t0) / (t1 - t0);
        return CatmullRom(controlPoints[i0], controlPoints[i1],
        ↪   controlPoints[i2], controlPoints[i3], localT);
    }

    // Implements the Catmull-Rom spline formula.
    public Vector3 CatmullRom(Vector3 p0, Vector3 p1, Vector3 p2,
    ↪   Vector3 p3, float t)
    {
        float t2 = t * t;
        float t3 = t2 * t;
```

```csharp
        return 0.5f * ((2f * p1) +
                       (-p0 + p2) * t +
                       (2f * p0 - 5f * p1 + 4f * p2 - p3) * t2 +
                       (-p0 + 3f * p1 - 3f * p2 + p3) * t3);
    }

    // Applies a simple exponential moving average as a low-pass
    // ↪ filter to smooth out raw velocity.
    public Vector3 LowPassFilter(Vector3 previousFiltered, Vector3
    ↪ rawVelocity)
    {
        return Vector3.Lerp(previousFiltered, rawVelocity,
        ↪ smoothingFactor);
    }

    // Integrates velocity using a simple Euler method to update
    // ↪ position.
    public Vector3 IntegratePosition(Vector3 currentPosition,
    ↪ Vector3 velocity, float deltaTime)
    {
        return currentPosition + velocity * deltaTime;
    }
}

public class LocomotionSimulation
{
    // Entry point for the simulation.
    public static void Main(string[] args)
    {
        // Define control points (sampled positions) and
        // ↪ corresponding time stamps.
        List<Vector3> controlPoints = new List<Vector3>()
        {
            new Vector3(0f, 0f, 0f),
            new Vector3(1f, 0f, 2f),
            new Vector3(3f, 0f, 3f),
            new Vector3(5f, 0f, 2f),
            new Vector3(7f, 0f, 0f)
        };
        List<float> timeStamps = new List<float>() { 0f, 1f, 2f, 3f,
        ↪ 4f };

        // Create an instance of TrajectorySmoother with a specified
        // ↪ low-pass smoothing factor.
        float smoothingFactor = 0.1f;
        TrajectorySmoother trajectory = new
        ↪ TrajectorySmoother(controlPoints, timeStamps,
        ↪ smoothingFactor);

        // Simulation parameters.
        float simulationTime = 0f;
        float simulationEnd = 4f;
        float dt = 0.02f;  // Time step (50 FPS).
```

148

```csharp
// Initialize simulation state.
Vector3 currentPosition = controlPoints[0];
Vector3 previousFilteredVelocity = Vector3.zero;
Vector3 previousVelocity = Vector3.zero;
Vector3 previousAcceleration = Vector3.zero;

// Simulation loop: mimics real-time continuous locomotion.
while (simulationTime < simulationEnd)
{
    // Determine target position using spline interpolation.
    Vector3 targetPosition =
    ↪   trajectory.EvaluateSpline(simulationTime);
    // Estimate raw velocity via finite differences.
    Vector3 rawVelocity = (targetPosition - currentPosition)
    ↪   / dt;
    // Apply low-pass filtering to smooth the velocity
    ↪   signal.
    Vector3 filteredVelocity =
    ↪   trajectory.LowPassFilter(previousFilteredVelocity,
    ↪   rawVelocity);
    previousFilteredVelocity = filteredVelocity;

    // Estimate acceleration as the rate of change of
    ↪   filtered velocity.
    Vector3 acceleration = (filteredVelocity -
    ↪   previousVelocity) / dt;
    // Estimate jerk (the third derivative) as the rate of
    ↪   change of acceleration.
    Vector3 jerk = (acceleration - previousAcceleration) /
    ↪   dt;

    // Update previous velocity and acceleration for the
    ↪   next iteration.
    previousVelocity = filteredVelocity;
    previousAcceleration = acceleration;

    // Update the position by integrating the filtered
    ↪   velocity.
    currentPosition =
    ↪   trajectory.IntegratePosition(currentPosition,
    ↪   filteredVelocity, dt);

    // Output the simulation state.
    Console.WriteLine("Time: {0:F2} | Position: {1} |
    ↪   Velocity: {2} | Acceleration: {3} | Jerk: {4}",
                      simulationTime, currentPosition,
                      ↪   filteredVelocity, acceleration,
                      ↪   jerk);

    // Increment simulation time.
    simulationTime += dt;
}
```

```
    }
}
```

```
// Summary: This C\# code snippet demonstrates how to implement
↪    smooth locomotion in virtual space.
// It integrates key mathematical models including spline
↪    interpolation for trajectory generation,
// low-pass filtering for smoothing user input derived velocity,
↪    Euler integration for position updates,
// and finite difference methods for acceleration and jerk
↪    estimation. The implementation ensures
// continuous motion with gradual transitions, thereby minimizing
↪    abrupt kinematic changes that affect user comfort.
```

Chapter 20

Implementing VR Snap Turning Mechanics

Conceptual Framework of Snap Turning

Snap turning mechanics in virtual reality are designed to mitigate issues related to continuous rotational motion, which can induce disorientation or discomfort in users. The mechanism achieves rapid reorientation by discretely updating the user's viewpoint in fixed angular increments. This approach replaces gradual rotation with instantaneous steps, thereby preventing the accumulation of minor angular deviations that may challenge the integrity of visual and vestibular feedback. The system relies on sophisticated input analysis that detects intentional turning commands and rapidly applies a predetermined angular shift. A central premise of this technique is the deliberate avoidance of transitional motion artifacts that are frequently associated with smooth rotational methods. The discrete update strategy originates from an understanding of user perceptual thresholds and aims to balance navigational efficiency with physiological ergonomics.

Mathematical Modeling of Discrete Rotations

The transformation underlying a snap turn can be rigorously modeled using the mathematical formalism of quaternions. Consider the current orientation of the user represented by a unit quaternion $q_{\text{current}} \in \mathbb{H}$. A predefined rotation by an angle θ around a unit vector $u \in \mathbb{R}^3$ is encapsulated in the rotation quaternion

$$\Delta q = \cos\left(\frac{\theta}{2}\right) + \sin\left(\frac{\theta}{2}\right) u,$$

which forms an element of the unit quaternion group. The new orientation, q_{new}, is then computed by the quaternion multiplication

$$q_{\text{new}} = \Delta q \otimes q_{\text{current}},$$

where $\otimes$ denotes the non-commutative quaternion product. This formulation not only ensures numerical stability when compared with rotation matrix formulations but also naturally adheres to the algebraic properties of the three-dimensional rotation group $SO(3)$. The precise formulation of the rotation allows for the seamless integration of discrete turning events into the broader VR system, preserving the order of rotational operations—a critical factor when multiple turns are executed in succession.

Architectural Considerations in Snap Turning Implementation

The integration of snap turning mechanics within a VR system necessitates an architectural framework that supports event-driven state transitions. The system continuously monitors input channels for signals that exceed a defined threshold, triggering a snap turning event. Upon detection of such an event, the input processing unit computes the corresponding angular increment and formulates the appropriate rotation quaternion using the model previously described. This rotation is then applied instantaneously to the existing orientation state. A key architectural challenge is the synchronization of these instantaneous updates with the rendering pipeline. Ensuring that the updated orientation is reflected coherently within the display frame requires precise timing mechanisms and careful calibration against the frame update cycle. Additionally, spatial constraints imposed by the VR environment are maintained by enforcing bounds on the cumulative rotational state, thereby preventing drift or disorientation in the virtual space.

Ergonomic and Usability Analysis of Discrete Turning

The ergonomic implications of snap turning systems are of paramount importance in virtual reality design. Discrete turning steps must be carefully calibrated to remain within the perceptual comfort zone of the user. The angular increment θ is a critical parameter, representing the fixed value by which orientation is altered during each snap turn. Empirical studies suggest that excessively large values of θ may lead to increased incidences of motion discomfort, whereas excessively small values might not sufficiently alleviate the issues caused by continuous rotation. To address this, the system incorporates adaptive scaling of θ, informed by real-time analysis of user motion profiles and environmental context. Complementary to this, hysteresis mechanisms are embedded within the input processing pipeline to preclude the rapid succession of snap turning events that could result in inadvertent over-rotation. The design framework also integrates feedback loops that correlate the discrete turning actions with user experience metrics, thereby ensuring that the angular dynamics remain within physiologically acceptable ranges. This approach results in a balanced system wherein rapid navigational adjustments coexist with a robust commitment to user comfort.

C# Code Snippet

```csharp
using UnityEngine;

public class SnapTurnController : MonoBehaviour
{
    // The fixed angle (in degrees) applied during each snap turn.
    public float snapAngle = 45f;

    // Threshold for detecting horizontal turning input (e.g., from
    //    a joystick or keyboard).
    public float inputThreshold = 0.8f;

    // Cooldown period (in seconds) to prevent rapid, successive
    //    snap turns.
    public float snapCooldown = 0.5f;

    // Internal timer to enforce the cooldown.
    private float cooldownTimer = 0f;
```

```csharp
// The axis around which the rotation occurs; typically the
↪   Y-axis for horizontal rotation.
public Vector3 turnAxis = Vector3.up;

// Update is called once per frame.
void Update()
{
    // Update the cooldown timer.
    if (cooldownTimer > 0f)
    {
        cooldownTimer -= Time.deltaTime;
    }

    // Capture horizontal input.
    float turnInput = Input.GetAxis("Horizontal");

    // Execute a snap turn if the absolute input exceeds the
    ↪   threshold and cooldown has elapsed.
    if (Mathf.Abs(turnInput) >= inputThreshold && cooldownTimer
    ↪   <= 0f)
    {
        // Determine the effective snap angle based on the input
        ↪   direction.
        float effectiveAngle = snapAngle *
        ↪   Mathf.Sign(turnInput);

        // Perform the snap turning operation.
        PerformSnapTurn(effectiveAngle);

        // Reset the cooldown timer to prevent immediate
        ↪   consecutive turns.
        cooldownTimer = snapCooldown;
    }
}

// This method performs the snap turn using quaternion
↪   mathematics.
void PerformSnapTurn(float angle)
{
    // Convert the snap angle from degrees to radians.
    float radAngle = angle * Mathf.Deg2Rad;

    // Compute half of the rotation angle.
    float halfAngle = radAngle / 2f;

    // Calculate cosine and sine of the half-angle.
    float cosHalf = Mathf.Cos(halfAngle);
    float sinHalf = Mathf.Sin(halfAngle);

    // Normalize the turn axis to ensure proper quaternion
    ↪   calculation.
    Vector3 normalizedAxis = turnAxis.normalized;
```

```
        // Compute the delta quaternion representing the discrete
        ↪    rotation.
        // The equation used is: deltaQ = cos(theta/2) +
        ↪    sin(theta/2) * (u)
        Quaternion deltaQ = new Quaternion(
            normalizedAxis.x * sinHalf,
            normalizedAxis.y * sinHalf,
            normalizedAxis.z * sinHalf,
            cosHalf
        );

        // Retrieve the current orientation of the GameObject.
        Quaternion currentOrientation = transform.rotation;

        // Compute the new orientation using quaternion
        ↪    multiplication:
        // newOrientation = deltaQ * currentOrientation
        Quaternion newOrientation = deltaQ * currentOrientation;

        // Apply the new, snap-turned orientation.
        transform.rotation = newOrientation;
    }
}
```

Chapter 21

Using VR Input Event Systems for Interaction

Architectural Foundations of Event-Driven Interaction

A central tenet in the construction of modern virtual reality systems is the adoption of an event-driven framework. In this paradigm, discrete input occurrences are detected, encapsulated, and dispatched via a structured event pipeline. Underlying this framework is the principle of decoupling; input detection is abstracted from the response mechanisms, thus permitting modular integration of interactive components. The architecture employs an event queue in which individual events, denoted as E_i, are enqueued with associated metadata such as timestamps t_i and priority levels p_i. This design decision not only enables scalable system composition but also facilitates a systematic handling of high-frequency input events characteristic of immersive environments.

Event Propagation and Handling in Virtual Reality

The propagation of input events within a VR context necessitates rigorous control over both the sequence and timing of event dispatch. Upon registration, an event is transmitted along a hierarchical chain, akin to the propagation models observed in established graphical frameworks. The event system employs both capturing and bubbling phases, ensuring that each interactive element within the scene graph has the opportunity to process an event. Mathematically, if an event E originates at a source node and is propagated through a sequence of n nodes, then the effective handling can be abstracted as

$$E_{\text{handled}} = f(E, n, \{w_i\}_{i=1}^{n}),$$

where each w_i represents the weight or processing efficiency at node i. Such a formulation aids in maintaining the integrity of interactive responses by enforcing a deterministic order, thereby mitigating potential disruptions in user experience.

Integration of the Event System with Interactive Components

The seamless integration of interactive components within the VR ecosystem is achieved through a well-defined registration mechanism that binds event listeners to specific types of input occurrences. Each interactive element subscribes to the central event dispatcher, thereby receiving notifications without establishing direct dependencies on the input detection subsystem. The decoupling achieved by this model is emblematic of the Observer design pattern, wherein observers are dynamically notified of state changes when an event is raised. Consequently, the communication between disparate components is streamlined, facilitating immediate responses and reducing the likelihood of latency-induced artifacts. The abstraction enforces a strict interface contract among components, ensuring that the transformation of raw input data into actionable commands adheres to a uniform protocol.

Temporal Dynamics and Synchronization of Input Events

The temporal dimension of input event processing plays a critical role in the fidelity of VR interactions. The asynchronous nature of input signal generation demands that the event system enforce precise synchronization with the rendering pipeline. To this end, the system timestamps each event and computes the interleaving delay Δt defined by

$$\Delta t = t_{\text{render}} - t_{\text{event}},$$

where t_{render} represents the time at which the next rendering cycle commences. Control over Δt is paramount, as excessive delays may result in perceptible lag, thereby compromising the immersive quality of the environment. The discrete event model ensures that each input occurrence is processed within the confines of a predetermined time window, thereby maintaining temporal consistency across the virtual scene. This synchronization underpins the responsive nature of the VR system, as it guarantees that input events lead to immediate and coherent updates across interactive components.

Enhancing Responsiveness through Event Prioritization

Given the variety and frequency of input events in virtual reality, it is imperative that the event system incorporates mechanisms for prioritizing important interactions. Each event is assigned a priority value p, where $p \in [0, 1]$, that dictates the order of processing relative to contemporaneous events. Through a combination of static priorities and dynamic adjustments based on contextual factors, the system is capable of resolving contention among simultaneous inputs. The prioritization algorithm can be conceptualized as an optimization problem, wherein the objective is to minimize the overall latency L subject to the constraint of maintaining responsiveness, formally represented by

$$\min_{p_i} L = \min_{p_i} \sum_{i=1}^{N} \delta_i(p_i),$$

with $\delta_i(p_i)$ denoting the processing delay associated with event i. The dynamic allocation of priority factors fosters an environment in which critical interactions are processed expeditiously, thereby ensuring that the user perceives a seamless and immediate response to their actions. This methodological approach to event prioritization underlines the system's commitment to delivering high-performance interactive experiences, a necessity in complex VR environments.

C# Code Snippet

```csharp
using System;
using System.Collections.Generic;
using System.Linq;
using System.Threading;

namespace VRInputEventSystem
{
    // Represents a VR input event with essential metadata.
    public class VREvent
    {
        public int Id { get; set; }
        public DateTime Timestamp { get; set; }
        public double Priority { get; set; }
        public string EventType { get; set; }
        public List<double> Weights { get; set; }

        public VREvent(int id, DateTime timestamp, double priority,
        ↳   string eventType, List<double> weights = null)
        {
            Id = id;
            Timestamp = timestamp;
            Priority = priority;
            EventType = eventType;
            Weights = weights ?? new List<double>();
        }
    }

    // Manages registration and dispatching of VR events.
    public class VREventDispatcher
    {
        private List<VREvent> eventQueue = new List<VREvent>();

        // Event handler using delegate to notify subscribers.
        public event Action<VREvent> OnEventDispatched;

        // Registers an event by adding it to the internal queue.
        public void RegisterEvent(VREvent vrEvent)
        {
            eventQueue.Add(vrEvent);
            // Sort events in descending order of priority (higher
            ↳   priority handled first)
            eventQueue = eventQueue.OrderByDescending(e =>
            ↳   e.Priority).ToList();
        }

        // Dispatches events to all subscribers using both capturing
        ↳   and bubbling phases.
        public void DispatchEvents()
        {
            foreach (var vrEvent in eventQueue)
```

```csharp
        {
            // Capture phase: early processing can be modeled
            ↪  here.
            PropagateEvent(vrEvent, isCapturing: true);
            // Bubbling phase: further handling as events bubble
            ↪  up.
            PropagateEvent(vrEvent, isCapturing: false);
        }
        eventQueue.Clear();
    }

    // Simulates the propagation of an event.
    private void PropagateEvent(VREvent vrEvent, bool
    ↪  isCapturing)
    {
        // In a full implementation, the phase flag could
        ↪  determine which parts of the scene graph process the
        ↪  event.
        OnEventDispatched?.Invoke(vrEvent);
    }

    // Computes the effective handling value using the abstract
    ↪  formulation:
    // E_handled = f(E, n, {w_i}_{i=1}^{n})
    // Here we demonstrate this by calculating a weighted
    ↪  average of the event's priority.
    public double ComputeEffectiveHandling(VREvent vrEvent, int
    ↪  n, List<double> processingWeights)
    {
        if (processingWeights == null || processingWeights.Count
        ↪  != n)
        {
            throw new ArgumentException("The number of
            ↪  processing weights must be equal to n.");
        }

        double weightSum = 0;
        for (int i = 0; i < n; i++)
        {
            weightSum += processingWeights[i];
        }
        double effectiveHandling = vrEvent.Priority * (weightSum
        ↪  / n);
        return effectiveHandling;
    }
}

// Processes input events with synchronization to a simulated
↪  rendering cycle.
public class VREventProcessor
{
    private VREventDispatcher dispatcher;
```

160

```csharp
    public VREventProcessor(VREventDispatcher dispatcher)
    {
        this.dispatcher = dispatcher;
        this.dispatcher.OnEventDispatched += HandleEvent;
    }

    // Handles an event: calculates temporal delay and effective
    ↪ handling.
    public void HandleEvent(VREvent vrEvent)
    {
        DateTime renderTime = DateTime.Now; // Simulate the next
        ↪ rendering cycle timestamp.
        double deltaT = (renderTime -
        ↪ vrEvent.Timestamp).TotalMilliseconds;
        Console.WriteLine($"Event ID: {vrEvent.Id}, Type:
        ↪ {vrEvent.EventType}, Priority:
        ↪ {vrEvent.Priority:F2}");
        Console.WriteLine($"Delta t (ms): {deltaT:F2}");

        // Assume a propagation chain of 3 nodes with defined
        ↪ processing efficiencies.
        int n = 3;
        List<double> processingWeights = new List<double> { 0.8,
        ↪ 0.9, 0.85 };
        double effectiveHandling =
        ↪ dispatcher.ComputeEffectiveHandling(vrEvent, n,
        ↪ processingWeights);
        Console.WriteLine($"Effective Handling Value:
        ↪ {effectiveHandling:F2}");
        Console.WriteLine();
    }
}

// Optimizes event priorities dynamically to minimize overall
↪ latency.
public class EventPriorityOptimizer
{
    // This method simulates a simple optimization by adjusting
    ↪ priorities based on measured latency.
    public void OptimizePriorities(List<VREvent> events)
    {
        double latencyThreshold = 50.0; // Threshold in
        ↪ milliseconds.
        foreach (var evt in events)
        {
            double currentLatency = (DateTime.Now -
            ↪ evt.Timestamp).TotalMilliseconds;

            if (currentLatency > latencyThreshold)
            {
                // Increase priority to expedite delayed events
                ↪ (ensuring it does not exceed the maximum
                ↪ value of 1.0).
```

```
            evt.Priority = Math.Min(evt.Priority + 0.1,
            ↪  1.0);
        }
        else
        {
            // Optionally lower the priority if latency is
            ↪  minimal, but not below 0.
            evt.Priority = Math.Max(evt.Priority - 0.05,
            ↪  0.0);
        }
    }
  }
}

// Simulates the full system: event creation, registration,
↪  optimization, and dispatch.
public class Program
{
    public static void Main(string[] args)
    {
        VREventDispatcher dispatcher = new VREventDispatcher();
        VREventProcessor processor = new
        ↪  VREventProcessor(dispatcher);
        EventPriorityOptimizer optimizer = new
        ↪  EventPriorityOptimizer();

        List<VREvent> events = new List<VREvent>();

        Random rand = new Random();

        // Create and register multiple VR events with simulated
        ↪  timestamps and random priorities.
        for (int i = 1; i <= 5; i++)
        {
            // Create a simulated past timestamp by subtracting
            ↪  a random number of milliseconds.
            DateTime eventTime =
            ↪  DateTime.Now.AddMilliseconds(-rand.Next(10,
            ↪  100));
            double priority = rand.NextDouble(); // Random
            ↪  priority between 0 and 1.
            VREvent newEvent = new VREvent(i, eventTime,
            ↪  priority, $"InputEvent_{i}");
            events.Add(newEvent);
            dispatcher.RegisterEvent(newEvent);
            Thread.Sleep(10); // Simulate a slight delay between
            ↪  event generations.
        }

        // Optimize event priorities based on the current
        ↪  latency measurements.
        optimizer.OptimizePriorities(events);
```

162

```
        // Dispatch all events, triggering propagation phases
        ↪   and corresponding handling.
        dispatcher.DispatchEvents();

        Console.WriteLine("Finished processing events with
        ↪   synchronized input and optimized priorities.");
        }
    }
}
```

Summary: The above C# code implements a comprehensive event-driven VR input system. It defines a VREvent class encapsulating event metadata including timestamps, priorities, and processing weights; a dispatcher that manages event registration and staged propagation (capturing and bubbling); a processor that computes temporal delays (t) and effective handling values according to the provided formula; and an optimizer that dynamically adjusts event priorities to minimize latency. This integrated approach reinforces decoupled design, modularity, and responsiveness essential for immersive VR interactions.

Chapter 22

Scripting Object Manipulation and Transformation

Mathematical Foundations of Object Transformations

Within dynamic virtual environments, object properties are represented in a three-dimensional Euclidean space, where each object is associated with a position vector $\mathbf{v} \in \mathbb{R}^3$. Transformation operations are formalized as mappings $T : \mathbb{R}^3 \to \mathbb{R}^3$, which systematically alter the spatial configuration of the object. By employing homogeneous coordinates—appending an additional coordinate to each vector—translations are incorporated within a matrix framework. This approach enables the consolidated representation of translation, rotation, and scaling in a single 4×4 matrix. The general structure of such a transformation matrix may be expressed as

$$
M = \begin{pmatrix} s_x r_{11} & s_y r_{12} & s_z r_{13} & t_x \\ s_x r_{21} & s_y r_{22} & s_z r_{23} & t_y \\ s_x r_{31} & s_y r_{32} & s_z r_{33} & t_z \\ 0 & 0 & 0 & 1 \end{pmatrix},
$$

where $\mathbf{t} = (t_x, t_y, t_z)$ denotes the translation vector, the coefficients r_{ij} encapsulate the rotational components, and s_x, s_y, and s_z define scaling factors along the principal axes.

Translation

Translation constitutes the operation that displaces an object from one location to another within its ambient space. For an object positioned at $\mathbf{v} = (x, y, z)$ and subject to a translation vector $\mathbf{t} = (t_x, t_y, t_z)$, the updated position $\mathbf{v}'$ is determined by the vector addition

$$\mathbf{v}' = \mathbf{v} + \mathbf{t}.$$

This operation is inherently linear and maintains the orientation of the object while effecting a uniform shift across the coordinate framework.

Rotation

Rotation involves reorienting an object about a defined pivot, frequently the object's center or the origin of its local coordinate system. The rotational action is mathematically represented either by rotation matrices or by unit quaternions. In the matrix representation, if $R \in SO(3)$ is a rotation matrix, then the effect of rotation on a vector $\mathbf{v}$ is conveyed by

$$\mathbf{v}' = R\mathbf{v}.$$

The properties

$$R^R = I \quad \text{and} \quad \det(R) = 1,$$

ensure that the transformation is orthogonal and preserves the intrinsic geometrical properties, such as lengths and angles. Moreover, an axis-angle formulation may be employed, where a rotation is encapsulated by an angle θ and a unitary axis $\mathbf{u}$, yielding a rotation matrix whose entries are explicit functions of these parameters.

Scaling

Scaling operations adjust the magnitude of an object's dimensions. When an object defined by the vector $\mathbf{v}$ is subjected to scaling factors (s_x, s_y, s_z), the transformation is performed via a diagonal matrix S, such that

$$\mathbf{v}' = S\mathbf{v} \quad \text{with} \quad S = \begin{pmatrix} s_x & 0 & 0 \\ 0 & s_y & 0 \\ 0 & 0 & s_z \end{pmatrix}.$$

Uniform scaling, represented by the condition $s_x = s_y = s_z$, preserves the object's proportionate dimensions, whereas non-uniform scaling facilitates anisotropic alterations that may intentionally distort the object's geometry.

Composite Transformations and Their Order

In practical scenarios, transformations are rarely isolated; rather, they are composed to achieve complex modifications. The sequential application of scaling, rotation, and translation is represented by a composite transformation matrix M, customarily formulated as

$$M = T \cdot R \cdot S,$$

where T, R, and S correspond to the translation, rotation, and scaling matrices, respectively. The ordering is of paramount significance due to the non-commutative nature of matrix multiplication; the resultant transformation is highly sensitive to the operational sequence. This composite structure ensures that scaling occurs in the object's local space, followed by a reorientation via rotation and subsequently by translation into the global coordinate frame.

Dynamic Object Manipulation in Virtual Reality

In the realm of immersive virtual reality, objects are subject to continuous transformation in response to dynamic inputs and environmental changes. The transformation parameters—translation vectors, rotation matrices, and scaling factors—are frequently updated to reflect real-time interactions, necessitating a robust computational framework for efficient recalculation. The dynamic transformation is characterized by a time-dependent composite matrix

$$M_{\text{dynamic}} = T(t) \cdot R(t) \cdot S(t),$$

where each constituent matrix evolves as a function of time. Ensuring numerical stability and minimizing computational latency during these updates is critical, particularly in high-performance VR systems where perceptual coherence is contingent on the fidelity of transformation propagation. Advanced techniques, such as interpolative transitions and incremental update algorithms, are employed to guarantee continuous and fluid transformations across the virtual scene.

C# Code Snippet

```csharp
using UnityEngine;

/// <summary>
/// This class encapsulates object transformations using
     translation, rotation, and scaling.
/// It constructs a composite transformation matrix using the order:
     Translation * Rotation * Scaling,
/// which corresponds to the equation M = T · R · S as discussed in
     the chapter.
/// </summary>
public class ObjectTransformation
{
    // The object's position vector (translation).
    public Vector3 position;

    // The object's rotation as a quaternion.
    public Quaternion rotation;

    // The object's scaling factors.
    public Vector3 scale;

    /// <summary>
    /// Initializes the transformation with default values.
    /// </summary>
    public ObjectTransformation()
    {
        position = Vector3.zero;
        rotation = Quaternion.identity;
        scale = Vector3.one;
    }

    /// <summary>
    /// Computes the composite transformation matrix M = T · R · S.
    /// T is the translation matrix, R is the rotation matrix, and S
         is the scaling matrix.
    /// </summary>
    /// <returns>A 4x4 transformation matrix representing the object
         transformation.</returns>
    public Matrix4x4 GetTransformationMatrix()
    {
        // Create the translation matrix T from the position vector.
        Matrix4x4 T = Matrix4x4.Translate(position);
        // Create the rotation matrix R from the quaternion.
        Matrix4x4 R = Matrix4x4.Rotate(rotation);
```

167

```csharp
    // Create the scaling matrix S from the scale vector.
    Matrix4x4 S = Matrix4x4.Scale(scale);

    // Composite Transformation: scaling is applied first, then
    ↪   rotation and finally translation.
    // This is critical because matrix multiplication is
    ↪   non-commutative.
    return T * R * S;
}


/// <summary>
/// Computes a dynamic composite transformation matrix that
↪   varies over time.
/// Each component (translation, rotation, scaling) is updated
↪   based on the time variable.
/// The dynamic matrix demonstrates M_dynamic = T(t) · R(t) ·
↪   S(t).
/// </summary>
/// <param name="time">The time variable, used to animate the
↪   transformation.</param>
/// <returns>A time-dependent 4x4 transformation
↪   matrix.</returns>
public Matrix4x4 GetDynamicTransformationMatrix(float time)
{
    // Dynamic translation: oscillates along the X axis.
    Vector3 dynamicTranslation = new Vector3(Mathf.Sin(time),
    ↪   position.y, position.z);
    Matrix4x4 T_dynamic =
    ↪   Matrix4x4.Translate(dynamicTranslation);

    // Dynamic rotation: rotates continuously around the Y axis.
    Quaternion dynamicRotation = Quaternion.Euler(0f, time *
    ↪   30f, 0f);
    Matrix4x4 R_dynamic = Matrix4x4.Rotate(dynamicRotation);

    // Dynamic scaling: pulsates uniformly based on a sine
    ↪   function.
    float scaleFactor = 1.0f + 0.3f * Mathf.Sin(time * 2f);
    Vector3 dynamicScale = new Vector3(scaleFactor, scaleFactor,
    ↪   scaleFactor);
    Matrix4x4 S_dynamic = Matrix4x4.Scale(dynamicScale);

    // Composite dynamic transformation: T(t) · R(t) · S(t)
    return T_dynamic * R_dynamic * S_dynamic;
}


/// <summary>
/// Transforms a given 3D point using the composite
↪   transformation matrix.
/// This applies the homogeneous coordinate operation v' = M ·
↪   v.
/// </summary>
/// <param name="point">The original 3D point.</param>
```

168

```
    /// <returns>The transformed 3D point.</returns>
    public Vector3 TransformPoint(Vector3 point)
    {
        Matrix4x4 M = GetTransformationMatrix();
        return M.MultiplyPoint3x4(point);
    }
}

/// <summary>
/// A MonoBehaviour to demonstrate object manipulation using
↪    transformation matrices in Unity.
/// </summary>
public class TransformationDemo : MonoBehaviour
{
    // Instance of ObjectTransformation to manage and compute
    ↪   transformations.
    private ObjectTransformation objTransform;

    void Start()
    {
        // Initialize and configure the transformation.
        objTransform = new ObjectTransformation();
        objTransform.position = new Vector3(1f, 2f, 3f);       //
        ↪   Translation: (t_x, t_y, t_z)
        objTransform.rotation = Quaternion.Euler(0f, 45f, 0f);  //
        ↪   Rotation: 45° about the Y axis
        objTransform.scale = new Vector3(2f, 2f, 2f);          //
        ↪   Uniform scaling

        // Example: Apply the static composite transformation to an
        ↪   origin point.
        Vector3 originalPoint = new Vector3(0f, 0f, 0f);
        Vector3 transformedPoint =
        ↪   objTransform.TransformPoint(originalPoint);
        Debug.Log("Transformed Point: " + transformedPoint);
    }

    void Update()
    {
        // Compute a dynamic transformation matrix based on the
        ↪   elapsed time.
        Matrix4x4 dynamicMatrix =
        ↪   objTransform.GetDynamicTransformationMatrix(Time.time);

        // Update the GameObject's position using the translation
        ↪   component of the dynamic matrix.
        transform.position = dynamicMatrix.GetColumn(3);
        // Note: Extracting full rotation and scale from the matrix
        ↪   is more complex.
        // In typical scenarios, these components are updated
        ↪   independently.
    }
```

}

Summary:

In this code snippet, we encapsulate the mathematical principles of object manipulation in immersive environments. The Object-Transformation class builds a 4x4 composite transformation matrix from translation, rotation, and scaling components ($M = T \cdot R \cdot S$), implementing the key equations discussed in the chapter. Both static and dynamic (time-varying) transformations are demonstrated, and the script shows how to apply these transformations to points in 3D space using homogeneous coordinates. This approach forms the basis for dynamic object manipulation in virtual reality applications.

Chapter 23

Adding Physics-Based Interactions to VR Objects

Newtonian Dynamics and Equations of Motion

The behavior of objects within a virtual reality environment is governed by the classical laws of mechanics. In this framework, the motion of an object with mass m is determined by the net force $\mathbf{F}$ acting upon it, as expressed by Newton's second law,

$$\mathbf{F} = m\,\mathbf{a},$$

where $\mathbf{a}$ is the acceleration. The evolution of an object's state is derived from differential equations that relate force, velocity, and position. In a discretized simulation, the instantaneous acceleration is integrated over a time step Δt to update the velocity $\mathbf{v}$ and position $\mathbf{x}$ of the object. Additionally, the impulse $\mathbf{J}$, defined as

$$\mathbf{J} = \int_t^{t+\Delta t} \mathbf{F}\, dt,$$

plays a central role in the calculation of momentum changes during discrete events such as collisions.

1 Newtonian Mechanics in Virtual Environments

Within the simulation context, the fundamental relation

$$\mathbf{a} = \frac{\mathbf{F}}{m}$$

serves as the basis for calculating instantaneous accelerations. The subsequent velocity update is performed using numerical integration methods, in which the updated velocity is given by

$$\mathbf{v}(t + \Delta t) = \mathbf{v}(t) + \frac{\mathbf{F}_{net}}{m} \Delta t.$$

The updated position is then determined by the equation

$$\mathbf{x}(t + \Delta t) = \mathbf{x}(t) + \mathbf{v}(t + \Delta t)\Delta t.$$

These formulations, while rooted in continuous dynamics, are discretized to accommodate the real-time requirements of physics simulation in virtual environments.

2 Impulse and Momentum Conservation

Collisions in a virtual scene are resolved through the calculation of impulses that alter the momentum of interacting bodies. For objects A and B, the conservation of momentum during an instantaneous collision is expressed as

$$m_A \mathbf{v}_A + m_B \mathbf{v}_B = m_A \mathbf{v}'_A + m_B \mathbf{v}'_B,$$

where the primed velocities denote the post-collision states. The collision response is further characterized by a coefficient of restitution e, which quantifies the elasticity of the impact. The impulse $\mathbf{J}$ necessary to resolve the collision is computed by the formula

$$\mathbf{J} = -(1 + e)\frac{(\mathbf{v}_{rel} \cdot \mathbf{n})}{\frac{1}{m_A} + \frac{1}{m_B}} \mathbf{n},$$

with $\mathbf{v}_{rel}$ representing the relative velocity and $\mathbf{n}$ the unit vector normal to the surface at the point of impact.

Collision Detection and Response Mechanisms

The detection and resolution of collisions require robust geometric analyses and efficient computational strategies. The simulation of physical interactions in virtual reality demands the precise detection of intersections between objects, followed by the computation of corrective responses that emulate real-world phenomena.

1 Geometric Collision Detection

The identification of collision events involves the analysis of the spatial relationships between objects. Mathematical techniques, such as the application of bounding volume hierarchies and the separating axis theorem, are utilized to determine whether pairs of objects have entered an intersection state. In simplified models, objects may be approximated by spheres or convex polyhedra, allowing the distance between objects to be characterized by

$$d = \|\mathbf{x}_A - \mathbf{x}_B\|,$$

where $\mathbf{x}_A$ and $\mathbf{x}_B$ denote the positions of the objects. The detection algorithm flags a collision when this distance falls below a predetermined threshold, taking into account the effective radii or extents of the objects.

2 Collision Response and Restitution Models

Upon the detection of a collision, a precise computation of the collision response is essential to preserve the realism of the simulation. The restitution model governs the elastic or inelastic nature of a collision, with the coefficient of restitution e determining the fraction of kinetic energy retained after impact. The resolution of overlapping geometries is achieved through the application of an impulse that modifies the velocities and momenta of the colliding bodies. The corrective impulse is judiciously computed so as to satisfy both the conservation of momentum and the specified restitution characteristics, ensuring that the resultant motion adheres to physical plausibility.

Force Fields, Constraints, and Energy Dissipation

In addition to collision-induced impulses, objects in immersive environments are subject to continuous force fields and constraints that further shape their behavior. Gravitational, drag, and frictional forces are integrated into the overall dynamics to produce a realistic simulation of movement and interaction.

1 Force Field Modeling and Constraints

A uniform gravitational force is typically modeled by a constant acceleration vector $\mathbf{g}$, such that the gravitational force on an object is

$$\mathbf{F}_g = m\,\mathbf{g}.$$

Beyond gravity, additional forces such as aerodynamic drag and viscous damping are incorporated to reflect the resistive interactions between objects and the ambient medium. Constraints, whether rigid or elastic, function to limit the degrees of freedom of an object or to maintain specified relationships between groups of objects. These constraints are often expressed through penalty functions or Lagrange multipliers within the simulation framework, imposing additional terms in the governing equations to ensure that physical linkages and boundaries are respected.

2 Energy Dissipation and Stability Considerations

The phenomenon of energy dissipation is critical when modeling inelastic interactions and frictional processes. Damping forces are introduced to account for the non-conservative aspects of force interactions, often characterized by a damping coefficient γ. The dissipative force can be approximated by

$$\mathbf{F}_d = -\gamma\,\mathbf{v},$$

effectively reducing kinetic energy and stabilizing the system over time. The simulation of these processes necessitates careful numerical treatment to avoid the accumulation of errors that could undermine the overall stability of the physics engine.

Numerical Integration and Stabilization Techniques

The accurate representation of physics-based interactions in virtual environments relies on robust numerical integration techniques that ensure both precision and computational efficiency. Real-time simulations impose stringent requirements on the integration schemes used to propagate the state of the system.

1 Temporal Discretization Methods

The semi-implicit (symplectic) Euler integration method is frequently employed due to its favorable stability characteristics. In this method, the velocity and position updates proceed with the equations

$$\mathbf{v}(t + \Delta t) = \mathbf{v}(t) + \frac{\mathbf{F}_{net}}{m}\Delta t,$$

$$\mathbf{x}(t + \Delta t) = \mathbf{x}(t) + \mathbf{v}(t + \Delta t)\Delta t.$$

This approach tends to better conserve energy, particularly in systems where oscillatory behavior is present, mitigating the numerical dissipation that would otherwise manifest in a purely explicit scheme.

2 Adaptive Integration and Error Control

The selection of the time step Δt represents a critical parameter in achieving the desired balance between simulation accuracy and performance. Adaptive integration techniques may be employed to dynamically adjust Δt in response to localized changes in force magnitudes or collision frequencies. Such adaptations minimize truncation errors while ensuring that high-speed collisions and rapid force variations are accurately captured. The careful calibration of these parameters is essential in maintaining a stable and realistic simulation in the context of interactive virtual environments.

C# Code Snippet

```
// This script demonstrates key physics calculations for VR
↪    interactions in Unity.
// It includes methods for applying forces, integrating motion using
↪    a semi-implicit Euler method,
// and handling collision response through impulse calculations
↪    based on conservation of momentum.
//
// Equations utilized:
//    - Newton's Second Law: F = m * a
//    - Velocity update: v(t+t) = v(t) + (F_net/m) * t
//    - Position update: x(t+t) = x(t) + v(t+t) * t
```

```
//    - Collision impulse: J = -(1+e) * ((v_rel   n) / (1/m_A +
↪    1/m_B)) * n

using UnityEngine;

public class PhysicsObject : MonoBehaviour
{
    // Mass of the object.
    public float mass = 1.0f;

    // Current velocity of the object.
    public Vector3 velocity = Vector3.zero;

    // Accumulated net force acting on the object during the frame.
    public Vector3 accumulatedForce = Vector3.zero;

    // Damping coefficient for energy dissipation.
    public float damping = 0.99f;

    // FixedUpdate serves as our simulation time step.
    void FixedUpdate()
    {
        // Time step.
        float deltaTime = Time.fixedDeltaTime;

        // Calculate acceleration: a = F_net / m.
        Vector3 acceleration = accumulatedForce / mass;

        // Semi-implicit (symplectic) Euler integration:
        // Update velocity: v(t+t) = v(t) + a * t.
        velocity += acceleration * deltaTime;

        // Apply damping to simulate energy dissipation (e.g., due
        ↪   to friction).
        velocity *= damping;

        // Update position: x(t+t) = x(t) + v(t+t) * t.
        transform.position += velocity * deltaTime;

        // Reset the force accumulator after integration.
        accumulatedForce = Vector3.zero;
    }

    // Method to apply an external force to the PhysicsObject.
    public void ApplyForce(Vector3 force)
    {
        accumulatedForce += force;
    }

    // Method to apply an instantaneous impulse, for example during
    ↪   collision response.
    public void ApplyImpulse(Vector3 impulse)
    {
```

```
        // Change in velocity due to impulse: v = J / m.
        velocity += impulse / mass;
    }
}

public class CollisionResolver : MonoBehaviour
{
    // Coefficient of restitution (e) determines the elasticity of
    ↪   the collision.
    // Value of 1 is perfectly elastic; 0 is perfectly inelastic.
    public float restitution = 0.8f;

    // Resolves collision between two PhysicsObjects using
    ↪   impulse-based response.
    public void ResolveCollision(PhysicsObject objA, PhysicsObject
    ↪   objB, Vector3 collisionNormal)
    {
        // Calculate relative velocity between the objects.
        Vector3 relativeVelocity = objB.velocity - objA.velocity;

        // Project the relative velocity onto the collision normal.
        float velocityAlongNormal = Vector3.Dot(relativeVelocity,
        ↪   collisionNormal);

        // If objects are moving apart, no collision resolution is
        ↪   needed.
        if(velocityAlongNormal > 0)
            return;

        // Inverse masses for use in impulse calculation.
        float invMassA = 1.0f / objA.mass;
        float invMassB = 1.0f / objB.mass;

        // Compute impulse scalar:
        // J = -(1+e) * (v_rel   n) / (1/m_A + 1/m_B).
        float impulseScalar = -(1 + restitution) *
        ↪   velocityAlongNormal / (invMassA + invMassB);

        // Calculate the impulse vector.
        Vector3 impulse = impulseScalar * collisionNormal;

        // Apply the impulse in opposite directions to both objects.
        objA.ApplyImpulse(-impulse);
        objB.ApplyImpulse(impulse);
    }
}

public class PhysicsManager : MonoBehaviour
{
    // Reference to all simulated PhysicsObjects in the scene.
    public PhysicsObject[] physicsObjects;

    // Reference to the CollisionResolver component.
```

```csharp
public CollisionResolver collisionResolver;

// Global gravitational acceleration vector.
public Vector3 gravity = new Vector3(0, -9.81f, 0);

void FixedUpdate()
{
    // Apply gravitational force to each PhysicsObject:
    ↪    F_gravity = m * g.
    foreach(PhysicsObject obj in physicsObjects)
    {
        Vector3 gravitationalForce = gravity * obj.mass;
        obj.ApplyForce(gravitationalForce);
    }

    // Simple pairwise collision detection using bounding
    ↪    spheres.
    for (int i = 0; i < physicsObjects.Length; i++)
    {
        for (int j = i + 1; j < physicsObjects.Length; j++)
        {
            PhysicsObject objA = physicsObjects[i];
            PhysicsObject objB = physicsObjects[j];

            // Compute the distance between the objects.
            float distance =
            ↪    Vector3.Distance(objA.transform.position,
            ↪    objB.transform.position);

            // Assume a fixed radius for each object (for a
            ↪    sphere approximation).
            float radiusA = 0.5f;
            float radiusB = 0.5f;

            // Collide if the distance is less than the sum of
            ↪    the radii.
            if (distance < (radiusA + radiusB))
            {
                // Calculate the collision normal (unit vector
                ↪    from objA to objB).
                Vector3 collisionNormal =
                ↪    (objB.transform.position -
                ↪    objA.transform.position).normalized;

                // Resolve the collision by applying an impulse
                ↪    based on the computed normal.
                collisionResolver.ResolveCollision(objA, objB,
                ↪    collisionNormal);
            }
        }
    }
}
```

}

Chapter 24

Implementing Collision Detection in VR Scenes

Mathematical Foundations of Collision Detection

Collision detection in immersive virtual reality necessitates a mathematically rigorous framework to ascertain the conditions under which objects and avatars intersect within a three-dimensional space. At the core of this framework lie distance metrics and geometric primitives that enable the determination of proximity and overlap. For example, when objects are approximated as spheres, their spatial interaction is governed by the relation

$$d = \|\mathbf{x}_A - \mathbf{x}_B\|,$$

where $\mathbf{x}_A$ and $\mathbf{x}_B$ denote the centers of the respective objects, and d represents the Euclidean distance between them. An intersection is detected when

$$d \leq r_A + r_B,$$

with r_A and r_B corresponding to the radii of the two spherical approximations. More intricate shapes are frequently encapsulated by axis-aligned or oriented bounding boxes, wherein collision tests involve verifying the overlap among intervals projected onto multiple axes.

A cornerstone of collision detection for convex geometries is provided by the separating axis theorem. This theorem holds that two convex bodies do not intersect if there exists an axis along which the projection of one body is completely separated from the projection of the other. Such projections are computed by determining the scalar values along candidate axes, and an absence of intersection on any one of these axes confirms non-intersection. The mathematical underpinnings of these methods reinforce the accuracy and reliability of collision calculations, which is critical when interactions must adhere to stringent virtual reality standards.

Spatial Partitioning and Hierarchical Techniques

The computational burden imposed by exhaustive pairwise collision checks in densely populated virtual environments can be significantly reduced through the implementation of spatial partitioning and hierarchical data structures. Spatial partitioning entails subdividing the scene into discrete regions based on the spatial locality of objects. Common data structures employed for this purpose include octrees, binary space partitioning (BSP) trees, and bounding volume hierarchies (BVHs). These structures aggregate objects into clusters, thereby allowing collision tests to be concentrated only on those objects residing within nearby or overlapping partitions.

Bounding volume hierarchies, in particular, facilitate efficient collision queries by encapsulating groups of objects within simple geometric containers, such as spheres or boxes. Each node in a BVH represents a bounded subset of the scene, and traversal of these hierarchies eliminates large segments of space from consideration, effectively reducing the number of candidate pairs that require detailed intersection testing. In many practical implementations, the computational complexity of collision detection can be reduced from an $O(n^2)$ scenario, applicable to naive pairwise comparisons, to an approximate $O(n \log n)$ pattern. This reduction is essential in virtual reality applications where rapid scene reactivity and real-time performance are of paramount importance.

Dynamic environments, characterized by the continuous motion of avatars and objects, further necessitate frequent updates to these spatial partitions. Incremental updating algorithms are employed to maintain the integrity of the partitioning, ensuring that the collision detection system remains both responsive and precise as the scene geometry evolves over time.

Temporal Coherence and Robustness in Dynamic Environments

The rapid motion inherent to immersive virtual reality introduces challenges that are not typically present in static or slow-moving scenarios. When objects or avatars traverse significant distances within a single time step, discrete collision detection methods may fail to register interactions, resulting in artifacts such as tunneling. To address such issues, continuous collision detection (CCD) methodologies are integrated into the collision framework.

Continuous detection accounts for the entire trajectory of an object over a time interval Δt, thereby capturing collisions that might occur between discrete sampling points. This is achieved by constructing a swept volume that represents all positions occupied by the object during its motion. The determination of a collision time, or time of impact, requires solving equations that encapsulate the object's kinematics. Frequently, this involves resolving a quadratic equation of the form

$$At^2 + Bt + C = 0,$$

where the constants A, B, and C are derived from the object's velocity, acceleration, and initial geometric configuration. The solutions to this equation provide candidate collision times which, when validated against the motion trajectories, yield accurate temporal information regarding when and how collisions occur.

Temporal coherence is further enhanced by leveraging the continuity of object trajectories across successive simulation frames. This coherence permits predictive algorithms to refine collision queries based on previous object states, thereby increasing both the robustness and precision of collision detection. In scenarios where rapid motions might otherwise introduce inaccuracies, these temporal strategies serve to mitigate the risk of missed collisions and ensure that interaction responses are enacted with the requisite level of accuracy.

The synthesis of rigorous mathematical analysis, efficient spatial partitioning, and continuous time-aware detection engenders a collision detection system capable of reliably and accurately managing interactions within immersive virtual reality scenes.

C# Code Snippet

```csharp
using UnityEngine;
using System.Collections.Generic;

public class CollisionDetectionUtility
{
    // Checks if two spheres intersect using the Euclidean distance
    ↪   between their centers.
    // Equation: d = || posA - posB ||, collision occurs if d <=
    ↪   (radiusA + radiusB)
    public static bool SphereCollision(Vector3 posA, float radiusA,
    ↪   Vector3 posB, float radiusB)
    {
        float distance = Vector3.Distance(posA, posB);
        return distance <= (radiusA + radiusB);
    }

    // Solves the quadratic equation A*t^2 + B*t + C = 0.
    // Returns true if real solutions exist and outputs the roots t0
    ↪   and t1 (with t0 <= t1).
    public static bool SolveQuadratic(float A, float B, float C, out
    ↪   float t0, out float t1)
    {
        t0 = t1 = 0f;
        float discriminant = B * B - 4f * A * C;
        if(discriminant < 0f)
            return false;

        float sqrtDiscriminant = Mathf.Sqrt(discriminant);
        t0 = (-B - sqrtDiscriminant) / (2f * A);
        t1 = (-B + sqrtDiscriminant) / (2f * A);

        if(t0 > t1)
        {
            float temp = t0;
            t0 = t1;
            t1 = temp;
        }
        return true;
    }

    // Implements Continuous Collision Detection (CCD) for two
    ↪   moving spheres.
    // Computes collision time by solving the equation for the swept
    ↪   volume:
    // |d + v*t|^2 = (radiusA + radiusB)^2,
    // which expands to: (v·v) * t^2 + 2*(d·v) * t + (d·d -
    ↪   (radiusA+radiusB)^2) = 0.
    // Returns true if a collision occurs within the provided
    ↪   timeDelta and outputs collisionTime.
```

183

```
public static bool ContinuousSphereCollision(Vector3 posA,
↪   Vector3 velA, float radiusA,
                                        Vector3 posB,
                                        ↪   Vector3 velB,
                                        ↪   float
                                        ↪   radiusB,
                                        float timeDelta,
                                        ↪   out float
                                        ↪   collisionTime)
{
    collisionTime = 0f;

    // Relative position and velocity.
    Vector3 d = posB - posA;
    Vector3 v = velB - velA;
    float combinedRadius = radiusA + radiusB;

    // Coefficients for the quadratic equation.
    float A = Vector3.Dot(v, v);
    float B = 2f * Vector3.Dot(d, v);
    float C = Vector3.Dot(d, d) - combinedRadius *
    ↪   combinedRadius;

    // Handle the near-zero relative velocity case (static or
    ↪   linear scenario).
    if(Mathf.Abs(A) < 1e-6f)
    {
        if(C <= 0f)
        {
            collisionTime = 0f;
            return true;
        }
        return false;
    }

    float t0, t1;
    if(!SolveQuadratic(A, B, C, out t0, out t1))
        return false;

    // Select the first collision time that falls within the
    ↪   interval [0, timeDelta].
    if(t0 >= 0f && t0 <= timeDelta)
    {
        collisionTime = t0;
        return true;
    }
    if(t1 >= 0f && t1 <= timeDelta)
    {
        collisionTime = t1;
        return true;
    }

    return false;
```

```csharp
}

// A simplified Bounding Volume Hierarchy (BVH) node for spatial
↪  partitioning in VR scenes.
// BVH reduces the number of collision checks by encapsulating
↪  objects in simple geometric bounds.
public class BVHNode
{
    public Bounds BoundingBox;
    public List<Collider> Colliders;
    public BVHNode Left;
    public BVHNode Right;

    // Constructs a BVH node by computing a bounding box that
    ↪  encapsulates all provided colliders.
    public BVHNode(List<Collider> colliders)
    {
        Colliders = colliders;
        if(colliders != null && colliders.Count > 0)
        {
            BoundingBox = colliders[0].bounds;
            for(int i = 1; i < colliders.Count; i++)
            {
                BoundingBox.Encapsulate(colliders[i].bounds);
            }
        }
    }

    // Traverses the BVH to collect colliders that intersect
    ↪  with the queryBounds.
    public void Query(Bounds queryBounds, List<Collider> result)
    {
        if(!BoundingBox.Intersects(queryBounds))
            return;

        if(Left == null && Right == null)
        {
            // Leaf node: add all colliders that overlap with
            ↪  queryBounds.
            foreach(var col in Colliders)
            {
                if(col.bounds.Intersects(queryBounds))
                    result.Add(col);
            }
        }
        else
        {
            if(Left != null)
                Left.Query(queryBounds, result);
            if(Right != null)
                Right.Query(queryBounds, result);
        }
    }
}
```

```
    }
}
```
_____

Chapter 25

Integrating Audio Spatialization in VR

Foundations of Audio Spatialization

Spatial audio is founded on principles derived from both classical acoustics and perceptual psychoacoustics. In immersive virtual reality systems, the simulation of auditory cues requires a precise replication of how sound propagates and interacts within three-dimensional spaces. The modeling of sound involves the consideration of directional attenuation, time delays, and frequency-dependent filtering that mimic the natural behavior of sound waves. By employing head-related transfer functions (HRTFs) and accounting for interaural time differences (Δt) as well as interaural level differences (ΔL), spatial audio systems can create the illusion of sound sources positioned accurately relative to the listener's virtual orientation.

Mathematical Modeling of Sound Propagation

A rigorous mathematical framework underpins the simulation of audio spatialization. One fundamental model is the inverse square law, which dictates that the intensity of sound (I) decays with the square of the distance (r) from the source, as governed by

$$I \propto \frac{1}{r^2}.$$

Moreover, the attenuation factor is often modulated by additional environmental variables that account for reflections, absorptions, and diffractions. The positional components of sound sources are represented as vectors in $\mathbb{R}^3$, such that the distance between a sound source at position $\mathbf{x}_s$ and a listener at position $\mathbf{x}_l$ is computed by

$$r = \|\mathbf{x}_l - \mathbf{x}_s\|.$$

These calculations serve not only to model volume attenuation but also to determine time-of-arrival differences, which are critical when synthesizing the directionality and movement of sound in a virtual environment. The superposition of multiple sound sources further introduces convolution operations where the combined auditory scene is derived as an integral over individual impulse responses, each indexed by its respective spatial parameters.

Spatial Audio Implementation in Unity

In the context of Unity, the integration of spatial audio entails a sophisticated orchestration of audio sources, listeners, and environmental acoustics. Unity's audio architecture leverages a three-dimensional sound model that computes spatial blending based on the relative orientation and distance between audio emitters and the listener position. Parameters such as spatial blend, volume rolloff, and Doppler effects are tuned to simulate realistic audio environments. The spatialization algorithm assigns weight to each sound source by evaluating the angular relationship between its emission vector and the listener's forward direction, thereby generating a stereo or binaural output that reflects spatial cues accurately.

Furthermore, the audio system incorporates configurable reverb zones and occlusion effects. These modifications utilize acoustic modeling to approximate how physical barriers and room configurations influence reverberation time (T_{60}) and frequency spectrum modifications. The integration process involves the calibration of these parameters to mirror natural sound propagation phenomena while maintaining computational efficiency necessary for real-time virtual reality applications.

Layered Dynamic Sound Environments

Constructing a dynamic auditory scene entails the creation of layered sound environments in which discrete audio elements interact harmoniously to support immersion. Each layer represents a distinct stratum of auditory information, ranging from ambient background textures to localized sound events that are context-sensitive and dynamically modulated. The layered approach utilizes a hierarchical mapping of audio sources where base layers establish a continuous spatial ambiance, while higher-order layers introduce transient and interactive auditory signals.

A key aspect of this methodology involves the temporal synchronization of multiple audio channels, ensuring that the composite soundscape remains coherent. Formally, the output sound field $S(t, \mathbf{x})$ at time t and spatial location $\mathbf{x}$ can be modeled as a summation

$$S(t, \mathbf{x}) = \sum_{i=1}^{N} s_i(t - \tau_i(\mathbf{x})) \cdot a_i(\mathbf{x}),$$

where $s_i(t)$ represents the ith sound component, $\tau_i(\mathbf{x})$ denotes the propagation delay attributable to the distance between the listener and the sound source, and $a_i(\mathbf{x})$ encapsulates the attenuation and directional filtering response. The precise calibration of these factors permits subtle transitions and dynamic modulations in response to virtual world interactions, thereby crafting a refined auditory environment that heightens the realism of the VR experience.

C# Code Snippet

```
using UnityEngine;
using System.Collections.Generic;

// This script simulates a basic spatial audio system in Unity using
↪    principles of sound attenuation,
// propagation delay, and directional filtering. It integrates the
↪    following key concepts from the chapter:
//
// 1. Inverse Square Law for Sound Intensity:
//     I  1 / r²,
//     where r = || listener.position - source.position ||.
//
// 2. Propagation Delay Computation:
//     delay = r / c,
```

189

```
//     where c is the speed of sound (approximately 343 m/s).
//
// 3. Composite Sound Field Calculation:
//     S(t, x) = ( s_i(t - _i(x))  a_i(x) ),
//     where s_i is the sound sample from the i-th source, _i is the
↪   delay due to distance, and a_i is the
//     attenuation factor computed via the inverse square law.
//
// 4. Directional Filtering:
//     A simplified head-related effect obtained by measuring the
↪   angle between the listener's forward direction
//     and the vector toward the sound source.
public class AudioSpatializer : MonoBehaviour
{
    // List of active spatial sound sources in the scene.
    public List<SpatialSoundSource> soundSources = new
    ↪   List<SpatialSoundSource>();

    // Transform representing the listener's position and
    ↪   orientation.
    public Transform listener;

    // Speed of sound in air in meters per second.
    public float speedOfSound = 343.0f;

    void Update()
    {
        // Get the current simulation time.
        float currentTime = Time.time;

        // Initialize the composite sound field amplitude.
        float compositeSoundField = 0.0f;

        // Iterate through each sound source to compute its
        ↪   contribution.
        foreach (SpatialSoundSource source in soundSources)
        {
            // Compute the distance between the sound source and the
            ↪   listener.
            float distance = Vector3.Distance(listener.position,
            ↪   source.position);

            // Calculate the propagation delay:  = r / c.
            float delay = distance / speedOfSound;

            // Compute the attenuation using the inverse square law:
            ↪   a = 1 / r².
            // An epsilon is used to avoid division by zero.
            float attenuation = 1.0f / Mathf.Max(distance *
            ↪   distance, 0.0001f);

            // Determine the directional factor based on the angle
            ↪   between the listener's forward vector
```

190

```csharp
        // and the vector from the listener to the source,
        ↪  simulating a simplified HRTF.
        Vector3 directionToSource = (source.position -
        ↪  listener.position).normalized;
        float angle = Vector3.Angle(listener.forward,
        ↪  directionToSource);
        float directionalFactor = Mathf.Clamp01(Mathf.Cos(angle
        ↪  * Mathf.Deg2Rad));

        // Retrieve the sound sample at time (t - delay) to
        ↪  simulate propagation.
        // s(t - ) = baseVolume * sin(2 * frequency * (t -
        ↪  delay))
        float sampleValue = source.GetSoundSample(currentTime -
        ↪  delay);

        // Compute the final amplitude for this sound source.
        float finalAmplitude = sampleValue * attenuation *
        ↪  directionalFactor;

        // Sum the contributions of all sources to form the
        ↪  composite sound field.
        compositeSoundField += finalAmplitude;
    }

    // For demonstration, output the computed composite sound
    ↪  field amplitude.
    Debug.Log("Composite Sound Field Amplitude: " +
    ↪  compositeSoundField.ToString("F4"));
    }
}

// Class representing an individual spatial sound source.
[System.Serializable]
public class SpatialSoundSource
{
    // The position of the sound source in the virtual environment.
    public Vector3 position;

    // The base volume of the sound source.
    public float baseVolume = 1.0f;

    // The frequency of the sound in Hertz (e.g., 440 Hz for
    ↪  standard A).
    public float frequency = 440.0f;

    // Returns a simulated sound sample at a given time t using a
    ↪  sine wave.
    public float GetSoundSample(float t)
    {
        // s(t) = baseVolume * sin(2 * frequency * t)
        return baseVolume * Mathf.Sin(2 * Mathf.PI * frequency * t);
    }
```

191

}

Summary: The above C# code integrates key acoustic formulas and spatial audio algorithms discussed in the chapter. It demonstrates the use of the inverse square law for calculating sound attenuation, computes propagation delays based on the distance between a sound source and a listener, and uses directional filtering to simulate head-related transfer effects. The composite sound field is generated by summing the contributions of individual sound sources, providing a basic framework for implementing immersive audio spatialization in Unity.

Chapter 26

Creating Immersive Spatial Soundscapes

Theoretical Foundations of Spatial Audio

The construction of spatial soundscapes within virtual reality necessitates a rigorous treatment of both physical acoustics and perceptual psychoacoustics. At the core of this treatment lies the modeling of sound as a propagating pressure wave, governed by classical principles such as the inverse square law, expressed as $I \propto \frac{1}{r^2}$, where I denotes the sound intensity and r the distance from the source. The model further captures the finite speed of sound, encapsulated in the propagation delay $\tau = \frac{r}{c}$, with c representing the speed of sound in the chosen medium. Such formulations form the basis for simulating the nuanced interplay between sound emission, attenuation, and the subsequent perception of spatial depth in a virtual environment. The dynamical behavior of these acoustic phenomena must be integrated with signal processing techniques that account for reflections, diffractions, and absorptive properties of the simulated space, thereby establishing an acoustically coherent framework.

Directional Sound Design

An essential aspect of immersive spatial soundscapes is the precise encoding of directional auditory cues. The localization of sound within a three-dimensional environment relies heavily on the exploitation of interaural time differences (ITD) and interaural level differences (ILD). These effects are computationally embodied in head-related transfer functions (HRTFs), which model the frequency-dependent filtering imposed by the anatomical structure of the head and ears. The angular positioning of sound sources relative to the listener is quantified by determining the geometric relationship between the listener's orientation and the sound emitter, thereby modulating the spectral content of the signal according to its angle of incidence. Filtering techniques that deftly alter the amplitude and phase of the incoming signal based on this angular offset ensure that lateral sound sources are perceived with a spectral balance distinct from those aligned with the listener's forward direction. Such directional modulation is critical for reproducing a realistic auditory scene where subtle differences in sound arrival times and intensities enhance the perception of spatial separation.

Ambient Sound Formation in Virtual Environments

Ambient sound plays a pivotal role in establishing the auditory context of a virtual environment. The creation of a layered ambient soundscape involves the careful blending of broad-spectrum noise fields, reverberant characteristics, and transient audio events to articulate the spatial atmosphere. Parameters such as reverberation time, commonly denoted as T_{60}, govern the decay rate of sound energy in enclosed spaces and are finely tuned to evoke the intended spatial enclosure or openness. The ambient layer is typically rendered as a continuous field that envelops the listener, providing subtle but persistent cues regarding the virtual environment's dimensions and material properties. This layer requires meticulous calibration of spectral content and temporal dynamics, ensuring that the ambient sounds coalesce into a cohesive background that does not overpower the directional cues yet significantly enhances the overall sense of presence.

Integration Strategies and Spatial Cohesion

The synthesis of directional audio elements with ambient sound fields culminates in an integrated auditory experience that is both coherent and immersive. The composite sound field, denoted as

$$S(t, \mathbf{x}) = \sum_{i=1}^{N} s_i\big(t - \tau_i(\mathbf{x})\big) \cdot a_i(\mathbf{x}),$$

is computed by aggregating the contributions of individual sound sources, each characterized by its own temporal delay $\tau_i(\mathbf{x})$ and attenuation factor $a_i(\mathbf{x})$, where $s_i(t)$ represents the signal generated by the ith source. This formulation ensures that the spatial interactions are maintained with high fidelity, as each source is weighted according to both its inherent signal characteristics and its spatial context relative to the listener. To achieve this integration, it is necessary to employ algorithms that reconcile the competing demands of computational efficiency and acoustic realism. The design process involves carefully balancing the contributions of transient directional cues with those of the persistent ambient layers, thereby forging an acoustically rich soundscape that accurately mirrors the complexity of real-world auditory experiences in a simulated virtual setting.

C# Code Snippet

```csharp
using System;
using System.Collections.Generic;
using UnityEngine;

public class SoundSource
{
    // Position of the sound source in the virtual space
    public Vector3 Position;
    // Frequency for the simulated sine wave signal (in Hz)
    public float Frequency;
    // Base amplitude of the sound signal
    public float Amplitude;
    // Name identifier for the source
    public string Name;

    public SoundSource(Vector3 position, float frequency, float
    ↪    amplitude, string name)
    {
        Position = position;
        Frequency = frequency;
        Amplitude = amplitude;
        Name = name;
    }
```

```csharp
// Simulates the sound signal as a sine wave at time t
public float GetSignal(float t)
{
    return Amplitude * Mathf.Sin(2f * Mathf.PI * Frequency * t);
}

// Applies a simplified Head-Related Transfer Function (HRTF) to
↪    modulate the signal
// based on the listener's orientation relative to the sound
↪    source.
public float ApplyHRTF(Vector3 listenerPosition, Vector3
↪    listenerForward, float signalValue)
{
    Vector3 direction = (listenerPosition -
    ↪    Position).normalized;
    // Calculate the angle (in degrees) between the listener's
    ↪    forward vector and the direction to the source
    float angle = Vector3.Angle(listenerForward, direction);
    // Approximate directional filtering using the cosine of the
    ↪    angle (converted to radians)
    float directionalFactor = Mathf.Abs(Mathf.Cos(angle *
    ↪    Mathf.Deg2Rad));
    return signalValue * directionalFactor;
}
}

public class SpatialAudioSimulator : MonoBehaviour
{
    // List of individual sound sources in the scene
    public List<SoundSource> soundSources = new List<SoundSource>();
    // Current position of the listener (e.g., the VR camera rig)
    public Vector3 ListenerPosition;
    // Listener's forward direction for orientation calculations
    public Vector3 ListenerForward = Vector3.forward;
    // Speed of sound in air (in meters per second)
    public float SpeedOfSound = 343f;

    void Start()
    {
        // Initialize sample sound sources with positions,
        ↪    frequencies, and amplitudes.
        soundSources.Add(new SoundSource(new Vector3(10f, 0f, 0f),
        ↪    440f, 1f, "Source1"));
        soundSources.Add(new SoundSource(new Vector3(-5f, 0f, 5f),
        ↪    523.25f, 0.8f, "Source2"));
        // An ambient sound source to represent the background audio
        ↪    field
        soundSources.Add(new SoundSource(new Vector3(0f, 0f, 0f),
        ↪    220f, 0.5f, "Ambient"));
    }

    // Computes the composite sound field S(t, x) at time t for the
    ↪    current listener position x.
```

196

```
// The composite signal is determined by summing the
↪   contributions of each sound source,
// factoring in propagation delay ( = r/c) and attenuation (a =
↪   1/r²) based on distance.
public float ComputeCompositeSoundField(float t)
{
    float compositeSignal = 0f;
    foreach (SoundSource source in soundSources)
    {
        // Calculate distance between the sound source and the
        ↪   listener
        float distance = Vector3.Distance(source.Position,
        ↪   ListenerPosition);
        // Prevent division by zero with a minimal distance
        ↪   threshold
        distance = Mathf.Max(distance, 0.1f);
        // Calculate propagation delay:  = r / c
        float propagationDelay = distance / SpeedOfSound;
        // Determine attenuation based on the inverse square
        ↪   law: a = 1 / r²
        float attenuation = 1f / (distance * distance);
        // Retrieve the delayed signal value from the sound
        ↪   source
        float sourceSignal = source.GetSignal(t -
        ↪   propagationDelay);
        // Apply directional filtering via a simple HRTF model
        ↪   based on listener orientation
        sourceSignal = source.ApplyHRTF(ListenerPosition,
        ↪   ListenerForward, sourceSignal);
        // Aggregate the weighted signal into the composite
        ↪   sound field
        compositeSignal += sourceSignal * attenuation;
    }
    return compositeSignal;
}

void Update()
{
    // Update the listener's position using the GameObject's
    ↪   current transform position
    ListenerPosition = transform.position;
    // Get the current simulation time
    float currentTime = Time.time;
    // Compute the overall composite sound field value at the
    ↪   current time
    float compositeField =
    ↪   ComputeCompositeSoundField(currentTime);
    // Output the computed value to the Unity debug console for
    ↪   demonstration purposes
    Debug.Log("Composite Sound Field Value: " + compositeField);
}
}
```

Chapter 27

Scripting Environmental Sound Triggers for VR

Acoustic and Computational Foundations

The establishment of real-time auditory feedback in virtual spaces is predicated upon a rigorous understanding of both the acoustic properties of sound and the computational paradigms required for event-driven processing. In virtual reality, sound is modeled not as an isolated phenomenon but as an interactive signal subject to environmental conditions and user-induced dynamics. Mathematical formulations such as the inverse square law, expressed as $I \propto \frac{1}{r^2}$, and the propagation delay, defined by $\tau = \frac{r}{c}$ where r denotes the distance from the source and c the speed of sound, provide a quantitative basis for simulating realistic auditory triggers. Signal processing frameworks further extend these models by incorporating algorithms for dynamic filtering, temporal synchronization, and thresholding mechanisms that ensure sound triggers are activated in response to specific stimuli or changes in the virtual environment.

Event Detection and Classification in Virtual Environments

The precision of environmental sound triggers is contingent upon the robust detection and classification of events occurring within the virtual space. This section outlines the underlying strategies for monitoring player actions and environmental changes that lead to auditory feedback. A thorough event detection mechanism utilizes sensor data, collision detection algorithms, and state transition analysis to map discrete and continuous events into a computational model. For example, let $E(t)$ represent the set of environmental events detected over time, with each event characterized by parameters such as intensity, duration, and spatial coordinates. A classification function $C : E(t) \rightarrow \{0, 1\}$ can be formally defined such that

$$C(e) = \begin{cases} 1, & \text{if } e \text{ satisfies the triggering criteria,} \\ 0, & \text{otherwise.} \end{cases}$$

This formulation enables the system to selectively process events by comparing them against a predetermined threshold, thereby ensuring that each significant interaction results in a corresponding sound trigger. The integration of statistical models and probabilistic thresholds further refines this process, allowing for adaptive adjustments in response to dynamic virtual conditions.

Real-Time Audio Feedback Mechanisms

The generation of immediate auditory responses in reaction to environmental stimuli requires a seamless integration of event handling and audio synthesis frameworks. In a real-time context, the system monitors the set of classified events and maps these to corresponding audio signals. Let the function $S(t)$ denote the resultant sound signal and $T_i(t)$ be the trigger function associated with the ith event. The composite auditory response can be mathematically expressed as

$$S(t) = \sum_{i=1}^{N} T_i(t) \cdot s_i(t - \tau_i),$$

where $s_i(t)$ represents the audio signal generated by the ith trigger and τ_i encapsulates the propagation delay influenced by the spatial separation between the event location and the listener. Careful consideration is given to minimizing computational latency; hence, efficient event polling and processing algorithms must be employed to ensure that the temporal resolution of the auditory feedback is maintained at a level congruent with the immersive requirements of virtual environments.

Temporal and Spatial Considerations in Sound Triggering

A critical aspect of scripting environmental sound triggers involves aligning the temporal and spatial dimensions of sound propagation with the dynamic nature of the virtual space. Spatial interpolation techniques and real-time filter adjustments are used to synchronize the onset of sound events with corresponding environmental changes. The system must account for the spatial coordinates of both the event and the listener, thereby modulating the amplitude and frequency spectrum of sound signals based on directional vectors and distance metrics. This modulation is fundamentally governed by the relationship

$$a = \frac{1}{\|\mathbf{p}_{\text{event}} - \mathbf{p}_{\text{listener}}\|^2},$$

where a denotes the attenuation factor and $\mathbf{p}_{\text{event}}$, $\mathbf{p}_{\text{listener}}$ denote the positional vectors of the event and the listener, respectively. Temporal alignment is equally critical; it necessitates the dynamic adjustment of trigger timing to offset computational delays and network latencies that could otherwise degrade the immersive experience. The synthesis of these spatial and temporal variables into a cohesive framework ensures that sound triggers provide veridical auditory cues that are perceptually congruent with the simulated physical environment.

C# Code Snippet

```
using UnityEngine;
using System.Collections;
using System.Collections.Generic;

public class SoundTriggerManager : MonoBehaviour
{
```

```csharp
// Speed of sound in meters per second.
public const float SpeedOfSound = 343.0f;

// Intensity threshold for triggering a sound event.
public float intensityThreshold = 0.5f;

// Reference to the listener (typically the VR camera).
public Transform listener;

// Structure representing an environmental event.
public struct EnvironmentalEvent
{
    public Vector3 position;   // Event location.
    public float intensity;    // Magnitude of the event (0 to
    ↪   1).
    public float duration;     // Duration of the event in
    ↪   seconds.

    public EnvironmentalEvent(Vector3 pos, float intensity,
    ↪   float duration)
    {
        this.position = pos;
        this.intensity = intensity;
        this.duration = duration;
    }
}

// List to hold detected environmental events.
public List<EnvironmentalEvent> eventList = new
↪   List<EnvironmentalEvent>();

// Calculate the attenuation factor using the inverse square law
↪   equation:
// a = 1 / (distance ^2)
public float CalculateAttenuation(Vector3 eventPos, Vector3
↪   listenerPos)
{
    float distance = Vector3.Distance(eventPos, listenerPos);
    if (distance < 0.0001f)
        distance = 0.0001f; // Prevent division by zero.
    return 1.0f / (distance * distance);
}

// Calculate the propagation delay based on the formula: tau =
↪   distance / speed of sound.
public float CalculatePropagationDelay(Vector3 eventPos, Vector3
↪   listenerPos)
{
    float distance = Vector3.Distance(eventPos, listenerPos);
    return distance / SpeedOfSound;
}

// Classification function for environmental events.
```

```csharp
// Returns true if the event intensity meets or exceeds the
//   triggering criteria.
public bool IsTriggerable(EnvironmentalEvent e)
{
    return e.intensity >= intensityThreshold;
}


// Process all detected events and trigger corresponding sound
//   outputs.
// This simulates the composite auditory response:
// S(t) = sum_{i=1}^{N} T_i(t) * s_i(t - tau_i)
// where T_i(t) is represented here as the trigger value (based
//   on intensity and attenuation)
// and s_i(t - tau_i) is simulated by playing a clip after a
//   calculated delay.
public void ProcessSoundTriggers()
{
    foreach (EnvironmentalEvent e in eventList)
    {
        if (IsTriggerable(e))
        {
            // Compute spatial attenuation and propagation
            //   delay.
            float attenuation = CalculateAttenuation(e.position,
                listener.position);
            float delay = CalculatePropagationDelay(e.position,
                listener.position);

            // Compute trigger value, analogous to T_i(t), as a
            //   function of intensity and attenuation.
            float triggerValue = e.intensity * attenuation;

            // Start coroutine to simulate playing the audio
            //   signal s_i(t - tau_i)
            // with the computed delay and adjusted "volume"
            //   based on triggerValue.
            StartCoroutine(PlaySoundWithDelay(e, delay,
                triggerValue));
        }
    }

    // Clear events after processing.
    eventList.Clear();
}


// Coroutine executing the delayed playback.
// This represents the real-time audio feedback mechanism.
private IEnumerator PlaySoundWithDelay(EnvironmentalEvent e,
    float delay, float volume)
{
    yield return new WaitForSeconds(delay);

    // Simulate playing sound with calculated volume.
```

```
    // In an actual implementation, this would interface with an
    ↪   AudioSource,
    // e.g., AudioSource.PlayClipAtPoint(audioClip, e.position,
    ↪   volume);
    Debug.Log("Playing sound for event at position: " +
    ↪   e.position +
            " with adjusted volume (after attenuation): " +
            ↪   volume);
}

// Example initialization and event simulation.
void Start()
{
    // Assign the listener if not set (default to main camera).
    if (listener == null && Camera.main != null)
    {
        listener = Camera.main.transform;
    }

    // Adding sample events to the event list.
    eventList.Add(new EnvironmentalEvent(new Vector3(5f, 0f,
    ↪   5f), 0.8f, 1.0f));
    eventList.Add(new EnvironmentalEvent(new Vector3(10f, 0f,
    ↪   10f), 0.3f, 1.0f));
    eventList.Add(new EnvironmentalEvent(new Vector3(3f, 0f,
    ↪   2f), 1.0f, 2.0f));

    // Process events to trigger sounds.
    ProcessSoundTriggers();
}
}
```

Summary: The code above demonstrates a comprehensive implementation of environmental sound triggers in a Unity-based VR setting. It calculates attenuation using the inverse square law, computes propagation delays, classifies events based on intensity thresholds, and simulates composite audio feedback by scheduling audio playback via coroutines—all essential for creating immersive, responsive auditory environments in virtual reality.

203

Chapter 28

Implementing 3D Positional Audio with Oculus

Architectural Foundations and Integration Strategy

The integration of Oculus audio tools within a virtual reality framework is achieved through a meticulous architectural synthesis of audio middleware and real-time spatial data. The audio subsystem is designed to operate in tandem with head-tracking and scene-management components, thereby ensuring that auditory stimuli are rendered in accordance with the listener's dynamic orientation. The system computes the relative position between an audio source at position $\mathbf{p}_s$ and a listener at position $\mathbf{p}_l$, obtaining the vector $\mathbf{r} = \mathbf{p}_s - \mathbf{p}_l$. Its Euclidean norm, $\|\mathbf{r}\|$, informs both the attenuation model and the delay computations in a free-field approximation. In practice, the integration leverages sophisticated head-related transfer function (HRTF) datasets and dynamically applies coordinate transformations, as represented by the relation

$$\mathbf{p}'_s = R\left(\mathbf{p}_s - \mathbf{p}_l\right)$$

where R is the rotation matrix derived from the listener's real-time orientation data. This methodology permits the precise alignment of spatial audio cues with an immersive visual environment.

Mathematical Modeling of Spatial Audio Cues

The formulation of 3D positional audio relies upon rigorous mathematical models that simulate the propagation, attenuation, and spectral modulation of sound. The intensity of an audio signal is modulated in proportion to the distance-dependent attenuation factor, frequently modeled as

$$a = \frac{1}{||\mathbf{p}_s - \mathbf{p}_l||^2}.$$

In addition, the propagation delay τ is computed as

$$\tau = \frac{||\mathbf{p}_s - \mathbf{p}_l||}{c},$$

with c representing the speed of sound in the medium. The angular positioning parameters are determined through the conversion of Cartesian coordinates to a spherical coordinate system, where the radial distance r, azimuthal angle θ, and elevation angle ϕ are given by

$$r = \sqrt{x^2 + y^2 + z^2}, \quad \theta = \arctan\left(\frac{y}{x}\right), \quad \phi = \arcsin\left(\frac{z}{r}\right).$$

These coordinates are essential for interpolating HRTF responses, denoted by $H(\theta, \phi, \omega)$, where ω is the angular frequency of the sound. The model thereby incorporates both interaural time differences (ITD) and interaural level differences (ILD) to yield a perceptually accurate spatial audio representation.

Signal Processing and Positional Audio Rendering

The transformation of raw audio streams into 3D positional sound is facilitated by a robust signal processing pipeline. Each audio source undergoes per-source filtering, wherein convolution operations with HRTF kernels adjust both the amplitude and phase of the signal based on the computed spatial parameters. The process is mathematically characterized by the superposition

$$S(t) = \sum_{i=1}^{n} A_i \cdot s_i\left(t - \tau_i\right),$$

where A_i represents the amplitude scaling factor derived from the attenuation model, $s_i(t)$ is the original audio signal for the ith source, and τ_i is the associated propagation delay. The use of fast Fourier transform (FFT) algorithms in the convolution process permits a reduction in computational latency, ensuring that updates to the audio scene remain synchronized with rapid changes in the listener's orientation and position. Advanced filtering techniques are employed to dynamically adjust the spectral content of the signal, thereby reinforcing the spatial cues essential for an immersive auditory experience.

Performance Optimization and System Synchronization

Maintaining real-time processing capabilities in the context of 3D positional audio necessitates rigorous performance optimization and precise synchronization of multi-source audio processing with sensor-driven positional updates. The design incorporates multi-threaded execution and hardware acceleration to manage the intensive digital signal processing (DSP) tasks. Parameter tuning—such as the adjustment of sampling rates and buffer sizes—plays a critical role in minimizing computational delays and ensuring that latency remains below perceptible levels. The system continuously monitors performance metrics related to audio rendering, and adaptive algorithms recalibrate processing pipelines to align with fluctuating computational loads. Such mechanisms guarantee that the spatial audio synthesis remains congruent with the visual rendering cycle and head-tracking outputs, thereby enhancing the fidelity of the immersive virtual experience.

C# Code Snippet

```csharp
using UnityEngine;
using System;

public class SpatialAudioProcessor
{
    public Vector3 listenerPosition;
    public Quaternion listenerRotation;
    public double speedOfSound = 343.0; // Speed of sound in m/s
```

```
public SpatialAudioProcessor(Vector3 listenerPosition,
↪    Quaternion listenerRotation)
{
    this.listenerPosition = listenerPosition;
    this.listenerRotation = listenerRotation;
}

// Computes the rotated source position using the formula:
// p'_s = R * (p_s - p_l)
public Vector3 GetRotatedSourcePosition(Vector3 sourcePosition)
{
    Vector3 relativePos = sourcePosition - listenerPosition;
    return listenerRotation * relativePos;
}

// Computes distance-dependent attenuation based on the formula:
// a = 1 / ||p_s - p_l||^2
public float ComputeAttenuation(Vector3 sourcePosition)
{
    Vector3 relativePos = sourcePosition - listenerPosition;
    float distanceSquared = relativePos.sqrMagnitude;
    if (distanceSquared < 0.0001f) // Avoid division by a
    ↪    near-zero distance
        return 1f;
    return 1f / distanceSquared;
}

// Computes the propagation delay using the formula:
//  = ||p_s - p_l|| / c
public float ComputePropagationDelay(Vector3 sourcePosition)
{
    Vector3 relativePos = sourcePosition - listenerPosition;
    float distance = relativePos.magnitude;
    return distance / (float)speedOfSound;
}

// Converts Cartesian coordinates to spherical coordinates:
// r = sqrt(x^2 + y^2 + z^2),  = arctan(y/x),  = arcsin(z/r)
public (float r, float theta, float phi)
↪    ComputeSphericalCoordinates(Vector3 relativePos)
{
    float r = relativePos.magnitude;
    float theta = Mathf.Atan2(relativePos.y, relativePos.x);
    float phi = (r > 0f) ? Mathf.Asin(relativePos.z / r) : 0f;
    return (r, theta, phi);
}

// Simulated HRTF response function: H(, , )
// For demonstration, this returns a simplified gain value based
↪    on angular parameters and frequency.
public float GetHRTFResponse(float theta, float phi, float
↪    frequency)
{
```

```csharp
        // Simplified directional gain: modulate by cosine of angles
        ↪   and a mild frequency-dependent factor.
        float gain = Mathf.Cos(theta) * Mathf.Cos(phi);
        gain *= 1.0f / (1.0f + 0.001f * frequency);
        return gain;
    }

    // Processes the audio buffer to synthesize 3D positional audio.
    // Implements a simplified convolution:
    // S(t) = [A_i * s_i(t - _i)]
    public float[] ProcessAudio(float[] audioBuffer, Vector3
    ↪   sourcePosition, float frequency)
    {
        float attenuation = ComputeAttenuation(sourcePosition);
        float delaySeconds =
        ↪   ComputePropagationDelay(sourcePosition);
        int delaySamples = (int)(delaySeconds *
        ↪   AudioSettings.outputSampleRate);

        Vector3 relativePos = sourcePosition - listenerPosition;
        var spherical = ComputeSphericalCoordinates(relativePos);
        float hrtfGain = GetHRTFResponse(spherical.theta,
        ↪   spherical.phi, frequency);

        // Prepare a processed buffer that accounts for the delay
        ↪   (using zero-padding).
        float[] processedBuffer = new float[audioBuffer.Length +
        ↪   delaySamples];

        // Apply the computed attenuation, HRTF gain, and delay to
        ↪   the audio samples.
        for (int i = 0; i < audioBuffer.Length; i++)
        {
            float sample = audioBuffer[i];
            sample *= attenuation * hrtfGain;
            if (i + delaySamples < processedBuffer.Length)
            {
                processedBuffer[i + delaySamples] += sample;
            }
        }

        return processedBuffer;
    }
}

public class SpatialAudioExample : MonoBehaviour
{
    public AudioSource audioSource;
    public Vector3 sourcePosition = new Vector3(5f, 2f, 3f);
    public float frequency = 1000f; // Frequency component in Hz for
    ↪   HRTF simulation

    private SpatialAudioProcessor audioProcessor;
```

```
void Start()
{
    // Initialize the spatial audio processor with the current
    ↪  listener's position and rotation.
    audioProcessor = new
    ↪  SpatialAudioProcessor(Camera.main.transform.position,
    ↪  Camera.main.transform.rotation);

    // Retrieve raw audio data from the AudioSource's clip.
    AudioClip originalClip = audioSource.clip;
    float[] samples = new float[originalClip.samples *
    ↪  originalClip.channels];
    originalClip.GetData(samples, 0);

    // Process the audio buffer with 3D positional effects.
    float[] processedSamples =
    ↪  audioProcessor.ProcessAudio(samples, sourcePosition,
    ↪  frequency);

    // Create a new AudioClip using the processed audio data.
    AudioClip processedClip = AudioClip.Create("ProcessedClip",
        processedSamples.Length / originalClip.channels,
        originalClip.channels,
        originalClip.frequency,
        false);
    processedClip.SetData(processedSamples, 0);

    // Assign the processed clip to the AudioSource and start
    ↪  playback.
    audioSource.clip = processedClip;
    audioSource.Play();
}

void Update()
{
    // Update the listener's position and orientation in real
    ↪  time to maintain synchronization.
    audioProcessor.listenerPosition =
    ↪  Camera.main.transform.position;
    audioProcessor.listenerRotation =
    ↪  Camera.main.transform.rotation;
}
}
```

Chapter 29

Creating Realistic Lighting in VR Environments

Directional Lighting Techniques

Directional lighting is employed to emulate an infinitely distant light source whose rays arrive with uniform directionality across all surfaces in the scene. The light vector, denoted as $\mathbf{L}$, is treated as a normalized constant that remains invariant for every fragment of the virtual environment. The diffuse component of the illumination is established through the Lambertian reflection model, where the intensity is computed as

$$I_d = k_d \cdot \max\{0, \mathbf{N} \cdot \mathbf{L}\},$$

with $\mathbf{N}$ representing the surface normal and k_d the diffuse reflectance coefficient. Additionally, the perceptual realism is enhanced by incorporating specular reflections via the Phong reflection model. This component is expressed as

$$I_s = k_s \cdot \max\{0, \mathbf{R} \cdot \mathbf{V}\}^n,$$

where $\mathbf{R}$ is the reflection vector, $\mathbf{V}$ indicates the view direction, k_s is the specular reflection coefficient, and n quantifies the shininess of the surface. The combination of these models, together with advanced shadow mapping and high dynamic range (HDR) techniques, facilitates the simulation of a convincing sunlight effect that uniformly illuminates large-scale virtual spaces.

Point Lighting Configurations

Point lights serve as localized sources that disseminate light isotropically from a specific position within the scene. The attenuation of light intensity from a point source is predominantly governed by the inverse square law. This relationship may be refined through the attenuation model

$$I_p = \frac{I_0}{a + br + cr^2},$$

where I_0 is the intrinsic luminance of the point source, r denotes the Euclidean distance from the light to a surface, and a, b, and c are tunable parameters that modulate the constant, linear, and quadratic attenuation factors respectively. The effective illumination on a surface is determined by applying a cosine correction factor, computed as

$$\max\{0, \mathbf{N} \cdot \hat{\mathbf{r}}\},$$

where $\hat{\mathbf{r}}$ symbolizes the normalized vector from the point light to the surface. This formulation ensures that the intensity of illumination decreases in a physically plausible manner as the distance increases, thereby preserving the natural gradation of light intensity essential for creating vivid and immersive virtual environments.

Ambient Illumination Considerations

Ambient lighting constitutes a global illumination term that fills shadowed regions and contributes to the overall luminance of the scene without regard for spatial orientation. This component is typically modeled as a uniform additive term in the illumination equation, represented by

$$I_a = k_a \cdot A,$$

where k_a is the ambient reflection coefficient and A symbolizes the base ambient light intensity. In virtual reality environments, refinement of ambient lighting is achieved through methods such as ambient occlusion and the application of spherical harmonics, which capture the influence of indirect light scattered by surrounding geometry. These methods calculate localized occlusion factors and enable a more nuanced blending of the ambient term with direct lighting components. The result is an environment where subtle variations in luminance contribute to the perception of depth and spatial coherence. Advanced techniques in ambient lighting ensure a balanced representation of light, mitigating the stark contrasts that can otherwise shatter the realism of a virtual scene while preserving the natural feel of real-world illumination.

C# Code Snippet

```csharp
using UnityEngine;

// VRLightingCalculator provides methods to compute lighting
↪    contributions for VR environments.
// It implements directional lighting using Lambertian and Phong
↪    reflection models,
// point lighting with distance attenuation, and ambient lighting
↪    calculations.
public class VRLightingCalculator
{
    // Calculates the directional light contribution using
    ↪    Lambertian (diffuse) and Phong (specular) models.
    // Parameters:
    //    normal: The surface normal vector at the fragment.
    //    viewDir: The direction from the fragment to the camera
    ↪    (should be normalized).
    //    lightDir: The directional light vector (should be
    ↪    normalized and point towards the surface).
    //    lightColor: The color/intensity of the directional light.
    //    k_d: The diffuse reflection coefficient.
    //    k_s: The specular reflection coefficient.
    //    shininess: The shininess exponent for the Phong specular
    ↪    term.
    public static Color CalculateDirectionalLight(Vector3 normal,
    ↪    Vector3 viewDir, Vector3 lightDir,
                                        Color
                                        ↪    lightColor,
                                        ↪    float k_d,
                                        ↪    float k_s,
                                        ↪    float
                                        ↪    shininess)
    {
        // Ensure vectors are normalized.
        normal = normal.normalized;
        viewDir = viewDir.normalized;
        lightDir = lightDir.normalized;
```

```
    // Lambertian Diffuse Reflection: I_d = k_d * max(0, dot(N,
    ↪   L))
    float diffuseFactor = Mathf.Max(0f, Vector3.Dot(normal,
    ↪   lightDir));
    float diffuse = k_d * diffuseFactor;

    // Phong Specular Reflection: I_s = k_s * max(0, dot(R,
    ↪   V))^n
    // Where R is the reflection vector computed using
    ↪   Vector3.Reflect.
    Vector3 reflectDir = Vector3.Reflect(-lightDir, normal);
    float specAngle = Mathf.Max(0f, Vector3.Dot(reflectDir,
    ↪   viewDir));
    float specular = k_s * Mathf.Pow(specAngle, shininess);

    // Total directional light intensity.
    float intensity = diffuse + specular;

    // Multiply the light color with the calculated intensity.
    return lightColor * intensity;
}

// Calculates the point light contribution with distance
↪   attenuation.
// Parameters:
//   surfacePos: The world position of the surface point.
//   normal: The surface normal at the point (should be
↪   normalized).
//   pointLightPos: The position of the point light source.
//   lightColor: The intrinsic color and intensity of the point
↪   light.
//   I0: The intrinsic luminance intensity of the point light.
//   a: Constant attenuation factor.
//   b: Linear attenuation factor.
//   c: Quadratic attenuation factor.
public static Color CalculatePointLight(Vector3 surfacePos,
↪   Vector3 normal, Vector3 pointLightPos,
                                    Color lightColor,
                                    ↪   float I0, float a,
                                    ↪   float b, float c)
{
    // Compute the vector and distance from the surface to the
    ↪   point light.
    Vector3 lightVector = pointLightPos - surfacePos;
    float distance = lightVector.magnitude;
    Vector3 dirToLight = lightVector.normalized;

    // Cosine Correction: max(0, dot(N, rHat))
    float cosFactor = Mathf.Max(0f,
    ↪   Vector3.Dot(normal.normalized, dirToLight));
```

```csharp
    // Attenuation based on distance: I_p = I0 / (a + b*r +
    ↪  c*r^2)
    float attenuation = I0 / (a + b * distance + c * distance *
    ↪  distance);

    // Return the point light contribution.
    return lightColor * attenuation * cosFactor;
}

// Calculates the ambient light contribution.
// Parameters:
//   ambientLight: The base ambient light color/intensity.
//   k_a: The ambient reflection coefficient.
public static Color CalculateAmbientLight(Color ambientLight,
↪  float k_a)
{
    // Ambient light uniformly contributes to the overall
    ↪  illumination.
    return ambientLight * k_a;
}

// Aggregates directional, point, and ambient lighting to
↪  compute the final color at a surface point.
// Parameters:
//   surfacePos: Position of the surface point.
//   normal: Surface normal at the point.
//   viewPos: Position of the camera/viewer.
//   directionalLightDir: Direction from which the directional
↪  light is coming.
//   directionalColor: Color/intensity of the directional light.
//   kd, ks, shininess: Coefficients for the directional light's
↪  diffuse and specular components.
//   pointLightPos: Position of the point light.
//   pointLightColor: Color/intensity of the point light.
//   I0, a, b, c: Intrinsic intensity and attenuation factors
↪  for the point light.
//   ambientLight: The base ambient light color.
//   ka: Ambient reflection coefficient.
public static Color ComputeFinalLighting(Vector3 surfacePos,
↪  Vector3 normal, Vector3 viewPos,
                                        Vector3
                                        ↪  directionalLightDir,
                                        ↪  Color
                                        ↪  directionalColor,
                                        float kd, float ks,
                                        ↪  float shininess,
                                        Vector3
                                        ↪  pointLightPos,
                                        ↪  Color
                                        ↪  pointLightColor,
                                        float I0, float a,
                                        ↪  float b, float c,
```

```
                                        Color ambientLight,
                                        ↪  float ka)
{
    // Calculate the view direction from the surface to the
    ↪  camera.
    Vector3 viewDir = (viewPos - surfacePos).normalized;

    // Compute contributions from each lighting component.
    Color directionalContribution =
    ↪  CalculateDirectionalLight(normal, viewDir,
    ↪  directionalLightDir, directionalColor, kd, ks,
    ↪  shininess);
    Color pointContribution = CalculatePointLight(surfacePos,
    ↪  normal, pointLightPos, pointLightColor, I0, a, b, c);
    Color ambientContribution =
    ↪  CalculateAmbientLight(ambientLight, ka);

    // Sum the contributions.
    Color finalColor = directionalContribution +
    ↪  pointContribution + ambientContribution;

    // Clamp the final color values between 0 and 1.
    finalColor.r = Mathf.Clamp01(finalColor.r);
    finalColor.g = Mathf.Clamp01(finalColor.g);
    finalColor.b = Mathf.Clamp01(finalColor.b);
    finalColor.a = Mathf.Clamp01(finalColor.a);

    return finalColor;
}
}

/*
```

Chapter 30

Working with Lightmapping for VR

Theoretical Underpinnings of Lightmapping

Lightmapping as a technique originates in the domain of global illumination and radiosity methods traditionally employed in offline rendering. The process entails the precomputation of both direct and indirect illumination effects, whereby light interaction with scene surfaces is captured in texture maps. The formulation of radiosity, expressed as

$$B_i = E_i + \rho_i \sum_{j=1}^{n} F_{ij} B_j,$$

serves as a fundamental model, where B_i denotes the radiosity (or total energy leaving surface i), E_i represents the self-emitted energy, ρ_i is the reflectance coefficient of the surface, and F_{ij} stands for the form factor quantifying the geometric relation between surface i and surface j. In the context of lightmapping for virtual reality, this precomputed illumination forms the basis of a baked lighting solution that obviates the need for costly real-time global illumination calculations.

Techniques for UV Unwrapping and Lightmap Baking

The generation of effective lightmaps requires a rigorous approach to UV unwrapping, ensuring that the mapping from three-dimensional surfaces to a two-dimensional texture space is both continuous and minimally distorted. Non-overlapping UV layouts are essential to prevent artifacts such as light leakage between adjacent surfaces. The optimization process involves careful consideration of texel density and aspect ratio in order to maximize the fidelity of the baked lighting. Techniques in spatial packing and the formation of a unified texture atlas are employed to consolidate disparate UV islands. The quality of the lightmap is directly influenced by the precision of this unwrapping process, with the goal of preserving the inherent spatial relationships and intensity gradients of the original scene illumination.

Baked Lighting Integration in VR Rendering Pipelines

The integration of baked lightmaps within a virtual reality rendering pipeline leverages the computational efficiencies afforded by precomputed illumination. By segregating indirect lighting computations from dynamic rendering, the system is able to allocate resources towards maintaining high frame rates necessary for immersive VR experiences. The composite lighting model, which can be represented as

$$I = I_{\text{direct}} + I_{\text{baked}},$$

combines real-time direct illumination with the static yet highly detailed baked radiance. High dynamic range (HDR) data is often incorporated into the baking process to accommodate a wide luminance range, thereby preserving subtle gradations and ensuring visual consistency under varying ambient conditions. This precomputation method is instrumental in reducing the per-frame computational load, which is of paramount importance in performance-constrained VR platforms.

Performance Optimization and Visual Fidelity in Lightmapping

The dual objectives of performance optimization and the maintenance of visual fidelity are central to the deployment of lightmapping in virtual reality. On one hand, the use of baked lightmaps eliminates the need for recurrent and expensive lighting calculations during runtime. On the other hand, it necessitates a meticulous balance between resolution and storage considerations. Compression algorithms and the judicious use of mipmapping are employed to minimize texture memory overhead while safeguarding against artifacts that could compromise the perceived quality of illumination. Metrics for evaluating performance improvements include frame-rate stability and reduced rendering overhead, as well as quantitative assessments of texture sampling accuracy. Through an iterative process of calibration—where resolution, compression, and lightmap blending parameters are refined—the system achieves an optimized equilibrium that fully exploits the benefits of precomputed lighting without sacrificing the immersive visual quality required of high-fidelity virtual reality environments.

C# Code Snippet

```csharp
using System;
using System.Collections.Generic;

namespace VRLightmapping
{
    // Class representing a surface with its lighting properties
    public class Surface
    {
        // Unique index for the surface
        public int Index { get; set; }
        // The self-emitted energy E_i
        public double Emission { get; set; }
        // The reflectance coefficient _i (range 0..1)
        public double Reflectance { get; set; }
        // The computed radiosity B_i
        public double Radiosity { get; set; }

        public Surface(int index, double emission, double
        ↪  reflectance)
        {
            Index = index;
            Emission = emission;
```

218

```
            Reflectance = reflectance;
            // Initial radiosity is set to the self-emitted energy
            Radiosity = emission;
        }
    }

    // Solver for computing radiosity using the iterative method.
    // It implements the equation:
    //    B_i = E_i + _i * _j (F_ij * B_j)
    public class RadiositySolver
    {
        private readonly List<Surface> surfaces;
        // Form factor matrix where formFactors[i,j] corresponds to
        ↪    F_ij
        private readonly double[,] formFactors;
        private readonly double tolerance;
        private readonly int maxIterations;

        public RadiositySolver(List<Surface> surfaces, double[,]
        ↪    formFactors, double tolerance = 1e-5, int maxIterations
        ↪    = 1000)
        {
            this.surfaces = surfaces;
            this.formFactors = formFactors;
            this.tolerance = tolerance;
            this.maxIterations = maxIterations;
        }

        // Iteratively compute the radiosity of each surface until
        ↪    convergence.
        public void Solve()
        {
            int n = surfaces.Count;
            double[] newRadiosity = new double[n];

            for (int iteration = 0; iteration < maxIterations;
            ↪    iteration++)
            {
                double maxDelta = 0;

                // Update radiosity for each surface based on
                ↪    current values
                for (int i = 0; i < n; i++)
                {
                    double sum = 0;
                    for (int j = 0; j < n; j++)
                    {
                        sum += formFactors[i, j] *
                        ↪    surfaces[j].Radiosity;
                    }
                    // Compute new radiosity using the radiosity
                    ↪    equation
```

```csharp
            newRadiosity[i] = surfaces[i].Emission +
            ↪    surfaces[i].Reflectance * sum;
        }

        // Compute the maximum change across all surfaces
        ↪    and update their radiosity
        for (int i = 0; i < n; i++)
        {
            double delta = Math.Abs(newRadiosity[i] -
            ↪    surfaces[i].Radiosity);
            if (delta > maxDelta)
            {
                maxDelta = delta;
            }
            surfaces[i].Radiosity = newRadiosity[i];
        }

        // Check if the solution has converged sufficiently
        if (maxDelta < tolerance)
        {
            Console.WriteLine("Radiosity converged after {0}
            ↪    iterations.", iteration);
            break;
        }
    }
}

// Print out the computed radiosity for each surface.
public void PrintResults()
{
    foreach (Surface s in surfaces)
    {
        Console.WriteLine("Surface {0}: Radiosity = {1:F4}",
        ↪    s.Index, s.Radiosity);
    }
}
}

// A simple class to demonstrate the composite lighting model:
// I = I_direct + I_baked
public static class IlluminationCalculator
{
    // Combines direct lighting and precomputed (baked) lighting
    ↪    into the final intensity.
    public static double ComputeFinalIllumination(double
    ↪    directLight, double bakedLight)
    {
        return directLight + bakedLight;
    }
}

// Main Program to test radiosity computation and composite
↪    illumination application.
```

```csharp
class Program
{
    static void Main(string[] args)
    {
        // Define a list of surfaces with their emission and
        // reflectance values.
        List<Surface> surfaces = new List<Surface>
        {
            new Surface(0, 10.0, 0.5), // High emission source
            new Surface(1, 5.0, 0.7),
            new Surface(2, 0.0, 0.6)    // Non-emissive surface
        };

        // Define a sample 3x3 form factor matrix F_ij.
        // These values represent the geometric interaction
        // between surfaces.
        double[,] formFactors = new double[3, 3]
        {
            { 0.0, 0.3, 0.2 },
            { 0.3, 0.0, 0.1 },
            { 0.2, 0.1, 0.0 }
        };

        // Create and run the RadiositySolver, which uses the
        // radiosity equation:
        // B_i + _i * _j (F_ij * B_j)
        RadiositySolver solver = new RadiositySolver(surfaces,
            formFactors);
        solver.Solve();
        solver.PrintResults();

        // Demonstrate the composite lighting equation:
        // I = I_direct + I_baked, where I_baked is taken from
        // one of the computed surfaces.
        double I_direct = 20.0;
        double I_baked = surfaces[0].Radiosity;
        double finalIllumination = IlluminationCalculator.
        ComputeFinalIllumination(
        I_direct, I_baked);
        Console.WriteLine("Final Illumination (Composite):
            {0:F4}", finalIllumination);

        // Wait for user input before closing the console
        // window.
        Console.WriteLine("Press any key to exit...");
        Console.ReadKey();
    }
}
}
```

221

Chapter 31

Optimizing Scene Lighting for Immersion

Challenges in VR Lighting Optimization

The optimization of scene lighting for immersive virtual reality environments demands a rigorous treatment of both computational complexity and perceptual quality. In a VR system, ensuring that high frame rates are consistently maintained places strict requirements on the computational budget allocated for lighting calculations. The graphical pipeline must process elaborate luminance interactions while preserving a temporal consistency that prevents perceptual discontinuities. In many instances, the lighting optimization problem can be abstracted as a multi-objective trade-off where the increase in computational costs, denoted as C, must be balanced against the enhancements in perceived realism R. Such a relationship may be conceptually framed as a diminishing return problem when C exceeds a certain threshold, thereby necessitating a careful calibration of algorithms that serve both objectives.

Techniques for Enhanced Visual Fidelity

Visual fidelity in VR is heavily dependent on the faithful reproduction of light behavior as observed in natural environments. The incorporation of physically-based rendering techniques allows for the simulation of light interaction with surfaces in a manner that honors the principles of conservation of energy and surface reflectance properties. Advanced shadow algorithms, including soft shadow mapping and percentage-closer filtering, contribute to the depth cues required for believable three-dimensional representation. Similarly, screen space ambient occlusion methods simulate the subtle shading variations that occur in shadowed crevices. The implementation of high dynamic range (HDR) imaging paired with sophisticated tone mapping operators effectively captures a broad luminance spectrum while remapping intensity values into a confined range appropriate for display devices. In this context, the transformation function $T(I)$, where I represents the scene luminance, is employed to compress the high dynamic range data into a perceptually linear output.

Optimization Strategies in Rendering Architectures

Architectural strategies aimed at light computation partitioning serve as the cornerstone of performance optimization. Deferred shading architectures, for instance, facilitate the decoupling of geometry processing from lighting calculations. In such approaches, the illumination of a scene is aggregated into separate buffers and later composited to yield the final image. The central equation governing this compositing stage can be represented as $I = I_{\text{direct}} + I_{\text{baked}}$, where I_{direct} corresponds to real-time computed illumination and I_{baked} denotes the precomputed lighting contributions. By offloading the bulk of indirect lighting computation to a preprocessing phase, the rendering pipeline effectively reduces the per-frame computational load. Moreover, techniques such as occlusion culling and view frustum culling are systematically applied to eliminate the computation of lighting for objects that fall outside of the viewer's immediate perception, further refining the allocation of graphical resources.

Balancing Computational Load through Hybrid Lighting Schemes

Hybrid lighting schemes represent a strategic synthesis wherein static and dynamic components of the scene are illuminated by different methods, thereby optimizing overall performance without sacrificing visual quality. Static scene elements, characterized by invariant geometry or identity over time, are rendered using lightmaps that encapsulate precomputed global illumination effects. This pre-baking process significantly diminishes runtime overhead. On the other hand, dynamic objects or interactive elements are subjected to real-time lighting computations that, while less computationally intense, maintain sufficient photorealism to ensure coherent integration within the static environment. The scene can be mathematically partitioned into regions R_s and R_d, where the performance metric P is expressed as

$$P = \alpha P_s + (1 - \alpha)P_d,$$

with P_s and P_d denoting the performance characteristics of static and dynamic lighting, respectively, and α representing the proportional weighting of the static component. This formalism underlines the primary goal of achieving an equilibrium whereby the combined approach maximizes system throughput while delivering a visually immersive experience.

C# Code Snippet

```
using System;

namespace VRLighting
{
    /// <summary>
    /// The LightingOptimizer class encapsulates methods for
    ↪    integrating different lighting
    /// computations and optimization algorithms used in immersive
    ↪    VR environments.
    /// It includes calculations for total illumination, tone
    ↪    mapping, performance metrics,
    /// and simulation of diminishing returns when computational
    ↪    cost exceeds an acceptable threshold.
    /// </summary>
    public class LightingOptimizer
    {
        /// <summary>
        /// Computes the total illumination of a scene by summing
        ↪    real-time (direct) illumination
        /// and precomputed (baked) illumination.
        /// Equation: I = I_direct + I_baked
        /// </summary>
        /// <param name="directIllumination">Real-time computed
        ↪    illumination (I_direct)</param>
        /// <param name="bakedIllumination">Precomputed lighting
        ↪    contribution (I_baked)</param>
```

```csharp
/// <returns>Total scene illumination</returns>
public static double ComputeTotalIllumination(double
↪    directIllumination, double bakedIllumination)
{
    return directIllumination + bakedIllumination;
}


/// <summary>
/// Applies a tone mapping operator to compress high dynamic
↪    range luminance data
/// into a perceptually linear output.
/// Here, we use a simplified Reinhard tone mapping:
/// T(I) = I / (I + 1)
/// </summary>
/// <param name="sceneLuminance">The total scene
↪    luminance</param>
/// <returns>Tone-mapped luminance value</returns>
public static double ToneMapping(double sceneLuminance)
{
    return sceneLuminance / (sceneLuminance + 1.0);
}


/// <summary>
/// Computes the overall performance metric for lighting
↪    computations based on the hybrid lighting scheme.
/// It blends the performance characteristics of static
↪    (baked) and dynamic (real-time) lighting.
/// Equation: P =   * P_s + (1 -  ) * P_d
/// </summary>
/// <param name="performanceStatic">Performance metric for
↪    static lighting (P_s)</param>
/// <param name="performanceDynamic">Performance metric for
↪    dynamic lighting (P_d)</param>
/// <param name="alpha">Weighting factor for the static
↪    lighting component (between 0 and 1)</param>
/// <returns>Combined performance metric</returns>
public static double ComputePerformanceMetric(double
↪    performanceStatic, double performanceDynamic, double
↪    alpha)
{
    if (alpha < 0 || alpha > 1)
        throw new ArgumentOutOfRangeException(nameof(alpha),
        ↪    "Alpha must be between 0 and 1.");

    return alpha * performanceStatic + (1 - alpha) *
    ↪    performanceDynamic;
}

/// <summary>
/// Simulates the effect of diminishing returns on perceived
↪    realism when computational cost exceeds a certain
↪    threshold.
```

```
/// When the computational cost (C) surpasses the
↪   costThreshold, additional cost yields less improvement
↪   to realism (R).
/// </summary>
/// <param name="computationalCost">The current
↪   computational cost (C)</param>
/// <param name="perceivedRealism">The estimated realism
↪   value (R) before cost adjustment</param>
/// <param name="costThreshold">The cost threshold beyond
↪   which diminishing returns occur</param>
/// <returns>Optimized realism value adjusted by
↪   computational cost</returns>
public static double OptimizeRealism(double
↪   computationalCost, double perceivedRealism, double
↪   costThreshold)
{
    if (computationalCost <= costThreshold)
        return perceivedRealism;
    else
    {
        // Diminishing return: scale realism by the ratio
        ↪   (costThreshold / computationalCost)
        return perceivedRealism * (costThreshold /
        ↪   computationalCost);
    }
}


/// <summary>
/// Simulates a hybrid lighting optimization process by
↪   combining several factors:
/// 1. Total illumination computation: I = I_direct +
↪   I_baked.
/// 2. Tone mapping of the computed illumination.
/// 3. Blending static and dynamic lighting performance
↪   using:
///     P =  * P_s + (1 - ) * P_d.
/// 4. Adjusting the perceived realism based on
↪   computational cost using diminishing returns.
/// Finally, the overall quality metric is computed as the
↪   product of tone-mapped illumination,
/// performance metric, and the optimized realism.
/// </summary>
/// <param name="directIllumination">Direct (real-time)
↪   illumination value</param>
/// <param name="bakedIllumination">Baked (precomputed)
↪   illumination value</param>
/// <param name="performanceStatic">Performance metric for
↪   static lighting</param>
/// <param name="performanceDynamic">Performance metric for
↪   dynamic lighting</param>
/// <param name="alpha">Weighting factor for static
↪   lighting</param>
```

```csharp
/// <param name="computationalCost">Current computational
↪   cost value (C)</param>
/// <param name="perceivedRealism">Perceived realism before
↪   adjustment (R)</param>
/// <param name="costThreshold">Cost threshold for
↪   diminishing returns</param>
/// <returns>Final quality metric (Q) representing overall
↪   visual fidelity and performance</returns>
public static double OptimizeHybridLighting(
    double directIllumination,
    double bakedIllumination,
    double performanceStatic,
    double performanceDynamic,
    double alpha,
    double computationalCost,
    double perceivedRealism,
    double costThreshold)
{
    // Compute total illumination: I = I_direct + I_baked
    double totalIllumination =
    ↪   ComputeTotalIllumination(directIllumination,
    ↪   bakedIllumination);

    // Apply tone mapping operator: T(I) = I / (I + 1)
    double mappedIllumination =
    ↪   ToneMapping(totalIllumination);

    // Compute performance metric: P =  * P_s + (1 - ) * P_d
    double performanceMetric =
    ↪   ComputePerformanceMetric(performanceStatic,
    ↪   performanceDynamic, alpha);

    // Adjust perceived realism based on computational cost
    ↪   and diminishing returns
    double optimizedRealism =
    ↪   OptimizeRealism(computationalCost, perceivedRealism,
    ↪   costThreshold);

    // Final quality metric is a synthesis of the above
    ↪   factors.
    // For demonstration, we define Q = mappedIllumination *
    ↪   performanceMetric * optimizedRealism.
    double finalQuality = mappedIllumination *
    ↪   performanceMetric * optimizedRealism;

    return finalQuality;
    }
}

class Program
{
    static void Main(string[] args)
    {
```

```
// Sample simulation parameters
double directIllumination = 2.5;      // I_direct:
↪  real-time computed illumination
double bakedIllumination = 1.8;       // I_baked:
↪  precomputed lighting contribution
double performanceStatic = 0.9;       // P_s:
↪  performance metric for static lighting
double performanceDynamic = 0.7;      // P_d:
↪  performance metric for dynamic lighting
double alpha = 0.6;                   // Weight factor
↪  for static lighting (0 <= alpha <= 1)
double computationalCost = 120.0;     // C: current
↪  computational cost (arbitrary units)
double costThreshold = 100.0;         // Threshold for
↪  cost beyond which diminishing returns apply
double perceivedRealism = 0.85;       // R: baseline
↪  perceived realism (normalized value)

// Compute the final quality metric using the hybrid
↪  lighting optimization algorithm.
double finalQuality =
↪  LightingOptimizer.OptimizeHybridLighting(
    directIllumination,
    bakedIllumination,
    performanceStatic,
    performanceDynamic,
    alpha,
    computationalCost,
    perceivedRealism,
    costThreshold
);

Console.WriteLine("Final Quality Metric: " +
↪  finalQuality.ToString("F4"));
        }
    }
}
```

Summary: This comprehensive C# code demonstrates the core equations and algorithms discussed in the chapter. It calculates the combined illumination from direct and baked lighting, applies a tone mapping transformation $(T(I) = I / (I + 1))$, computes a hybrid performance metric $(P = * P\_s + (1 -) * P\_d)$, and adjusts perceived realism based on a diminishing returns model when computational cost exceeds a threshold. The final quality metric is produced as a synthesis of these factors, effectively simulating an optimization strategy for immersive VR scene lighting.

228

Chapter 32

Implementing Shadow Effects in Virtual Reality

Mathematical Foundations of Shadow Computation in VR

A rigorous mathematical framework underpins the computation and implementation of dynamic shadows within virtual reality environments. The formation of shadows can be modeled by examining the interaction between incident light and scene geometry. At a given surface point $\mathbf{x}$, the intensity of light, after occlusion effects are incorporated, is expressed as

$$I_{\text{shadow}}(\mathbf{x}) = I_{\text{light}} \cdot V(\mathbf{x}),$$

where I_{light} represents the incident illumination and $V(\mathbf{x}) \in [0, 1]$ denotes the visibility function at point $\mathbf{x}$. The transformation of world coordinates into the coordinate system of the light source is achieved using a transformation matrix $\mathbf{T}_L$, which projects scene geometry into light space. This projection enables efficient depth comparison across projected coordinates, and it is instrumental in the calculation of occlusion. Artifacts such as shadow bias and aliasing require careful treatment, often necessitating the incorporation of a small bias term ϵ in depth comparisons to ensure the integrity of shadow edges.

Dynamic Shadow Generation Techniques

Dynamic shadow generation is predicated on simulating the real-time evolution of shadows as scene geometry and lighting conditions change. A prevalent method in this domain is shadow mapping, which involves rendering the scene from the light source's perspective to generate a depth texture. The primary computation in shadow mapping is the determination of the shadow visibility function $V(\mathbf{x})$, derived from the depth comparison between the fragment depth $d(\mathbf{x})$ and the corresponding depth value $D(\mathbf{x}_L)$ extracted from the shadow map under the projected coordinate $\mathbf{x}_L$. This process is mathematically captured by the relationship

$$V(\mathbf{x}) = \begin{cases} 1, & \text{if } d(\mathbf{x}) - \epsilon > D(\mathbf{x}_L), \\ 0, & \text{otherwise,} \end{cases}$$

where ϵ is introduced to circumvent self-shadowing artifacts. Alternative methodologies, such as the construction of shadow volumes, provide a geometric interpretation of shadowed regions by extruding the silhouette edges of occluders. These techniques demand precise handling of triangulation and tessellation to preserve the quality of shadow edges in real time. The inherent trade-off between visual fidelity and computational complexity is an essential consideration when selecting an appropriate dynamic shadow generation technique for immersive virtual reality applications.

Enhancing Depth Perception Through Shadow Cues

Dynamic shadows serve as a crucial mechanism for enhancing both depth perception and spatial awareness within virtual environments. The gradual transition of shadow intensity offers a subtle yet powerful cue regarding the relative positioning of objects and surfaces. The soft transition zones, or penumbras, are generated through gradated light attenuation that is often modeled using an exponential decay form. Specifically, the attenuation of shadow intensity as a function of distance can be formulated as

$$V(\mathbf{x}) = e^{-\lambda \cdot d(\mathbf{x})},$$

where λ is an attenuation coefficient, and $d(\mathbf{x})$ quantifies the distance from the occluding geometry. This exponential attenuation generates naturalistic gradients that contribute to the perception of object scale, distance, and the spatial interrelation between elements in the scene. The interplay between shadow hardness and softness, governed by the light source characteristics and the precision of depth comparisons, plays a central role in establishing a layered, coherent three-dimensional visual field.

Optimization Strategies and Performance Considerations

The real-time rendering of dynamic shadows in virtual reality necessitates a balanced approach to optimization, as the computational cost of accurate shadow generation may significantly impact frame rates and overall system responsiveness. Performance optimization strategies are designed to reconcile the trade-off between rendering quality and computational efficiency. One common strategy involves the use of multi-resolution shadow maps, whereby distant or less significant elements in the scene are rendered with a reduced level of detail. Such approaches preserve critical shadow details in areas of immediate focus while economizing on computational resources for peripheral regions. Another effective optimization technique is the deployment of deferred shading architectures, which separate geometry processing from subsequent lighting calculations. This decoupling enables the aggregation of lighting contributions into dedicated buffers, thereby streamlining the compositing process. The optimization challenge is often formalized as a multi-objective function

$$Q = f(P, R),$$

where P denotes a performance metric, and R encapsulates the perceptual realism of the shadow effects. Filtering techniques, such as percentage-closer filtering and adaptive shadow map resolution, further ameliorate the adverse effects of aliasing and flickering, ensuring that the final shadow output is both visually coherent and computationally tractable. Detailed profiling of rendering pipelines allows for the iterative refinement of these techniques, ensuring that the implementation of dynamic shadows sustains a high level of immersive realism without compromising system throughput.

C# Code Snippet

```csharp
using UnityEngine;

public class ShadowEffectsVR : MonoBehaviour
{
    // Transformation matrix to convert world coordinates into light
    ↪ space.
    public Matrix4x4 lightMatrix;

    // Shadow map texture generated from the light's perspective
    ↪ (depth values).
    public Texture2D shadowMap;

    // Bias to prevent self-shadowing artifacts.
    public float shadowBias = 0.005f;

    // Attenuation coefficient for soft shadow (penumbra) effects.
    public float softnessLambda = 50.0f;

    // Ambient light intensity (I_light in the equation I_shadow(x)
    ↪ = I_light * V(x)).
    public float lightIntensity = 1.0f;

    /// <summary>
    /// Computes the shadow intensity at a given world position
    ↪ using shadow mapping.
    /// This method implements:
    ///    1. The binary shadow visibility:
    ///        V(x) = 1 if (fragmentDepth - epsilon) <=
    ↪ shadowMapDepth, else 0.
    ///    2. A smooth exponential decay for soft shadows:
    ///        V(x) = exp(-lambda * |fragmentDepth - shadowMapDepth|).
    ///    3. The final shadow intensity: I_shadow(x) = I_light *
    ↪ V(x).
    /// </summary>
    /// <param name="worldPos">The world-space position where the
    ↪ shadow is to be computed.</param>
    /// <returns>The computed shadow intensity.</returns>
    public float ComputeShadowIntensity(Vector3 worldPos)
    {
        // Transform world position into light space.
        Vector4 posLS = lightMatrix * new Vector4(worldPos.x,
        ↪ worldPos.y, worldPos.z, 1.0f);
        posLS /= posLS.w;

        // Convert from clip space [-1, 1] to texture space [0, 1].
        float u = posLS.x * 0.5f + 0.5f;
        float v = posLS.y * 0.5f + 0.5f;

        // Sample the shadow map depth using bilinear filtering.
        float shadowMapDepth = shadowMap.GetPixelBilinear(u, v).r;
```

```
    // Get the fragment depth in light space (d(x) in the
    ↪   equations).
    float fragmentDepth = posLS.z;

    // Compute binary visibility function:
    // If the depth of the fragment, adjusted by bias, is
    ↪   greater than the shadow map depth,
    // the fragment is in shadow.
    float visibilityBinary = (fragmentDepth - shadowBias) >
    ↪   shadowMapDepth ? 0.0f : 1.0f;

    // Compute smooth visibility using exponential decay
    ↪   (penumbra effect):
    // V(x) = exp(-lambda * |d(x) - D(x_L)|)
    float depthDifference = Mathf.Abs(fragmentDepth -
    ↪   shadowMapDepth);
    float visibilitySmooth = Mathf.Exp(-softnessLambda *
    ↪   depthDifference);
    visibilitySmooth = Mathf.Clamp01(visibilitySmooth);

    // Here we choose the smooth visibility to create a soft
    ↪   shadow appearance.
    float visibility = visibilitySmooth;

    // Compute final shadow intensity: I_shadow(x) = I_light *
    ↪   V(x)
    float shadowIntensity = lightIntensity * visibility;
    return shadowIntensity;
}

/// <summary>
/// Demonstrates an approach to multi-resolution shadow mapping.
/// The softness coefficient (lambda) is adjusted based on the
↪   desired resolution level.
/// </summary>
/// <param name="worldPos">The world-space position.</param>
/// <param name="resolutionLevel">Resolution level indicator (0:
↪   high, 1: medium, 2: low).</param>
/// <returns>The computed shadow intensity with resolution-based
↪   adjustments.</returns>
public float ComputeShadowIntensityMultiResolution(Vector3
↪   worldPos, int resolutionLevel)
{
    float adjustedLambda = softnessLambda;
    switch (resolutionLevel)
    {
        case 1:
            adjustedLambda *= 1.5f;
            break;
        case 2:
            adjustedLambda *= 2.0f;
            break;
```

233

```
        default:
            break;
    }

    // Transform into light space and convert coordinates.
    Vector4 posLS = lightMatrix * new Vector4(worldPos.x,
    ↪   worldPos.y, worldPos.z, 1.0f);
    posLS /= posLS.w;
    float u = posLS.x * 0.5f + 0.5f;
    float v = posLS.y * 0.5f + 0.5f;
    float shadowMapDepth = shadowMap.GetPixelBilinear(u, v).r;
    float fragmentDepth = posLS.z;

    // Use the adjusted lambda for smooth transition.
    float depthDifference = Mathf.Abs(fragmentDepth -
    ↪   shadowMapDepth);
    float visibilitySmooth = Mathf.Exp(-adjustedLambda *
    ↪   depthDifference);
    visibilitySmooth = Mathf.Clamp01(visibilitySmooth);

    // Final shadow intensity calculation.
    float shadowIntensity = lightIntensity * visibilitySmooth;
    return shadowIntensity;
}

/// <summary>
/// Simulates deferred shadow updates in a deferred shading
↪   pipeline.
/// In practice, this computation would be embedded within a
↪   shader program.
/// </summary>
void UpdateShadowDeferred()
{
    Vector3 samplePosition = transform.position;
    float intensity = ComputeShadowIntensity(samplePosition);
    Debug.Log("Deferred Shadow Intensity: " + intensity);
}

// Update is called once per frame.
void Update()
{
    // Compute shadow intensity at the object's current world
    ↪   position.
    float currentShadow =
    ↪   ComputeShadowIntensity(transform.position);

    // Optionally simulate deferred shading shadow updates.
    UpdateShadowDeferred();

    // The resulting shadow intensity can then drive material
    ↪   shading or influence lighting computations.
    // For example, one might adjust ambient light or shadow
    ↪   color using 'currentShadow'.
```

234

```
    }
}
```

Chapter 33

Creating Custom Shaders for VR Immersion

Fundamentals of Shader Development in Unity

Shader development in Unity is grounded in the principles of real-time rendering and programmable graphics pipelines. The shader programs serve as specialized routines that determine the final appearance of objects by dynamically calculating pixel-level properties such as color, transparency, and reflectance. In the context of virtual reality, shader development entails additional considerations with respect to stereoscopic rendering and the preservation of frame rate performance. The process begins with the decomposition of the rendering task into modular stages, each governed by specific shader types that collectively encompass vertex manipulation, geometry processing, and fragment-level color computations. A thorough comprehension of the underlying graphics API and Unity's shader abstraction layer is pivotal for constructing custom materials that seamlessly integrate with the engine's rendering pipeline.

Mathematical Foundations of Shader Computations

At the core of custom shader design is a rigorous mathematical framework which governs the computation of light-material interactions. The fundamental equation for the computation of the final color at a given pixel is expressed as

$$C = \sum_{i=1}^{n} L_i \cdot f_r(\omega_i, \omega_o) \cdot \max(0, \mathbf{n} \cdot \omega_i),$$

where L_i is the intensity of the ith light source, $f_r(\omega_i, \omega_o)$ represents the Bidirectional Reflectance Distribution Function (BRDF) that defines the material's reflective properties, $\mathbf{n}$ is the surface normal, and ω_i and ω_o denote the incident and outgoing light directions respectively. The BRDF itself is often modeled by a combination of diffuse and specular components, each adhering to established physical approximations such as Lambertian reflection, given by

$$f_{\text{diffuse}} = \frac{\rho}{\pi},$$

where ρ is the albedo of the material, and a specular term which may be approximated by models such as the Cook-Torrance microfacet model. These equations require precise numerical integration and are highly sensitive to parameters that determine the level of realism and performance, particularly under the high demands imposed by immersive VR environments.

Physically Based Material Representation and Light Interaction

The construction of custom shaders for virtual reality necessitates the employment of physically based material representations. Such materials are designed to adhere to the laws of energy conservation and reciprocity, ensuring that the computed light interactions are not only visually plausible but also physically consistent. The integration of properties such as roughness, metalness, and anisotropy into shader algorithms permits the simulation of complex surface characteristics. The layered structure of many modern shader models is captured by the equation

$$C_{\text{material}} = \alpha \cdot C_{\text{diffuse}} + (1 - \alpha) \cdot C_{\text{specular}},$$

where α balances the contribution of the diffuse and specular components based on material properties. Such formulations allow for the dynamic modulation of material appearance in response to varying lighting conditions, enhancing the perception of depth and realism within a VR scene. Meticulous calibration of these parameters is essential in achieving a harmonious interplay between custom shader outputs and the intricate lighting setups typical of immersive environments.

Integration of Custom Shaders in the VR Rendering Pipeline

The integration of custom shaders within the Unity rendering pipeline must account for the distinctive challenges posed by virtual reality. The high frame rate and low latency requirements of VR demand that shader computations are both efficient and robust. Custom shaders are integrated into the deferred or forward rendering paths by material assignment and proper setup within Unity's rendering configuration. In a deferred rendering scenario, the custom shader contributes to the generation of intermediate buffers that contain geometric and lighting information, which are later synthesized to produce the final image. This integration process involves careful management of shader parameters, transformation matrices, and lighting models to ensure that the custom materials interact correctly with pre-existing scene data. The deployment of custom shaders is further complicated by the dual-camera nature of stereoscopic displays, necessitating that all shader computations are replicated and optimized for two distinct viewports.

Performance Considerations in Custom Shader Implementation

The implementation of custom shaders in virtual reality environments is subject to stringent performance constraints. The computational overhead introduced by additional shader complexity must be balanced against the necessity for high-fidelity visual effects. Optimization strategies involve the minimization of arithmetic and texture sampling operations, the efficient use of conditional operations within shader code, and the adoption of approximative techniques that reduce computational intensity without a perceptible loss of realism. Mathematical approximations, such as substituting complex integrals with precomputed lookup tables or employing lower precision arithmetic where appropriate, are common practices. The cost function for optimizing shader performance can be formalized as

$$Q = \lambda_1 T + \lambda_2 E,$$

where T represents the processing time per frame, E denotes the energy consumed by the GPU during rendering, and λ_1, λ_2 are weights assigned to performance metrics relevant across various hardware configurations. This formulation guides the iterative refinement of custom shader algorithms with the objective of achieving an optimal trade-off between computational expense and visual quality in highly immersive VR settings.

C# Code Snippet

```csharp
using System;
using System.Collections.Generic;
using UnityEngine;

public class CustomShaderSimulator : MonoBehaviour
{
    [Serializable]
    public struct LightSource
    {
        // Normalized direction from the surface towards the light.
        public Vector3 direction;
        // Intensity of the light source.
        public float intensity;
    }

    [Header("Material Properties")]
    public Color albedo = Color.white;        // Base color used for
    ↪ diffuse reflection.
    [Range(0f, 1f)]
    public float roughness = 0.5f;            // Controls specular
    ↪ highlight sharpness.
    [Range(0f, 1f)]
    public float metalness = 0.0f;            // Factor for
    ↪ metal-like reflections.
    [Range(0f, 1f)]
    public float alpha = 0.8f;                // Balances diffuse and
    ↪ specular contributions in layered model.

    [Header("Performance Optimization Weights")]
    public float lambda1 = 1.0f;              // Weight for
    ↪ processing time in cost function Q.
```

```csharp
public float lambda2 = 1.0f;              // Weight for energy
↪ consumption in cost function Q.


[Header("Scene Lights")]
public List<LightSource> lights = new List<LightSource>();

// -------------------------------------------
// BRDF Simulation:
// Computes a simplified Bidirectional Reflectance Distribution
↪ Function (BRDF)
// combining a Lambertian (diffuse) term and a specular term
↪ (approximated via Blinn-Phong).
// -------------------------------------------
float BRDF(Vector3 lightDir, Vector3 viewDir, Vector3 normal)
{
    // Diffuse component: Lambertian reflection (f_diffuse = /)
    ↪ using the red channel for example.
    float diffuseBRDF = albedo.r / Mathf.PI;

    // Specular component approximation:
    // Calculate the half-vector between light direction and
    ↪ view direction.
    Vector3 halfDir = (lightDir + viewDir).normalized;
    // Clamp dot product between normal and half-vector.
    float specAngle = Mathf.Max(Vector3.Dot(normal, halfDir),
    ↪ 0f);
    // Use roughness to control shininess (inverse relation).
    float specularBRDF = Mathf.Pow(specAngle, 1.0f /
    ↪ Mathf.Max(roughness, 0.0001f));

    return diffuseBRDF + specularBRDF;
}


// -------------------------------------------
// Final Color Computation:
// Implements the equation:
//   C = ( L_i * f_r(_i, _o) * max(0, n · _i) )
// where the sum runs over all light sources.
// -------------------------------------------
public float ComputeFinalColor(Vector3 fragNormal, Vector3
↪ viewDir)
{
    float finalColor = 0f;
    foreach (var light in lights)
    {
        Vector3 lightDir = light.direction.normalized;
        float NdotL = Mathf.Max(Vector3.Dot(fragNormal,
        ↪ lightDir), 0f);
        float brdf = BRDF(lightDir, viewDir, fragNormal);
        finalColor += light.intensity * brdf * NdotL;
    }
    return finalColor;
}
```

```csharp
// -------------------------------------------
// Material Color via Layered Representation:
// Uses the formula:
//    C_material =  * C_diffuse + (1 - ) * C_specular
// Diffuse is computed using Lambert's cosine law; specular is
// ↪  approximated with a Blinn-Phong model.
// -------------------------------------------
public Color ComputeMaterialColor(Vector3 fragNormal, Vector3
↪  viewDir)
{
    float diffuseComponent = 0f;
    float specularComponent = 0f;

    foreach (var light in lights)
    {
        Vector3 lightDir = light.direction.normalized;
        float NdotL = Mathf.Max(Vector3.Dot(fragNormal,
        ↪  lightDir), 0f);
        // Diffuse contribution.
        diffuseComponent += light.intensity * (albedo.r /
        ↪  Mathf.PI) * NdotL;

        // Specular contribution.
        Vector3 halfDir = (lightDir + viewDir).normalized;
        float specAngle = Mathf.Max(Vector3.Dot(fragNormal,
        ↪  halfDir), 0f);
        specularComponent += light.intensity *
        ↪  Mathf.Pow(specAngle, 1.0f / Mathf.Max(roughness,
        ↪  0.0001f));
    }

    float diffuseBalance = alpha;
    float specularBalance = 1f - alpha;

    // Combine both terms to simulate the layered material
    ↪  appearance.
    float combinedValue = diffuseBalance * diffuseComponent +
    ↪  specularBalance * specularComponent;
    return new Color(combinedValue, combinedValue,
    ↪  combinedValue, 1f);
}


// -------------------------------------------
// Performance Cost Function:
// Implements the optimization cost function:
//    Q =  * T +  * E
// T: processing time (per frame), E: energy consumption from
// ↪  GPU during rendering.
// -------------------------------------------
public float ComputePerformanceCost(float processingTime, float
↪  energyConsumption)
{
```

```csharp
    return lambda1 * processingTime + lambda2 *
    ↪   energyConsumption;
}

// ------------------------------------------
// Update:
// Demonstrates the shader computation and performance
↪   evaluation per frame.
// ------------------------------------------
void Update()
{
    // Assume fragment's normal is the object's up vector for
    ↪   demonstration.
    Vector3 fragNormal = transform.up;
    // Compute the view direction from the fragment to the main
    ↪   camera.
    Vector3 viewDir = (Camera.main.transform.position -
    ↪   transform.position).normalized;

    float pixelColorIntensity = ComputeFinalColor(fragNormal,
    ↪   viewDir);
    Color materialColor = ComputeMaterialColor(fragNormal,
    ↪   viewDir);

    // Simulate performance metrics: processing time (ms) and
    ↪   energy consumption (arbitrary units).
    float simulatedProcessingTime = 1.5f;
    float simulatedEnergyConsumption = 0.8f;
    float performanceCost =
    ↪   ComputePerformanceCost(simulatedProcessingTime,
    ↪   simulatedEnergyConsumption);

    Debug.Log("Pixel Color Intensity: " + pixelColorIntensity);
    Debug.Log("Computed Material Color: " +
    ↪   materialColor.ToString());
    Debug.Log("Performance Cost (Q): " + performanceCost);
}
}
```

Chapter 34

Scripting Post-Processing Effects for VR

Bloom: Dynamic Luminance Enhancement

The bloom effect is employed to simulate the scattering of light from intensely bright regions, thereby reinforcing a sense of realism and intensity in virtual reality scenes. Bright pixels are first isolated using a luminance threshold operation, mathematically expressed as

$$I_{\text{thresh}} = \max(I - T, 0),$$

where I denotes the incident pixel intensity and T is the predefined threshold. The thresholded image is subsequently subjected to a convolution process with a Gaussian kernel, $G(\sigma)$, defined by its standard deviation σ. The convolution smooths the high-luminance areas, effectively creating a halo effect around bright sources. In stereoscopic rendering, it is critical that this operation is performed separately for each view to prevent incongruities between the dual perspectives. The additive recomposition step then merges the blurred luminance with the original image according to a linear blend model, preserving both the local detail and the overall light distribution.

Depth of Field: Simulating Optical Focus

Depth of field (DoF) is implemented to emulate the optical phenomena observed in camera systems, wherein objects at varying distances exhibit different levels of sharpness. The computation commences with the extraction of a depth map from the scene, enabling the determination of the spatial disparity between an object and the focal plane. The blur radius, r, is typically modeled as

$$r = k \cdot |d - d_f|,$$

where d represents the depth value at a given pixel, d_f is the target focal depth, and k is a scaling constant that moderates the extent of blurring. A spatial filter (often Gaussian in nature) is applied with intensity modulated by r, thereby replicating the gradual transition between sharp and blurred regions. Rigorous attention is given to the preservation of stereo alignment across both eye views, ensuring that the depth-based blurring does not compromise the coherence between left and right images. In complex scenes, refinements in the sampling process are necessary to account for discontinuities and to mitigate artifacts that could arise from abrupt depth transitions.

Color Grading: Tonal Harmonization in VR

Color grading constitutes a systematic adjustment of the image's color profile to achieve a unified tonal atmosphere. The process typically involves remapping the input color vector, $\mathbf{C}_{\text{in}}$, to an output color, $\mathbf{C}_{\text{out}}$, via a transfer function defined as

$$\mathbf{C}_{\text{out}} = f(\mathbf{C}_{\text{in}}).$$

This mapping may incorporate linear transformations, nonlinear adjustments such as gamma correction, and modifications to parameters including contrast, saturation, and hue. Techniques leveraging three-dimensional lookup tables (3D LUTs) provide a mechanism for complex, nuanced transformations that maintain perceptual uniformity. The modified color space must be compatible with the overall lighting model and post-composition effects applied later in the rendering pipeline. In a VR context, ensuring the consistency of color transformations across dual viewports is paramount, necessitating that all adjustments be computed with high precision and in synchronization with other post-processing passes.

Mathematical Modeling of Post-Processing Effects

The integration of post-processing effects into a VR system is underpinned by a composite mathematical framework that aggregates individual transformations. The final pixel intensity, I_{final}, can be modeled as

$$I_{\text{final}} = I_{\text{original}} + G_{\text{bloom}}(I_{\text{original}}) + B_{\text{DoF}}(I_{\text{original}}, D) + T_{\text{grade}}(I_{\text{original}}),$$

where I_{original} represents the raw rendered image, G_{bloom} refers to the bloom transformation achieved via Gaussian blurring, B_{DoF} denotes the depth-dependent blur function modulated by the depth buffer D, and T_{grade} encapsulates the color grading operation. Each component function is designed to be continuously differentiable, a property that is advantageous for gradient-based performance optimizations. Moreover, the individual processing stages are interdependent; for instance, the parameters governing the bloom effect and the depth of field must be jointly calibrated to ensure that the final composite image adheres to the desired aesthetic and performance criteria.

Optimization Strategies for VR Post-Processing

The computational complexity inherent in post-processing pipelines necessitates the adoption of various optimization strategies to achieve real-time rendering performance in VR environments. For the bloom effect, the convolution operation is frequently decomposed into two successive one-dimensional passes—first horizontal and then vertical. This separation reduces the computational overhead from $O(n)$ per pixel, with n representing the total number of samples in a two-dimensional kernel, to $O(\sqrt{n})$ per pass. A similar approach is applied to depth of field processing, where adaptive sampling is utilized based on the variance of the depth values to minimize redundant computations.

Furthermore, the overall performance of post-processing is quantitatively assessed via a cost function,

$$C = \lambda_T T + \lambda_E E + \lambda_Q \Delta Q,$$

in which T denotes the processing time per frame, E represents the energy consumption on the GPU, and ΔQ quantifies the degradation in visual quality relative to an ideal, artifact-free output. The coefficients λ_T, λ_E, and λ_Q are determined through empirical evaluation and characterize the trade-offs among speed, efficiency, and visual fidelity. Optimization efforts focus on reducing T and E while constraining ΔQ to acceptable limits, ensuring that sophisticated post-processing effects are delivered without compromising the low-latency requirements critical to immersive virtual reality experiences.

C# Code Snippet

```csharp
using UnityEngine;

public class VRPostProcessingEffects : MonoBehaviour
{
    // Adjustable parameters based on the chapter's formulas.

    [Header("Bloom Settings")]
    // Bloom threshold: I_thresh = max(I - T, 0)
    public float bloomThreshold = 0.8f;
    // Standard deviation for the Gaussian kernel, G()
    public float sigma = 2.0f;

    [Header("Depth of Field Settings")]
    // Focal depth (d_f) used in the blur radius equation r = k * |d
    ↪    - d_f|
    public float focalDepth = 5.0f;
    // Scaling constant (k) for the depth-based blur radius
    ↪    calculation
    public float dofScale = 0.05f;

    [Header("Color Grading Settings")]
    // 3D Lookup Table for advanced color remapping: C_out = f(C_in)
    public Texture3D colorLUT;

    // Coefficients for performance cost function: C = _T T + _E E +
    ↪    _Q Q
    private float lambdaT = 0.5f;
    private float lambdaE = 0.3f;
    private float lambdaQ = 0.2f;
```

```
// Material that leverages a custom shader implementing multiple
↪   post-processing passes.
public Shader postProcessShader;
private Material postProcessMaterial;

// Initialization: create material instance based on the
↪   provided shader.
void Start()
{
    if (postProcessShader != null)
    {
        postProcessMaterial = new Material(postProcessShader);
    }
}

// OnRenderImage is called after the scene is rendered.
// This method simulates the complete VR post-processing
↪   pipeline:
// I_final = I_original + G_bloom(I_original) +
↪   B_DoF(I_original, D) + T_grade(I_original)
void OnRenderImage(RenderTexture src, RenderTexture dest)
{
    // Create temporary render textures for each effect stage.
    RenderTexture bloomRT =
    ↪   RenderTexture.GetTemporary(src.width, src.height);
    RenderTexture dofRT = RenderTexture.GetTemporary(src.width,
    ↪   src.height);
    RenderTexture colorGradeRT =
    ↪   RenderTexture.GetTemporary(src.width, src.height);

    // ===============================================
    // Bloom Effect Implementation
    // ===============================================
    // Step 1: Isolate bright pixels using the luminance
    ↪   threshold:
    // I_thresh = max(I - bloomThreshold, 0)
    postProcessMaterial.SetFloat("_BloomThreshold",
    ↪   bloomThreshold);
    // Shader pass 0: Extracts regions of high luminance.
    Graphics.Blit(src, bloomRT, postProcessMaterial, 0);

    // Step 2: Apply Gaussian convolution:
    // This mimics the behavior of convolving the thresholded
    ↪   image with G()
    postProcessMaterial.SetFloat("_Sigma", sigma);
    // Perform horizontal blur (shader pass 1)
    RenderTexture tempRT = RenderTexture.GetTemporary(src.width,
    ↪   src.height);
    Graphics.Blit(bloomRT, tempRT, postProcessMaterial, 1);
    // Perform vertical blur (shader pass 2)
    Graphics.Blit(tempRT, bloomRT, postProcessMaterial, 2);
    RenderTexture.ReleaseTemporary(tempRT);
```

```csharp
// ===============================================
// Depth of Field (DoF) Effect Implementation
// ===============================================
// Compute the blur radius based on depth differences:
// r = dofScale * |d - focalDepth|
postProcessMaterial.SetFloat("_FocalDepth", focalDepth);
postProcessMaterial.SetFloat("_DOFScale", dofScale);
// Shader pass 3: Applies depth-dependent blurring using the
// ↪ scene's depth buffer.
Graphics.Blit(src, dofRT, postProcessMaterial, 3);

// ===============================================
// Color Grading Implementation
// ===============================================
// Utilize a transfer function for tonal harmonization:
// C_out = f(C_in) via a 3D LUT mapping.
if (colorLUT != null)
{
    postProcessMaterial.SetTexture("_ColorLUT", colorLUT);
}
// Shader pass 4: Adjusts color properties like contrast,
// ↪ saturation, and gamma.
Graphics.Blit(src, colorGradeRT, postProcessMaterial, 4);

// ===============================================
// Final Composite: Combining All Effects
// ===============================================
// Composite the original image with the processed effects:
// I_final = I_original + G_bloom(I_original) +
// ↪ B_DoF(I_original, D) + T_grade(I_original)
postProcessMaterial.SetTexture("_BloomTex", bloomRT);
postProcessMaterial.SetTexture("_DoFTex", dofRT);
postProcessMaterial.SetTexture("_ColorGradeTex",
    ↪ colorGradeRT);
// Shader pass 5: Merges all inputs into the final output.
Graphics.Blit(src, dest, postProcessMaterial, 5);

// Release temporary render textures.
RenderTexture.ReleaseTemporary(bloomRT);
RenderTexture.ReleaseTemporary(dofRT);
RenderTexture.ReleaseTemporary(colorGradeRT);

// Log performance metrics using a cost function:
// C = _T * T + _E * E + _Q * Q
LogPerformanceMetrics(Time.deltaTime,
    ↪ GetGPUEnergyConsumption(), EstimateQualityLoss(dest));
}

// Simulated method to obtain GPU energy consumption.
// In practice, this would interface with hardware-level APIs.
float GetGPUEnergyConsumption()
{
    return Random.Range(0.1f, 0.5f);
```

248

```
        }

        // Simulated method to estimate visual quality degradation.
        // A real implementation might analyze artifact presence in the
        ↪    final RenderTexture.
        float EstimateQualityLoss(RenderTexture processedImage)
        {
            return Random.Range(0.0f, 0.1f);
        }

        // Logs the overall post-processing cost based on processing
        ↪    time (T),
        // GPU energy consumption (E), and quality loss (Q).
        void LogPerformanceMetrics(float processingTime, float
        ↪    energyConsumption, float qualityLoss)
        {
            float cost = lambdaT * processingTime + lambdaE *
            ↪    energyConsumption + lambdaQ * qualityLoss;
            Debug.Log("Post-Processing Cost: " + cost.ToString("F4"));
        }
    }
```

Summary

This code snippet demonstrates the implementation of a VR post-processing pipeline in Unity, encompassing Bloom, Depth of Field, and Color Grading effects. The code breaks down the workflow into multiple shader passes that execute thresholding, Gaussian blurring, depth-based blur, and color remapping. Finally, the effects are composited into a final image while performance is monitored via a cost function that accounts for processing time, energy consumption, and visual quality.

Chapter 35

Integrating Particle Systems in VR Scenes

Theoretical Framework of Particle Systems

The integration of particle systems within virtual reality (VR) environments is predicated on the mathematical modeling of transient visual phenomena. These systems simulate dynamic effects, such as smoke, fire, or ethereal magic, by treating each visual element as an individual particle governed by a set of physical parameters. In a formal sense, each particle is characterized by its position $\mathbf{x}(t)$, velocity $\mathbf{v}(t)$, acceleration $\mathbf{a}(t)$, and an associated lifetime parameter. The fundamental evolution of a particle's state can be described by the classical kinematic equations. For instance, the position update over a discrete time interval Δt is given by

$$\mathbf{x}(t + \Delta t) = \mathbf{x}(t) + \Delta t \, \mathbf{v}(t) + \frac{1}{2}\Delta t^2 \, \mathbf{a}(t),$$

while the velocity is updated as

$$\mathbf{v}(t + \Delta t) = \mathbf{v}(t) + \Delta t \, \mathbf{a}(t).$$

The stochastic elements inherent in phenomena such as turbulent smoke or flickering flames are incorporated via probabilistic models that govern particle emission rates, initial velocity distributions, and decay functions. A commonly employed decay model is the exponential decay, represented as

$$L(t) = L_0\, e^{-\lambda t},$$

where L_0 denotes the initial luminosity and λ is the decay constant.

Architectural Integration in Virtual Reality Environments

The architectural integration of particle systems within VR necessitates careful consideration of both spatial coherence and computational efficiency. In contrast to traditional single-view rendering approaches, VR environments require that each visual effect is rendered from two slightly different perspectives to achieve stereoscopic depth. Consequently, particle effects must be replicated and maintained consistently across both viewports. This is accomplished by leveraging parallel processing mechanisms and optimized data structures designed for high-throughput computations. The underlying architecture is responsible for managing the lifecycle of potentially thousands of individual particles, each of which contributes to the overall atmospheric quality of the scene. The synchronization of these particles with the scene's lighting and occlusion systems further ensures that their contribution remains visually congruent with the surrounding environment.

Mathematical Modeling and Simulation Dynamics

The simulation dynamics of particle systems are underpinned by numerical integration techniques that compute the evolution of individual particles over time. Euler integration provides the most direct approach, approximating the continuous dynamics through discrete updates:

$$\mathbf{x}(t + \Delta t) \approx \mathbf{x}(t) + \Delta t\, \mathbf{v}(t).$$

For applications where higher precision is necessary, more sophisticated schemes such as Runge–Kutta methods are adopted. These methods offer improved stability and accuracy in scenarios where rapid changes in acceleration occur due to varying environmental forces. Moreover, the emission of particles is frequently modeled as a Poisson process, ensuring that particles are generated at random intervals in accordance with a specified average emission rate. This stochastic process is crucial for replicating the natural variability observed in phenomena like dissipating smoke or crackling fire. The mathematical formalism extends to the modulation of particle properties over time, where variables such as color fade, translucency, and size scaling are computed as functions of time, position, and external influences.

Visual and Atmospheric Enhancement Techniques

Particle systems serve as the primary mechanism for enhancing the atmospheric quality of VR scenes. Their contribution is not merely ornamental but integral to achieving a rich, immersive visual experience. The rendering of each particle involves the computation of its individual color, opacity, and blending factor with the scene. Alpha blending, governed by the equation

$$I_{\text{final}} = I_{\text{background}}(1 - \alpha) + I_{\text{particle}}\,\alpha,$$

facilitates the seamless integration of particles with the underlying scene, preserving both lighting continuity and depth cues. Texture mapping and volumetric rendering techniques supplement the basic particle simulation by imparting realistic variations in density and turbulence. Spatial distribution is refined through the use of noise functions and gradient-based control fields, which dictate the movement and dispersion of particles in a manner that mimics natural environmental dynamics. The resultant effects yield a heightened sense of realism, as particles interact with ambient light sources and scene geometry in complex and visually compelling ways.

Performance Optimizations and Computational Constraints

Given the computational intensity associated with simulating large numbers of particles, performance optimization is a critical consideration in VR applications. The computational complexity involved in updating and rendering particle systems is intrinsically linear with respect to the number of particles, denoted as $O(N)$, where N represents the total particle count. To manage this load effectively, modern implementations employ GPU-based parallel processing, allowing simultaneous computation of particle dynamics. Techniques such as billboarding enable the efficient rendering of particles by approximating three-dimensional effects using two-dimensional textures that always face the viewer. Moreover, level-of-detail (LOD) strategies dynamically adjust particle simulation fidelity based on the viewer's distance, thereby conserving processing resources while maintaining visual quality. Memory access patterns are optimized through spatial partitioning and buffer reuse, reducing latency and ensuring smooth visual updates even under conditions of high particle density. These measures collectively ensure that the integration of particle systems does not compromise the stringent performance criteria required by immersive VR applications.

C# Code Snippet

```
using System;
using System.Collections.Generic;
using System.Threading;

namespace VRParticleSystem
{
    // A simple 3D vector struct to support basic arithmetic
    ↪   operations.
    public struct Vector3
    {
        public float x, y, z;

        public Vector3(float x, float y, float z)
        {
            this.x = x;
            this.y = y;
            this.z = z;
        }

        public static Vector3 operator +(Vector3 a, Vector3 b)
        {
            return new Vector3(a.x + b.x, a.y + b.y, a.z + b.z);
        }

        public static Vector3 operator *(Vector3 a, float scalar)
        {
            return new Vector3(a.x * scalar, a.y * scalar, a.z *
            ↪   scalar);
        }
```

253

```csharp
    public static Vector3 operator *(float scalar, Vector3 a)
    {
        return a * scalar;
    }

    public override string ToString()
    {
        return $"({x:F2}, {y:F2}, {z:F2})";
    }
}

// The Particle class encapsulates the dynamics and visual
//   properties of a particle.
public class Particle
{
    public Vector3 Position;
    public Vector3 Velocity;
    public Vector3 Acceleration;
    public float Lifetime;              // Remaining lifetime in
    //   seconds.
    public float InitialLifetime;       // Used to compute elapsed
    //   time.
    public float InitialLuminosity;   // L in the exponential
    //   decay equation.
    public float DecayConstant;        //    in the decay equation.

    // Constructor sets initial state in accordance with
    //   provided parameters.
    public Particle(Vector3 position, Vector3 velocity, Vector3
    //   acceleration, float lifetime, float initialLuminosity,
    //   float decayConstant)
    {
        Position = position;
        Velocity = velocity;
        Acceleration = acceleration;
        Lifetime = lifetime;
        InitialLifetime = lifetime;
        InitialLuminosity = initialLuminosity;
        DecayConstant = decayConstant;
    }

    // Update method calculates the next state of the particle.
    // Implements:
    //   Position: x(t+t) = x(t) + t * v(t) + 0.5 * t² * a(t)
    //   Velocity: v(t+t) = v(t) + t * a(t)
    //   Exponential decay: L(t) = L * exp(- * t)
    public float Update(float deltaTime)
    {
        // Update position using the kinematic equation.
        Position += Velocity * deltaTime + Acceleration * (0.5f
        //   * deltaTime * deltaTime);
```

254

```csharp
        // Update velocity via Euler integration.
        Velocity += Acceleration * deltaTime;

        // Reduce the remaining lifetime.
        Lifetime -= deltaTime;

        // Calculate the elapsed time.
        float elapsedTime = InitialLifetime - Lifetime;

        // Compute current luminosity using exponential decay.
        float currentLuminosity = InitialLuminosity *
        ↪   (float)Math.Exp(-DecayConstant * elapsedTime);
        return currentLuminosity;
    }

    public bool IsAlive()
    {
        return Lifetime > 0;
    }
}

// ParticleEmitter simulates generation and management of
↪   particles over time.
public class ParticleEmitter
{
    private List<Particle> particles = new List<Particle>();
    private Random random = new Random();
    private float emissionAccumulator = 0.0f;

    // Controls the average rate of particle creation (particles
    ↪   per second).
    public float EmissionRate = 50.0f;

    // Update emitter: manage particle creation according to a
    ↪   Poisson-like process and update all particles.
    public void Update(float deltaTime)
    {
        // Increment accumulator based on emission rate.
        emissionAccumulator += EmissionRate * deltaTime;
        int particlesToEmit = (int)emissionAccumulator;
        emissionAccumulator -= particlesToEmit;

        // Emit new particles.
        for (int i = 0; i < particlesToEmit; i++)
        {
            particles.Add(CreateParticle());
        }

        // Update each particle and remove ones that are no
        ↪   longer alive.
        for (int i = particles.Count - 1; i >= 0; i--)
        {
            float luminosity = particles[i].Update(deltaTime);
```

255

```csharp
            if (!particles[i].IsAlive())
            {
                particles.RemoveAt(i);
            }
        }
    }
}

// CreateParticle generates a new particle with random
↪   initial conditions.
private Particle CreateParticle()
{
    // Emitter position at origin.
    Vector3 pos = new Vector3(0, 0, 0);

    // Randomize initial velocity to simulate variation.
    float vx = RandomRange(-1.0f, 1.0f);
    float vy = RandomRange(2.0f, 5.0f);
    float vz = RandomRange(-1.0f, 1.0f);
    Vector3 vel = new Vector3(vx, vy, vz);

    // Use constant acceleration to simulate gravity.
    Vector3 acc = new Vector3(0, -9.81f, 0);

    // Assign a random lifetime between 2 and 5 seconds.
    float lifetime = RandomRange(2.0f, 5.0f);

    // Set initial luminosity; decay will simulate fading.
    float initialLuminosity = 1.0f;
    float decayConstant = 0.5f; // Controls rate of
    ↪   luminosity decay.

    return new Particle(pos, vel, acc, lifetime,
    ↪   initialLuminosity, decayConstant);
}

// Utility function to return a random float between min and
↪   max.
private float RandomRange(float min, float max)
{
    return (float)(min + random.NextDouble() * (max - min));
}

// Render simulates drawing particles in the VR scene by
↪   printing their status.
public void Render()
{
    Console.Clear();
    Console.WriteLine("Simulated VR Particle System
    ↪   State:");
    foreach (var particle in particles)
    {
        // Retrieve current luminosity without advancing
        ↪   time.
```

```csharp
                float luminosity = particle.Update(0);
                Console.WriteLine($"Particle Position:
                ↪   {particle.Position}, Luminosity:
                ↪   {luminosity:F2}");
            }
        }
    }

// Main simulation loop that continuously updates and renders
↪   the particle system.
class Program
{
    static void Main(string[] args)
    {
        ParticleEmitter emitter = new ParticleEmitter();
        float deltaTime = 0.016f; // Assuming ~60 FPS, so 16ms
        ↪   per frame.

        while (true)
        {
            emitter.Update(deltaTime);
            emitter.Render();
            Thread.Sleep(16); // Pause to simulate frame rate.
        }
    }
}
```

Chapter 36

Scripting Environmental Effects: Fog, Rain, and Fire

Fog Simulation: Physical and Optical Considerations

Fog simulation in virtual environments relies on the accurate representation of light scattering phenomena within a participating medium. The optical depth of fog is frequently modeled using an exponential attenuation function, given by

$$I = I_0 \, e^{-\beta d},$$

where I_0 denotes the incident light intensity, β is the scattering coefficient, and d represents the distance traversed by the light. This model encapsulates the gradual dissipation of light as it penetrates the medium, resulting in a spatially varying visibility function that is integrated into the rendering pipeline. In some circumstances, a linear attenuation model may be employed to approximate the gradient of the fog density when computational simplicity is prioritized. The implementation of these models requires the precise computation of cumulative optical thickness over complex scene geometries, often accomplished through ray-marching techniques that discretize the intervening volumetric space.

The interplay between ambient illumination and localized light sources further complicates the simulation. The scattering function is enriched by phase functions such as the Henyey-Greenstein function, defined as

$$P(\theta) = \frac{1}{4\pi} \frac{1 - g^2}{(1 + g^2 - 2g\cos\theta)^{\frac{3}{2}}},$$

where g is the anisotropy factor and θ represents the scattering angle. Such formulations capture the directional dependence of light scattering and contribute to establishing a realistic gradient of fog density as a function of both position and view angle. Calibration of these parameters requires rigorous mathematical analysis and iterative tuning to achieve atmospheric consistency within the virtual scene.

Rain Dynamics and Simulation

The simulation of rain encompasses both the micro-scale kinematics of individual droplets and the macro-scale aggregation of precipitation effects. At its core, the motion of each raindrop is governed by classical dynamics. The velocity update can be described by

$$\mathbf{v}(t + \Delta t) = \mathbf{v}(t) + \mathbf{g}\,\Delta t,$$

where $\mathbf{v}(t)$ is the velocity vector at time t, $\mathbf{g}$ is the gravitational acceleration, and Δt is the time increment. This deterministic update is often supplemented with stochastic components that account for aerodynamic drag and turbulent fluctuations. Probabilistic models determine the distribution of droplet sizes, initial velocities, and directional deviations, thereby introducing natural variability into the simulation.

In addition to free-fall dynamics, rain simulation addresses secondary effects such as droplet collision, splash generation upon impact, and transient water film formation on surfaces. The momentum transfer during impact is quantified using the principles of conservation of momentum, whereas the generation of secondary droplets is modeled through controlled random processes. Furthermore, the optical appearance of rain is augmented via volumetric rendering techniques that simulate the collective scattering of light by a multitude of droplets. These techniques ensure that the rain effect is not treated as a mere overlay but as an integrated component of the virtual atmosphere with spatially varying intensity and translucency.

Fire Simulation: Combustion Dynamics and Visual Effects

The simulation of fire involves a synthesis of combustion dynamics, heat transfer, and advanced visual rendering techniques. Fire is inherently a highly dynamic phenomenon, exhibiting rapid temporal and spatial variation. The underlying thermal diffusion and combustion processes are captured via partial differential equations. For example, the evolution of the temperature field T within a burning medium may be approximated by

$$\frac{\partial T}{\partial t} = \nabla \cdot (k \, \nabla T) - \lambda (T - T_{\text{ambient}}),$$

where k denotes the thermal conductivity, λ is a cooling constant, and T_{ambient} represents the ambient temperature. This equation forms the basis for modulating both the luminance and color gradients associated with a flame, whereby hotter regions emit more light and shift toward higher energy color spectra.

In addition to these deterministic models, fire simulation routinely incorporates procedural noise to replicate the characteristic flicker and turbulent undulations associated with combustion. Noise functions modulate emissive intensity, spectral variance, and spatial coherence, thereby generating a composite effect that mimics the randomness of natural fire while remaining computationally tractable. Volumetric lighting models further enhance the integration of fire with its surroundings by accounting for light scattering, absorption, and the gradual occlusion of background elements. This layered approach facilitates a rich visual tapestry in which the dynamic behavior of fire is rendered with convincing depth and vibrancy.

Synthesis and Integration of Atmospheric Effects

The integration of fog, rain, and fire within a cohesive virtual atmosphere demands the unification of diverse simulation paradigms into a single rendering framework. Each environmental effect relies on distinct mathematical formulations and numerical techniques, yet they converge in the overall scene through coherent compositing and light attenuation strategies. A representative model for handling combined volumetric effects is expressed as

$$I(\mathbf{x}) = I_0 \, e^{-\int_0^\ell \sigma(\mathbf{x}(s)) \, ds},$$

where $\sigma(\mathbf{x}(s))$ is the cumulative attenuation coefficient along the ray path of length ℓ. This formulation serves as a common denominator for integrating disparate phenomena, ensuring that the contributions of fog, rain, and fire are blended appropriately to reinforce atmospheric realism.

The simultaneous simulation of multiple weather effects presents significant computational challenges. To maintain the fidelity required for immersive environments, real-time systems often rely on parallelized computations executed on dedicated graphics processing units (GPUs). Adaptive level-of-detail (LOD) schemes are employed to dynamically adjust simulation complexity based on the viewer's focus, thereby mitigating performance overhead while preserving key visual details. Spatial partitioning techniques optimize memory access patterns, and temporal filtering is applied to smooth transitions between discrete simulation states. The orchestration of these strategies allows for the robust synthesis of environmental effects, yielding an immersive atmosphere where each element reinforces the perception of a living, dynamic world.

C# Code Snippet

```
using System;
using System.Numerics;
using System.Collections.Generic;

namespace VREnvironmentSimulation
{
    // Fog simulation class to compute light attenuation through
    ↪    fog.
    public static class FogSimulator
    {
        // Computes light intensity using the exponential
        ↪    attenuation model:
        // I = I0 * exp(-beta * distance)
        public static double ComputeLightIntensity(double I0, double
        ↪    beta, double distance)
        {
            return I0 * Math.Exp(-beta * distance);
        }

        // Computes integrated light intensity along a ray path
        ↪    using discrete summation.
```

```csharp
// Approximates I(x) = I0 * exp(- sigma(x) ds) as:
// I = I0 * exp(-sum(sigma * ds))
public static double ComputeIntegratedIntensity(double I0,
↪  double[] sigmaValues, double ds)
{
    double cumulativeSigma = 0.0;
    foreach (var sigma in sigmaValues)
    {
        cumulativeSigma += sigma * ds;
    }
    return I0 * Math.Exp(-cumulativeSigma);
}
}


// Rain simulation class representing a raindrop with position
↪  and velocity.
public class RainSimulator
{
    // Static Random instance for generating turbulence.
    private static Random rnd = new Random();

    public Vector3 Position { get; private set; }
    public Vector3 Velocity { get; private set; }

    public RainSimulator(Vector3 initialPosition, Vector3
    ↪  initialVelocity)
    {
        Position = initialPosition;
        Velocity = initialVelocity;
    }

    // Update the raindrop's position and velocity based on
    ↪  gravitational acceleration
    // and random turbulence to simulate aerodynamic drag and
    ↪  fluctuations.
    public void Update(double dt)
    {
        // Gravitational acceleration vector.
        Vector3 gravity = new Vector3(0f, -9.81f, 0f);
        // Update velocity using: v(t+t) = v(t) + g * t.
        Velocity += gravity * (float)dt;

        // Add a small random component to simulate turbulence.
        float turbulenceX = 0.1f * (float)(rnd.NextDouble() -
        ↪  0.5);
        float turbulenceZ = 0.1f * (float)(rnd.NextDouble() -
        ↪  0.5);
        Velocity += new Vector3(turbulenceX, 0f, turbulenceZ);

        // Update position based on new velocity.
        Position += Velocity * (float)dt;
    }
}
```

```csharp
// Fire simulation class using a simple finite-difference method
↪    on a 2D temperature field.
public class FireSimulator
{
    private int gridWidth;
    private int gridHeight;
    private double[,] temperature;
    private double k;              // Thermal conductivity.
    private double lambda;         // Cooling constant.
    private double ambientTemperature;

    public FireSimulator(int width, int height, double
    ↪    initialTemperature, double conductivity, double cooling,
    ↪    double ambientTemp)
    {
        gridWidth = width;
        gridHeight = height;
        temperature = new double[width, height];
        for (int i = 0; i < width; i++)
        {
            for (int j = 0; j < height; j++)
            {
                temperature[i, j] = initialTemperature;
            }
        }
        k = conductivity;
        lambda = cooling;
        ambientTemperature = ambientTemp;
    }

    // Computes the Laplacian at a given grid cell (i, j) via
    ↪    finite differences.
    private double Laplacian(int i, int j)
    {
        double center = temperature[i, j];
        double up = (j > 0) ? temperature[i, j - 1] : center;
        double down = (j < gridHeight - 1) ? temperature[i, j +
        ↪    1] : center;
        double left = (i > 0) ? temperature[i - 1, j] : center;
        double right = (i < gridWidth - 1) ? temperature[i + 1,
        ↪    j] : center;
        return (up + down + left + right - 4 * center);
    }

    // Updates the temperature field using the equation:
    // dT/dt = k * Laplacian(T) - lambda * (T -
    ↪    ambientTemperature)
    public void Update(double dt)
    {
        double[,] newTemp = new double[gridWidth, gridHeight];
        for (int i = 0; i < gridWidth; i++)
        {
```

```
            for (int j = 0; j < gridHeight; j++)
            {
                double lap = Laplacian(i, j);
                newTemp[i, j] = temperature[i, j] + dt * (k *
                ↪ lap - lambda * (temperature[i, j] -
                ↪ ambientTemperature));
            }
        }
        temperature = newTemp;
    }

    // Returns the current temperature field.
    public double[,] GetTemperatureField()
    {
        return temperature;
    }
}

// Environmental effects simulator integrating fog, rain, and
↪ fire effects.
public class EnvironmentalEffectsSimulator
{
    public List<RainSimulator> RainDrops { get; private set; }
    public FireSimulator FireSim { get; set; }

    public EnvironmentalEffectsSimulator()
    {
        RainDrops = new List<RainSimulator>();
    }

    // Performs simulation updates for rain and fire effects
    ↪ over a time step.
    public void RunSimulationStep(double dt)
    {
        foreach (var rain in RainDrops)
        {
            rain.Update(dt);
        }
        FireSim?.Update(dt);
    }

    // Computes combined attenuation from volumetric effects:
    // I(x) = I0 * exp(- sigma ds) => computed as I0 *
    ↪ exp(-sum(sigma * ds))
    public double ComputeCombinedAttenuation(double I0, double[]
    ↪ sigmaValues, double ds)
    {
        double cumulativeSigma = 0.0;
        foreach (var sigma in sigmaValues)
        {
            cumulativeSigma += sigma * ds;
        }
        return I0 * Math.Exp(-cumulativeSigma);
```

264

```
        }
    }

    // Main program demonstrating simulation of fog, rain, and fire
    ↪   effects.
    class Program
    {
        static void Main(string[] args)
        {
            // Fog simulation: Compute light intensity after fog
            ↪   attenuation.
            double initialIntensity = 1.0;
            double beta = 0.2;
            double distance = 10.0;
            double fogIntensity =
            ↪   FogSimulator.ComputeLightIntensity(initialIntensity,
            ↪   beta, distance);
            Console.WriteLine("Fog Intensity: " + fogIntensity);

            // Fog simulation using integrated attenuation over
            ↪   discrete sigma values.
            double[] sigmaValues = new double[] { 0.1, 0.15, 0.2,
            ↪   0.1, 0.05 };
            double integratedFogIntensity =
            ↪   FogSimulator.ComputeIntegratedIntensity(
            initialIntensity, sigmaValues, 1.0);
            Console.WriteLine("Integrated Fog Intensity: " +
            ↪   integratedFogIntensity);

            // Rain simulation: Update a raindrop over one frame
            ↪   (~60fps).
            RainSimulator raindrop = new RainSimulator(new
            ↪   Vector3(0, 10, 0), new Vector3(0, 0, 0));
            raindrop.Update(0.016); // time step ~16ms
            Console.WriteLine("Raindrop Position: " +
            ↪   raindrop.Position);

            // Fire simulation: Initialize a fire simulation on a
            ↪   10x10 grid.
            FireSimulator fireSim = new FireSimulator(10, 10, 1000,
            ↪   0.1, 0.05, 300);
            fireSim.Update(0.016);
            double[,] temperatureField =
            ↪   fireSim.GetTemperatureField();
            Console.WriteLine("Fire Temperature at (5,5): " +
            ↪   temperatureField[5, 5]);

            // Combined environmental simulation integrating fog,
            ↪   rain, and fire effects.
            EnvironmentalEffectsSimulator envSim = new
            ↪   EnvironmentalEffectsSimulator();
            envSim.RainDrops.Add(raindrop);
            envSim.FireSim = fireSim;
```

265

```
envSim.RunSimulationStep(0.016);

// Compute combined attenuation for an integrated
↪  volumetric effect.
double combinedIntensity =
↪  envSim.ComputeCombinedAttenuation(initialIntensity,
↪  sigmaValues, 1.0);
Console.WriteLine("Combined Attenuated Intensity: " +
↪  combinedIntensity);
        }
    }
}
```

Summary: The above C# code demonstrates core simulation algorithms for fog (using both the exponential attenuation model and the integrated optical depth approach), rain (by updating droplet dynamics with gravitational and stochastic turbulence components), and fire (through a finite-difference method updating a 2D temperature field based on thermal diffusion and cooling). These algorithms are integrated into a cohesive simulation framework, illustrating how multiple environmental effects can be synchronized to enhance immersive VR experiences.

Chapter 37

Animating VR Characters and Objects

Overview of VR Animation Systems

The animation systems employed in immersive virtual reality environments are constructed upon a rigorous framework that integrates both deterministic keyframe methodologies and algorithmically driven procedural techniques. Within such a system, the objective is to simulate lifelike motion for both characters and inanimate entities under real-time constraints. The underlying architecture leverages transformation hierarchies, temporal interpolation of motion data, and continuous adjustments of object states. This approach is essential in ensuring that all animated elements react coherently to the dynamic stimuli present within a virtual scene, thereby reinforcing the perceptual integrity of the immersive experience.

Skeletal Animation Techniques for Avatars

Skeletal animation forms the cornerstone of animating articulated figures within virtual reality systems. This technique involves the use of a hierarchical bone structure, where each bone is associated with its own transformation matrix. The pose of an avatar is determined by the composition of these matrices through successive multiplications. For a given bone B_i, the effective transformation can be mathematically expressed as

$$T_i = T_{p(i)} \cdot M_{\text{bind}}(B_i) \cdot M_{\text{current}}(B_i),$$

where $T_{p(i)}$ is the transformation matrix of the parent bone, $M_{\text{bind}}(B_i)$ represents the bind pose of the bone, and $M_{\text{current}}(B_i)$ signifies the keyframe-specific transformation. In addition, vertex skinning relies on a weighted blend of the influences exerted by multiple bones. This deformation process is typically modeled as

$$D(v) = \sum_j w_j \, T_j \, v,$$

with w_j indicating the weight of the jth bone's influence and T_j its respective transformation matrix. Such formulations are critical in achieving smooth and realistic deformations of the animated character during complex motion sequences.

Procedural Animation for Inanimate Objects

Inanimate objects in virtual environments often exhibit motion that is driven by procedural animation techniques, which are rooted in the principles of classical mechanics. The dynamic behavior of such objects can be derived from physical simulations based on Newtonian dynamics. For instance, when an object is subjected to an external force $\mathbf{F}$, its acceleration is determined from the equation

$$\mathbf{a} = \frac{\mathbf{F}}{m},$$

where m is the mass of the object. The integration of this acceleration over time yields a continuous motion profile that adheres to realistic physical behavior. The incorporation of collision responses, frictional effects, and other constraints further refines the simulated movement, ensuring that the resultant animation exhibits a naturalistic quality. These procedural methods serve to augment keyframed animations by introducing emergent behaviors that are inherently unpredictable and adaptive to environmental interactions.

Animation Blending and Transitioning

The fluidity of motion in immersive environments is significantly enhanced through the application of animation blending techniques. This process involves the interpolation between discrete animation states to achieve smooth transitions. A common approach employs linear interpolation, where the blended transformation T_{blend} is defined by

$$T_{\text{blend}} = (1 - \alpha)\, T_1 + \alpha\, T_2,$$

with $\alpha \in [0, 1]$ serving as the interpolation factor between the two animations T_1 and T_2. For rotational transformations, spherical linear interpolation (slerp) is frequently utilized in order to maintain a constant angular velocity and to prevent distortions in the orientation space. The precise control over the weighting factors and the temporal alignment of key poses is crucial in guaranteeing that the transition between animations preserves both visual continuity and physical plausibility in a virtual scenario.

Inverse Kinematics for Realistic Motion

Inverse kinematics (IK) plays an indispensable role in refining the realism of animated characters by enabling the adaptation of joint configurations in response to spatial targets. The IK problem involves computing the joint angles necessary for positioning an end-effector at a desired location. The forward kinematics function is described by

$$\mathbf{x} = f(\theta),$$

where θ denotes the vector of joint angles and $\mathbf{x}$ the resultant end-effector position. The inverse problem requires solving for θ such that

$$f(\theta) = \mathbf{x},$$

a task typically addressed through iterative numerical methods such as the Jacobian transpose or pseudo-inverse strategies. The optimization process minimizes an error function, for example,

$$E = \| f(\theta) - \mathbf{x} \|,$$

thereby ensuring that the computed joint configurations conform to both the target positional constraints and the biomechanical limits inherent to the skeletal model. The integration of inverse kinematics within a VR animation pipeline permits nuanced adjustments that are critical for achieving lifelike and contextually appropriate motion across various interactive scenarios.

C# Code Snippet

```csharp
using System;
using System.Numerics;
using System.Collections.Generic;

namespace VRAnimationExample
{
    // Represents a bone in the skeletal hierarchy.
    // Implements the equation: T_i = T_{p(i)} * M_bind(B_i) *
    ↪ M_current(B_i)
    public class Bone
    {
        public string Name { get; set; }
        public Matrix4x4 BindPose { get; set; }
        public Matrix4x4 CurrentPose { get; set; }
        public Bone Parent { get; set; }

        public Bone(string name, Matrix4x4 bindPose, Matrix4x4
        ↪ currentPose, Bone parent = null)
        {
            Name = name;
            BindPose = bindPose;
            CurrentPose = currentPose;
            Parent = parent;
        }

        // Recursively computes the combined transformation for this
        ↪ bone.
        public Matrix4x4 GetCombinedTransform()
        {
            if (Parent != null)
            {
                // T_i = T_{p(i)} * M_bind * M_current
                return
                ↪ Matrix4x4.Multiply(Parent.GetCombinedTransform(),
                ↪ Matrix4x4.Multiply(BindPose, CurrentPose));
            }
            else
            {
                return Matrix4x4.Multiply(BindPose, CurrentPose);
            }
        }
    }

    public static class AnimationUtilities
    {
```

270

```
// Vertex Skinning:
// D(v) = sum_j weight_j * (T_j * v)
// Applies weighted bone transformations to a vertex.
public static Vector3 SkinVertex(Vector3 vertex, Bone[]
↪   influencingBones, float[] weights)
{
    if (influencingBones.Length != weights.Length)
        throw new ArgumentException("Bones and weights
        ↪   arrays must be of the same length.");

    Vector3 skinnedVertex = Vector3.Zero;
    for (int i = 0; i < influencingBones.Length; i++)
    {
        Matrix4x4 transform =
        ↪   influencingBones[i].GetCombinedTransform();
        Vector3 transformedVertex =
        ↪   Vector3.Transform(vertex, transform);
        skinnedVertex += weights[i] * transformedVertex;
    }
    return skinnedVertex;
}


// Procedural Animation for Inanimate Objects:
// Using the formula a = F/m, then integrating over time.
public static void SimulateProceduralAnimation(ref Vector3
↪   position, ref Vector3 velocity, Vector3 force, float
↪   mass, float deltaTime)
{
    // Calculate acceleration: a = F / m
    Vector3 acceleration = force / mass;
    // Update velocity: v += a * dt
    velocity += acceleration * deltaTime;
    // Update position: p += v * dt
    position += velocity * deltaTime;
}


// Animation Blending:
// Linear blend of two transformation matrices:
// T_blend = (1 - alpha) * T1 + alpha * T2 (applied
↪   element-wise)
public static Matrix4x4 BlendTransforms(Matrix4x4 t1,
↪   Matrix4x4 t2, float alpha)
{
    return new Matrix4x4(
        Lerp(t1.M11, t2.M11, alpha), Lerp(t1.M12, t2.M12,
        ↪   alpha), Lerp(t1.M13, t2.M13, alpha),
        ↪   Lerp(t1.M14, t2.M14, alpha),
        Lerp(t1.M21, t2.M21, alpha), Lerp(t1.M22, t2.M22,
        ↪   alpha), Lerp(t1.M23, t2.M23, alpha),
        ↪   Lerp(t1.M24, t2.M24, alpha),
        Lerp(t1.M31, t2.M31, alpha), Lerp(t1.M32, t2.M32,
        ↪   alpha), Lerp(t1.M33, t2.M33, alpha),
        ↪   Lerp(t1.M34, t2.M34, alpha),
```

```
            Lerp(t1.M41, t2.M41, alpha), Lerp(t1.M42, t2.M42,
            ↪   alpha), Lerp(t1.M43, t2.M43, alpha),
            ↪   Lerp(t1.M44, t2.M44, alpha)
        );
    }

    private static float Lerp(float a, float b, float alpha)
    {
        return a * (1 - alpha) + b * alpha;
    }

    // For rotations, blending is handled by spherical linear
    ↪   interpolation (slerp):
    public static Quaternion BlendRotations(Quaternion q1,
    ↪   Quaternion q2, float alpha)
    {
        return Quaternion.Slerp(q1, q2, alpha);
    }
}

// A simple 2D IK chain demonstrating inverse kinematics.
// The forward kinematics function f() computes the position of
↪   the end-effector.
public class IKChain
{
    public float[] JointAngles; // Joint angles in radians.
    public Vector3 BasePosition;
    public float[] BoneLengths;

    public int JointCount { get { return JointAngles.Length; } }

    public IKChain(Vector3 basePos, float[] boneLengths, float[]
    ↪   initialAngles)
    {
        BasePosition = basePos;
        BoneLengths = boneLengths;
        JointAngles = initialAngles;
    }

    // Computes the end-effector position using forward
    ↪   kinematics (assumes motion in the XY plane).
    public Vector3 ForwardKinematics()
    {
        Vector3 pos = BasePosition;
        float angleSum = 0f;
        for (int i = 0; i < JointCount; i++)
        {
            angleSum += JointAngles[i];
            pos.X += BoneLengths[i] * (float)Math.Cos(angleSum);
            pos.Y += BoneLengths[i] * (float)Math.Sin(angleSum);
        }
        return pos;
    }
```

```
// Computes the position of joint at index 'jointIndex' via
↳  forward kinematics.
private Vector3 ComputeJointPosition(int jointIndex)
{
    Vector3 pos = BasePosition;
    float angleSum = 0f;
    for (int i = 0; i < jointIndex; i++)
    {
        angleSum += JointAngles[i];
        pos.X += BoneLengths[i] * (float)Math.Cos(angleSum);
        pos.Y += BoneLengths[i] * (float)Math.Sin(angleSum);
    }
    return pos;
}

// Inverse Kinematics:
// Solves for the joint angles such that f() approximates
↳  the target position.
// Minimizes the error E = || f() - target || using an
↳  iterative Jacobian Transpose approach.
public void SolveIK(Vector3 target, int maxIterations, float
↳  threshold)
{
    for (int iter = 0; iter < maxIterations; iter++)
    {
        Vector3 endEffector = ForwardKinematics();
        Vector3 error = target - endEffector;
        if (error.Length() < threshold)
            break;

        // Update joints from end-effector backwards.
        for (int i = JointCount - 1; i >= 0; i--)
        {
            Vector3 jointPos = ComputeJointPosition(i);
            Vector3 toEnd = endEffector - jointPos;
            Vector3 toTarget = target - jointPos;

            // Compute the current and target angles.
            float currentAngle = (float)Math.Atan2(toEnd.Y,
            ↳  toEnd.X);
            float targetAngle =
            ↳  (float)Math.Atan2(toTarget.Y, toTarget.X);
            float angleError = targetAngle - currentAngle;

            // Update the joint angle with a learning rate.
            float learningRate = 0.1f;
            JointAngles[i] += learningRate * angleError;

            // Update end-effector position after adjusting
            ↳  the joint.
            endEffector = ForwardKinematics();
        }
```

```
            }
        }
    }

class Program
{
    static void Main(string[] args)
    {
        // Demonstration of Skeletal Animation and Vertex
        ↪    Skinning.
        Bone rootBone = new Bone("Root", Matrix4x4.Identity,
        ↪    Matrix4x4.Identity);
        Bone childBone = new Bone("Child",
        ↪    Matrix4x4.CreateTranslation(0, 1, 0),
        ↪    Matrix4x4.CreateRotationZ(0.5f), rootBone);
        Bone[] bones = new Bone[] { rootBone, childBone };
        float[] weights = new float[] { 0.4f, 0.6f };
        Vector3 vertex = new Vector3(1, 0, 0);
        Vector3 skinnedVertex =
        ↪    AnimationUtilities.SkinVertex(vertex, bones,
        ↪    weights);
        Console.WriteLine("Skinned Vertex: " + skinnedVertex);

        // Demonstration of Procedural Animation (Newtonian
        ↪    dynamics: a = F/m).
        Vector3 position = new Vector3(0, 0, 0);
        Vector3 velocity = new Vector3(0, 0, 0);
        Vector3 force = new Vector3(10, 0, 0); // Force applied
        ↪    along the X-axis.
        float mass = 2.0f;
        float deltaTime = 0.016f; // Approximate frame time (~60
        ↪    FPS).
        AnimationUtilities.SimulateProceduralAnimation(ref
        ↪    position, ref velocity, force, mass, deltaTime);
        Console.WriteLine("New Position: " + position + ", New
        ↪    Velocity: " + velocity);

        // Demonstration of Transform Blending.
        Matrix4x4 transform1 = Matrix4x4.CreateTranslation(0, 0,
        ↪    0);
        Matrix4x4 transform2 = Matrix4x4.CreateTranslation(10,
        ↪    0, 0);
        float alpha = 0.5f;
        Matrix4x4 blendedTransform =
        ↪    AnimationUtilities.BlendTransforms(transform1,
        ↪    transform2, alpha);
        Console.WriteLine("Blended Transform Translation X: " +
        ↪    blendedTransform.M41);

        // Demonstration of Inverse Kinematics on a 2D 3-joint
        ↪    chain.
        float[] boneLengths = new float[] { 2.0f, 1.5f, 1.0f };
        float[] initialAngles = new float[] { 0f, 0f, 0f };
```

274

```
        IKChain ikChain = new IKChain(new Vector3(0, 0, 0),
        ↪  boneLengths, initialAngles);
        Vector3 target = new Vector3(3, 2, 0);
        ikChain.SolveIK(target, maxIterations: 100, threshold:
        ↪  0.01f);
        Console.WriteLine("IK Solved End Effector Position: " +
        ↪  ikChain.ForwardKinematics());
        Console.WriteLine("Joint Angles (radians): " +
        ↪  string.Join(", ", ikChain.JointAngles));
    }
  }
}
```

Chapter 38

Developing Dynamic Animation Controllers for VR

Architectural Foundations of Dynamic Controllers

Dynamic animation controllers in virtual reality environments are predicated on architectures that integrate modular state representations with adaptive transition mechanisms. The design adopts a finite state framework, wherein the set of animation states S is rigorously defined and the transition function $T : S \times I \to S$ maps player inputs I into distinct state changes. The architecture encapsulates not only discrete keyframe-based states but also incorporates parameters for continuous motion interpolation. This duality is essential in encapsulating both deterministic and emergent animation patterns within a cohesive state model.

The underlying system architecture leverages layered abstractions, where low-level motion synthesis is decoupled from high-level interaction semantics. By enforcing a modular design, each state of the animation controller can be independently optimized and subsequently integrated into a larger behavioral framework. Such an approach ensures that computational complexity is managed effectively while maintaining consistency in visual output and behavioral responsiveness.

Integration of Player Interaction Data

The interfacing of player interaction data with animation controllers requires an intricate mapping from raw interaction input to meaningful behavioral modifications. In this paradigm, the temporal dynamics of interaction are captured through a function $I(t)$, which quantifies input as a continuous variable over time. The state update scheme is thereby reformulated as

$$s(t + \Delta t) = F(s(t), I(t)),$$

where F is an update function that computes the subsequent animation state based on the current state $s(t)$ and the instantaneous input $I(t)$.

This integration necessitates the implementation of pre-processing and filtering mechanisms to ensure that transient or noisy inputs do not precipitate abrupt or non-physical state changes. The dynamism afforded to the controller by this method ensures that the animation response is finely tuned to the nuances of player actions, thus preserving the immersive quality and perceptual continuity of the virtual environment.

Interpolation and Transition Dynamics

Transitioning between animation states within a dynamic controller is a process that critically hinges on sophisticated interpolation techniques. Linear interpolation, defined by

$$T_{\text{blend}} = (1 - \alpha) T_1 + \alpha T_2,$$

where $0 \leq \alpha \leq 1$, serves as the basis for blending transformations between key poses. For rotational transformations, the adoption of spherical linear interpolation (slerp) is paramount to maintain constant angular velocity and improved perceptual consistency.

The blending function is not limited to a simple weighted average; rather, it must account for synchronization of motion trajectories and the temporal alignment of state transitions. In a dynamic animation controller, the evolution of animation states is modeled as a continuous function, where the derivative $\dot{T}_{\text{blend}}(t)$ is regulated to ensure that acceleration and velocity constraints are upheld. The mathematical treatment of these transitions involves minimizing smoothness criteria, often formulated as the minimization of a cost functional

$$J(\alpha) = \int_0^T \left\| \dot{T}_{\text{blend}}(t) \right\|^2 dt,$$

which enforces consistency and minimizes visual discontinuities during state transitions.

Context-Sensitive State Management

Context sensitivity in dynamic animation controllers is achieved by augmenting the state transition mechanisms with environmental and interaction-based parameters. This enhancement transforms the conventional state update function into a more comprehensive form:

$$T : S \times I \times C \to S,$$

where C represents a vector of context-sensitive variables. These variables may include spatial orientation, proximity metrics, and relative motion data, which are critical in formulating a context-aware response.

The system employs real-time analysis of contextual cues to modulate animation behavior dynamically. The integration of context allows for adaptive adjustments in the blending parameters and underpins the transition function with conditional constraints that alter the animation state based on situational demands. This methodology ensures that animations not only synchronize with explicit player input but also harmonize with the environmental conditions, thereby facilitating immersive and contextually appropriate visual behavior.

Mathematical Modeling and Controller Calibration

The efficacy of dynamic animation controllers is further enhanced through precise mathematical modeling and systematic controller calibration. The underlying models incorporate state estimation, error minimization, and continuous feedback mechanisms to maintain fidelity in motion transitions. Calibration is performed by tuning the parameters of the transition functions and the interpolation weights to minimize the error in state reproduction, quantified by an error metric

$$E = \|T_{\text{desired}} - T_{\text{actual}}\|,$$

where T_{desired} represents the target transformation and T_{actual} is the outcome produced by the controller.

Incorporating optimization techniques, the system iteratively refines the control parameters to achieve a balance between responsiveness and smooth transitional behavior. The calibration process is governed by both empirical evaluations and theoretical constraints derived from biomechanical models, ensuring that the dynamic animation controllers adhere to physical plausibility while delivering high-fidelity visual performance.

C# Code Snippet

```csharp
using System;
using System.Threading;

namespace VRAnimationController
{
    // Define the available animation states.
    public enum AnimationState
    {
        Idle,
        Walking,
        Running,
        Jumping,
        Interacting
    }

    // Structure representing a simple transformation (e.g.,
    ↪    position and rotation).
    public struct Transformation
    {
        public float Position;
        public float Rotation;

        // Linear interpolation between two transformations.
        // Implements: T_blend = (1 - ) * T1 +  * T2
        public static Transformation Lerp(Transformation T1,
        ↪    Transformation T2, float alpha)
        {
            return new Transformation
            {
                Position = (1 - alpha) * T1.Position + alpha *
                ↪    T2.Position,
```

```
            Rotation = (1 - alpha) * T1.Rotation + alpha *
            ↪   T2.Rotation
        };
    }

    // Placeholder for spherical linear interpolation.
    // In practice, implement proper slerp for rotations.
    public static Transformation Slerp(Transformation T1,
    ↪   Transformation T2, float alpha)
    {
        return Lerp(T1, T2, alpha);
    }

    // Error metric: E = ||T_desired - T_actual||
    // Here we use a simple sum of absolute differences.
    public static float Cost(Transformation desired,
    ↪   Transformation actual)
    {
        return Math.Abs(desired.Position - actual.Position) +
               Math.Abs(desired.Rotation - actual.Rotation);
    }
}

// DynamicAnimationController simulates state transitions,
↪   blending, and calibration.
public class DynamicAnimationController
{
    // Time step simulation: 16ms per frame (~60 FPS)
    private readonly float deltaTime = 0.016f;

    // Current animation state and transformation.
    public AnimationState CurrentState { get; private set; }
    public Transformation CurrentTransformation { get; private
    ↪   set; }

    // Finite state transition function: s(t+t) = F(s(t), I(t))
    public AnimationState UpdateState(AnimationState
    ↪   currentState, float input)
    {
        // Transition logic based on input thresholds.
        if (input > 0.8f)
            return AnimationState.Running;
        if (input > 0.3f)
            return AnimationState.Walking;
        return AnimationState.Idle;
    }

    // Simulate a continuous player input as a function I(t).
    public float GetInputAtTime(float time)
    {
        // Example: a sine function to simulate fluctuating
        ↪   input.
        return (float)(0.5 * Math.Sin(time) + 0.5);
```

```
}

// Blends current transformation with target based on alpha.
// Implements T_blend = (1 - ) * T_current +  * T_target.
public Transformation UpdateTransformation(Transformation
 ↪  current, Transformation target, float alpha)
{
    return Transformation.Lerp(current, target, alpha);
}

// Compute a cost function to evaluate the smoothness of the
 ↪  blend.
// This simulates a simplified version of the cost
 ↪  functional:
// J() =  || d/dt T_blend ||~2 dt, here approximated via
 ↪  acceleration differences.
public float ComputeBlendCost(Transformation previous,
 ↪  Transformation current, Transformation next, float
 ↪  timeInterval)
{
    float velocity1 = (current.Position - previous.Position)
     ↪  / timeInterval;
    float velocity2 = (next.Position - current.Position) /
     ↪  timeInterval;
    return Math.Abs(velocity2 - velocity1);
}

// Calibrate the blend factor () by minimizing the error:
// E = || T_desired - T_blend || where T_blend is computed
 ↪  with a given .
public float CalibrateBlend(Transformation target,
 ↪  Transformation current, float initialAlpha)
{
    float alpha = initialAlpha;
    float bestAlpha = alpha;
    float minCost = Transformation.Cost(target,
     ↪  UpdateTransformation(current, target, alpha));

    // Simple line search around the initial alpha value.
    for (float delta = -0.1f; delta <= 0.1f; delta += 0.01f)
    {
        float testAlpha = Math.Max(0, Math.Min(1, alpha +
         ↪  delta));
        Transformation blended =
         ↪  UpdateTransformation(current, target,
         ↪  testAlpha);
        float cost = Transformation.Cost(target, blended);
        if (cost < minCost)
        {
            minCost = cost;
            bestAlpha = testAlpha;
        }
    }
```

281

```
    return bestAlpha;
}

// Returns a target transformation based on the current
↪    animation state.
private Transformation
↪    GetTargetTransformation(AnimationState state)
{
    switch (state)
    {
        case AnimationState.Running:
            return new Transformation { Position = 10.0f,
            ↪    Rotation = 45.0f };
        case AnimationState.Walking:
            return new Transformation { Position = 5.0f,
            ↪    Rotation = 20.0f };
        case AnimationState.Idle:
        default:
            return new Transformation { Position = 0.0f,
            ↪    Rotation = 0.0f };
    }
}

// Main simulation loop demonstrating state updates,
↪    blending, and calibration.
public void UpdateSimulation(float totalTime)
{
    float time = 0.0f;
    // Initialize state and transformation.
    CurrentState = AnimationState.Idle;
    CurrentTransformation = new Transformation { Position =
    ↪    0.0f, Rotation = 0.0f };

    while (time < totalTime)
    {
        // Acquire continuous player input I(t).
        float input = GetInputAtTime(time);

        // Update the animation state: s(t+t) = F(s(t),
        ↪    I(t))
        CurrentState = UpdateState(CurrentState, input);

        // Determine the target transformation based on
        ↪    state (includes context in extended model).
        Transformation targetTransformation =
        ↪    GetTargetTransformation(CurrentState);

        // Calibrate blend factor to minimize error: E =
        ↪    ||T_desired - T_actual||
        float optimalAlpha =
        ↪    CalibrateBlend(targetTransformation,
        ↪    CurrentTransformation, 0.5f);
```

```csharp
            // Compute the updated transformation using the
            ↪   optimal blend factor.
            Transformation updatedTransformation =
            ↪   UpdateTransformation(CurrentTransformation,
            ↪   targetTransformation, optimalAlpha);

            // Optionally compute blending cost to assess
            ↪   smoothness.
            float blendCost =
            ↪   ComputeBlendCost(CurrentTransformation,
            ↪   updatedTransformation, targetTransformation,
            ↪   deltaTime);

            // Update current transformation.
            CurrentTransformation = updatedTransformation;

            // Output simulation data for debugging.
            Console.WriteLine($"Time: {time:F2}s | State:
            ↪   {CurrentState} | Alpha: {optimalAlpha:F2} | " +
              $"Position: {CurrentTransformation.Position:F2} |
              ↪   Rotation: {CurrentTransformation.Rotation:F2}
              ↪   | " +
              $"Cost: {blendCost:F4}");

            time += deltaTime;
            Thread.Sleep((int)(deltaTime * 1000));
        }
    }
}

// Program entry point that runs the simulation.
internal class Program
{
    static void Main(string[] args)
    {
        DynamicAnimationController controller = new
        ↪   DynamicAnimationController();
        // Run the simulation for a total of 5 seconds.
        controller.UpdateSimulation(5.0f);
    }
}
}
```

Summary

This C# code snippet demonstrates a dynamic animation controller for VR applications. It integrates a finite-state architecture with adaptive transition mechanisms, incorporates player interaction data, applies linear and (placeholder) spherical interpolation techniques, and utilizes a simple optimization routine for calibration. All concepts—state transitions, blending interpolation, and error minimization—mirror the mathematical framework discussed in the chapter.

Chapter 39

Scripting Physics-Based Animations in Unity VR

Foundational Concepts in Physics-Driven Animation

Within the context of virtual reality, animation systems have progressed beyond conventional keyframe techniques to embrace physics-driven methodologies that synthesize motion in accordance with established physical laws. These systems rely on the integration of rigid body dynamics and procedural animation to generate natural, reactive movements. In such frameworks, the evolution of an object's state is dictated by both predefined control parameters and emergent responses based on the simulation of forces, collisions, and energy exchange. The discrete time update for a rigid body is typically modeled as

$$\mathbf{x}(t + \Delta t) = \mathbf{x}(t) + \mathbf{v}(t)\Delta t + \frac{1}{2}\mathbf{a}(t)\Delta t^2,$$

where $\mathbf{x}(t)$ represents the spatial state, $\mathbf{v}(t)$ denotes the velocity, and $\mathbf{a}(t)$ is the acceleration derived from applied forces. Such formulations establish the mathematical underpinning that allows for the synthesis of animations which adhere to the constraints of physical realism in immersive environments.

Integration of Physics Simulation with Animation Systems

The architectural design of contemporary animation frameworks in Unity VR is characterized by the decoupling of the low-level physics simulation from the high-level animation control logic. A physics engine is deployed to compute collision responses, force accumulations, and impulse propagations. The resultant data is then mapped to an animation state space via a transformation function

$$A : S \times F \to S,$$

where S represents the set of animation states and F is the collection of net force vectors computed from both environmental interactions and user inputs. This mapping permits a responsive animation system that dynamically updates the character or object state based on the instantaneous physical influences present within the virtual scene.

1   Modeling Reactive Dynamics

A key element in achieving believable reactive animations is the formal incorporation of dynamic forces into animation blending processes. The instantaneous force, given by

$$\mathbf{F} = m\mathbf{a},$$

where m is the effective mass and $\mathbf{a}$ is the calculated acceleration, is employed to modulate the interpolation between distinct animation transforms. An adaptive blending function may be formulated as

$$B(t) = \alpha(t)T_1 + (1 - \alpha(t))T_2,$$

in which T_1 and T_2 denote the transformation matrices corresponding to pre- and post-interaction states, and the scalar $\alpha(t)$ is computed dynamically based on the measured force magnitude and impulse characteristics. This adaptive modulation ensures that transitions between animation states are governed by the underlying physical interactions, resulting in motion trajectories that are resilient to abrupt changes and exhibit smooth, continuous evolution.

2　Temporal Coherence and Numerical Stability

Temporal coherence is critical when synthesizing physics-based animations, necessitating an emphasis on the numerical stability of the integration techniques employed. Methods such as Verlet integration or higher-order Runge-Kutta schemes are utilized to approximate continuous system dynamics within discretized time intervals. For instance, the incremental position update,

$$\Delta \mathbf{x} = \Delta t \, \mathbf{v} + \frac{1}{2} \Delta t^2 \, \mathbf{a},$$

must be computed while ensuring that the timestep Δt is sufficiently small to mitigate the risk of numerical instabilities. Furthermore, the computation of kinetic energy,

$$E_k = \frac{1}{2} m \|\mathbf{v}\|^2,$$

serves as a verification tool for preserving energy conservation properties, thereby preventing unrealistic accelerations or oscillatory behavior during state transitions. Such integration and validation techniques collectively underpin the fidelity of the physics-based animation framework.

Physical Constraints and Energy Minimization in Animation Blending

The incorporation of physical constraints within the animation blending process is achieved by formulating an optimization problem where the objective is to minimize discrepancies between the desired physical energy profile and that produced by the simulation. This is expressed through a cost function,

$$J = \|E_{\text{desired}} - E_{\text{computed}}\|^2,$$

which quantifies the error between the target energy state and the actual energy measured from the physics engine. By iteratively adjusting animation parameters to minimize J, the system achieves transitions that honor conservation laws and maintain physical plausibility. Constraint solvers, implemented via iterative optimization routines, ensure adherence to momentum and energy conservation, thereby producing animation transitions that are seamless and exhibit a high degree of natural motion.

Empirical Calibration of Physics-Driven Animations

Empirical calibration represents an indispensable phase in the deployment of physics-driven animation frameworks. Within this phase, numerous parameters—such as damping coefficients, frictional forces, and blending weights—are systematically tuned to optimize the responsiveness and naturalism of animations. The calibration process is guided by an objective minimization expressed as

$$\epsilon = \min_{\theta} \|\mathbf{x}_{\text{target}} - \mathbf{x}_{\theta}\|,$$

where θ denotes the vector of calibration parameters, $\mathbf{x}_{\text{target}}$ is the intended motion trajectory, and $\mathbf{x}_{\theta}$ is the computed trajectory resultant from the current parameter configuration. The minimization of ϵ ensures that the dynamic behavior produced by the physics-driven animation closely replicates target motion profiles under a variety of interaction scenarios. This rigorous calibration facilitates the convergence of the animation system towards a state where reactive movements are not only mathematically consistent but also perceptually realistic within immersive virtual environments.

C# Code Snippet

```
using UnityEngine;

public class PhysicsBasedAnimation : MonoBehaviour
{
    // Simulation parameters
    public float mass = 1.0f;
    public Vector3 velocity = Vector3.zero;
    public Vector3 acceleration = Vector3.zero;
    public float damping = 0.98f; // Damping factor for velocity

    // Transforms representing pre- and post-interaction states
    public Transform preInteractionTransform;
    public Transform postInteractionTransform;
    public float blendFactor = 0.0f; // Computed blending weight

    // Target state for empirical calibration
    public Vector3 targetPosition = Vector3.zero;

    // Internal state tracking
```

```csharp
private Vector3 currentPosition;

void Start()
{
    // Initialize current position from the object's starting
    ↪   location
    currentPosition = transform.position;
}

void FixedUpdate()
{
    float dt = Time.fixedDeltaTime;

    // --- Discrete Time Integration ---
    // Update position using the formula:
    // x(t + t) = x(t) + v(t)t + 0.5 a(t)t²
    Vector3 newPosition = currentPosition + velocity * dt + 0.5f
    ↪   * acceleration * dt * dt;

    // Approximate new velocity based on position change
    velocity = (newPosition - currentPosition) / dt;

    // Apply damping to simulate friction and energy dissipation
    velocity *= damping;

    // Set the object's new position
    transform.position = newPosition;
    currentPosition = newPosition;

    // --- Kinetic Energy Calculation ---
    // Compute kinetic energy: E_k = 0.5 * m * ||v||²
    float kineticEnergy = 0.5f * mass * velocity.sqrMagnitude;
    Debug.Log("Kinetic Energy: " + kineticEnergy);

    // --- Force Computation ---
    // Compute the instantaneous force: F = m * a
    Vector3 force = mass * acceleration;
    float forceMagnitude = force.magnitude;

    // --- Adaptive Blending ---
    // Compute blending factor based on force magnitude.
    // Blending function: B(t) = (t) T + (1-(t)) T
    float alpha = ComputeAlpha(forceMagnitude);
    blendFactor = alpha;

    // Blend the two transformation matrices corresponding to
    ↪   pre- and post-interaction states
    Matrix4x4 blendedMatrix =
    ↪   BlendTransforms(preInteractionTransform.localToWorldMatrix,
      postInteractionTransform.localToWorldMatrix,
      alpha);
```

```
    // Apply the blended transformation to the object (for
    ↪    demonstration purposes)
    ApplyBlendedMatrix(blendedMatrix);

    // --- Empirical Calibration ---
    // Calibrate parameters to minimize the error:  = ||x_target
    ↪    - x_computed||
    CalibrateParameters();
}

// Computes the alpha blending factor based on the magnitude of
↪    the applied force.
float ComputeAlpha(float forceMag)
{
    // Define a maximum force threshold to scale alpha between 0
    ↪    and 1
    float maxForce = 10f;
    return Mathf.Clamp01(forceMag / maxForce);
}

// Blends two transformation matrices using linear interpolation
↪    for positions
// and spherical linear interpolation (Slerp) for rotations.
Matrix4x4 BlendTransforms(Matrix4x4 T1, Matrix4x4 T2, float
↪    alpha)
{
    // Extract positions from matrices (4th column)
    Vector3 pos1 = T1.GetColumn(3);
    Vector3 pos2 = T2.GetColumn(3);
    Vector3 blendedPos = Vector3.Lerp(pos1, pos2, alpha);

    // Extract forward and up vectors to construct rotations
    Quaternion rot1 = Quaternion.LookRotation(T1.GetColumn(2),
    ↪    T1.GetColumn(1));
    Quaternion rot2 = Quaternion.LookRotation(T2.GetColumn(2),
    ↪    T2.GetColumn(1));
    Quaternion blendedRot = Quaternion.Slerp(rot1, rot2, alpha);

    // Create a transformation matrix from blended position and
    ↪    rotation (assuming uniform scale)
    Matrix4x4 blendedMatrix = Matrix4x4.TRS(blendedPos,
    ↪    blendedRot, Vector3.one);
    return blendedMatrix;
}

// Applies a blended transformation matrix to the game object's
↪    transform.
void ApplyBlendedMatrix(Matrix4x4 matrix)
{
    // Set the transform's position from the matrix's
    ↪    translation column
    transform.position = matrix.GetColumn(3);
```

```csharp
    // Reconstruct rotation from direction vectors (columns 2
    ↪  and 1)
    Quaternion blendedRotation =
    ↪  Quaternion.LookRotation(matrix.GetColumn(2),
    ↪  matrix.GetColumn(1));
    transform.rotation = blendedRotation;
}

// Calibrates simulation parameters by minimizing the positional
↪  error relative to a target position.
void CalibrateParameters()
{
    // Compute the error:  = ||targetPosition -
    ↪  currentPosition||
    float error = Vector3.Distance(transform.position,
    ↪  targetPosition);

    // Adjust damping based on the error magnitude (simple
    ↪  adjustment for demonstration)
    if (error > 0.1f)
    {
        damping = Mathf.Lerp(damping, 0.99f, 0.01f);
    }
    else
    {
        damping = Mathf.Lerp(damping, 0.95f, 0.01f);
    }

    Debug.Log("Calibration error: " + error + " | Updated
    ↪  Damping: " + damping);
}
}
```

Summary: The above C# code snippet demonstrates a comprehensive implementation of physics-driven animation in Unity VR. It integrates fundamental equations such as the discrete time update for rigid bodies, computes kinetic energy and dynamic forces, applies adaptive blending between pre- and post-interaction transforms, and uses a simple calibration routine to minimize state deviations—all of which contribute to achieving realistic and reactive animations in immersive environments.

Chapter 40

Implementing IK Systems for VR Avatars

Foundations of Inverse Kinematics in Virtual Reality

In the domain of virtual reality, the precise representation of avatar motion necessitates an accurate mapping between high-level spatial targets and the joint configurations of articulated bodies. Inverse kinematics (IK) addresses this requirement by computing the set of joint parameters that yield a desired position and orientation for an end-effector within an articulated chain. The conceptual framework is rooted in the formulation of forward kinematics, where a mapping $f(\mathbf{q})$ defines the relationship between the vector of joint parameters $\mathbf{q}$ and the resultant spatial state of the limb. The central challenge of IK lies in determining the inverse mapping such that $f(\mathbf{q}) = \mathbf{p}_d$, with $\mathbf{p}_d$ representing the target position defined by the spatial constraints of the virtual environment. This inverse mapping is critical for attaining realistic limb positioning and enhanced user representation in immersive contexts.

Mathematical Formulation of Inverse Kinematics

The IK problem is mathematically formalized by considering the non-linear relationship between joint parameters and end-effector positioning. In many systems, the forward kinematics function, denoted by $f(\mathbf{q})$, is differentiable, which allows for the linearization of the problem around a current configuration. This linear relationship is expressed as

$$\Delta\mathbf{p} = \mathbf{J}(\mathbf{q})\,\Delta\mathbf{q},$$

where $\Delta\mathbf{p}$ denotes the differential change in the end-effector position, $\Delta\mathbf{q}$ is the corresponding change in joint parameters, and $\mathbf{J}(\mathbf{q})$ is the Jacobian matrix that encodes the sensitivity of the end-effector position with respect to variations in $\mathbf{q}$. In scenarios where the system exhibits redundancy or encounters singularities, a damped least-squares approach is employed to stabilize the solution:

$$\Delta\mathbf{q} = \mathbf{J}^{\mathrm{T}}\left(\mathbf{J}\,\mathbf{J}^{\mathrm{T}} + \lambda^2\mathbf{I}\right)^{-1}\Delta\mathbf{p},$$

with λ representing a damping factor and $\mathbf{I}$ the identity matrix. This formulation ensures that computed adjustments to the joint parameters remain stable even in the vicinity of singular configurations, thereby preserving the fidelity of the avatar's motion.

Constraint Optimization in Inverse Kinematics

In virtual environments, the optimization of joint configurations must account for a variety of biomechanical and environmental constraints. Articulated figures are subject to joint limits, collision avoidance requirements, and the maintenance of anatomical plausibility. These constraints are integrated into the IK framework by formulating an optimization problem that minimizes the deviation between the computed end-effector position and the desired target:

$$\min_{\mathbf{q}} \| f(\mathbf{q}) - \mathbf{p}_d \|^2,$$

subject to the bounds

$$\mathbf{q}_{\min} \leq \mathbf{q} \leq \mathbf{q}_{\max}.$$

The incorporation of inequality constraints such as $A\mathbf{q} \leq \mathbf{b}$ further refines the solution space to exclude configurations that would violate physical or anatomical limitations. Iterative optimization techniques, commonly based on gradient descent or quadratic programming, are utilized to obtain solutions that satisfy both the kinematic equation and the imposed constraints. This constrained optimization process ensures that the computed joint configurations yield realistic and biomechanically feasible motion trajectories.

Dynamic Integration and Temporal Continuity

The implementation of an IK system in a virtual reality context requires not only static accuracy but also dynamic consistency over time. To preserve temporal continuity, the joint parameter vector is updated incrementally according to the relation

$$\mathbf{q}(t + \Delta t) = \mathbf{q}(t) + \Delta\mathbf{q}(t),$$

where Δt denotes a small time increment. This iterative update facilitates a smooth transition between successive configurations, thereby preventing abrupt changes in the avatar's posture that could disrupt visual plausibility. The integration of the IK solution with sensor data and real-time user input is achieved through predictive models that compensate for system latency and ensure that motion remains coherent across time steps. Such an approach mitigates the influence of numerical instabilities and contributes to the continuous and responsive adjustment of the avatar's limbs.

Enhanced User Representation through Inverse Kinematics

The application of IK techniques to virtual avatars significantly elevates the realism of user representation by ensuring that limb movements accurately reflect the intended spatial targets. The interplay of sensor-derived positional data and the computational determination of joint parameters results in avatar motions that are both natural and reflective of underlying biomechanical principles. Quantitative measures of performance are derived from the residual error

$$\epsilon = \|f(\mathbf{q}) - \mathbf{p}_d\|,$$

which is iteratively minimized to achieve high-precision alignment between user commands and avatar posture. The successful integration of inverse kinematics into VR avatars relies on a fusion of high-dimensional optimization, constraint adherence, and dynamic temporal integration, all of which coalesce to produce a system where limb positioning is rendered with exceptional realism.

C# Code Snippet

```
using System;
using MathNet.Numerics.LinearAlgebra;

namespace VRAvatarIK
{
    // The IKSolver class encapsulates the inverse kinematics
    //   solution using the damped least squares method.
    public class IKSolver
    {
        public Vector<double> JointAngles { get; private set; }
        public Vector<double> JointMin { get; private set; }
        public Vector<double> JointMax { get; private set; }
        public double Lambda { get; private set; }
        public double DeltaTime { get; private set; }

        public IKSolver(Vector<double> initialAngles, Vector<double>
            jointMin, Vector<double> jointMax, double lambda = 0.1,
            double deltaTime = 0.02)
        {
            JointAngles = initialAngles;
            JointMin = jointMin;
            JointMax = jointMax;
            Lambda = lambda;
            DeltaTime = deltaTime;
        }

        // Computes the damped least squares solution using:
        // q = J^T (J*J^T + ^2 I)^{-1} p
        public Vector<double> ComputeDeltaQ(Matrix<double> jacobian,
            Vector<double> deltaP)
        {
            var jTranspose = jacobian.Transpose();
            var jjT = jacobian * jTranspose;
            var identity =
                Matrix<double>.Build.DenseIdentity(jjT.RowCount);
            var dampingMatrix = identity * (Lambda * Lambda);
            var jjTDamped = jjT + dampingMatrix;
```

```csharp
        var inverted = jjTDamped.Inverse();
        Vector<double> deltaQ = jTranspose * (inverted *
        ↪   deltaP);
        return deltaQ;
    }


    // Updates joint angles using the computed q and then
    ↪   enforces the joint limits.
    public void UpdateJointAngles(Vector<double> deltaQ)
    {
        JointAngles = JointAngles + deltaQ;
        for (int i = 0; i < JointAngles.Count; i++)
        {
            if(JointAngles[i] < JointMin[i])
                JointAngles[i] = JointMin[i];
            else if(JointAngles[i] > JointMax[i])
                JointAngles[i] = JointMax[i];
        }
    }


    // Executes one iteration of the IK update:
    // Calculates the error p = p_d - f(q), computes q via
    ↪   damped LS and updates the joint state.
    public void IterateIK(Func<Vector<double>, Vector<double>>
    ↪   ForwardKinematics,
                        Func<Vector<double>, Matrix<double>>
                        ↪   ComputeJacobian,
                        Vector<double> targetPosition)
    {
        // Compute current end-effector position using forward
        ↪   kinematics.
        Vector<double> currentPosition =
        ↪   ForwardKinematics(JointAngles);
        // Error vector: p = targetPosition - f(q)
        Vector<double> deltaP = targetPosition -
        ↪   currentPosition;

        // Compute the Jacobian matrix at the current joint
        ↪   configuration.
        Matrix<double> jacobian = ComputeJacobian(JointAngles);

        // Solve for q using the damped least squares algorithm.
        Vector<double> deltaQ = ComputeDeltaQ(jacobian, deltaP);

        // Dynamically integrate: q(t+t) = q(t) + q.
        UpdateJointAngles(deltaQ);

        // Output the current error magnitude for debugging
        ↪   purposes.
        double error = deltaP.L2Norm();
        Console.WriteLine("Error: " + error);
    }
}
```

```csharp
// The VRAvatarExample class demonstrates a simple 2-DOF planar
↪    arm as an example of a VR avatar limb.
public static class VRAvatarExample
{
    // ForwardKinematics computes the end-effector position for
    ↪    a 2-link planar arm.
    // f(q) = [l1*cos(theta1) + l2*cos(theta1+theta2),
    ↪    l1*sin(theta1) + l2*sin(theta1+theta2)]
    public static Vector<double>
    ↪    ForwardKinematics(Vector<double> jointAngles)
    {
        double l1 = 1.0, l2 = 1.0;
        double theta1 = jointAngles[0];
        double theta2 = jointAngles[1];
        double x = l1 * Math.Cos(theta1) + l2 * Math.Cos(theta1
        ↪    + theta2);
        double y = l1 * Math.Sin(theta1) + l2 * Math.Sin(theta1
        ↪    + theta2);
        return Vector<double>.Build.DenseOfArray(new double[] {
        ↪    x, y });
    }

    // ComputeJacobian returns the 2x2 Jacobian matrix for the
    ↪    2-link planar arm.
    public static Matrix<double> ComputeJacobian(Vector<double>
    ↪    jointAngles)
    {
        double l1 = 1.0, l2 = 1.0;
        double theta1 = jointAngles[0];
        double theta2 = jointAngles[1];
        double j11 = -l1 * Math.Sin(theta1) - l2 *
        ↪    Math.Sin(theta1 + theta2);
        double j12 = -l2 * Math.Sin(theta1 + theta2);
        double j21 = l1 * Math.Cos(theta1) + l2 *
        ↪    Math.Cos(theta1 + theta2);
        double j22 = l2 * Math.Cos(theta1 + theta2);

        return Matrix<double>.Build.DenseOfArray(new double[,] {
            { j11, j12 },
            { j21, j22 }
        });
    }

    // The Main method performs iterative IK updates until
    ↪    convergence to the target end-effector position.
    public static void Main()
    {
        // Define initial joint angles (in radians) for the
        ↪    2-DOF arm.
        var initialAngles =
        ↪    Vector<double>.Build.DenseOfArray(new double[] {
        ↪    0.0, 0.0 });
```

```csharp
// Define joint limits.
var jointMin = Vector<double>.Build.DenseOfArray(new
↪  double[] { -Math.PI, -Math.PI });
var jointMax = Vector<double>.Build.DenseOfArray(new
↪  double[] { Math.PI, Math.PI });

// Instantiate the IK solver with predefined damping ()
↪  and time step (t).
IKSolver solver = new IKSolver(initialAngles, jointMin,
↪  jointMax, lambda: 0.1, deltaTime: 0.02);

// Set the desired target position for the end-effector.
Vector<double> targetPosition =
↪  Vector<double>.Build.DenseOfArray(new double[] {
↪  1.5, 1.0 });

// Run iterative IK updates.
for (int i = 0; i < 100; i++)
{
    solver.IterateIK(ForwardKinematics, ComputeJacobian,
    ↪  targetPosition);
    Console.WriteLine("Iteration " + i + ": Joint Angles
    ↪  = " + solver.JointAngles);

    // Check for convergence based on the residual
    ↪  error.
    Vector<double> currentPos =
    ↪  ForwardKinematics(solver.JointAngles);
    if ((targetPosition - currentPos).L2Norm() < 0.001)
    {
        Console.WriteLine("Converged to target
        ↪  position.");
        break;
    }
}
        }
    }
}
```

Chapter 41

Handling Object Interactions with Inverse Kinematics

Theoretical Underpinnings of Object Interaction via IK

In immersive environments where object manipulation must be rendered with high fidelity, inverse kinematics (IK) emerges as a pivotal computational paradigm. The framework models an articulated representation of a virtual avatar or mechanical manipulator, wherein the relationship between the joint configuration vector $\mathbf{q}$ and the resultant end-effector position $f(\mathbf{q})$ is encapsulated by a forward kinematics function. Object interaction requires that this function be effectively inverted in order to achieve precise alignment between the end-effector and the object of interest. The complexity of this inversion is amplified by the necessity to accommodate multitiered constraints, including kinematic reachability, joint limit boundaries, and the accommodation of non-linearly coupled interactions that arise in natural manipulation tasks.

Mathematical Formulation and Constraint Integration

The formulation of IK in the context of object interaction involves the resolution of the non-linear mapping defined by the forward kinematics function $f(\mathbf{q})$. The goal is to determine a joint configuration $\mathbf{q}$ such that the end-effector successfully contacts the object in a desired manner. This is mathematically expressed as the solution to the equation

$$f(\mathbf{q}) = \mathbf{p}_d,$$

where $\mathbf{p}_d$ represents the target position associated with the object. The inherent non-linearity is often addressed through local linearization via the Jacobian matrix $\mathbf{J}(\mathbf{q})$, which approximates the differential relationship

$$\Delta \mathbf{p} \approx \mathbf{J}(\mathbf{q}) \, \Delta \mathbf{q}.$$

The presence of redundant degrees of freedom and potential singularities necessitates the application of robust numerical techniques such as the damped least-squares method. This technique stabilizes the solution using the formulation

$$\Delta \mathbf{q} = \mathbf{J}^{\mathrm{T}}(\mathbf{q}) \left(\mathbf{J}(\mathbf{q}) \, \mathbf{J}^{\mathrm{T}}(\mathbf{q}) + \lambda^2 \mathbf{I} \right)^{-1} \Delta \mathbf{p},$$

where λ denotes a damping parameter and $\mathbf{I}$ is the identity matrix. In object manipulation scenarios, additional constraints are embedded to ensure that the resulting joint configuration adheres to physical limitations and produces natural motion profiles.

Integration of Object Interaction Constraints

A critical aspect of applying IK to object interactions is the integration of constraints that govern both the anatomical or mechanical structure and the task-specific requirements of the manipulation. The realized pose must be biomechanically plausible or mechanically feasible, and must preserve properties such as balance and grasp stability. These requirements are frequently incorporated via inequality constraints of the form

$$\mathbf{q}_{\min} \leq \mathbf{q} \leq \mathbf{q}_{\max}$$

and by enforcing task-specific restrictions, expressed as

$$A\mathbf{q} \le \mathbf{b},$$

where A represents a matrix encoding interaction-related constraints, and $\mathbf{b}$ is a vector defining the permissible ranges. The constrained optimization problem may be formally stated as

$$\min_{\mathbf{q}} \|f(\mathbf{q}) - \mathbf{p}_d\|^2 \quad \text{subject to} \quad \mathbf{q}_{\min} \le \mathbf{q} \le \mathbf{q}_{\max},$$

which is typically solved through iterative methods such as gradient descent or quadratic programming. Such approaches ensure that the resultant object manipulation is rendered with a natural and precise correspondence to the intended spatial target.

Dynamic Considerations and Temporal Continuity

Object interactions in virtual environments are inherently dynamic, requiring the IK system to update joint configurations in real time while synchronizing with the evolving configuration of the environment. The temporal evolution of the joint states is governed by the relation

$$\mathbf{q}(t + \Delta t) = \mathbf{q}(t) + \Delta \mathbf{q}(t),$$

which facilitates smooth transitions and mitigates potential instabilities introduced by abrupt state changes. In object manipulation tasks, temporal continuity plays an essential role in preserving the naturalness of the interaction, particularly when contact with objects must remain consistent as either the manipulator or the environment undergoes motion. Predictive and adaptive techniques are employed to counteract the effects of computational latency and sensor noise, ensuring that the end-effector's trajectory remains coherent relative to the object's position. The integration of the IK solution within a dynamic framework hence contributes significantly to the realistic portrayal of object interactions.

Optimization of Joint Trajectories for Precise Manipulation

Achieving precise and natural object manipulation through IK necessitates the continuous optimization of joint trajectories over time. The error metric

$$\epsilon = \|f(\mathbf{q}) - \mathbf{p}_d\|$$

serves as the primary quantitative measure for evaluating the quality of the solution. Minimization of ϵ through iterative refinement of $\mathbf{q}$ ensures that manipulative actions are executed with high spatial accuracy. During such refinement, the damping factor λ is carefully tuned to balance convergence speed with the stability of the manipulation, particularly in scenarios where configurations approach singular regions. The interplay between the Jacobian matrix structure and the imposed constraints is central to attaining joint trajectories that not only minimize the residual error but also conform to the natural motion patterns expected in object interaction tasks. This optimization procedure results in joint movements that are both precise and adaptive, enabling complex manipulations with discernible realism in immersive environments.

C# Code Snippet

```
using System;

namespace VRInverseKinematics
{
    // Inverse kinematics solver for a 3DOF manipulator using the
    ↪   Damped Least Squares method
    class InverseKinematicsSolver
    {
        // Link lengths for the manipulator
        private double l1 = 1.0;
        private double l2 = 1.0;

        // Joint limits: q0 [-,], q1 [-/2, /2], q2 [0,2]
        private double[] qMin = new double[] { -Math.PI, -Math.PI /
        ↪   2, 0.0 };
        private double[] qMax = new double[] { Math.PI, Math.PI / 2,
        ↪   2.0 };

        // Forward kinematics for a 3DOF manipulator:
        // q[0] controls the base rotation around the vertical axis,
        // q[1] affects the horizontal reach and vertical elevation,
        // q[2] is a prismatic joint influencing vertical extension.
        // The end-effector position is computed as:
        //    x = cos(q0) * (l1 + l2*cos(q1))
        //    y = sin(q0) * (l1 + l2*cos(q1))
        //    z = l2*sin(q1) + q2
        public double[] ForwardKinematics(double[] q)
```

```
{
    double theta = q[0];
    double jointAngle = q[1];
    double prismatic = q[2];

    double horizontal = l1 + l2 * Math.Cos(jointAngle);
    double x = Math.Cos(theta) * horizontal;
    double y = Math.Sin(theta) * horizontal;
    double z = l2 * Math.Sin(jointAngle) + prismatic;
    return new double[] { x, y, z };
}

// Compute the Jacobian matrix for the current joint
↪    configuration q.
// Its formulation is derived from the partial derivatives
↪    of the forward kinematics:
//  x/q0 = -sin(q0)*(l1+l2*cos(q1))
//  y/q0 =  cos(q0)*(l1+l2*cos(q1))
//  x/q1 = -cos(q0)*l2*sin(q1)
//  y/q1 = -sin(q0)*l2*sin(q1)
//  z/q1 =  l2*cos(q1) and z/q2 = 1.
public double[,] ComputeJacobian(double[] q)
{
    double[,] J = new double[3, 3];
    double theta = q[0];
    double jointAngle = q[1];

    double horizontal = l1 + l2 * Math.Cos(jointAngle);

    // Derivatives with respect to q0
    J[0, 0] = -Math.Sin(theta) * horizontal;
    J[1, 0] =  Math.Cos(theta) * horizontal;
    J[2, 0] = 0;

    // Derivatives with respect to q1
    J[0, 1] = -Math.Cos(theta) * l2 * Math.Sin(jointAngle);
    J[1, 1] = -Math.Sin(theta) * l2 * Math.Sin(jointAngle);
    J[2, 1] =  l2 * Math.Cos(jointAngle);

    // Derivatives with respect to q2 (prismatic joint)
    J[0, 2] = 0;
    J[1, 2] = 0;
    J[2, 2] = 1;

    return J;
}

// Solves the IK problem iteratively by minimizing the error
//  = ||f(q) - target|| using the damped least squares
↪    update:
// q = J^T * (J * J^T + ^2 I)^(-1) * (target - f(q))
public double[] SolveIK(double[] qInitial, double[] target,
↪    double lambda, int maxIterations, double tolerance)
```

303

```csharp
{
    double[] q = (double[])qInitial.Clone();
    for (int iter = 0; iter < maxIterations; iter++)
    {
        double[] currentPos = ForwardKinematics(q);
        double[] error = Subtract(target, currentPos);
        double errorNorm = Norm(error);
        if (errorNorm < tolerance)
        {
            Console.WriteLine("Converged in " + iter + "
            ↪   iterations.");
            return q;
        }
        double[,] J = ComputeJacobian(q);
        double[] deltaQ = DampedLeastSquaresUpdate(J, error,
        ↪   lambda);

        // Update joint configuration with the computed q
        ↪   and clamp to joint limits.
        for (int i = 0; i < q.Length; i++)
        {
            q[i] += deltaQ[i];
            q[i] = Clamp(q[i], qMin[i], qMax[i]);
        }
    }
    Console.WriteLine("Max iterations reached without full
    ↪   convergence.");
    return q;
}

// Computes the Damped Least Squares update:
// q = J^T * (J*J^T + ^2 I)^(-1) * p , where p = target -
↪   f(q)
public double[] DampedLeastSquaresUpdate(double[,] J,
↪   double[] deltaP, double lambda)
{
    // Compute J * J^T
    double[,] JJt = MultiplyMatrices(J, Transpose(J));
    int n = JJt.GetLength(0);
    double[,] dampingMatrix = IdentityMatrix(n);
    for (int i = 0; i < n; i++)
        dampingMatrix[i, i] *= (lambda * lambda);

    // Add damping: A = J*J^T + ^2 I
    double[,] A = AddMatrices(JJt, dampingMatrix);
    double[,] AInv = InvertMatrix3x3(A);
    double[,] J_T = Transpose(J);
    double[] temp = MultiplyMatrixVector(AInv, deltaP);
    // Compute q = J^T * temp
    double[] deltaQ = MultiplyMatrixVector(J_T, temp);
    return deltaQ;
}
```

```csharp
// Helper: Compute the Euclidean norm of a vector.
public static double Norm(double[] v)
{
    double sum = 0;
    for (int i = 0; i < v.Length; i++)
        sum += v[i] * v[i];
    return Math.Sqrt(sum);
}

// Helper: Subtract vector b from vector a.
public static double[] Subtract(double[] a, double[] b)
{
    double[] result = new double[a.Length];
    for (int i = 0; i < a.Length; i++)
        result[i] = a[i] - b[i];
    return result;
}

// Helper: Multiply matrix M and vector v.
public static double[] MultiplyMatrixVector(double[,] M,
↪   double[] v)
{
    int rows = M.GetLength(0);
    int cols = M.GetLength(1);
    double[] result = new double[rows];
    for (int i = 0; i < rows; i++)
    {
        double sum = 0;
        for (int j = 0; j < cols; j++)
            sum += M[i, j] * v[j];
        result[i] = sum;
    }
    return result;
}

// Helper: Transpose the matrix M.
public static double[,] Transpose(double[,] M)
{
    int rows = M.GetLength(0);
    int cols = M.GetLength(1);
    double[,] T = new double[cols, rows];
    for (int i = 0; i < rows; i++)
        for (int j = 0; j < cols; j++)
            T[j, i] = M[i, j];
    return T;
}

// Helper: Multiply two matrices A and B.
public static double[,] MultiplyMatrices(double[,] A,
↪   double[,] B)
{
    int rowsA = A.GetLength(0);
    int colsA = A.GetLength(1);
```

```csharp
        int colsB = B.GetLength(1);
        double[,] result = new double[rowsA, colsB];
        for (int i = 0; i < rowsA; i++)
            for (int j = 0; j < colsB; j++)
            {
                double sum = 0;
                for (int k = 0; k < colsA; k++)
                    sum += A[i, k] * B[k, j];
                result[i, j] = sum;
            }
        return result;
    }

    // Helper: Add two matrices A and B.
    public static double[,] AddMatrices(double[,] A, double[,]
    ↪ B)
    {
        int rows = A.GetLength(0);
        int cols = A.GetLength(1);
        double[,] result = new double[rows, cols];
        for (int i = 0; i < rows; i++)
            for (int j = 0; j < cols; j++)
                result[i, j] = A[i, j] + B[i, j];
        return result;
    }

    // Helper: Create an identity matrix of the given size.
    public static double[,] IdentityMatrix(int size)
    {
        double[,] I = new double[size, size];
        for (int i = 0; i < size; i++)
            I[i, i] = 1;
        return I;
    }

    // Helper: Invert a 3x3 matrix using an analytical method.
    public static double[,] InvertMatrix3x3(double[,] M)
    {
        double a = M[0, 0], b = M[0, 1], c = M[0, 2];
        double d = M[1, 0], e = M[1, 1], f = M[1, 2];
        double g = M[2, 0], h = M[2, 1], i = M[2, 2];

        double det = a * (e * i - f * h) - b * (d * i - f * g) +
        ↪ c * (d * h - e * g);
        if (Math.Abs(det) < 1e-8)
            throw new Exception("Matrix is singular and cannot
            ↪ be inverted.");

        double invDet = 1.0 / det;
        double[,] inv = new double[3, 3];
        inv[0, 0] =  (e * i - f * h) * invDet;
        inv[0, 1] = -(b * i - c * h) * invDet;
        inv[0, 2] =  (b * f - c * e) * invDet;
```

306

```
        inv[1, 0] = -(d * i - f * g) * invDet;
        inv[1, 1] =  (a * i - c * g) * invDet;
        inv[1, 2] = -(a * f - c * d) * invDet;
        inv[2, 0] =  (d * h - e * g) * invDet;
        inv[2, 1] = -(a * h - b * g) * invDet;
        inv[2, 2] =  (a * e - b * d) * invDet;
        return inv;
    }

    // Helper: Clamp a value within the specified min and max
    ↪    bounds.
    public static double Clamp(double value, double min, double
    ↪    max)
    {
        if (value < min)
            return min;
        if (value > max)
            return max;
        return value;
    }
}

class Program
{
    static void Main(string[] args)
    {
        InverseKinematicsSolver solver = new
        ↪    InverseKinematicsSolver();

        // Initial joint configuration: [q0 (radians), q1
        ↪    (radians), q2 (meters)]
        double[] qInitial = new double[] { 0.0, 0.0, 0.5 };

        // Desired target position for the end-effector in 3D
        ↪    space.
        double[] target = new double[] { 1.0, 1.0, 1.0 };

        double lambda = 0.1;        // Damping factor to ensure
        ↪    stability.
        int maxIterations = 100;    // Maximum number of
        ↪    iterations to update q.
        double tolerance = 1e-3;    // Convergence tolerance for
        ↪    the error norm.

        double[] solution = solver.SolveIK(qInitial, target,
        ↪    lambda, maxIterations, tolerance);

        Console.WriteLine("Final joint configuration:");
        Console.WriteLine("q0: " + solution[0]);
        Console.WriteLine("q1: " + solution[1]);
        Console.WriteLine("q2: " + solution[2]);

        double[] finalPos = solver.ForwardKinematics(solution);
```

```
        Console.WriteLine("Final end-effector position:");
        Console.WriteLine("x: " + finalPos[0]);
        Console.WriteLine("y: " + finalPos[1]);
        Console.WriteLine("z: " + finalPos[2]);
      }
    }
  }
```

Summary

This C# code snippet implements a robust inverse kinematics solver based on the damped least squares method. It formulates the forward kinematics for a 3DOF manipulator, computes the Jacobian matrix, and iteratively updates the joint configuration while enforcing joint limits. The algorithm minimizes the error between the current end-effector position and a desired target, ensuring smooth, realistic object interactions in a VR environment.

Chapter 42

Creating Realistic Avatar Movements in Oculus VR

Motion Capture and Sensor Fusion Techniques

A fundamental aspect of generating realistic avatar movements is the precise acquisition and fusion of motion data from multiple tracking modalities. The analytical framework developed for this purpose integrates information from inertial measurement units (IMUs), optical tracking systems, and other sensor arrays. The resulting sensor fusion algorithm reconciles spatial and temporal discrepancies inherent in individual sensors, thereby producing a coherent estimate of the skeletal joint configuration denoted by

$$q = \{q_1, q_2, \ldots, q_n\}.$$

The process involves statistical approaches to attenuate sensor noise and systematic calibration errors. Bayesian inference and Kalman filtering techniques are utilized to compute robust estimates of joint positions and orientations, which are subsequently mapped onto the avatar model. This rigorous fusion procedure ensures that the acquired motion data accurately reflects real-world dynamics before being applied to the digital representation.

Temporal Alignment and Interpolation Mechanisms

The fidelity of avatar animation critically depends on the accurate synchronization of motion data over time. Discrete sensor outputs, sampled at non-uniform intervals $t_0, t_1, \ldots, t_k$, require conversion into a continuous temporal representation. This conversion is achieved through the application of high-order interpolation schemes such as cubic splines, which yield a smooth estimation $\hat{q}(t)$ of the joint configuration over continuous time. The interpolation is governed by the minimization of an error function expressed as

$$E(t) = \|q(t) - \hat{q}(t)\|,$$

where $q(t)$ represents the temporally sampled joint data. The iterative minimization process provides a uniform time base for the avatar's movement, ensuring the elimination of temporal discontinuities and lag that could impair the realism of the animation.

Kinematic Consistency and Constraint Enforcement

Ensuring that avatar animations adhere to the physical constraints of human biomechanics is essential for achieving realistic representation. The joint configurations of the avatar must satisfy predefined kinematic constraints, typically expressed in the form

$$q_{min} \leq q \leq q_{max},$$

which enforce physiologically plausible range-of-motion boundaries for each joint. In addition to angle constraints, dynamic considerations derived from principles of Lagrangian mechanics impose further restrictions on the allowable accelerations and torques. These restrictions are integrated into the motion synthesis process via inverse kinematics, where optimization routines adjust the joint angles to minimize discrepancies between the prescribed posture and sensor-derived motion data. This multiconstraint optimization guarantees that the avatar exhibits natural, biomechanically consistent movements while capturing the nuances of the user's behavior.

Adaptive Kinematics and Dynamic Adjustment

The continuous adaptation of the avatar's kinematic configuration in response to fluctuating motion data is critical for maintaining a responsive virtual presence. Small variations in sensor readings necessitate instantaneous recalibration, which is typically modeled by computing incremental adjustments Δq to the current joint configuration q. This adjustment is determined by solving a regularized least-squares problem of the form

$$\min_{\Delta q} \| J(q)\Delta q - \Delta p \|^2 + \lambda \|\Delta q\|^2,$$

where $J(q)$ is the Jacobian matrix of the current configuration and Δp represents the discrepancy in end-effector position derived from the sensor measurements. The regularization parameter λ is carefully tuned to balance sensor fidelity against the smoothness of the transition. Such adaptive kinematic correction mechanisms ensure that the avatar's movements remain immediately responsive to real-world inputs while preserving a high degree of natural motion continuity.

Representation Fidelity and Accuracy Assessment

Quantitative assessment of the avatar's motion accuracy is performed by comparing the synthesized joint trajectories with the original motion capture data. Metrics such as the mean squared error (MSE) are computed over the duration T of the recorded motion, where

$$\text{MSE} = \frac{1}{T} \int_0^T \| q_{\text{real}}(t) - q_{\text{avatar}}(t) \|^2 \, dt.$$

This metric provides a rigorous measure of the deviation between the real-world motion data $q_{\text{real}}(t)$ and the avatar's animated joint positions $q_{\text{avatar}}(t)$. In addition, spatial and temporal correlation analyses are conducted to assess the degree of synchronization between the user and avatar, thereby serving as a baseline for further refinement of the motion synthesis algorithms. The statistical evaluation of these metrics supports iterative improvements in the underlying techniques, ultimately leading to an avatar representation that faithfully mirrors user behavior with high temporal coherence and biomechanical accuracy.

C# Code Snippet

```csharp
using System;

namespace VRAvatarMotion
{
    public class AvatarMotionProcessor
    {
        public int JointCount { get; private set; }
        public float[] CurrentJoints;
        public float[] qMin;
        public float[] qMax;
        public float Lambda = 0.1f; // Regularization parameter

        public AvatarMotionProcessor(int jointCount)
        {
            JointCount = jointCount;
            CurrentJoints = new float[jointCount];
            qMin = new float[jointCount];
            qMax = new float[jointCount];
        }

        // -----------------------------
        // Sensor Fusion and Filtering
        // -----------------------------
        // Combines sensor data from an IMU and an optical tracking
        ↪  system using a simple average,
        // representing the fusion algorithm which can be extended
        ↪  with Bayesian or Kalman filtering.
        public float[] SensorFusion(float[] imuData, float[]
        ↪  opticalData)
        {
            if (imuData.Length != JointCount || opticalData.Length
            ↪  != JointCount)
                throw new ArgumentException("Sensor data length must
                ↪  equal the number of joints.");

            float[] fused = new float[JointCount];
            for (int i = 0; i < JointCount; i++)
            {
                // Equation: q = {q1, q2, ..., qn} is estimated by
                ↪  fusing sensor inputs.
                fused[i] = (imuData[i] + opticalData[i]) / 2f;
            }
            return fused;
        }
    }
```

312

```
// -------------------------
// Temporal Alignment and Cubic Spline Interpolation
// -------------------------
// This function performs interpolation of joint
↪   configuration data using Catmull-Rom splines,
// which is a high-order cubic interpolation scheme.
// times: an array of time stamps, jointData: an array of
↪   joint configurations (each is an array of floats)
// queryTime: the time at which we want the interpolated
↪   joint configuration.
public float[] InterpolateSpline(float[] times, float[][]
↪   jointData, float queryTime)
{
    int n = times.Length;
    if (n == 0)
        throw new ArgumentException("Empty times array.");
    if (jointData.Length != n)
        throw new ArgumentException("Length of jointData
        ↪   must match times array.");

    // If queryTime is outside the provided time range,
    ↪   return the first or last configuration.
    if (queryTime <= times[0])
        return jointData[0];
    if (queryTime >= times[n - 1])
        return jointData[n - 1];

    // Find the index i so that times[i] <= queryTime <
    ↪   times[i+1]
    int i;
    for (i = 0; i < n - 1; i++)
    {
        if (queryTime < times[i + 1])
            break;
    }

    // Determine indices for Catmull-Rom spline: p0, p1, p2,
    ↪   p3.
    int i0 = (i - 1) < 0 ? 0 : i - 1;
    int i1 = i;
    int i2 = i + 1;
    int i3 = (i + 2) >= n ? n - 1 : i + 2;

    // Compute local parameter t in [0,1] over the segment
    ↪   times[i] to times[i+1]
    float t0 = times[i];
    float t1 = times[i + 1];
    float tLocal = (queryTime - t0) / (t1 - t0);

    float[] interpolated = new float[JointCount];
    for (int joint = 0; joint < JointCount; joint++)
    {
        float p0 = jointData[i0][joint];
```

313

```
            float p1 = jointData[i1][joint];
            float p2 = jointData[i2][joint];
            float p3 = jointData[i3][joint];
            interpolated[joint] = CatmullRom(p0, p1, p2, p3,
            ↪  tLocal);
        }
        return interpolated;
    }

    // Catmull-Rom spline interpolation formula.
    private float CatmullRom(float p0, float p1, float p2, float
    ↪  p3, float t)
    {
        return 0.5f * ((2f * p1) +
                    (-p0 + p2) * t +
                    (2f * p0 - 5f * p1 + 4f * p2 - p3) * t *
                    ↪  t +
                    (-p0 + 3f * p1 - 3f * p2 + p3) * t * t *
                    ↪  t);
    }

    // -------------------------
    // Kinematic Consistency: Constraint Enforcement
    // -------------------------
    // Clamps each joint angle between its minimum and maximum
    ↪  allowable values.
    public float[] EnforceKinematicConstraints(float[]
    ↪  jointConfig)
    {
        float[] constrained = new float[JointCount];
        for (int i = 0; i < JointCount; i++)
        {
            constrained[i] = Math.Min(Math.Max(jointConfig[i],
            ↪  qMin[i]), qMax[i]);
        }
        return constrained;
    }

    // ----------------------------------------
    // Adaptive Kinematics: Regularized Least-Squares Adjustment
    // ----------------------------------------
    // Solves for q in: min_{q} ||J(q)q - p||^2 + ||q||^2
    // using the solution: q = (J^T J + I)^{-1} J^T p.
    public float[] AdaptiveKinematicsAdjustment(float[,] J,
    ↪  float[] deltaP)
    {
        // Dimensions:
        // J should be m x n where m is the number of
        ↪  end-effector dimensions and n equals JointCount.
        int m = J.GetLength(0);
        int n = J.GetLength(1);
        if (n != JointCount)
```

314

```
        throw new ArgumentException("Jacobian column count
        ↪   must equal JointCount.");
    if (deltaP.Length != m)
        throw new ArgumentException("DeltaP vector length
        ↪   must match the number of Jacobian rows.");

    // Compute the transpose of J: JT.
    float[,] JT = Transpose(J);

    // Compute A = J^T * J.
    float[,] A = MultiplyMatrices(JT, J);

    // Add regularization term: A + I.
    float[,] lambdaI = IdentityMatrix(n, Lambda);
    A = AddMatrices(A, lambdaI);

    // Invert A.
    float[,] invA = InvertMatrix(A);

    // Compute b = J^T * deltaP.
    float[] b = MultiplyMatrixVector(JT, deltaP);

    // Compute q = invA * b.
    float[] deltaQ = MultiplyMatrixVector(invA, b);
    return deltaQ;
}


// ------------------------------
// Representation Fidelity: Mean Squared Error Calculation
// ------------------------------
// Computes the MSE between real joint configurations and
↪   the avatar's joint configurations.
public float CalculateMSE(float[][] realData, float[][]
↪   avatarData)
{
    int n = realData.Length;
    if(n == 0 || avatarData.Length != n)
        throw new ArgumentException("Data array length
        ↪   mismatch.");
    float mse = 0f;
    int totalElements = 0;
    for (int i = 0; i < n; i++)
    {
        if(realData[i].Length != JointCount ||
        ↪   avatarData[i].Length != JointCount)
            throw new ArgumentException("Joint configuration
            ↪   length mismatch.");
        for (int j = 0; j < JointCount; j++)
        {
            float diff = realData[i][j] - avatarData[i][j];
            mse += diff * diff;
            totalElements++;
        }
    }
```

```
    }
    mse /= totalElements;
    return mse;
}

// ---------------------------
// Matrix and Vector Helpers
// ---------------------------

// Transposes a 2D matrix.
public float[,] Transpose(float[,] matrix)
{
    int rows = matrix.GetLength(0);
    int cols = matrix.GetLength(1);
    float[,] transposed = new float[cols, rows];
    for (int i = 0; i < rows; i++)
        for (int j = 0; j < cols; j++)
            transposed[j, i] = matrix[i, j];
    return transposed;
}

// Multiplies two matrices.
public float[,] MultiplyMatrices(float[,] A, float[,] B)
{
    int rowsA = A.GetLength(0);
    int colsA = A.GetLength(1);
    int rowsB = B.GetLength(0);
    int colsB = B.GetLength(1);
    if (colsA != rowsB)
        throw new ArgumentException("Invalid dimensions for
        ↪  matrix multiplication.");

    float[,] result = new float[rowsA, colsB];
    for (int i = 0; i < rowsA; i++)
    {
        for (int j = 0; j < colsB; j++)
        {
            result[i, j] = 0f;
            for (int k = 0; k < colsA; k++)
            {
                result[i, j] += A[i, k] * B[k, j];
            }
        }
    }
    return result;
}

// Adds two matrices element-wise.
public float[,] AddMatrices(float[,] A, float[,] B)
{
    int rows = A.GetLength(0);
    int cols = A.GetLength(1);
    if (rows != B.GetLength(0) || cols != B.GetLength(1))
```

```
            throw new ArgumentException("Matrices must have the
            ↪   same dimensions.");
        float[,] result = new float[rows, cols];
        for (int i = 0; i < rows; i++)
            for (int j = 0; j < cols; j++)
                result[i, j] = A[i, j] + B[i, j];
        return result;
}

// Creates an identity matrix of size n with the diagonal
↪   elements multiplied by a factor.
public float[,] IdentityMatrix(int n, float factor = 1f)
{
    float[,] I = new float[n, n];
    for (int i = 0; i < n; i++)
        I[i, i] = factor;
    return I;
}

// Multiplies a matrix with a vector.
public float[] MultiplyMatrixVector(float[,] A, float[] v)
{
    int rows = A.GetLength(0);
    int cols = A.GetLength(1);
    if (cols != v.Length)
        throw new ArgumentException("Matrix and vector
        ↪   dimensions do not match.");
    float[] result = new float[rows];
    for (int i = 0; i < rows; i++)
    {
        result[i] = 0f;
        for (int j = 0; j < cols; j++)
        {
            result[i] += A[i, j] * v[j];
        }
    }
    return result;
}

// Inverts a square matrix using Gauss-Jordan elimination.
public float[,] InvertMatrix(float[,] A)
{
    int n = A.GetLength(0);
    if (n != A.GetLength(1))
        throw new ArgumentException("Matrix must be
        ↪   square.");

    float[,] result = new float[n, n];
    // Initialize result as the identity matrix.
    for (int i = 0; i < n; i++)
        for (int j = 0; j < n; j++)
            result[i, j] = (i == j) ? 1f : 0f;
```

```
    // Create a copy of A to avoid modifying the original
    ↳  matrix.
    float[,] A_copy = new float[n, n];
    for (int i = 0; i < n; i++)
        for (int j = 0; j < n; j++)
            A_copy[i, j] = A[i, j];

    // Perform Gauss-Jordan elimination.
    for (int i = 0; i < n; i++)
    {
        float pivot = A_copy[i, i];
        if (Math.Abs(pivot) < 1e-6)
            throw new Exception("Matrix is singular or
            ↳  nearly singular.");

        // Normalize the pivot row.
        for (int j = 0; j < n; j++)
        {
            A_copy[i, j] /= pivot;
            result[i, j] /= pivot;
        }

        // Eliminate pivot column entries in other rows.
        for (int k = 0; k < n; k++)
        {
            if (k == i) continue;
            float factor = A_copy[k, i];
            for (int j = 0; j < n; j++)
            {
                A_copy[k, j] -= factor * A_copy[i, j];
                result[k, j] -= factor * result[i, j];
            }
        }
    }
    return result;
    }
}


// --------------------------
// Example Program to Demonstrate Use
// --------------------------
public class Program
{
    public static void Main()
    {
        // Create an instance for a 3-joint avatar.
        int jointCount = 3;
        AvatarMotionProcessor processor = new
        ↳  AvatarMotionProcessor(jointCount);

        // Set joint limits.
        processor.qMin = new float[] { -90f, -45f, -30f };
        processor.qMax = new float[] { 90f, 45f, 30f };
```

```
processor.CurrentJoints = new float[] { 0f, 0f, 0f };

// Simulate sensor data from the IMU and optical
↪   tracking systems.
float[] imuData = new float[] { 10f, 5f, -2f };
float[] opticalData = new float[] { 9f, 6f, -1f };
float[] fusedData = processor.SensorFusion(imuData,
↪   opticalData);

// Adaptive kinematics adjustment.
// Define a dummy 3x3 Jacobian matrix and a deltaP
↪   vector.
float[,] J = new float[,] { { 1f, 0.1f, 0f }, { 0.2f,
↪   1f, 0.3f }, { 0f, 0.1f, 1f } };
float[] deltaP = new float[] { 0.5f, -0.3f, 0.2f };
float[] deltaQ =
↪   processor.AdaptiveKinematicsAdjustment(J, deltaP);

// Update the current joint configuration with the
↪   computed deltaQ.
float[] newJointConfig = new float[jointCount];
for (int i = 0; i < jointCount; i++)
{
    newJointConfig[i] = processor.CurrentJoints[i] +
    ↪   deltaQ[i];
}
// Enforce the kinematic constraints (range-of-motion
↪   boundaries).
newJointConfig =
↪   processor.EnforceKinematicConstraints(newJointConfig);

// Cubic spline interpolation for joint data.
float[] times = new float[] { 0f, 1f, 2f, 3f };
float[][] jointData = new float[][] {
    new float[] { 0f, 0f, 0f },
    new float[] { 10f, 5f, -2f },
    new float[] { 15f, 7f, -1f },
    new float[] { 20f, 10f, 0f }
};
float queryTime = 1.5f;
float[] interpolatedJoints =
↪   processor.InterpolateSpline(times, jointData,
↪   queryTime);

// Calculate Mean Squared Error between sample 'real'
↪   sensor data and the avatar data.
float[][] realData = new float[][] {
    new float[] { 10f, 5f, -2f },
    new float[] { 11f, 5.5f, -1.5f }
};
float[][] avatarData = new float[][] {
    fusedData,
    newJointConfig
```

```
    };
    float mse = processor.CalculateMSE(realData,
    ↪   avatarData);

    // Output the results.
    Console.WriteLine("Fused Data: " + string.Join(", ",
    ↪   fusedData));
    Console.WriteLine("Delta Q: " + string.Join(", ",
    ↪   deltaQ));
    Console.WriteLine("New Joint Configuration: " +
    ↪   string.Join(", ", newJointConfig));
    Console.WriteLine("Interpolated Joints at t = " +
    ↪   queryTime + ": " + string.Join(", ",
    ↪   interpolatedJoints));
    Console.WriteLine("Mean Squared Error: " + mse);
    }
  }
}
```

Summary: - This C# code demonstrates sensor fusion using a simple averaging method, cubic spline interpolation via Catmull-Rom splines, enforcement of biomechanical joint constraints, adaptive kinematic adjustments via a regularized least-squares approach, and the computation of mean squared error for assessing the fidelity of avatar motion relative to captured real-world data.

Chapter 43

Optimizing VR Performance: Rendering Pipeline Basics

Overview of Unity's Rendering Pipeline

The rendering pipeline in Unity embodies a multifaceted architecture that transforms three-dimensional scene descriptions into a two-dimensional visual output. At its core, the process commences with the assembly and classification of scene geometry, which is then subjected to vertex transformations, lighting calculations, and fragment shading. This sequential processing leverages both fixed-function hardware and programmable shader units, enabling a flexible approach to rendering that accommodates diverse visual styles. The integration between the central processing unit (CPU) and the graphics processing unit (GPU) is critical, as it ensures that data flows efficiently through the pipeline while sustaining the high performance demanded by virtual reality applications. The design of the pipeline inherently balances computational load and visual fidelity to meet the rigorous performance thresholds required for immersive environments.

Geometry Processing and Spatial Partitioning Techniques

The preliminary stages of the rendering pipeline involve an intricate manipulation of geometric data, where scene primitives are parsed and organized to optimize subsequent computations. Spatial partitioning techniques, such as octrees and bounding volume hierarchies, are employed to decompose the scene into manageable segments. These structures facilitate rapid frustum culling by mathematically evaluating whether objects reside within the camera's field of view. As objects external to the view frustum are efficiently discarded from processing, the burden of vertex transformations and shading computation is significantly reduced. Such systematic organization not only mitigates the computational complexity associated with large and dynamic scenes but also ensures that each frame is rendered within the tight time constraints inherent to high-performance virtual reality.

Advanced Culling Mechanisms and Their Computational Impact

Culling mechanisms are pivotal in eliminating redundant processing of off-screen or obscured objects. Frustum culling operates by defining the camera's view volume through a set of planes and subsequently determining the intersection of these planes with the bounding volumes of scene objects. Complementary to this, occlusion culling assesses whether objects, although within the view frustum, are blocked by nearer geometry. The computational impact of these techniques is substantial; by reducing the number of draw calls and the volume of unnecessary shading calculations, these algorithms directly contribute to decreased latency and enhanced frame stability. The mathematical rigor underlying these methods—often involving operations on vector spaces and planar equations—serves to optimize the rendering process while preserving the visual integrity expected from virtual reality experiences.

Shader and Material Optimization

Shaders function as the programmable core of material rendering in Unity, dictating the appearance of surfaces through complex calculations executed on the GPU. The performance of a shader is directly correlated with its complexity, which encompasses the number of computational instructions, texture lookups, and conditional branches. In high-performance VR scenarios, the imperative to maintain elevated frame rates necessitates a reduction in shader complexity without compromising the visual quality of materials. Techniques such as minimizing texture sampling operations, consolidating multiple effects into a single rendering pass, and streamlining conditional logic are integral to achieving this balance. The careful calibration of shader programs ensures that the processing overhead remains bounded, thereby allowing the rendering pipeline to deliver consistent and immersive visual outputs.

Batching, Draw Call Reduction, and Resource Management

A critical aspect of optimizing rendering performance lies in the reduction of draw calls issued to the GPU. In Unity, effective batching techniques—both static and dynamic—consolidate multiple objects with similar render states into a single draw call. This consolidation diminishes the overhead associated with state changes and vertex buffer bindings, elements that are computationally expensive in the context of real-time rendering. Moreover, a judicious management of memory resources, particularly the minimization of data transfers between the CPU and GPU, is essential. By optimizing the scheduling of these transfers and employing strategies to reduce redundant data processing, the overall rendering throughput is enhanced. These measures, taken in concert, serve to alleviate potential bottlenecks in the pipeline and support the stringent performance criteria characteristic of immersive VR systems.

Optimization of Post-Processing Effects and Overhead Mitigation

Post-processing effects provide the final visual enhancements through operations such as anti-aliasing, bloom, and tone mapping. While these effects greatly contribute to the aesthetic quality of the rendered scene, they also impose additional computational demands. In the context of high-performance virtual reality, it is imperative that post-processing pipelines be meticulously optimized to avoid degrading frame rates. Techniques that streamline these processes include single-pass optimizations and the dynamic scaling of post-processing intensity based on scene complexity. By carefully managing these overheads, the rendering pipeline is enabled to maintain a balance between visual enrichment and computational efficiency, thereby ensuring that the immersive experience remains both vibrant and fluid.

C# Code Snippet

```csharp
// VR Rendering Performance Optimization Algorithms

using System;
using System.Collections.Generic;
using UnityEngine;

public static class FrustumCulling
{
    // Extracts the 6 view frustum planes from the given camera by
    //   combining its projection and view matrices.
    // The planes are computed using the matrix rows, based on the
    //   plane equation: A*x + B*y + C*z + D = 0.
    public static Plane[] ExtractFrustumPlanes(Camera cam)
    {
        Plane[] planes = new Plane[6];
        Matrix4x4 matrix = cam.projectionMatrix *
            cam.worldToCameraMatrix;

        // Left plane: row4 + row1
        planes[0] = CreatePlane(
            matrix.m30 + matrix.m00,
            matrix.m31 + matrix.m01,
            matrix.m32 + matrix.m02,
            matrix.m33 + matrix.m03
        );

        // Right plane: row4 - row1
```

```csharp
    planes[1] = CreatePlane(
        matrix.m30 - matrix.m00,
        matrix.m31 - matrix.m01,
        matrix.m32 - matrix.m02,
        matrix.m33 - matrix.m03
    );

    // Bottom plane: row4 + row2
    planes[2] = CreatePlane(
        matrix.m30 + matrix.m10,
        matrix.m31 + matrix.m11,
        matrix.m32 + matrix.m12,
        matrix.m33 + matrix.m13
    );

    // Top plane: row4 - row2
    planes[3] = CreatePlane(
        matrix.m30 - matrix.m10,
        matrix.m31 - matrix.m11,
        matrix.m32 - matrix.m12,
        matrix.m33 - matrix.m13
    );

    // Near plane: row4 + row3
    planes[4] = CreatePlane(
        matrix.m30 + matrix.m20,
        matrix.m31 + matrix.m21,
        matrix.m32 + matrix.m22,
        matrix.m33 + matrix.m23
    );

    // Far plane: row4 - row3
    planes[5] = CreatePlane(
        matrix.m30 - matrix.m20,
        matrix.m31 - matrix.m21,
        matrix.m32 - matrix.m22,
        matrix.m33 - matrix.m23
    );

    return planes;
}


// Normalizes the derived plane coefficients and creates a
↪    UnityEngine.Plane.
private static Plane CreatePlane(float a, float b, float c,
↪    float d)
{
    // Normalize the plane (A, B, C, D) so that the normal
    ↪    vector has unit length.
    float magnitude = Mathf.Sqrt(a * a + b * b + c * c);
    a /= magnitude;
    b /= magnitude;
    c /= magnitude;
```

```csharp
        d /= magnitude;
        // The Unity Plane is defined via a normal and a distance
        ↪  such that for any point P: normal·P + distance = 0.
        return new Plane(new Vector3(a, b, c), d);
    }

    // Determines if a bounding volume is visible within the camera
    ↪  frustum.
    // It tests the object's bounds against each frustum plane using
    ↪  the support point strategy.
    public static bool IsBoundsVisible(Bounds bounds, Plane[]
    ↪  frustumPlanes)
    {
        foreach (Plane plane in frustumPlanes)
        {
            // Determine the support point (most positive vertex)
            ↪  for the plane normal.
            Vector3 testPoint = bounds.center;
            Vector3 extents = bounds.extents;

            if (plane.normal.x >= 0)
                testPoint.x += extents.x;
            else
                testPoint.x -= extents.x;

            if (plane.normal.y >= 0)
                testPoint.y += extents.y;
            else
                testPoint.y -= extents.y;

            if (plane.normal.z >= 0)
                testPoint.z += extents.z;
            else
                testPoint.z -= extents.z;

            // If the test point is outside the plane, the bounds
            ↪  are not visible.
            if (plane.GetDistanceToPoint(testPoint) < 0)
                return false;
        }
        return true;
    }
}

// A simple Octree implementation for spatial partitioning of scene
↪  objects.
public class OctreeNode<T>
{
    public Bounds NodeBounds;
    public List<T> Objects;
    public OctreeNode<T>[] Children;
    public int Depth;
    private int maxObjects = 8;
```

```csharp
private int maxDepth = 5;

public OctreeNode(Bounds bounds, int depth = 0)
{
    NodeBounds = bounds;
    Depth = depth;
    Objects = new List<T>();
    Children = null;
}

// Inserts an object along with its bounding region into the
↪   octree.
public void Insert(T obj, Bounds objBounds)
{
    if (!NodeBounds.Intersects(objBounds))
        return;

    if (Children == null && (Objects.Count < maxObjects || Depth
    ↪   >= maxDepth))
    {
        Objects.Add(obj);
        return;
    }

    if (Children == null)
        Subdivide();

    bool inserted = false;
    foreach (var child in Children)
    {
        if (child.NodeBounds.Intersects(objBounds))
        {
            child.Insert(obj, objBounds);
            inserted = true;
        }
    }

    if (!inserted)
        Objects.Add(obj);
}

// Subdivides the current node into 8 child nodes.
private void Subdivide()
{
    Children = new OctreeNode<T>[8];
    Vector3 size = NodeBounds.size / 2f;
    Vector3 center = NodeBounds.center;
    int index = 0;

    for (int x = -1; x <= 1; x += 2)
    {
        for (int y = -1; y <= 1; y += 2)
        {
```

```
                    for (int z = -1; z <= 1; z += 2)
                    {
                        Vector3 childCenter = center + Vector3.Scale(new
                        ↪   Vector3(x, y, z), size / 2f);
                        Bounds childBounds = new Bounds(childCenter,
                        ↪   size);
                        Children[index++] = new
                        ↪   OctreeNode<T>(childBounds, Depth + 1);
                    }
                }
            }

            // Reinsert existing objects into children
            List<T> tempObjects = new List<T>(Objects);
            Objects.Clear();
            foreach (T obj in tempObjects)
            {
                // In a complete implementation, each object's own
                ↪   bounds would be used.
                Insert(obj, NodeBounds);
            }
        }

        // Queries and collects all objects within a specified region.
        public void Query(Bounds queryBounds, List<T> results)
        {
            if (!NodeBounds.Intersects(queryBounds))
                return;

            foreach (T obj in Objects)
                results.Add(obj);

            if (Children != null)
            {
                foreach (var child in Children)
                    child.Query(queryBounds, results);
            }
        }
    }

    // BatchManager reduces draw calls by grouping GameObjects that
    ↪   share materials.
    public static class BatchManager
    {
        public static void BatchRender(List<GameObject> objects)
        {
            Dictionary<Material, List<MeshFilter>> batches = new
            ↪   Dictionary<Material, List<MeshFilter>>();
            foreach (GameObject go in objects)
            {
                MeshRenderer renderer = go.GetComponent<MeshRenderer>();
                MeshFilter filter = go.GetComponent<MeshFilter>();
                if (renderer != null && filter != null)
```

328

```csharp
        {
            Material mat = renderer.sharedMaterial;
            if (!batches.ContainsKey(mat))
                batches[mat] = new List<MeshFilter>();
            batches[mat].Add(filter);
        }
    }

    // Here we simulate batching by logging the count per
    //     material.
    foreach (KeyValuePair<Material, List<MeshFilter>> kvp in
    //     batches)
    {
        Debug.Log("Batching " + kvp.Value.Count + " objects with
        //     material: " + kvp.Key.name);
        // Real-world usage could combine meshes or call GPU
        //     instancing to reduce draw calls.
    }
    }
}

// PostProcessingOptimizer adjusts post-processing effect parameters
//     to maintain performance.
public static class PostProcessingOptimizer
{
    public static void OptimizeEffects(Camera camera, int
    //     qualityLevel)
    {
        // For high-performance VR, dynamically adjust
        //     post-processing based on scene complexity.
        Debug.Log("Optimizing post-processing effects with quality
        //     level " + qualityLevel);
        // Actual adjustments such as dynamic resolution scaling or
        //     single-pass optimizations would be implemented here.
    }
}

// Example usage within a Unity MonoBehaviour to integrate the above
//     algorithms.
public class VRRenderingOptimization : MonoBehaviour
{
    public Camera vrCamera;
    public List<GameObject> sceneObjects;
    public Bounds sceneBounds;

    private Plane[] frustumPlanes;
    private OctreeNode<GameObject> octree;

    void Start()
    {
        // Calculate the camera's view frustum planes.
        frustumPlanes =
        //     FrustumCulling.ExtractFrustumPlanes(vrCamera);
```

329

```
    // Initialize an octree covering the defined scene bounds.
    octree = new OctreeNode<GameObject>(sceneBounds);

    // Insert each scene object into the octree using its
    ↪   renderer bounds.
    foreach (GameObject obj in sceneObjects)
    {
        Renderer rend = obj.GetComponent<Renderer>();
        if (rend != null)
            octree.Insert(obj, rend.bounds);
    }
}

void Update()
{
    // Perform frustum culling by enabling or disabling objects
    ↪   based on their visibility.
    foreach (GameObject obj in sceneObjects)
    {
        Renderer rend = obj.GetComponent<Renderer>();
        if (rend != null)
        {
            bool visible =
            ↪   FrustumCulling.IsBoundsVisible(rend.bounds,
            ↪   frustumPlanes);
            obj.SetActive(visible);
        }
    }

    // Optimize draw calls by batching objects with shared
    ↪   materials.
    BatchManager.BatchRender(sceneObjects);

    // Dynamically adjust post-processing effects to balance
    ↪   visual fidelity and performance.
    PostProcessingOptimizer.OptimizeEffects(vrCamera,
    ↪   qualityLevel: 2);
    }
}
```

Summary: This C# code snippet demonstrates key VR rendering performance optimization algorithms, including frustum culling using view frustum plane extraction and bounding-volume testing, spatial partitioning through an octree structure, batching techniques for reducing draw calls, and runtime adjustment of post-processing effects to secure an optimal balance between visual quality and computational efficiency.

Chapter 44

Implementing Occlusion Culling in VR Scenes

Fundamental Concepts of Occlusion Culling

Occlusion culling is a technique that systematically reduces rendering overhead by dynamically excluding objects that are not visible from the current viewpoint. This process is predicated on the observation that, in a three-dimensional scene, many objects are entirely obscured by nearer geometry and therefore do not contribute to the final rendered image. In the context of virtual reality, where the rendering pipeline must operate under stringent performance constraints, the implementation of occlusion culling is essential. The efficacy of this technique derives from its advanced utilization of depth information and spatial relationships, which permits the rapid assessment of object visibility. The process involves identifying occluder objects, constructing an occlusion volume, and executing visibility queries that determine whether the projected screen space representation of a candidate object intersects with the occlusion volume. When such intersections are absent, the object is omitted from subsequent rendering passes.

Mathematical Formulation and Algorithmic Approaches

The theoretical foundation of occlusion culling relies on well-defined mathematical constructs and efficient algorithmic strategies. A rigorous formulation involves mapping elements in the three-dimensional scene into a view-dependent representation, typically via the transformation afforded by the camera projection matrix. Let $V \subset \mathbb{R}^3$ denote the volume occupied by an individual scene object, and let $O \subset \mathbb{R}^3$ represent the aggregate occlusion region computed from nearer geometry. An object V is considered occluded if

$$V \cap O =,$$

where the absence of a non-empty intersection indicates complete occlusion.

1 Geometric Representations and Bounding Volumes

To facilitate rapid occlusion tests, each object is associated with a simplified geometric representation, commonly in the form of an axis-aligned bounding box (AABB) or an oriented bounding box (OBB). These bounding volumes are computed such that they encapsulate the detailed geometry of the object with minimal excess. The mathematical test for occlusion then reduces to verifying whether a bounding volume B, defined by a center point and extents along the three axes, intersects the occlusion volume O. By leveraging inequalities derived from the plane equations that define the sides of O, one may efficiently compute a conservative estimate of object visibility. This conservative approach guarantees that only objects guaranteed to be visible are processed further in the rendering pipeline.

2 Spatial Data Structures and Visibility Coherence

The performance and scalability of occlusion culling are greatly enhanced by the use of spatial partitioning schemes. Data structures such as octrees or binary space partitioning (BSP) trees facilitate hierarchical organization of the scene. By recursively subdividing the spatial domain, these structures permit the early rejection of entire regions in which all enclosed objects are occluded. The recursive nature of such algorithms exploits visibility coherence over successive frames; that is, the relative spatial arrangement of scene objects often remains stable over short time intervals. This stability allows the reuse of visibility information, reducing the computational load associated with performing full occlusion tests on a per-frame basis. In essence, if a node within an octree is determined to lie completely outside the visible region, all objects contained within that node are excluded from further processing, thereby amortizing the cost of occlusion determination.

Architectural Integration within VR Rendering Pipelines

The seamless incorporation of occlusion culling into the virtual reality rendering pipeline requires a careful orchestration of GPU and CPU resources. Given the dual-eye rendering paradigm intrinsic to stereoscopic displays, the occlusion culling algorithms must accommodate dual perspectives, ensuring that the visibility tests are performed consistently across both views. A typical integration involves the initial execution of a depth pre-pass, wherein the scene's depth buffer is populated to capture the distance data of nearby occluding objects. Subsequent stages employ the depth buffer to define occlusion volumes, which in turn are used to evaluate candidate objects against the pre-established criteria for visibility. The outcome of these evaluations informs the scheduling of rendering tasks, ultimately reducing the number of fragment shader invocations and draw calls. In this manner, the architectural design not only preserves computational resources but also mitigates the latency issues that are particularly detrimental in virtual reality environments.

Computational Analysis and Performance Considerations

The implementation of occlusion culling introduces additional computational steps; however, its net effect is a significant reduction in rendering workload. Quantitatively, the algorithmic complexity associated with spatial queries can be characterized by an average-case time complexity of $O(n \log n)$, where n corresponds to the number of scene objects. By minimizing the number of objects that undergo detailed shading and rasterization, the load on the GPU is markedly reduced. This reduction is critical in VR applications, where maintaining high and consistent frame rates is imperative for both performance and user comfort. The interplay between the occlusion culling module and the rest of the rendering pipeline is governed by trade-offs between the overhead of performing the culling tests and the savings accrued from avoided processing. Empirical evidence from high-fidelity VR systems indicates that judiciously parameterized occlusion culling can lead to substantial reductions in draw calls, improved memory bandwidth usage, and a consequential stabilization of frame rates without compromising the visual fidelity of the scene.

C# Code Snippet

```csharp
using System;
using System.Collections.Generic;
using UnityEngine;

public class OcclusionCullingManager : MonoBehaviour
{
    // Array of occlusion planes computed from the camera's view
    ↪    frustum.
    // These planes represent the occlusion volume O in the equation
    ↪    V O = .
    private Plane[] occlusionPlanes;

    // Root node of an octree structure for spatial partitioning of
    ↪    scene renderers.
    private OctreeNode octreeRoot;

    void Start()
    {
        // Compute initial occlusion planes based on the main
        ↪    camera.
        ComputeViewFrustumPlanes();
        // Build an octree that encompasses all renderers in the
        ↪    scene.
        BuildOctree();
    }

    void Update()
    {
        // Update occlusion planes every frame (to account for
        ↪    camera movement).
        ComputeViewFrustumPlanes();
```

```csharp
    // Perform occlusion culling on all objects using the
    ↪    octree.
    if (octreeRoot != null)
    {
        CullOctree(octreeRoot);
    }
}

// Computes the view frustum planes using Unity's built-in
↪    method.
void ComputeViewFrustumPlanes()
{
    Camera cam = Camera.main;
    if (cam != null)
    {
        // The frustum planes serve as our occlusion volume O.
        occlusionPlanes =
        ↪    GeometryUtility.CalculateFrustumPlanes(cam);
    }
}

// Custom occlusion test based on the mathematical formulation:
// An object with volume V is considered occluded if V  O = ,
// meaning all 8 corners of its bounding box lie completely
↪    outside at least one plane of O.
bool CustomOcclusionTest(Bounds bounds, Plane[] planes)
{
    Vector3[] corners = GetCorners(bounds);
    foreach (var plane in planes)
    {
        int outsideCount = 0;
        foreach (var corner in corners)
        {
            // GetDistanceToPoint returns a negative value if
            ↪    the point is behind the plane.
            if (plane.GetDistanceToPoint(corner) < 0)
            {
                outsideCount++;
            }
        }
        // If all corners are outside (i.e., not intersecting
        ↪    the occlusion volume), the object is occluded.
        if (outsideCount == 8)
        {
            return true;
        }
    }
    return false;
}

// Returns the eight corner points of a bounding box.
Vector3[] GetCorners(Bounds b)
```

```
{
    Vector3[] corners = new Vector3[8];
    Vector3 min = b.min;
    Vector3 max = b.max;
    corners[0] = new Vector3(min.x, min.y, min.z);
    corners[1] = new Vector3(max.x, min.y, min.z);
    corners[2] = new Vector3(min.x, max.y, min.z);
    corners[3] = new Vector3(max.x, max.y, min.z);
    corners[4] = new Vector3(min.x, min.y, max.z);
    corners[5] = new Vector3(max.x, min.y, max.z);
    corners[6] = new Vector3(min.x, max.y, max.z);
    corners[7] = new Vector3(max.x, max.y, max.z);
    return corners;
}

// Builds an octree from all renderers in the scene to optimize
↪    spatial queries.
void BuildOctree()
{
    Renderer[] renderers = FindObjectsOfType<Renderer>();
    if (renderers.Length == 0)
        return;

    // Calculate the scene's collective bounds.
    Bounds sceneBounds = renderers[0].bounds;
    foreach (Renderer rend in renderers)
    {
        sceneBounds.Encapsulate(rend.bounds);
    }

    // Initialize the octree root node with the calculated scene
    ↪    bounds.
    octreeRoot = new OctreeNode(sceneBounds);
    foreach (Renderer rend in renderers)
    {
        octreeRoot.Insert(rend);
    }
}

// Recursively traverses the octree to disable renderers for
↪    nodes that are completely occluded.
void CullOctree(OctreeNode node)
{
    if (node == null)
        return;

    // If the entire octree node's bounds are occluded, disable
    ↪    all contained renderers.
    if (CustomOcclusionTest(node.bounds, occlusionPlanes))
    {
        node.SetRenderersEnabled(false);
        return;
    }
```

```
        // If this is a leaf node, perform individual occlusion
        ↪   tests on each renderer.
        if (node.IsLeaf())
        {
            foreach (Renderer rend in node.objects)
            {
                if (CustomOcclusionTest(rend.bounds,
                ↪   occlusionPlanes))
                    rend.enabled = false;
                else
                    rend.enabled = true;
            }
        }
        else
        {
            // Recursively process child nodes.
            foreach (OctreeNode child in node.children)
            {
                CullOctree(child);
            }
        }
    }
}

// A basic octree node implementation for spatial partitioning.
public class OctreeNode
{
    public Bounds bounds;              // The spatial boundaries
    ↪   of this node.
    public List<Renderer> objects;     // Renderers contained in
    ↪   this node.
    public OctreeNode[] children;      // Child nodes (null if
    ↪   this is a leaf).

    // Maximum number of objects a leaf node may contain before
    ↪   subdividing.
    private const int Capacity = 4;

    public OctreeNode(Bounds bounds)
    {
        this.bounds = bounds;
        objects = new List<Renderer>();
        children = null;
    }

    // Returns true if the node has not been subdivided.
    public bool IsLeaf()
    {
        return children == null;
    }

    // Inserts a renderer into the octree, subdividing if necessary.
```

337

```
public void Insert(Renderer rend)
{
    if (!bounds.Intersects(rend.bounds))
        return;

    if (IsLeaf() && objects.Count < Capacity)
    {
        objects.Add(rend);
    }
    else
    {
        if (IsLeaf())
        {
            Subdivide();
            // Reassign existing objects into appropriate child
            ↪   nodes.
            foreach (Renderer obj in objects)
            {
                foreach (OctreeNode child in children)
                {
                    child.Insert(obj);
                }
            }
            objects.Clear();
        }
        foreach (OctreeNode child in children)
        {
            child.Insert(rend);
        }
    }
}

// Subdivides the current node into 8 equally sized children.
public void Subdivide()
{
    children = new OctreeNode[8];
    Vector3 size = bounds.size / 2f;
    Vector3 center = bounds.center;
    int index = 0;
    for (int x = -1; x <= 1; x += 2)
    {
        for (int y = -1; y <= 1; y += 2)
        {
            for (int z = -1; z <= 1; z += 2)
            {
                Vector3 offset = new Vector3(x, y, z) * size /
                ↪   2f;
                Bounds childBounds = new Bounds(center + offset,
                ↪   size);
                children[index++] = new OctreeNode(childBounds);
            }
        }
    }
```

```
    }

    // Enables or disables all renderers contained within this node
    ↪   (recursively for children).
    public void SetRenderersEnabled(bool enabled)
    {
        if (IsLeaf())
        {
            foreach (Renderer rend in objects)
            {
                if (rend != null)
                    rend.enabled = enabled;
            }
        }
        else
        {
            foreach (OctreeNode child in children)
            {
                child.SetRenderersEnabled(enabled);
            }
        }
    }
}
```

Summary

This C# code snippet integrates the mathematical foundations and algorithmic strategies outlined in the chapter. It demonstrates how to compute occlusion using view frustum planes, perform a custom occlusion test based on bounding volume intersection (V O =), and leverage an octree for spatial partitioning—together ensuring efficient integration of occlusion culling within VR rendering pipelines.

Chapter 45

Managing Level of Detail for Immersive VR

Fundamental Concepts of Level-of-Detail Strategies

Level-of-detail (LOD) management is predicated on the observation that, in three-dimensional renderings, the fidelity of an object's representation may be attenuated as a function of its distance from the observer without incurring perceptible loss in visual quality. In immersive virtual reality environments—characterized by expansive, complex scenes and dual stereoscopic viewpoints—the selective reduction of geometric, shading, and textural complexity is indispensable. The underlying rationale is that an object M, defined by a high polygon count N, can be approximated by a simplified representation M' with a reduced polygon count N' such that

$$N' = \alpha N, \quad \alpha \in (0, 1).$$

This proportional scaling mitigates the computational load associated with detailed rendering, while preserving the salient visual attributes necessary for maintaining immersion. Conceptually, the efficacy of LOD strategies emerges from the non-linear relationship between the apparent size of rendered objects and their actual spatial dimensions, where the projected screen area diminishes with the square of the distance from the observer.

Geometric Simplification and Hierarchical Representations

The generation of multiple representations for a single object relies on geometric simplification methods designed to preserve the object's perceptual features across varying scales. Traditional decimation algorithms, vertex clustering, and edge collapse techniques transform the high-fidelity model M into a series of approximations $\{M_0, M_1, \ldots, M_k\}$ where each successive model M_i embodies reduced detail while approximating the original mesh within an allowable error margin. The error associated with a given simplification is commonly measured by an error metric

$$E = \|M - M_i\|,$$

which quantifies the deviation between the original and the simplified versions. Hierarchical representations, such as progressive meshes or multiresolution analysis, further serve to encapsulate these varying levels of abstraction within a coherent data structure. These structures facilitate rapid selection and switching between models, enabling efficient real-time updates as the observer's viewpoint shifts and the rendered screen space occupied by objects evolves.

Adaptive LOD Selection and Evaluation Metrics

The determination of an appropriate LOD is governed by adaptive techniques that dynamically evaluate the projected prominence of objects. A prevalent measure is the screen-space error metric E_{ss}, which relates the geometric error to the distance d between the object and the observer. This metric is often expressed as

$$E_{ss} = \frac{S}{d^2},$$

where S corresponds to the projected area or a representative scale factor of the object on the display plane. When the computed error E_{ss} exceeds a predefined threshold T, a transition to a higher-fidelity model is triggered; conversely, when $E_{ss} \leq T$, a lower-fidelity version is deemed acceptable. Such adaptive selection mechanisms are crucial in ensuring that the rendering pipeline consistently allocates computational resources to objects that contribute substantively to the visual composition, while simultaneously reducing the overhead associated with extraneous details. Additional evaluation criteria may incorporate angular deviation, occlusion status, and temporal coherence, ensuring that LOD transitions occur seamlessly and do not engender distracting visual artifacts.

Integration of LOD Strategies in Immersive VR Rendering

The integration of LOD management within a virtual reality rendering pipeline mandates a sophisticated orchestration of both spatial data structures and view-dependent algorithms. Given the necessity for stereoscopic rendering, the LOD system must reconcile the requirements of dual camera viewpoints, ensuring uniformity in detail selection to mitigate perceptual discontinuities. Spatial partitioning mechanisms, such as octrees or bounding volume hierarchies (BVH), are often employed to segment the scene into manageable regions. Each region is associated with its own LOD parameters based on its distance from the observer and its relative contribution to the overall scene. In this context, the adaptive LOD algorithm continuously computes screen-space error measures for each object, evaluates potential transitions between LOD levels, and coordinates these updates across both eye buffers. The resultant interplay between the LOD selection criteria and the hierarchical organization of scene elements serves to optimize rendering performance while safeguarding the visual fidelity that is paramount in immersive VR applications.

C# Code Snippet

```
using System.Collections.Generic;
using UnityEngine;

/// <summary>
/// Represents a single Level-of-Detail (LOD) representation for an
↪    object.
```

```csharp
/// It stores the GameObject for this LOD level, the original
↪   high-fidelity polygon count,
/// and a simplification factor "alpha" which is used in the
↪   formula:
///      N' = alpha * N,
/// where N is the original polygon count and N' is the simplified
↪   count.
/// </summary>
public class LODLevel
{
    public GameObject model;                // The GameObject
    ↪   representing this LOD level.
    public int originalPolygonCount;        // Polygon count for the
    ↪   original high-fidelity model.
    public float simplificationFactor;      // Factor (alpha) in (0,1)
    ↪   used to compute simplified polygon count.

    public LODLevel(GameObject model, int originalPolygonCount,
    ↪   float simplificationFactor)
    {
        this.model = model;
        this.originalPolygonCount = originalPolygonCount;
        // Ensure alpha is between 0 and 1.
        this.simplificationFactor =
        ↪   Mathf.Clamp(simplificationFactor, 0.01f, 0.99f);
    }

    // Computes the simplified polygon count using the formula: N' =
    ↪   alpha * N.
    public int GetSimplifiedPolygonCount()
    {
        return Mathf.Max(1, Mathf.RoundToInt(simplificationFactor *
        ↪   originalPolygonCount));
    }
}


/// <summary>
/// Manages LOD selection for an object based on the screen-space
↪   error metric.
/// It demonstrates the evaluation of:
///      E_ss = S / d^2,
/// where S is an approximate screen area factor (derived from the
↪   renderer's bounds)
/// and d is the distance from the observer (camera) to the object.
/// When E_ss is less than an adaptive threshold (scaled per LOD
↪   level),
/// a lower-fidelity model is selected; otherwise, a higher-fidelity
↪   one is used.
/// </summary>
public class LODObject : MonoBehaviour
{
    // List of LOD levels (ordered from highest to lowest fidelity).
    public List<LODLevel> lodLevels = new List<LODLevel>();
```

343

```csharp
// Reference to the main camera (assigned in the inspector or
↳  auto-assigned at runtime).
public Camera mainCamera;

// Base threshold value for screen-space error. The adaptive
↳  criterion multiplies this value
// by the LOD index (i+1) to allow lower LOD models a higher
↳  error tolerance.
public float screenSpaceErrorThreshold = 0.5f;

// Current active LOD index.
private int currentActiveLOD = -1;

void Start()
{
    if (mainCamera == null)
    {
        mainCamera = Camera.main;
    }

    // Activate the highest detail model at startup if
    ↳  available.
    if (lodLevels != null && lodLevels.Count > 0)
    {
        ActivateLOD(0);
    }
}

void Update()
{
    UpdateLOD();
}


/// <summary>
/// Evaluates the current screen-space error and switches LOD
↳  levels if necessary.
/// The screen-space error is computed as:
///     E_ss = S / (d * d),
/// where S is approximated using the magnitude of the
↳  renderer's bounds and d is the distance from the camera.
/// </summary>
void UpdateLOD()
{
    // Compute distance from the camera to this object.
    float distance =
    ↳  Vector3.Distance(mainCamera.transform.position,
    ↳  transform.position);

    // Obtain a renderer component to estimate screen area
    ↳  factor S.
    Renderer objectRenderer =
    ↳  GetComponentInChildren<Renderer>();
```

```
if (objectRenderer == null)
{
    return;
}

// Estimate S as the magnitude of the bounds' size.
float S = objectRenderer.bounds.size.magnitude;

// Compute screen-space error: E_ss = S / (d^2).
float screenSpaceError = S / (distance * distance);

// Determine the appropriate LOD level based on the adaptive
↪   criterion.
int selectedLOD = 0;
for (int i = 0; i < lodLevels.Count; i++)
{
    // Allowed error increases with lower fidelity:
    ↪   allowedError = screenSpaceErrorThreshold * (i+1).
    float allowedError = screenSpaceErrorThreshold * (i +
    ↪   1);
    if (screenSpaceError < allowedError)
    {
        selectedLOD = i;
        break;
    }
}

// If the selected LOD differs from the current one, update
↪   the active model.
if (selectedLOD != currentActiveLOD)
{
    ActivateLOD(selectedLOD);
}
}

/// <summary>
/// Activates the LOD model at the specified index and
↪   deactivates others.
/// </summary>
/// <param name="lodIndex">Index of the LOD level to
↪   activate.</param>
void ActivateLOD(int lodIndex)
{
    for (int i = 0; i < lodLevels.Count; i++)
    {
        if (lodLevels[i].model != null)
        {
            lodLevels[i].model.SetActive(i == lodIndex);
        }
    }

    currentActiveLOD = lodIndex;
}
```

```
}

/// <summary>
/// Utility class providing helper functions for LOD computations.
/// </summary>
public static class LODUtility
{
    /// <summary>
    /// Computes the simplified polygon count using the equation:
    ///     N' = alpha * N,
    /// where N is the original polygon count and alpha is the
    ↪ simplification factor.
    /// </summary>
    /// <param name="originalCount">Original polygon count
    ↪ (N).</param>
    /// <param name="alpha">Simplification factor (alpha), expected
    ↪ to be in (0,1).</param>
    /// <returns>Simplified polygon count (N').</returns>
    public static int ComputeSimplifiedPolygonCount(int
    ↪ originalCount, float alpha)
    {
        alpha = Mathf.Clamp(alpha, 0.01f, 0.99f); // Ensure alpha is
        ↪ within (0,1)
        return Mathf.Max(1, Mathf.RoundToInt(alpha *
        ↪ originalCount));
    }

    /// <summary>
    /// Computes an error metric between the high-fidelity model and
    ↪ its simplified version.
    /// This dummy metric is defined as:
    ///     E = |N - N'|,
    /// where N is the polygon count of the original model and N' is
    ↪ that of the simplified model.
    /// </summary>
    /// <param name="highFidelityCount">Polygon count of the
    ↪ original model (N).</param>
    /// <param name="simplifiedCount">Polygon count of the
    ↪ simplified model (N').</param>
    /// <returns>Error value representing the deviation between
    ↪ models.</returns>
    public static float ComputeModelError(int highFidelityCount, int
    ↪ simplifiedCount)
    {
        return Mathf.Abs(highFidelityCount - simplifiedCount);
    }
}
```

Chapter 46

Implementing VR-Friendly Material Systems

Material Abstraction and Representation in Virtual Reality

In immersive virtual reality, material systems must encapsulate both the physical nuances of surface appearance and the stringent performance requirements imposed by real-time rendering. The design of material representations is governed by physically based rendering (PBR) principles, where each material is characterized by its diffuse, specular, and emissive properties. A key aspect of material abstraction lies in the integration of the bidirectional reflectance distribution function, expressed as

$$f_r(\omega_i, \omega_o),$$

where ω_i and ω_o denote the incident and exitant light directions, respectively. This formalism enables a detailed reproduction of light-surface interactions while allowing the system to interpolate material properties across varying levels of detail. In a virtual reality context, the material model must be robust enough to incorporate layered textures, normal maps, and roughness parameters, yet sufficiently flexible to support dynamic adjustments based on real-time performance metrics.

Optimization Techniques for Shader Design

Shaders form the computational backbone for rendering material appearances in real time. The inherent complexity of realistic materials necessitates a careful balance between visual fidelity and computational efficiency. Techniques such as conditional branching, precomputation of complex mathematical functions, and the use of approximation algorithms are crucial when implementing shaders for virtual reality. The computational cost associated with a shader implementation is often modeled by the relation

$$C = k \cdot P \cdot S,$$

where C represents the cost, P denotes the polygon count of the scene geometry, S signifies the intrinsic complexity of the shader, and k is a proportionality constant reflective of hardware characteristics. The deliberate selection of shader parameters, including the strategic simplification of lighting equations and the omission of less perceptible reflective terms, contributes to lower processing overheads without compromising the overall visual composition.

Texture Management and Compression Strategies

Textures serve to convey surface details beyond the capabilities of geometric modeling and shader execution. In virtual reality, texture resources must be optimized not only for resolution but also for memory bandwidth and storage efficiency. The practical implementation of texture management involves the use of compression algorithms and mipmapping techniques. Mipmaps, where each subsequent level is defined as a reduction by a scale factor of 2^{-i} relative to the original texture size, facilitate continuous texture sampling in accordance with the viewer's distance. By ensuring that only textures commensurate with the current screen-space coverage are utilized, the rendering engine maintains high throughput while minimizing aliasing effects. The use of texture atlases further consolidates multiple materials into a single data block, reducing state changes and draw calls during the rendering process.

Adaptive Parameterization and Material State Management

The dynamic nature of virtual reality environments necessitates an adaptive approach to material parameterization. Material properties can be scaled and modified according to both spatial and temporal constraints. For example, the level of specular intensity and surface roughness may be adjusted in real time based on the distance between the camera and the object, thereby modulating the perceived material quality. Let λ represent a parameter that quantifies the degree of adaptation relative to computational constraints; then the effective material property M_{eff} may be formalized as

$$M_{eff} = M_{base} \cdot \lambda,$$

with M_{base} indicating the baseline material characteristic. Through state management systems that monitor and update these adaptive parameters, material systems can dynamically balance between high-fidelity visual detail and the imperative for optimal performance. This approach ensures that materials contributing less prominently to the current scene are rendered with simplified properties, thereby conserving processing resources and stabilizing the overall frame rate.

Integration of Material Systems with Rendering Pipelines

The final stage in the implementation of VR-friendly material systems involves seamless integration with the rendering pipeline. This integration demands an orchestrated management of multiple material states in parallel with the view-dependent rendering processes. Data structures such as directed acyclic graphs (DAGs) or scene trees are employed to maintain relations between high-fidelity materials and their simplified counterparts. The rendering engine evaluates scene complexity through metrics such as screen-space error and object importance, and subsequently selects an appropriate material variant. The underlying algorithm continuously updates material parameters and binds texture resources under the constraints of real-time feedback loops. This systematic integration minimizes latency and ensures that material transitions occur transparently, thereby upholding the aesthetic integrity and

349

performance robustness requisite for a compelling virtual reality experience.

C# Code Snippet

```csharp
using System;
using System.Numerics;

namespace VRMaterials
{
    // Class representing material properties used in rendering
    public class MaterialProperties
    {
        // Diffuse reflectance coefficient (0 to 1)
        public float Diffuse { get; set; }
        // Specular reflectance coefficient (0 to 1)
        public float Specular { get; set; }
        // Emissive factor
        public float Emissive { get; set; }
        // Surface roughness parameter (higher means rougher)
        public float Roughness { get; set; }
        // Baseline material property for adaptive parameterization
        ↪  (M_base)
        public float BaseProperty { get; set; }

        public MaterialProperties(float diffuse, float specular,
        ↪  float emissive, float roughness, float baseProp)
        {
            Diffuse = diffuse;
            Specular = specular;
            Emissive = emissive;
            Roughness = roughness;
            BaseProperty = baseProp;
        }
    }

    // VRMaterialSystem integrates the equations, formulas, and
    ↪  algorithms
    // discussed in this chapter to manage VR-friendly material
    ↪  systems.
    public class VRMaterialSystem
    {
        /// <summary>
        /// Calculates the Bidirectional Reflectance Distribution
        ↪  Function (BRDF) value.
        /// Approximated using the combination of Lambertian diffuse
        ↪  and a simple specular term.
        ///
        /// Formula:
```

```csharp
///   f_r(_i, _o) = (Diffuse/) + Specular * (max(0, dot(_i,
↪   _o)))^(1/(Roughness + ))
/// </summary>
public static float CalculateBRDF(Vector3 incident, Vector3
↪   exitant, MaterialProperties material)
{
    // Normalize the light direction vectors.
    incident = Vector3.Normalize(incident);
    exitant = Vector3.Normalize(exitant);

    // Lambertian term: diffuse reflection is approximated
    ↪   by Diffuse/.
    float lambertian = material.Diffuse / MathF.PI;

    // Specular term: simple power function of the cosine of
    ↪   the angle between the directions.
    float cosTheta = MathF.Max(0, Vector3.Dot(incident,
    ↪   exitant));
    // Add a small epsilon (0.001f) to avoid division by
    ↪   zero in roughness.
    float specular = material.Specular * MathF.Pow(cosTheta,
    ↪   1.0f / (material.Roughness + 0.001f));

    // Combine both terms.
    return lambertian + specular;
}

/// <summary>
/// Calculates the shader computational cost.
///
/// Formula:
///   C = k * P * S
/// where:
///   C = computational cost,
///   k = hardware-dependent constant,
///   P = polygon count,
///   S = intrinsic shader complexity.
/// </summary>
public static float CalculateShaderCost(int polygonCount,
↪   int shaderComplexity, float k)
{
    return k * polygonCount * shaderComplexity;
}

/// <summary>
/// Calculates the effective material property for adaptive
↪   parameterization.
///
/// Formula:
///   M_eff = M_base *
/// where:
///   M_eff = effective material property,
///   M_base = baseline material property,
```

```csharp
///     = adaptation factor based on computational
↪   constraints.
/// </summary>
public static float CalculateEffectiveMaterialProperty(float
↪   baseProperty, float lambda)
{
    return baseProperty * lambda;
}


/// <summary>
/// Computes the texture size at a given mipmap level.
/// Each mip level is reduced by a scale factor of 2^{-i}.
/// </summary>
public static int CalculateMipMapSize(int textureSize, int
↪   mipLevel)
{
    // Ensure that the computed size is at least 1.
    return Math.Max(1, (int)(textureSize * MathF.Pow(0.5f,
    ↪   mipLevel)));
}


/// <summary>
/// Demonstrates adaptive material state management based on
↪   camera distance.
/// Adjusts the effective material property via an
↪   adaptation factor .
/// </summary>
public static void UpdateMaterialLOD(MaterialProperties
↪   material, float distance)
{
    // Determine adaptation factor  based on distance
    ↪   thresholds.
    float lambda = 1.0f;
    if (distance > 20f)
        lambda = 0.5f;
    else if (distance > 10f)
        lambda = 0.75f;

    float effectiveProperty =
    ↪   CalculateEffectiveMaterialProperty(
    material.BaseProperty, lambda);
    Console.WriteLine($"Distance: {distance:F2} units,
    ↪   Effective Material Property:
    ↪   {effectiveProperty:F2}");
    }
}

// Main Program to demonstrate the VR Material System functions
public class Program
{
    public static void Main(string[] args)
    {
```

```csharp
// Initialize sample material properties: Diffuse,
↪    Specular, Emissive, Roughness, BaseProperty.
MaterialProperties material = new
↪    MaterialProperties(0.8f, 0.5f, 0.2f, 0.3f, 1.0f);

// Define example light directions for BRDF calculation.
Vector3 incident = new Vector3(0, 0, -1);
Vector3 exitant = new Vector3(0, 0, 1);

// Calculate and display the BRDF value.
float brdf = VRMaterialSystem.CalculateBRDF(incident,
↪    exitant, material);
Console.WriteLine($"Calculated BRDF: {brdf:F4}");

// Calculate and display shader computational cost (C =
↪    k * P * S).
int polygonCount = 1000;
int shaderComplexity = 5;
float k = 0.0001f; // Example hardware constant.
float shaderCost =
↪    VRMaterialSystem.CalculateShaderCost(polygonCount,
↪    shaderComplexity, k);
Console.WriteLine($"Calculated Shader Cost:
↪    {shaderCost:F4}");

// Demonstrate mipmap size calculation for a texture of
↪    512 pixels.
int baseTextureSize = 512;
for (int mipLevel = 0; mipLevel < 5; mipLevel++)
{
    int mipSize = VRMaterialSystem.CalculateMipMapSize(
    baseTextureSize, mipLevel);
    Console.WriteLine($"MipMap Level {mipLevel}: Texture
    ↪    Size = {mipSize}");
}

// Update and display adaptive LOD based on different
↪    camera distances.
float[] distances = { 5f, 12f, 25f };
foreach (float distance in distances)
{
    VRMaterialSystem.UpdateMaterialLOD(material,
    ↪    distance);
}

// Simulate integration with the rendering pipeline.
Console.WriteLine("Integrating Material System with
↪    Rendering Pipeline...");
// In an actual VR application, this section would
↪    manage material states,
// bind textures, and update rendering data in real
↪    time.
}
```

```
        }
}
```
_____

Chapter 47

Scripting Interactive Environment Triggers

Event Detection and Classification

The fundamental challenge in designing interactive trigger systems for virtual environments lies in the accurate detection and classification of events. In this context, an event may be defined as any discrete state change originating from either a player action or an environmental fluctuation. The system must continually sample a high-dimensional set of sensor inputs and user interactions, mapping these diverse signals to a well-defined set $E = \{e_1, e_2, \ldots, e_n\}$ of events. Each event e_i is associated with an attribute vector $a_i \in \mathbb{R}^m$ that encapsulates parameters such as position, velocity, intensity, and temporal duration. The detection process is therefore conceived as a function

$$D : \mathbb{R}^k \to E,$$

where D operates on a continuous stream of high-frequency data and yields a discretized output. Emphasis is placed on filtering techniques and statistical thresholding to mitigate the effects of sensor noise and to ensure the robustness of classification in scenarios of partial occlusion or rapid motion.

Architectural Design of Interactive Trigger Systems

The architecture underlying interactive trigger systems must reconcile the dual requirements of high responsiveness with scalability in complex environments. Central to the design is the partitioning of the environment into discrete regions of interest, each governed by its own trigger logic. A hierarchical organization is often realized via a directed acyclic graph (DAG) where nodes represent spatial zones, and edges define the propagation of trigger events across boundaries. Within this framework, modular design principles dictate that each trigger module encapsulates the detection logic, state transformation, and subsequent response instantiation. In the formal sense, a trigger module can be abstracted as a tuple

$$T = \langle I, P, R \rangle,$$

where I denotes the set of input events, P encapsulates the processing function, and R represents the resulting action or state change. The integration of such modules into the broader scene graph ensures that dynamic responses propagate seamlessly, thereby enabling modifications to the virtual world that are both responsive and contextually coherent.

Mathematical Modeling of Trigger Conditions

A rigorous treatment of interactive triggers necessitates the formulation of precise mathematical models that describe both the conditions for activation and the resultant modifications of the virtual environment. Let Γ denote the state space of the environment and consider a trigger condition defined as a predicate function

$$\Theta : \Gamma \to \{0, 1\},$$

where $\Theta(\gamma) = 1$ if and only if the specific environmental or player-action criteria are met at state $\gamma \in \Gamma$. The response mechanism is then formulated as an operator

$$\Delta : \Gamma \times E \to \Gamma,$$

which maps the current environment state and the triggering event to a new state. The overall trigger system is thus expressible as the composite function

$$\Lambda(\gamma, e) = \Delta(\gamma, e) \quad \text{if} \quad \Theta(\gamma) = 1.$$

This formalism allows for a deterministic and predictable modification of the environment in response to a matrix of interactive stimuli. The model supports the inclusion of probabilistic elements as well, by extending Θ to account for stochastic processes that govern uncertainty in player behavior and sensor fidelity.

Dynamic Response and Adaptive Scene Modification

Once an event has been detected and formally classified, the subsequent phase involves the execution of adaptive response algorithms that dynamically alter aspects of the virtual scene. The design of these algorithms is predicated on the need to balance computational efficiency with the intricacy of the modifications being applied. Consider an adaptation factor $\alpha \in [0, 1]$, which modulates the intensity or scale of the response based on available processing resources and real-time performance metrics. The effective transformation of the scene can then be described by the function

$$\Phi : \Gamma \times E \to \Gamma, \quad \Phi(\gamma, e) = \gamma' = \gamma + \alpha \cdot \Delta(\gamma, e),$$

where the addition symbol denotes a suitable operation on the state space that reflects incremental modifications. Such modifications may involve changes to lighting conditions, alterations to physics parameters, or adjustments to object positioning, thereby facilitating a highly interactive and immersive virtual reality experience. The system is typically implemented within a continuous feedback loop that monitors aggregate scene complexity and dynamically regulates α, ensuring that spatial fidelity and interactivity are maintained within predefined performance constraints.

C# Code Snippet

```
using System;
using System.Collections.Generic;
```

```csharp
using System.Linq;
using System.Threading;

namespace VRTriggers
{
    // Represents a discrete event with an attribute vector a_i   ^m.
    public class Event
    {
        public string Name { get; set; }
        public float[] Attributes { get; set; }

        public Event(string name, float[] attributes)
        {
            Name = name;
            Attributes = attributes;
        }
    }

    // Implements the detection function D: ^k → E from sensor data.
    public class Detector
    {
        private float threshold;

        public Detector(float threshold)
        {
            this.threshold = threshold;
        }

        public Event DetectEvent(float[] sensorData)
        {
            // Calculate the average of the sensor inputs as a
            ↪   simple metric.
            float avg = sensorData.Average();
            if (avg > threshold)
            {
                return new Event("HighEvent", sensorData);
            }
            return new Event("NormalEvent", sensorData);
        }
    }

    // Represents the state space   of the environment.
    public class EnvironmentState
    {
        public float LightIntensity { get; set; }
        public float ObjectPosition { get; set; }

        public EnvironmentState(float lightIntensity, float
        ↪   objectPosition)
        {
            LightIntensity = lightIntensity;
            ObjectPosition = objectPosition;
        }
```

```
}

// Delegate defining the processing function P: ( × E) → .
public delegate EnvironmentState
↪  ProcessingFunction(EnvironmentState currentState, Event
↪  triggerEvent);

// Represents a trigger module T = (I, P, R).
public class TriggerModule
{
    public List<Event> InputEvents { get; set; }
    public ProcessingFunction ProcessEvent { get; set; }
    public Action<EnvironmentState> Response { get; set; }

    public TriggerModule(ProcessingFunction processEvent,
    ↪  Action<EnvironmentState> response)
    {
        InputEvents = new List<Event>();
        ProcessEvent = processEvent;
        Response = response;
    }

    // Predicate function :  → {0,1} to check trigger
    ↪  conditions.
    public bool Theta(EnvironmentState state)
    {
        // For demonstration, activate trigger if light
        ↪  intensity is below 0.5.
        return state.LightIntensity < 0.5f;
    }

    // Operator : ( × E) →  to compute the state change given a
    ↪  triggering event.
    public EnvironmentState Delta(EnvironmentState state, Event
    ↪  triggerEvent)
    {
        // Compute a new state based on the sum of event
        ↪  attributes.
        float sumAttributes = triggerEvent.Attributes.Sum();
        float newLight = state.LightIntensity + 0.1f *
        ↪  sumAttributes;
        float newPosition = state.ObjectPosition + 0.05f *
        ↪  sumAttributes;
        return new EnvironmentState(newLight, newPosition);
    }

    // Composite function (, e) = (, e) if () = 1.
    public EnvironmentState Execute(EnvironmentState
    ↪  currentState, Event triggerEvent, float
    ↪  adaptationFactor)
    {
        if (Theta(currentState))
        {
```

```csharp
        // Calculate the state change using the trigger's
        ↪  processing function.
        EnvironmentState deltaState =
        ↪  ProcessEvent(currentState, triggerEvent);
        // Apply the adaptive transformation : ' = +  · ((,
        ↪  e) - ).
        EnvironmentState adaptedState =
        ↪  ApplyAdaptation(currentState, deltaState,
        ↪  adaptationFactor);
        // Execute the associated response action.
        Response(adaptedState);
        return adaptedState;
    }
    return currentState;
}

// Function :  × E → , implementing the adaptation factor
↪  [0,1].
private EnvironmentState ApplyAdaptation(EnvironmentState
↪  oldState, EnvironmentState newState, float alpha)
{
    float adaptedLight = oldState.LightIntensity + alpha *
    ↪  (newState.LightIntensity - oldState.LightIntensity);
    float adaptedPosition = oldState.ObjectPosition + alpha
    ↪  * (newState.ObjectPosition -
    ↪  oldState.ObjectPosition);
    return new EnvironmentState(adaptedLight,
    ↪  adaptedPosition);
}
}

// Main program simulating sensor input and trigger response in
↪  a VR environment.
class Program
{
    static void Main(string[] args)
    {
        // Initialize the environment state    .
        EnvironmentState state = new EnvironmentState(0.3f,
        ↪  5.0f);

        // Create a detector with a predefined threshold to
        ↪  process sensor data.
        Detector detector = new Detector(0.6f);

        // Initialize the trigger module.
        // The processing function P is set to use the Delta
        ↪  operator.
        TriggerModule trigger = new TriggerModule(
            (currentState, triggerEvent) =>
            ↪  trigger.Delta(currentState, triggerEvent),
            (newState) =>
            {
```

```
                Console.WriteLine("Response executed: New Light
                ↪   Intensity = "
                    + newState.LightIntensity + ", New Object
                    ↪   Position = " + newState.ObjectPosition);
        }
    );

    // Define an adaptation factor   [0,1] for dynamic
    ↪   response scaling.
    float adaptationFactor = 0.8f;

    // Simulation loop to represent continuous sensor
    ↪   sampling and trigger execution.
    Random rand = new Random();
    for (int i = 0; i < 10; i++)
    {
        // Simulate a 3-dimensional sensor input vector.
        float[] sensorData = new float[3];
        for (int j = 0; j < sensorData.Length; j++)
        {
            sensorData[j] = (float)rand.NextDouble();
        }

        // Use the detector to map sensor data to an event e
        ↪   E.
        Event detectedEvent =
        ↪   detector.DetectEvent(sensorData);
        Console.WriteLine("Detected event: " +
        ↪   detectedEvent.Name);

        // Update the environment state using the trigger
        ↪   module.
        state = trigger.Execute(state, detectedEvent,
        ↪   adaptationFactor);
        Console.WriteLine("Updated Environment State: Light
        ↪   = "
            + state.LightIntensity + ", Position = " +
            ↪   state.ObjectPosition);
        Console.WriteLine("----------------------");

        // Pause to simulate real-time sampling.
        Thread.Sleep(1000);
    }
    }
    }
}
```

Chapter 48

Integrating Particle Collision Systems

Particle Representations and Collision Primitives

Particle systems are modeled as collections of discrete elements, each characterized by a spatial position $p_i \in \mathbb{R}^3$, a velocity vector $v_i \in \mathbb{R}^3$, and an effective collision radius $r_i \in \mathbb{R}$. In many implementations, the collision primitive is chosen to be a sphere due to the mathematical simplicity of its intersection tests. Two particles, indexed by i and j, are considered to be in collision when the condition

$$\|p_i - p_j\| < (r_i + r_j)$$

is satisfied. This relation employs the Euclidean norm to measure the distance between the particles, thereby providing an efficient and robust criterion for collision detection. The abstraction of complex objects via composite bounding volumes further enhances the versatility of these models in dynamic settings.

Spatial Partitioning and Optimization Strategies

The high computational cost associated with evaluating collisions among large numbers of particles necessitates the use of spatial partitioning techniques. Spatial data structures, such as uniform grids, k-d trees, and bounding volume hierarchies, partition the state space $\mathbb{R}^3$ into disjoint regions $\{R_1, R_2, \ldots, R_k\}$. Given a set of particles $\mathcal{P}$, candidate collision pairs are limited to those particles residing within the same region or in adjacent regions, thereby reducing the number of pairwise comparisons required. The collision detection function

$$C : \mathcal{P} \times \mathcal{P} \to \{0, 1\}$$

is consequently applied only to these localized subsets, yielding significant improvements in computational efficiency. Such partitioning strategies are analyzed in terms of their average case complexity, which, under favorable conditions, approaches $O(n \log n)$ relative to the number of particles n.

Collision Detection Algorithms and Theoretical Considerations

The core of particle collision detection lies in the rigorous formulation of detection algorithms that operate on the system state

$$S(t) = \{(p_i(t), v_i(t), r_i) : i = 1, 2, \ldots, n\}.$$

Time integration methods, including Euler and Runge-Kutta schemes, are employed to predict future states via a temporal projection function

$$\Psi : S(t) \times \Delta t \to S(t + \Delta t).$$

This predictive capability enhances the detection of imminent collisions, allowing the system to pre-emptively evaluate interactions within the time interval Δt. The collision condition for a pair of particles is formally expressed as

$$C(p_i, p_j, t) = \begin{cases} 1, & \text{if } \|p_i(t) - p_j(t)\| < (r_i + r_j), \\ 0, & \text{otherwise.} \end{cases}$$

For situations involving simultaneous collisions, iterative resolution methods are implemented, incorporating factors such as conservation of momentum and energy. The utilization of restitution coefficients, denoted by $e \in [0, 1]$, modulates the post-collision velocity vectors, ensuring that the physical responses adhere to realistic dynamics.

Integration of Collision Responses with Interactive Visual Effects

Collision events serve as pivotal triggers for a wide spectrum of interactive visual effects within the simulation environment. Upon detection, a collision event E, containing both spatial and kinetic data, is mapped by a transformation operator

$$\Phi : S \times E \to S',$$

which synthesizes the current system state S with the collision information to produce an updated state S'. The operator Φ is responsible for adjusting visual properties such as luminosity, color, and trajectory of particles, thereby conveying the perceptible impact of the collision. The propagation of collision-induced state changes into visual effects is governed by a complex interplay between real-time rendering systems and dynamic state updates. This framework ensures that interactive visual phenomena are tightly coupled with the underlying physics, allowing for immediate and coherent visual feedback in response to both automated in-game events and user interactions.

Real-Time Considerations and Interaction Dynamics

The integration of particle collision systems within an interactive environment imposes stringent real-time processing constraints. For a fixed update interval Δt, the collision detection and resolution pipeline must operate with sufficient efficiency to maintain smooth system dynamics. The continuous monitoring of performance metrics allows the system to adapt its computational strategies, optimizing for both accuracy and speed. In scenarios induced by user actions, where particle distributions may change rapidly, the collision system must seamlessly scale to accommodate increased computational loads without introducing perceptible latency. Analytical models, supported by empirical benchmarks, offer guidance in tuning the parameters of spatial partitioning algorithms and collision response mechanisms. The resulting synchronization between physical simulation and visual representation is critical for preserving the integrity of interactive visual effects in dynamic virtual environments.

C# Code Snippet

```csharp
using UnityEngine;
using System.Collections.Generic;

/// <summary>
/// Represents a particle with a position, velocity, collision
↪   radius, and visual color.
/// </summary>
public class Particle
{
    public Vector3 Position;
    public Vector3 Velocity;
    public float Radius;
    public Color Color;

    public Particle(Vector3 position, Vector3 velocity, float
    ↪   radius, Color color)
    {
        Position = position;
        Velocity = velocity;
        Radius = radius;
        Color = color;
    }
}

/// <summary>
/// Simulates particle collisions using both naive and spatial
↪   partitioning methods,
/// integrates particle motion via Euler's method, and applies
↪   collision responses
/// with restitution. This class is designed to be attached to a
↪   Unity GameObject.
/// </summary>
public class ParticleCollisionSimulator : MonoBehaviour
{
    // List of all particles in the simulation.
    public List<Particle> Particles = new List<Particle>();

    // Time step for Euler integration.
    public float DeltaTime = 0.02f;

    // Restitution coefficient (in [0,1]) controlling bounciness.
    public float Restitution = 0.8f;

    // Grid cell size used for spatial partitioning.
    public float GridCellSize = 1.0f;

    // Toggle between naive collision detection and spatial
    ↪   partitioning.
    public bool UseSpatialPartitioning = true;
```

```csharp
// Dictionary used for partitioning space; key is cell index,
↪  value is the list of particles in that cell.
private Dictionary<Vector3Int, List<Particle>> grid = new
↪  Dictionary<Vector3Int, List<Particle>>();

/// <summary>
/// Initialize the simulation with a set of randomly generated
↪  particles.
/// </summary>
void Start()
{
    // Create an ensemble of 50 particles placed randomly within
    ↪  a defined volume.
    for (int i = 0; i < 50; i++)
    {
        Vector3 pos = new Vector3(
            Random.Range(-5f, 5f),
            Random.Range(-5f, 5f),
            Random.Range(-5f, 5f)
        );
        Vector3 vel = new Vector3(
            Random.Range(-1f, 1f),
            Random.Range(-1f, 1f),
            Random.Range(-1f, 1f)
        );
        float radius = Random.Range(0.2f, 0.5f);
        Color col = Color.white;
        Particles.Add(new Particle(pos, vel, radius, col));
    }
}

/// <summary>
/// Update is called once per frame, handling particle motion,
↪  collision detection,
/// collision resolution, and triggering of visual effects.
/// </summary>
void Update()
{
    // Update particle positions using Euler integration:
    // p(t + t) = p(t) + v(t) * t.
    foreach (Particle p in Particles)
    {
        p.Position += p.Velocity * DeltaTime;
    }

    // Detect collisions: choose between naive O(n^2) approach
    ↪  and spatial partitioning.
    if (UseSpatialPartitioning)
    {
        BuildSpatialGrid();
        DetectCollisionsUsingSpatialPartitioning();
    }
    else
```

```
    {
        DetectCollisionsNaive();
    }

    // Update visual effects to reflect any collision responses.
    UpdateVisualEffects();
}

/// <summary>
/// Implements naive collision detection by checking all unique
↪   particle pairs.
/// Uses the collision condition:
///   ||p_i - p_j|| < (r_i + r_j)
/// </summary>
void DetectCollisionsNaive()
{
    int count = Particles.Count;
    for (int i = 0; i < count; i++)
    {
        for (int j = i + 1; j < count; j++)
        {
            if (CheckCollision(Particles[i], Particles[j]))
            {
                ResolveCollision(Particles[i], Particles[j]);
                TriggerCollisionEffect(Particles[i],
↪                   Particles[j]);
            }
        }
    }
}

/// <summary>
/// Constructs a spatial grid to partition particles, reducing
↪   the number of collision checks.
/// </summary>
void BuildSpatialGrid()
{
    grid.Clear();
    foreach (Particle p in Particles)
    {
        Vector3Int cell = GetCellIndex(p.Position);
        if (!grid.ContainsKey(cell))
        {
            grid[cell] = new List<Particle>();
        }
        grid[cell].Add(p);
    }
}

/// <summary>
/// Uses the spatial grid to detect collisions by checking
↪   particles within the same and adjacent cells.
/// </summary>
```

```
void DetectCollisionsUsingSpatialPartitioning()
{
    foreach (KeyValuePair<Vector3Int, List<Particle>> cellEntry
    ↪  in grid)
    {
        Vector3Int cell = cellEntry.Key;
        List<Particle> cellParticles = cellEntry.Value;

        // Check collisions within the same cell.
        for (int i = 0; i < cellParticles.Count; i++)
        {
            for (int j = i + 1; j < cellParticles.Count; j++)
            {
                if (CheckCollision(cellParticles[i],
                ↪  cellParticles[j]))
                {
                    ResolveCollision(cellParticles[i],
                    ↪  cellParticles[j]);
                    TriggerCollisionEffect(cellParticles[i],
                    ↪  cellParticles[j]);
                }
            }
        }

        // Check collisions with neighboring cells.
        for (int x = -1; x <= 1; x++)
        {
            for (int y = -1; y <= 1; y++)
            {
                for (int z = -1; z <= 1; z++)
                {
                    // Skip the current cell.
                    if (x == 0 && y == 0 && z == 0)
                        continue;

                    Vector3Int neighborCell = new
                    ↪  Vector3Int(cell.x + x, cell.y + y,
                    ↪  cell.z + z);
                    if (grid.ContainsKey(neighborCell))
                    {
                        List<Particle> neighborParticles =
                        ↪  grid[neighborCell];
                        foreach (Particle p1 in cellParticles)
                        {
                            foreach (Particle p2 in
                            ↪  neighborParticles)
                            {
                                if (CheckCollision(p1, p2))
                                {
                                    ResolveCollision(p1, p2);
                                    TriggerCollisionEffect(p1,
                                    ↪  p2);
                                }
```

```
                            }
                        }
                    }
                }
            }
        }
    }
}
```

```
/// <summary>
/// Converts a world position to a cell index for spatial
↪    partitioning.
/// </summary>
/// <param name="position">The world space position.</param>
/// <returns>A Vector3Int representing the cell index.</returns>
Vector3Int GetCellIndex(Vector3 position)
{
    int x = Mathf.FloorToInt(position.x / GridCellSize);
    int y = Mathf.FloorToInt(position.y / GridCellSize);
    int z = Mathf.FloorToInt(position.z / GridCellSize);
    return new Vector3Int(x, y, z);
}
```

```
/// <summary>
/// Checks whether two particles are colliding based on the
↪    distance criterion:
///     ||p_i - p_j|| < (r_i + r_j)
/// </summary>
/// <param name="p1">First particle.</param>
/// <param name="p2">Second particle.</param>
/// <returns>True if a collision is detected; otherwise,
↪    false.</returns>
bool CheckCollision(Particle p1, Particle p2)
{
    float distance = Vector3.Distance(p1.Position, p2.Position);
    return distance < (p1.Radius + p2.Radius);
}
```

```
/// <summary>
/// Resolves a collision between two particles using an elastic
↪    collision model with restitution.
/// The impulse-based resolution follows:
///     v1' = v1 - (1+e) * (dot(v1-v2, n)/(2)) * n,
/// where n is the normalized vector from p1 to p2.
/// </summary>
/// <param name="p1">First particle.</param>
/// <param name="p2">Second particle.</param>
void ResolveCollision(Particle p1, Particle p2)
{
    Vector3 n = p2.Position - p1.Position;
    float distance = n.magnitude;
    if (distance == 0f) return;
    n.Normalize();
```

```
        // Compute relative velocity and its component along the
        ↪   collision normal.
        Vector3 relativeVelocity = p1.Velocity - p2.Velocity;
        float velAlongNormal = Vector3.Dot(relativeVelocity, n);

        // Do not resolve if particles are moving away from each
        ↪   other.
        if (velAlongNormal > 0)
            return;

        // Compute impulse scalar (assumes equal mass for both
        ↪   particles).
        float j = -(1 + Restitution) * velAlongNormal / 2f;
        Vector3 impulse = j * n;
        p1.Velocity += impulse;
        p2.Velocity -= impulse;
    }

    /// <summary>
    /// Triggers collision-induced visual effects. In this example,
    ↪   particle colors are temporarily
    /// changed to red to indicate a collision event.
    /// </summary>
    /// <param name="p1">First colliding particle.</param>
    /// <param name="p2">Second colliding particle.</param>
    void TriggerCollisionEffect(Particle p1, Particle p2)
    {
        p1.Color = Color.red;
        p2.Color = Color.red;
        // In a complete implementation, additional visual feedback
        ↪   (such as particle bursts or dynamic lighting)
        // could be triggered here.
    }

    /// <summary>
    /// Updates the visual representation of particles in the scene.
    /// This placeholder function would typically interface with
    ↪   Unity's rendering engine,
    /// updating GameObjects or UI elements to reflect the current
    ↪   state of each particle.
    /// </summary>
    void UpdateVisualEffects()
    {
        // Placeholder: In a full application, update the positions,
        ↪   colors, and other properties
        // of the GameObjects representing each particle.
    }
}
```

Summary

This code snippet demonstrates the implementation of core equations and algorithms for a particle collision system. Key features include Euler-based time integration, collision detection using the sphere intersection criterion ($\|p\_i - p\_j\| < r\_i + r\_j$), impulse-based collision resolution with restitution, and an optional spatial partitioning system to optimize collision checks. The snippet also outlines where interactive visual effects can be integrated to reflect real-time collision events in a virtual environment.

Chapter 49

Scripting Real-Time Environmental Reactions

Overview of Real-Time Reaction Mechanisms

The fundamental challenge in designing environments that react in real time to player interactions lies in the tight coupling between event detection and state transformation. Complex virtual worlds must continuously evaluate a stream of discrete events, each associated with varying degrees of spatial and temporal significance. In this context, an event is formalized as an element $e \in \mathcal{E}$, where the set $\mathcal{E}$ encapsulates all triggers generated by interactive entities, environmental sensors, and auxiliary input devices. The virtual environment maintains a dynamic state $S(t)$ at time t, which is modified reactively in response to these events. The framework employs high-frequency update loops whereby state transitions, denoted by the operator Ψ, are computed as

$$S(t + \Delta t) = \Psi(S(t), e(t)),$$

illustrating that the system dynamics are inherently dependent on both the current state and the incoming event signals. Such continuous evaluation enforces a stringent real-time processing paradigm that is critical for preserving the immersive nature of the simulation.

Event-Driven Architectures in Virtual Environments

A robust implementation of real-time environmental reactions is predicated on an event-driven architecture that supports asynchronous processing. In this paradigm, events are not polled in a rigid sequence; instead, they are received and processed concurrently to maximize responsiveness. Each event e_i is annotated with parameters such as timestamp t_i, location vector $\mathbf{x_i} \in \mathbb{R}^3$, and a set of context descriptors that inform the reaction logic. The architecture is designed to propagate these events through a series of middleware layers, each tasked with filtering, prioritizing, and dispatching events to the appropriate subsystems. Such a design encourages modularity and scalability, ensuring that the computational overhead of processing event streams does not compromise the system's overall responsiveness.

Modeling Environmental Dynamics and State Transitions

In complex interactive simulations, the environment is regarded as a composite system whose state $S(t)$ comprises a high-dimensional vector containing spatial layouts, ambient lighting parameters, material properties, and behavioral modifiers. State transitions are modeled by mapping relationships of the form

$$S(t + \Delta t) = \Phi\big(S(t), \{e_i(t)\}_{i=1}^{k}\big),$$

where the transformation operator Φ assimilates the cumulative effect of multiple events over the interval Δt. This formulation allows the synthesis of intricate responses such as alterations in weather conditions, dynamic modifications of terrain, or shifts in acoustic profiles. The operator Φ is typically instantiated via a combination of finite state machines and differential equation solvers, ensuring that the environmental updates adhere to rigorously defined physical or aesthetic heuristics. The precision of these transition models is paramount, as even minimal deviations can disrupt the perceptual continuity essential for immersive experiences.

Temporal Synchronization and Coherent Update Cycles

Temporal coherence in environmental reactions is achieved by enforcing a strict synchronization between the computational update cycle and the perceived real-time progression of the simulation. The system is designed to operate at a fixed refresh rate, with the time increment Δt determined by a target frequency f, such that

$$\Delta t = \frac{1}{f}.$$

This temporal granularity ensures that discrete events are integrated with minimal latency, allowing for immediate modifications to the environment upon the occurrence of a trigger. The architecture incorporates event buffering and timestamp correction mechanisms to manage potential discrepancies arising from asynchronous event arrivals. Moreover, iterative refinement techniques are applied to reconcile the state of the environment across successive update cycles, thereby guaranteeing that the environmental dynamics remain both spatially and temporally coherent.

Adaptive Control of Visual and Auditory Feedback

Adaptive control of sensory feedback constitutes a critical facet of real-time environmental reactions. The environment is configured to modulate visual and auditory parameters in direct correspondence to the intensity and nature of incoming events. The feedback functions, denoted by F_v for visual cues and F_a for auditory signals, are defined as

$$F_v(t) = \Phi_v(S(t), e(t)) \quad \text{and} \quad F_a(t) = \Phi_a(S(t), e(t)),$$

where Φ_v and Φ_a are transformation operators that map the current state and event data onto modifications in brightness, color tone, spatial positioning of sound sources, and dynamic range of acoustic elements. These functions are designed to adapt continuously to evolving interaction patterns, ensuring that each player action is met with an appropriate and perceptually coherent response. By establishing a direct correlation between interactive triggers and sensory outputs, the system reinforces immersion and enables a richer, more engaging virtual experience.

C# Code Snippet

```csharp
using System;
using System.Collections.Generic;
using UnityEngine;

// Represents the dynamic state S(t) of the virtual environment.
public class EnvironmentState
{
    // Ambient color and light intensity define the visual state.
    public Color AmbientColor { get; set; }
    public float LightIntensity { get; set; }

    // Sound volume represents the auditory state.
    public float SoundVolume { get; set; }

    // TerrainModifier can simulate dynamic changes in spatial
    ↪   layout.
    public Vector3 TerrainModifier { get; set; }

    // Constructor initializing default state values.
    public EnvironmentState()
    {
        AmbientColor = Color.gray;
        LightIntensity = 1.0f;
        SoundVolume = 1.0f;
        TerrainModifier = Vector3.zero;
    }
}

// Represents an event e   that triggers reactions in the
↪   environment.
public class InteractiveEvent
{
    public float Timestamp { get; set; }
    public Vector3 Location { get; set; }
    public string EventType { get; set; }

    // Additional context descriptors to refine reaction logic.
    public Dictionary<string, object> ContextDescriptors { get; set;
    ↪   }

    public InteractiveEvent(float timestamp, Vector3 location,
    ↪   string eventType)
    {
        Timestamp = timestamp;
        Location = location;
        EventType = eventType;
        ContextDescriptors = new Dictionary<string, object>();
    }
}
```

```csharp
// Manages real-time environmental reactions via state updates and
↪    feedback mechanisms.
public class EnvironmentManager : MonoBehaviour
{
    // Target refresh frequency f (with t = 1/f).
    public float TargetFrequency = 60.0f;
    private float DeltaTime;

    // Current state S(t) of the environment.
    private EnvironmentState currentState;

    // A queue to store incoming events e(t).
    private List<InteractiveEvent> eventQueue;

    void Start()
    {
        // Initialize t = 1 / f for precise temporal
        ↪    synchronization.
        DeltaTime = 1.0f / TargetFrequency;

        // Set up the initial environment state S(0).
        currentState = new EnvironmentState();

        // Initialize the event queue.
        eventQueue = new List<InteractiveEvent>();
    }

    void Update()
    {
        // For demonstration: simulate event generation.
        SimulateEventGeneration();

        // Process all queued events and update the environment
        ↪    state.
        // Implements S(t + t) = (S(t), e(t)) and its aggregated
        ↪    version.
        ProcessEventQueue();

        // Apply adaptive visual feedback, corresponding to F_v(t) =
        ↪    _v(S(t), e(t)).
        ApplyVisualFeedback();

        // Apply adaptive auditory feedback, corresponding to F_a(t)
        ↪    = _a(S(t), e(t)).
        ApplyAudioFeedback();
    }

    // -------------------------------------
    // Simulation helper: Generate events at runtime.
    void SimulateEventGeneration()
    {
        // Trigger a "lightChange" event every second.
```

```csharp
    if (Time.frameCount % Mathf.RoundToInt(TargetFrequency) ==
    ↪   0)
    {
        var lightEvent = new InteractiveEvent(
            Time.time,
            new Vector3(UnityEngine.Random.Range(-5, 5), 0,
            ↪   UnityEngine.Random.Range(-5, 5)),
            "lightChange"
        );
        eventQueue.Add(lightEvent);
    }

    // Trigger a "soundChange" event roughly every half-second.
    if (Time.frameCount % Mathf.RoundToInt(TargetFrequency *
    ↪   0.5f) == 0)
    {
        var soundEvent = new InteractiveEvent(
            Time.time,
            new Vector3(UnityEngine.Random.Range(-10, 10), 0,
            ↪   UnityEngine.Random.Range(-10, 10)),
            "soundChange"
        );
        eventQueue.Add(soundEvent);
    }
}

// Public method to add events externally.
public void AddEvent(InteractiveEvent interactiveEvent)
{
    eventQueue.Add(interactiveEvent);
}

// Processes the event queue and updates state using the
↪   transformation operator :
// S(t + t) = (S(t), {e_i(t)}).
void ProcessEventQueue()
{
    if (eventQueue.Count == 0) return;

    // Sequentially process each event.
    foreach (var e in eventQueue)
    {
        // Update state based on each event.
        currentState = Phi(currentState, e);
    }

    // Clear the queue after processing.
    eventQueue.Clear();
}

// Transformation operator  that maps the current state and an
↪   event to a new state.
EnvironmentState Phi(EnvironmentState state, InteractiveEvent e)
```

377

```
{
    // Determine the type of event and update state properties
    ↪    accordingly.
    switch (e.EventType)
    {
        case "lightChange":
            {
                // Calculate distance to simulate spatial
                ↪    influence on light intensity.
                float distance = Vector3.Distance(e.Location,
                ↪    Vector3.zero);
                state.LightIntensity = Mathf.Clamp(1.0f -
                ↪    distance / 10.0f, 0.0f, 1.0f);
                // Gradually shift ambient color towards white.
                state.AmbientColor =
                ↪    Color.Lerp(state.AmbientColor, Color.white,
                ↪    0.5f);
                break;
            }
        case "soundChange":
            {
                // Adjust sound volume based on the event's
                ↪    spatial attributes.
                float distance = Vector3.Distance(e.Location,
                ↪    Vector3.zero);
                state.SoundVolume = Mathf.Clamp(1.0f - distance
                ↪    / 20.0f, 0.0f, 1.0f);
                break;
            }
        case "terrainMod":
            {
                // Modify terrain characteristics as an example
                ↪    of state change.
                state.TerrainModifier = new Vector3(1, 0, 0);
                break;
            }
        default:
            {
                // Handle other event types if necessary.
                break;
            }
    }
    return state;
}

// Applies visual changes to the environment (e.g., ambient
↪    lighting).
void ApplyVisualFeedback()
{
    RenderSettings.ambientLight = currentState.AmbientColor *
    ↪    currentState.LightIntensity;
}
```

```
// Applies auditory changes (e.g., global audio volume
↪    adjustment).
void ApplyAudioFeedback()
{
    AudioListener.volume = currentState.SoundVolume;
}
}
```

Summary: The above C# code snippet implements a comprehensive event-driven architecture for real-time environmental reactions in a VR setting. It models the environment's dynamic state S(t) and processes incoming interactive events to update the state via a transformation operator (). The code also demonstrates adaptive visual and auditory feedback mechanisms, ensuring that state changes are synchronized with a fixed update cycle (t = 1/f), thereby maintaining immersive, responsive virtual experiences.

Chapter 50

Implementing Dynamic Object Spawning in VR

Theoretical Underpinnings and Architectural Considerations

Dynamic object instantiation within virtual reality environments can be rigorously modeled as a transformation function

$$\Theta : S(t) \times \Omega \to S(t + \Delta t),$$

where $S(t)$ denotes the state of the environment at time t, and Ω represents the domain of spawning criteria derived from spatial, contextual, and interaction-driven analyses. The architectural framework supporting dynamic spawning seamlessly integrates event detection, spatial reasoning, and resource management into a unified system. In this formalism, each instantiation event influences the progression of the environment by modifying state variables in a manner that preserves both consistency and interactivity. The design necessitates precise mathematical characterizations of instantiation triggers and their corresponding state transitions to ensure that every spawned object adheres to the established environmental semantics.

Event-Driven Object Instantiation Mechanisms

Within this paradigm, real-time responsiveness arises from an event-driven approach whereby instantiation events are detected as elements

$$e \in \mathcal{E},$$

of a pre-defined set of triggers. Each event is evaluated in the context of spatial proximity and the prevailing environmental conditions before the instantiation process is initiated. A conditional spawning function may be formulated as

$$\Theta^*(e, S(t)) = \begin{cases} 1, & \text{if } \|\mathbf{x}_{\text{user}} - \mathbf{x}_{\text{trigger}}\| < \varepsilon \text{ and } \chi(e) \geq \xi, \\ 0, & \text{otherwise,} \end{cases}$$

where $\mathbf{x}_{\text{user}}$ and $\mathbf{x}_{\text{trigger}}$ signify the respective positions of the user and the event generator, ε is a predetermined spatial threshold, and $\chi(e)$ quantifies the intensity of the event relative to a threshold ξ. This formalism ensures that object spawning occurs only when environmental and spatial criteria are simultaneously satisfied, yielding a controlled and purposeful object instantiation process.

Resource Allocation, Object Pooling, and Optimization Constraints

Efficient resource management is paramount within performance-sensitive VR applications. The inherent latency associated with dynamic memory allocation is mitigated through the implementation of object pooling, wherein pre-initialized object instances are recycled to accommodate successive instantiation events. The object pool, denoted by

$$\mathcal{P},$$

comprises a finite set of objects $O_i \in \mathcal{P}$ that are maintained in a dormant state until activated by a spawning event. The dynamic adjustment of the pool can be mathematically represented as

$$\mathcal{P}(t + \Delta t) = \Gamma\big(\mathcal{P}(t), \lambda(t)\big),$$

where $\lambda(t)$ models the temporal demand for object instantiation, and Γ encapsulates the reallocation and replenishment strategies.

Such optimization ensures that the instantiation overhead remains minimal, thereby preserving the high-performance standards essential for immersive VR experiences.

Spatial Modeling and Contextual Criteria for Spawning

The spatial distribution and contextual relevance of spawned objects are determined by integrating spatial modeling techniques into the instantiation pipeline. The mapping function

$$P : \mathbb{R}^3 \to \mathbb{R}^3$$

assigns precise coordinates for newly instantiated objects by factoring in the user's current location, environmental topology, and ancillary contextual parameters. Formally, the spawn position is computed as

$$\mathbf{x}_{\text{spawn}} = P(\mathbf{x}_{\text{user}}, \mathbf{C}),$$

where $\mathbf{C}$ denotes an array of contextual descriptors that include ambient conditions, density metrics, and thematic constraints. Advanced spatial partitioning methodologies, such as grid-based decompositions and hierarchical octree structures, facilitate the rapid evaluation of viable spawn locations. These techniques ensure that any instantiation aligns harmoniously with the surrounding virtual landscape, thereby sustaining both visual coherence and interactive integrity.

Temporal Dynamics and Feedback Integration

Temporal synchrony is critical to the seamless incorporation of dynamically spawned objects into the virtual scene. The continuous update cycle of the simulation defines a discrete time increment

$$\Delta t = \frac{1}{f},$$

with f representing the refresh frequency of the simulation. Within each update cycle, the instantiation mechanism evaluates pending events and integrates new objects into the scene in concordance with this temporal discretization. Feedback integration further refines the spawning process by incorporating real-time performance metrics and interaction data. These are assimilated into adaptive control loops that modulate spawning parameters based on evolving environmental conditions. The resulting system dynamically calibrates the frequency, positioning, and characteristics of spawned objects, ensuring that they contribute to a continuously evolving and interactive virtual reality experience.

C# Code Snippet

```csharp
using UnityEngine;
using System.Collections.Generic;

// This class encapsulates the dynamic object spawning mechanism,
//    integrating event-driven triggers,
// spatial mapping, object pooling, and temporal regulation based on
//    theoretical formalisms.
public class DynamicObjectSpawner : MonoBehaviour
{
    // Configuration Parameters (thresholds and simulation timing)
    public GameObject objectPrefab;                 // Prefab to be
    //    spawned
    public float spawnThresholdDistance = 5.0f;    // : Maximum
    //    distance between user and event trigger
    public float eventIntensityThreshold = 0.5f;   // : Minimum
    //    intensity chi(e) required for spawning
    public float refreshFrequency = 60.0f;         // f: Refresh
    //    frequency of the simulation
    public int initialPoolSize = 10;               // Initial pool
    //    size for object pooling

    private List<GameObject> objectPool;            // Represents the
    //    pool of pre-initialized objects
    private float deltaTime;                         // t computed as
    //    1/f (temporal discretization)
    private Transform userTransform;                // Represents
    //    S(t): the current state (user's position)

    void Start()
    {
        // Initialize temporal dynamics and reference to the user
        //    (main camera)
        deltaTime = 1.0f / refreshFrequency;
        userTransform = Camera.main.transform;
        InitializeObjectPool();
    }

    void Update()
```

383

```
{
    // In an actual VR application, events would come from
    ↪   interaction or environmental triggers.
    // For demonstration, we simulate an event when the user
    ↪   presses the Space key.
    if (Input.GetKeyDown(KeyCode.Space))
    {
        // Simulate an event e  with a random trigger position
        ↪   offset and intensity value.
        EventData e = new EventData();
        e.triggerPosition = userTransform.position + new
        ↪   Vector3(
            Random.Range(1.0f, 3.0f),
            0,
            Random.Range(1.0f, 3.0f));
        e.intensity = Random.Range(0.0f, 1.0f);

        // Process the event by evaluating it and, if conditions
        ↪   are met, spawning an object.
        ProcessSpawnEvent(e);
    }
}


// Initializes the object pool: (t) is pre-populated with
↪   inactive objects.
void InitializeObjectPool()
{
    objectPool = new List<GameObject>();
    for (int i = 0; i < initialPoolSize; i++)
    {
        GameObject obj = Instantiate(objectPrefab);
        obj.SetActive(false);
        objectPool.Add(obj);
    }
}


// Evaluates a spawn event using the conditional function *
↪   defined as:
// *(e, S(t)) = 1 if || x_user - x_trigger || <  and (e)  , else
↪   0.
bool EvaluateSpawn(EventData e)
{
    float distance = Vector3.Distance(userTransform.position,
    ↪   e.triggerPosition);
    if (distance < spawnThresholdDistance && e.intensity >=
    ↪   eventIntensityThreshold)
    {
        return true;
    }
    return false;
}
```

```csharp
// Computes the spawn position using the mapping function P: ˉ3
↪   → ˉ3,
// which considers the user's current position and contextual
↪   descriptors.
Vector3 ComputeSpawnPosition(Vector3 userPos)
{
    // For demonstration, an offset within the defined threshold
    ↪   is calculated.
    Vector3 contextOffset = new Vector3(
        Random.Range(-spawnThresholdDistance,
        ↪   spawnThresholdDistance),
        0,
        Random.Range(-spawnThresholdDistance,
        ↪   spawnThresholdDistance));
    return userPos + contextOffset;
}

// Processes an event by evaluating its eligibility and spawning
↪   an object if conditions are met.
// This mimics the transformation : S(t) x  → S(t+t) by updating
↪   scene state.
void ProcessSpawnEvent(EventData e)
{
    if (EvaluateSpawn(e))
    {
        // Retrieve an available object from the pool  or expand
        ↪   the pool if necessary.
        GameObject obj = GetPooledObject();
        if (obj != null)
        {
            // Compute the dynamic spawn position using the
            ↪   spatial model P.
            Vector3 spawnPosition =
            ↪   ComputeSpawnPosition(userTransform.position);
            obj.transform.position = spawnPosition;
            obj.SetActive(true);

            // Feedback Integration: Log instantiation details
            ↪   for debugging purposes.
            Debug.Log("Spawned object at " + spawnPosition + "
            ↪   with event intensity " + e.intensity);
        }
    }
    else
    {
        // Condition not met: No instantiation occurs.
        Debug.Log("Event did not meet spawning criteria.
        ↪   Distance or intensity threshold not reached.");
    }
}

// Retrieves an inactive object from the object pool, reflecting
↪   the reallocation strategy
```

```csharp
    // represented by (P(t), (t)) in our resource management
    ↪    formalism.
    GameObject GetPooledObject()
    {
        foreach (GameObject obj in objectPool)
        {
            if (!obj.activeInHierarchy)
            {
                return obj;
            }
        }
        // If none are available, instantiate a new one, expand the
        ↪    pool, and return it.
        GameObject newObj = Instantiate(objectPrefab);
        newObj.SetActive(false);
        objectPool.Add(newObj);
        return newObj;
    }
}


// Definition of EventData representing an event e   with its
↪    spatial and intensity parameters.
// This struct encapsulates x_trigger and (e) used within the
↪    spawning condition *.
public struct EventData
{
    public Vector3 triggerPosition; // Represents x_trigger in the
    ↪    environment.
    public float intensity;         // Represents (e), the intensity
    ↪    value of the event.
}
```

Chapter 51

Scripting Procedural Environment Modifications

Theoretical Foundations of Procedural Generation

Procedural generation constitutes an algorithmic methodology for the systematic creation and modification of virtual environments. By abstracting the generation process into a mathematically formalized mapping, the generation of unique virtual configurations can be denoted as

$$\Psi : \mathcal{I} \times \mathcal{P} \to \mathcal{E},$$

where $\mathcal{I}$ represents a set of input parameters and constraints, $\mathcal{P}$ the procedural algorithm, and $\mathcal{E}$ the ensemble of generated environmental states. This formulation permits the synthesis of virtual reality scenes that evolve continuously through the interplay of deterministic rules and controlled randomness, thus enabling dynamically varying spatial structures that are unique across instantiations.

Mathematical Models and State Transformations in Virtual Environments

The evolution of a virtual environment subject to procedural modifications is well described within the framework of state transformation. Denote the state of the environment at a given time t as $S(t)$. A procedural modification can then be modeled by a state transition operator

$$\Lambda : S(t) \times M \to S(t + \Delta t),$$

where M encapsulates the modifications prescribed by the procedural engine. Within this operator, both additive and subtractive modifications may be accommodated, and the transformation is frequently influenced by random variables $r \in \mathcal{R}$ drawn from predefined probability distributions. The integration of these stochastic elements within the otherwise deterministic transformation yields an evolution of $S(t)$ that is governed by the composite dynamics of fixed algorithmic rules and probabilistic variability.

Algorithmic Strategies for Procedural Modifications

A variety of algorithmic strategies have been developed to facilitate the procedural alteration of virtual environments. These strategies include rule-based systems, recursive grammars, fractal algorithms, and noise-driven techniques. In rule-based systems, a series of conditionals and transformations are applied recursively; such systems are frequently encapsulated by formal grammars that dictate the growth of architectural motifs. Fractal algorithms, on the other hand, capitalize on self-similarity and scaling properties to generate complex structures from simple recursive rules, while noise-driven methods leverage continuous functions such as Perlin or simplex noise to produce smooth, naturalistic variations. Each strategy is selected on the basis of scalability, computational efficiency, and the specific aesthetic or functional objectives required by the virtual environment.

Parameterization and Randomization Techniques

Central to the procedural generation process is the careful integration of parameterization and randomization. The parameter space, denoted by

$$\Theta = \{\theta_1, \theta_2, \ldots, \theta_n\},$$

comprises the collection of configurational variables that determine baseline structural attributes, material properties, and spatial distributions. Randomization is introduced by means of pseudo-random generators, whose output is statistically controlled to conform to desired distributions. This dual approach allows the environment to be both rigorously defined and richly variable. The implementation of noise functions ensures that transitions between generated states are smooth, thereby preserving visual coherence while still offering significant diversity in the resulting spatial configurations.

Dynamic Integration and Real-Time Evolution

The integration of procedural modifications into a real-time virtual environment is characterized by the continuous evaluation and update of environmental state. Given a fixed temporal discretization, where the time step is defined as

$$\Delta t = \frac{1}{f},$$

with f being the simulation refresh rate, the environment is updated iteratively. During each update cycle, the procedural generation engine computes the necessary state modifications by applying the transformation operator Λ, thereby evolving $S(t)$ into $S(t + \Delta t)$. These dynamic updates are often supplemented by real-time feedback loops that adjust the parameter set Θ based on current performance metrics and interaction data. The resulting system embodies an adaptive architecture wherein the continuous interplay of algorithmic procedures and stochastic variations produces a virtual environment that evolves organically, ensuring that each instantiation yields a unique spatial experience.

C# Code Snippet

```csharp
using System;
using System.Collections.Generic;

namespace ProceduralVR
{
    // Represents the state of the environment: S(t)
    public class EnvironmentState
    {
        public int Seed { get; set; }
        public float NoiseValue { get; set; }
        public List<float> Parameters { get; set; }

        public EnvironmentState(int seed, List<float> parameters)
        {
            Seed = seed;
            Parameters = new List<float>(parameters);
            NoiseValue = 0f;
        }

        public override string ToString()
        {
            return $"Seed: {Seed}, Noise: {NoiseValue:F3}, Params:
            ↪ [{string.Join(", ", Parameters)}]";
        }
    }

    // Encapsulates modification parameters M used in state
    ↪ transitions.
    public class ModificationParameters
    {
        public float DeltaValue { get; set; }
        public float RandomInfluence { get; set; }
    }

    // ProceduralEngine implements the procedural algorithm.
    // It encapsulates both the mapping : I x P -> E
    ↪ (GenerateEnvironment)
    // and the state transformation operator : S(t) x M -> S(t+t)
    ↪ (TransformState).
    public class ProceduralEngine
    {
        private Random _random;

        // Initialize the procedural engine with a given seed.
        public ProceduralEngine(int seed)
        {
            _random = new Random(seed);
        }

        // GenerateEnvironment implements the mapping:
```

390

```csharp
    //    : I x P -> E, where I are input parameters (theta) and P
    //    is the algorithm.
    public EnvironmentState GenerateEnvironment(List<float>
        inputParameters)
    {
        int newSeed = _random.Next();
        EnvironmentState state = new EnvironmentState(newSeed,
            inputParameters);
        // Simulate noise value generation (e.g., via Perlin
        //   noise) as a placeholder.
        state.NoiseValue = (float)_random.NextDouble();
        return state;
    }

    // TransformState simulates the operator : S(t) x M ->
    //    S(t+t)
    // It updates the current state based on deterministic delta
    //    and stochastic randomness.
    public EnvironmentState TransformState(EnvironmentState
        currentState, ModificationParameters modParams)
    {
        EnvironmentState newState = new
            EnvironmentState(currentState.Seed, new
            List<float>(currentState.Parameters));
        float randomFactor = (float)_random.NextDouble();
        // Apply transformation: new state's noise value is
        //    computed by adding a deterministic delta and a
        //    random influence.
        newState.NoiseValue = currentState.NoiseValue +
            modParams.DeltaValue + randomFactor *
            modParams.RandomInfluence;
        return newState;
    }
}

class Program
{
    static void Main(string[] args)
    {
        // Define the parameterization space  = {1, 2, ..., n}
        List<float> theta = new List<float> { 0.5f, 1.0f, 1.5f
            };

        // Create the procedural engine with a fixed initial
        //    seed.
        ProceduralEngine engine = new ProceduralEngine(42);

        // Use the procedural mapping  to generate the initial
        //    environment state.
        EnvironmentState currentState =
            engine.GenerateEnvironment(theta);
        Console.WriteLine("Initial Environment State:");
        Console.WriteLine(currentState);
```

```csharp
        // Define modification parameters M for state
        ↪    transition.
        ModificationParameters modParams = new
        ↪    ModificationParameters
        {
            DeltaValue = 0.1f,
            RandomInfluence = 0.05f
        };

        // Define simulation parameters.
        int simulationSteps = 10;
        float frameRate = 60f;
        // Compute time step t = 1 / f.
        float deltaTime = 1f / frameRate;

        // Simulate the evolution of the environment state over
        ↪    time.
        for (int i = 0; i < simulationSteps; i++)
        {
            currentState = engine.TransformState(currentState,
            ↪    modParams);
            Console.WriteLine($"State at step {i + 1} (t = {(i +
            ↪    1) * deltaTime:F3}s):");
            Console.WriteLine(currentState);
        }

        Console.WriteLine("Procedural environment modification
        ↪    simulation completed.");
    }
  }
}
```

Summary: This C# code demonstrates a procedural environment modification system. The procedural engine generates an initial state using the mapping : × → and then applies iterative state transformations via the operator : $S(t) \times M \rightarrow S(t+t)$, where t is computed as $1/f$. It integrates both deterministic changes and stochastic variability to simulate evolving VR environments.

Chapter 52

Managing Object States in VR Scenes

Formal Representation and Modelling of Object States

In virtual reality (VR) environments, each interactive object is characterized by a set of parameters that collectively define its state. Formally, let an object o in the scene be associated with a state function

$$f(o, t) \in \mathcal{S},$$

where $\mathcal{S}$ denotes the state space encompassing geometric properties, physical dynamics, and semantic attributes, and t represents time. The state $f(o, t)$ is typically expressed as a multidimensional vector capturing attributes such as spatial position, orientation, velocity, and material properties. For instance, a complete state may be represented by

$$S = \begin{bmatrix} x & y & z & \theta & \phi & \psi & v_x & v_y & v_z & \lambda_1 \\ \lambda_2 \end{bmatrix}^T,$$

where (x, y, z) defines the object's position, (θ, ϕ, ψ) its orientation in Euler angles, (v_x, v_y, v_z) its linear velocity components, and λ_i additional state variables pertinent to the context of interactivity. This rigorous formalization provides a foundation for representing individual object states that evolve in a continuous and quantifiable manner.

Mechanisms of State Transition and Tracking

The evolution of an object's state is governed by state transition operators that encapsulate both deterministic processes and stochastic influences. Consider the operator

$$\Gamma : \mathcal{S} \times \mathcal{I} \to \mathcal{S},$$

where $\mathcal{I}$ represents an input or modification space that accounts for environmental stimuli, user interactions, and internal dynamics. Consequently, for a discrete time increment Δt, the update of an object's state is modeled as

$$S(t + \Delta t) = \Gamma\big(S(t), i(t)\big),$$

with $i(t) \in \mathcal{I}$ comprising both controlled and random variables. This formulation ensures that state transitions are both measurable and predictable in terms of system response while allowing for the inherent variability introduced by interactive contexts. The mapping Γ can encapsulate various phenomena such as collision responses, user-triggered modifications, and physical simulations, thus providing a unified framework for state updates.

Patterns and Paradigms for State Management in VR

A variety of design patterns are applicable to the management of object states in immersive VR systems. Among these, the state design pattern provides a modular approach, in which an object's behavior is encapsulated within discrete state objects that define its current mode of operation. This paradigm supports the decoupling of state-specific logic from the object's core functionalities, thereby facilitating both ease of maintenance and extension for varying interactivity requirements.

Furthermore, the observer pattern is frequently employed to ensure that updates to an object's state propagate reliably to dependent components, such as collision detection modules and rendering systems. Under this paradigm, observers subscribe to state change events and apply necessary adjustments promptly. In distributed VR systems, such architectures accommodate divergence between local and global states via synchronization mechanisms that govern the consistency of state information across multiple subsystems.

The adoption of event-driven architectures further reinforces responsive interactivity. In such systems, state transitions are triggered by discrete events, with each event potentially invoking transformations represented by the operator Γ. The resulting framework supports both incremental and batch updates, ensuring that state changes occur fluidly and are consistent with real-time interaction demands.

Consistency and Responsiveness in Dynamic Environments

Maintaining consistency across the multitude of interacting objects in a VR scene requires the implementation of robust state validation and synchronization strategies. Let the global state of the VR environment at time t be defined as

$$\mathcal{S}_{\text{global}}(t) = \big\{ S_1(t), S_2(t), \ldots, S_n(t) \big\},$$

where $S_i(t)$ is the state of the ith object. A consistency invariant, denoted by

$$C\big(\mathcal{S}_{\text{global}}(t)\big) = \top,$$

must be enforced after each state transition to ensure that inter-object constraints, such as non-overlapping conditions and conservation of energy, remain valid.

Mechanisms such as atomic state updates and transactional modifications are crucial in environments where multiple state transitions occur simultaneously. The application of these techniques minimizes intermediate inconsistencies and mitigates artifacts that may arise from asynchronous updates. By enforcing strict invariants and employing synchronization primitives, VR systems achieve a high degree of responsiveness to user input while preserving the integrity of the overall scene.

Temporal Integration and Real-Time Constraints

The continuous and dynamic nature of VR scenes imposes stringent real-time constraints on state management processes. With state updates performed at discrete time intervals, the temporal evolution of each object requires careful calibration of the update rate. Let the time between updates be denoted by

$$\Delta t = \frac{1}{f},$$

where f is the refresh rate of the simulation. The necessity for rapid state evaluations is underscored by the need to balance computational load with the perceptual requirements of a smooth interactive experience.

Real-time integration demands that the operator Γ execute within the confines of the allocated time step while still ensuring that state transitions honor the underlying physics and interaction logic. Adaptive techniques, such as dynamic adjustment of state update frequencies and prioritization of critical state transitions, assist in maintaining responsiveness under variable computational conditions. Consequently, effective temporal integration facilitates an immersive environment in which objects react instantaneously to stimuli, thereby underpinning the overall fidelity and interactivity of the VR experience.

C# Code Snippet

```csharp
using System.Collections.Generic;
using UnityEngine;

namespace VRStateManagement
{
    // Represents the formal state of a VR object.
    public class VRObjectState
    {
        // Geometric properties.
        public Vector3 Position;
        public Vector3 Rotation; // Euler angles in degrees.

        // Physical dynamics.
        public Vector3 Velocity;

        // Additional semantic state variables.
        public float Lambda1;
        public float Lambda2;

        public VRObjectState(Vector3 position, Vector3 rotation,
        ↪ Vector3 velocity, float lambda1, float lambda2)
        {
```

```csharp
        Position = position;
        Rotation = rotation;
        Velocity = velocity;
        Lambda1 = lambda1;
        Lambda2 = lambda2;
    }

    // Creates a copy of the current state.
    public VRObjectState Clone()
    {
        return new VRObjectState(Position, Rotation, Velocity,
        ↪   Lambda1, Lambda2);
    }

    public override string ToString()
    {
        return $"Pos: {Position}, Rot: {Rotation}, Vel:
        ↪   {Velocity}, Lambda1: {Lambda1}, Lambda2: {Lambda2}";
    }
}

// Represents input or modifications acting on a VR object.
public class VRInput
{
    // External force applied (e.g., from user interaction or
    ↪   environmental influence).
    public Vector3 Force;
    // External torque influencing rotation.
    public Vector3 Torque;
    // Modifications to additional parameters.
    public float DeltaLambda1;
    public float DeltaLambda2;

    public VRInput(Vector3 force, Vector3 torque, float
    ↪   deltaLambda1, float deltaLambda2)
    {
        Force = force;
        Torque = torque;
        DeltaLambda1 = deltaLambda1;
        DeltaLambda2 = deltaLambda2;
    }
}

// Delegate for notifying observers when a state changes.
public delegate void StateChangedEventHandler(VRObjectState
↪   newState);

// VRObject encapsulates the state and state transition
↪   mechanism using a Gamma operator.
public class VRObject
{
    public VRObjectState State;
    public event StateChangedEventHandler OnStateChanged;
```

397

```csharp
public VRObject(VRObjectState initialState)
{
    State = initialState;
}

/// <summary>
/// Updates the state of the object using the state
↪   transition operator .
/// The update model: S(t + t) = (S(t), i(t)).
/// For demonstration, Euler integration is applied with
↪   assumed unit mass.
/// </summary>
/// <param name="input">Input modifications and forces
↪   acting on the object.</param>
/// <param name="deltaTime">Discrete time increment
↪   t.</param>
public void UpdateState(VRInput input, float deltaTime)
{
    // Compute acceleration based on input force.
    Vector3 acceleration = input.Force; // Assuming mass =
    ↪   1.

    // Update position using: pos += velocity * t + 0.5 *
    ↪   acceleration * t^2
    Vector3 newPosition = State.Position + State.Velocity *
    ↪   deltaTime + 0.5f * acceleration * deltaTime *
    ↪   deltaTime;

    // Update velocity: v += acceleration * t
    Vector3 newVelocity = State.Velocity + acceleration *
    ↪   deltaTime;

    // Update rotation using provided torque (simple
    ↪   additive integration).
    Vector3 newRotation = State.Rotation + input.Torque *
    ↪   deltaTime;

    // Update additional state variables.
    float newLambda1 = State.Lambda1 + input.DeltaLambda1 *
    ↪   deltaTime;
    float newLambda2 = State.Lambda2 + input.DeltaLambda2 *
    ↪   deltaTime;

    // Assign the updated state.
    State = new VRObjectState(newPosition, newRotation,
    ↪   newVelocity, newLambda1, newLambda2);

    // Notify any listeners that the object's state has
    ↪   changed.
    OnStateChanged?.Invoke(State);
}
}
```

```csharp
// Manages a collection of VR objects and ensures global
↪   consistency and responsiveness.
public class VRSceneManager : MonoBehaviour
{
    // List of all VR objects in the scene.
    public List<VRObject> VRObjects = new List<VRObject>();
    // Update frequency in Hertz.
    public float UpdateFrequency = 90f; // Typical for VR
    ↪   applications.
    private float _deltaTime;

    void Start()
    {
        _deltaTime = 1f / UpdateFrequency;

        // Initialize VR objects with sample starting states.
        VRObject obj1 = new VRObject(new VRObjectState(new
        ↪   Vector3(0, 0, 0), Vector3.zero, Vector3.zero, 0f,
        ↪   0f));
        VRObject obj2 = new VRObject(new VRObjectState(new
        ↪   Vector3(2, 0, 0), Vector3.zero, Vector3.zero, 0f,
        ↪   0f));
        VRObjects.Add(obj1);
        VRObjects.Add(obj2);

        // Subscribe observers to state change events.
        foreach (var obj in VRObjects)
        {
            obj.OnStateChanged += HandleStateChanged;
        }
    }

    // Update is called once per frame.
    void Update()
    {
        // Simulate input for each VR object.
        foreach (var obj in VRObjects)
        {
            VRInput simulatedInput = new VRInput(
                // Random force to simulate user interaction or
                ↪   environmental influence.
                new Vector3(Random.Range(-0.5f, 0.5f), 0,
                ↪   Random.Range(-0.5f, 0.5f)),
                // Random torque for rotation update.
                new Vector3(0, Random.Range(-1f, 1f), 0),
                // Change in additional state variables.
                Random.Range(-0.1f, 0.1f),
                Random.Range(-0.1f, 0.1f)
            );
            obj.UpdateState(simulatedInput, _deltaTime);
        }
```

```csharp
    // Perform a global consistency check after state
    ↪  updates.
    CheckConsistency();
}


// Event handler that logs state changes.
void HandleStateChanged(VRObjectState newState)
{
    Debug.Log("State Updated: " + newState.ToString());
}


/// <summary>
/// Checks global consistency invariants. In this example,
↪  verifies that objects maintain a minimum separation.
/// </summary>
void CheckConsistency()
{
    float minDistance = 0.5f; // Minimum allowable distance
    ↪  between objects.
    for (int i = 0; i < VRObjects.Count; i++)
    {
        for (int j = i + 1; j < VRObjects.Count; j++)
        {
            float dist =
            ↪  Vector3.Distance(VRObjects[i].State.Position,
            ↪  VRObjects[j].State.Position);
            if (dist < minDistance)
            {
                Debug.LogWarning($"Consistency Invariant
                ↪  Failed: Objects {i} and {j} are too
                ↪  close. Distance: {dist}");
            }
        }
    }
}
```

Chapter 53

Implementing Save and Load Systems for VR Worlds

Formalization of Persistent VR States

The state of an immersive virtual reality environment can be conceptualized as a mapping from time to a set of numerical descriptors, where each object is characterized by a state vector $S(t) \in \mathcal{S}$. A global VR scene is formally represented as

$$\mathcal{S}_{\text{global}}(t) = \{S_1(t), S_2(t), \ldots, S_n(t)\},$$

with each $S_i(t)$ encapsulating geometric parameters, dynamic properties, and semantic attributes relevant to a given object or subsystem. In order to reliably persist these states, it is essential to construct a formal model that reduces the complexity of $S(t)$ into a structured, storable representation without compromising the intrinsic fidelity of the original dynamic data.

Serialization Methodologies and Data Fidelity Preservation

Serialization is the process that translates an in-memory structure into a format suitable for long-term storage or transmission. In the context of saving VR states, this entails mapping each element of a state vector $S(t)$ onto a structured schema—whether in text, binary, or hybrid formats—that preserves the precision of numerical values and the integrity of interdependent relationships. The adopted serialization approach must guarantee that the serialized representation maintains a one-to-one correspondence with the original state, ensuring that metrics such as positions, velocities, orientations, and auxiliary parameters remain quantitatively accurate. The schema is typically augmented with descriptive metadata to facilitate future deserialization, version control, and validation against potential data corruption.

Atomicity and Consistency Constraints in State Persistence

Dynamic VR environments frequently encounter concurrent state transitions that necessitate robust transactional mechanisms during the save operation. Atomicity in state persistence refers to the requirement that the entire scene state be saved as an indivisible operation, thereby precluding the possibility of partial or inconsistent state capture. This condition can be formally described by ensuring that a global consistency invariant $C\big(\mathcal{S}_{\text{global}}(t)\big) = \top$ is satisfied upon completion of any save operation. To enforce this invariant, techniques inspired by distributed system protocols and database transactions are applied so that either all components of $\mathcal{S}_{\text{global}}(t)$ are successfully persisted or none are, thus eliminating transient inconsistencies. Such approaches mitigate issues arising from concurrent modifications and asynchronous interactions within the VR scene.

Reloading Mechanisms and Reconstruction of VR Scenes

The reloading stage constitutes the inverse process of serialization, wherein stored data is deserialized to reconstruct the dynamic state of the VR environment. During this phase, the persistent representation is methodically parsed and each state vector $S(t)$ is reinstated into its corresponding in-memory format. The reconstitution process is performed with rigorous validation procedures to ensure that the reconstructed state maintains the original structural and semantic properties. Furthermore, inter-object relationships and environmental constraints must be re-established to guarantee continuity in simulation dynamics. The methodology employed for deserialization supports iterative refinement, allowing for verification that the restored state meets the same consistency criteria and invariants that were enforced during state persistence.

Performance, Scalability, and Real-time Constraints in Save/Load Operations

The operational efficiency of state persistence is paramount in virtual reality applications, where real-time performance is governed by the refresh rate f and the corresponding time step $\Delta t = \frac{1}{f}$. In these environments, it is critical that the processes of saving and loading do not impose excessive computational burden on the system. Advanced techniques, such as incremental and asynchronous saving, are employed to reduce input/output overhead and to distribute the persistence workload across available computational resources. Incremental saving strategies focus on isolating only those segments of the state that have undergone significant change, rather than persisting the entire scene state at every interval. Additionally, parallel processing and optimized data handling algorithms are leveraged to ensure that the scaling of persistence operations remains manageable even as the complexity and size of $S_{\text{global}}(t)$ increase. These performance considerations are essential to uphold the responsiveness and stability of VR worlds during both routine save operations and the subsequent reloading phase.

C# Code Snippet

```csharp
using System;
using System.Collections;
using System.Collections.Generic;
using System.IO;
using UnityEngine;

[Serializable]
public class VRObjectState {
    // Represents the state vector S(t) for an individual VR object.
    // Each object comprises geometric parameters, dynamic
    ↪    properties, and semantic attributes.
    public string objectID;
```

```
        public Vector3 position;
        public Quaternion rotation;
        public Vector3 velocity;
        public Vector3 scale;

        public VRObjectState(string id, Vector3 pos, Quaternion rot,
        ↪  Vector3 vel, Vector3 scl) {
            objectID = id;
            position = pos;
            rotation = rot;
            velocity = vel;
            scale = scl;
        }
    }


[Serializable]
public class VRSceneState {
    // Represents the global VR state S_global(t) as a collection of
    ↪  all object states.
    public List<VRObjectState> objects = new List<VRObjectState>();
}

public static class StatePersistenceManager {
    // File path where the global scene state will be saved.
    private static string filePath =
    ↪  Path.Combine(Application.persistentDataPath,
    ↪  "vrscene_state.json");

    // Serializes and atomically persists the global VR state.
    // This ensures that the operation is completed as an
    ↪  indivisible unit.
    public static bool SaveSceneState(VRSceneState sceneState) {
        // Convert the in-memory state structure into a JSON string
        ↪  with high fidelity.
        string json = JsonUtility.ToJson(sceneState, true);

        // Temporary file path for atomic write operation.
        string tempPath = filePath + ".tmp";

        try {
            // Write the complete serialized state to a temporary
            ↪  file.
            File.WriteAllText(tempPath, json);

            // Remove any existing state file to prevent partial
            ↪  updates.
            if (File.Exists(filePath)) {
                File.Delete(filePath);
            }
            // Atomically move the temporary file to the designated
            ↪  persistent path.
            File.Move(tempPath, filePath);
            Debug.Log("VR Scene State saved successfully.");
```

```
            return true;
        } catch (Exception e) {
            Debug.LogError("Error saving VR Scene State: " +
            ↪  e.Message);
            return false;
        }
    }

    // Deserializes the stored VR scene state, reconstructing the
    ↪  dynamic VR environment.
    public static VRSceneState LoadSceneState() {
        if (!File.Exists(filePath)) {
            Debug.LogWarning("Save file does not exist. Returning a
            ↪  new scene state.");
            return new VRSceneState();
        }

        try {
            string json = File.ReadAllText(filePath);
            VRSceneState sceneState =
            ↪  JsonUtility.FromJson<VRSceneState>(json);
            if (sceneState == null) {
                Debug.LogWarning("Deserialized scene state is null.
                ↪  Returning a new scene state.");
                sceneState = new VRSceneState();
            }
            Debug.Log("VR Scene State loaded successfully.");
            return sceneState;
        } catch (Exception e) {
            Debug.LogError("Error loading VR Scene State: " +
            ↪  e.Message);
            return new VRSceneState();
        }
    }

    // Validates the global consistency invariant C(global(t)) =
    ↪  true.
    // Ensures that every VR object has a valid identifier and
    ↪  finite position values.
    public static bool CheckGlobalInvariant(VRSceneState sceneState)
    ↪  {
        if (sceneState == null || sceneState.objects == null)
            return false;
        foreach (VRObjectState obj in sceneState.objects) {
            if (string.IsNullOrEmpty(obj.objectID))
                return false;
            if (float.IsNaN(obj.position.x) ||
            ↪  float.IsNaN(obj.position.y) ||
            ↪  float.IsNaN(obj.position.z))
                return false;
        }
        return true;
    }
```

405

```csharp
    // Implements an asynchronous save operation to meet real-time
    ↪   constraints.
    // This approach reduces the I/O overhead by deferring the
    ↪   persistence task until the end of the frame.
    public static IEnumerator SaveSceneStateAsync(VRSceneState
    ↪   sceneState) {
        yield return new WaitForEndOfFrame();
        SaveSceneState(sceneState);
    }
}

public class VRStatePersistenceDemo : MonoBehaviour {
    // Demonstrates the usage of state persistence in a VR
    ↪   environment.
    public VRSceneState currentSceneState = new VRSceneState();

    void Start() {
        // Initialize the VR environment with sample objects
        ↪   representing S(t) for each entity.
        currentSceneState.objects.Add(new VRObjectState(
            "Object_1",
            new Vector3(0, 1, 0),
            Quaternion.identity,
            new Vector3(0, 0, 0),
            Vector3.one
        ));
        currentSceneState.objects.Add(new VRObjectState(
            "Object_2",
            new Vector3(2, 3, 4),
            Quaternion.Euler(0, 45, 0),
            new Vector3(0.5f, 0, 0),
            new Vector3(1, 2, 1)
        ));

        // Before persisting, enforce consistency constraints on the
        ↪   global state.
        if (StatePersistenceManager.
        CheckGlobalInvariant(currentSceneState)) {
            StatePersistenceManager.
            SaveSceneState(currentSceneState);
        } else {
            Debug.LogError("Scene state failed consistency check.
            ↪   Save aborted.");
        }
    }

    void Update() {
        // On pressing the 'R' key, trigger the reload operation to
        ↪   reconstruct the VR environment.
        if (Input.GetKeyDown(KeyCode.R)) {
            VRSceneState loadedState =
            ↪   StatePersistenceManager.LoadSceneState();
```

```
        if (StatePersistenceManager.
        CheckGlobalInvariant(loadedState)) {
            currentSceneState = loadedState;
            Debug.Log("Scene state reloaded and verified.");
        } else {
            Debug.LogError("Loaded scene state failed
            ↪  consistency check.");
        }
    }
  }
}
```

Chapter 54

Scripting Contextual Object Interactions

Formal Framework for Contextual Interactions

Within advanced virtual reality systems, interactive behaviors are defined not solely by static object properties but by the interplay between an object's current state and a multidimensional contextual space. An object state may be represented as a vector $S(t) \in \mathcal{S}$, where $\mathcal{S}$ denotes the state space encompassing geometric, dynamic, and semantic properties. Contextual parameters, denoted by $c \in \mathcal{C}$ with $\mathcal{C}$ representing a defined space of environmental and user-derived cues, introduce external modifiers that influence interactive outcomes. In a formal sense, the mapping of a state-context pair to a set of responses can be expressed as

$$I : \mathcal{S} \times \mathcal{C} \to \mathcal{A},$$

where $\mathcal{A}$ is the set of all possible actions. This abstraction serves as the foundation upon which context-dependent interaction dynamics are built, providing a mathematically robust framework that facilitates the systematic treatment of variable interaction modalities.

Proximity-Based Interaction Paradigms

Spatial relationships within a virtual environment play a definitive role in modulating object behavior. The distance between interacting entities is quantified using a metric function $d : \mathcal{S} \times \mathcal{S} \to \mathbb{R}$, where for an object o_i and a reference point p, the value $d(o_i, p)$ is computed using classical Euclidean distance. A specified threshold parameter $\delta \in \mathbb{R}^+$ determines the effective range of influence, such that when

$$d(o_i, p) < \delta,$$

the associated interaction scheme transitions into a state of heightened responsiveness. In this regime, underlying interaction functions may be redefined to incorporate a gradient of behavioral intensities, with the intensity function $I_p(S, c)$ being a monotonically decreasing function of $d(o_i, p)$. This formulation ensures that the perceptual and responsive quality of the virtual system is intimately coupled to spatial proximities, thereby enabling a nuanced, distance-sensitive control mechanism for interaction scripting.

Modeling User State for Adaptive Interactions

In addition to spatial coordinates, the state of the user constitutes a significant contextual variable capable of modulating VR interactions. The user is characterized by a time-dependent state vector $U(t) \in \mathcal{U}$, where $\mathcal{U}$ encompasses variables such as biometric signals, orientation, gesture profiles, and other behavioral metrics. The integration of $U(t)$ into the interaction model extends the mapping to

$$I : \mathcal{S} \times \mathcal{C} \times \mathcal{U} \to \mathcal{A},$$

thereby permitting the interactive behavior of objects to be dynamically adjusted based on current user dispositions. Incorporating user state into the interaction framework allows for the modulation of object responses—ranging from subtle adjustments in animation states to significant behavioral shifts—based on recent user activity and expressed intent. This results in a system where interactive outputs not only reflect spatial context but also adapt in real time to the evolving profile of the user.

Synthesis of Contextual Dynamics

The concurrent influence of spatial parameters and user state necessitates a synthesis mechanism that harmonizes disparate contextual sources into a unified response. A weighted aggregation model is utilized to reconcile these contributions, described by the expression

$$A = w_p \, I_p(S, c_p) + w_u \, I_u(S, U),$$

where w_p and w_u are non-negative weights satisfying $w_p + w_u = 1$. Here, $I_p(S, c_p)$ represents the interaction intensity driven by proximity-based cues c_p, while $I_u(S, U)$ encapsulates the influences stemming from the user state. This formulation allows the interaction system to dynamically recalibrate the relative importance of spatial and behavioral contexts. Refinements to this model may include adaptive weight adjustments based on temporal stability metrics or environmental perturbations, ensuring that the contextual interactions remain both flexible and resistant to transient fluctuations.

Environmental Semantics in Contextual Modeling

Complementary to proximity and user state, the broader environmental semantics contribute additional layers of context to interactive behaviors. The environment is treated as a distinct contextual subset $\mathcal{E}$, which consists of static attributes and dynamic properties of the virtual world. An enriched interaction function can therefore be articulated as

$$I : \mathcal{S} \times \mathcal{C} \times \mathcal{E} \to \mathcal{A},$$

where the inclusion of $\mathcal{E}$ permits the derivation of nuanced behavioral responses that are reflective of ambient conditions and contextual narratives imbued within the VR experience. The composite framework leverages a layered approach, wherein each contextual dimension—whether it be spatial, user-specific, or environmental—contributes to the overall interaction model in a manner that enhances responsiveness and preserves the fidelity of the immersive simulation.

C# Code Snippet

```csharp
using UnityEngine;

public class ContextualInteractionManager : MonoBehaviour
{
    [Header("Interaction Parameters")]
    // : Effective range for proximity-based interaction.
    public float proximityThreshold = 5.0f;

    // Weights for aggregating influences, where w + w = 1.
    [Range(0f, 1f)]
    public float weightProximity = 0.6f;      // w: Proximity
    ↪  influence weight.
    [Range(0f, 1f)]
    public float weightUser = 0.4f;           // w: User state
    ↪  influence weight.

    [Header("User and Environmental Factors")]
    // Reference to the player (or camera) transform representing
    ↪  the spatial context.
    public Transform playerTransform;

    // User state (e.g., engagement or biometric signal), normalized
    ↪  between 0 and 1.
    [Range(0f, 1f)]
    public float userEngagement = 0.8f;

    // Environmental semantic factor representing ambient
    ↪  conditions.
    [Range(0f, 1f)]
    public float environmentalFactor = 1.0f;

    // Internal reference representing the object's state S (e.g.,
    ↪  its position, orientation, etc.).
    private Transform objectTransform;

    void Start()
    {
        // Initialize the object state.
        objectTransform = transform;
    }

    void Update()
    {
        // Map the state, context, and user parameters to an
        ↪  interaction intensity (A)
        // using the framework: I: S × C × U → A.
        float interactionIntensity =
        ↪  CalculateInteractionIntensity();

        // Execute an action based on the computed intensity.
```

411

```
        PerformAction(interactionIntensity);
}


// Calculates the overall interaction intensity based on:
// I(S, c): Proximity-based interaction intensity.
// I(S, U): User state-based interaction intensity.
// Aggregated via A = w·I + w·I, further modulated by
↪    environmental semantics.
float CalculateInteractionIntensity()
{
    // Compute the Euclidean distance d(o, p) where o is the
    ↪    object and p is the player.
    float distance = Vector3.Distance(objectTransform.position,
    ↪    playerTransform.position);

    // Proximity-based component I: decreases monotonically with
    ↪    distance.
    float intensityProximity =
    ↪    ComputeProximityIntensity(distance);

    // User-based component I: derived directly from the user
    ↪    engagement level.
    float intensityUser = ComputeUserIntensity(userEngagement);

    // Weighted aggregation and modulation by environmental
    ↪    factor.
    float aggregatedIntensity =
        (weightProximity * intensityProximity + weightUser *
        ↪    intensityUser) * environmentalFactor;

    // Ensure the intensity is between 0 and 1.
    return Mathf.Clamp01(aggregatedIntensity);
}


// Implements the proximity intensity function:
// I = ( - d) /   if d < , otherwise I = 0.
float ComputeProximityIntensity(float distance)
{
    if (distance < proximityThreshold)
    {
        return (proximityThreshold - distance) /
        ↪    proximityThreshold;
    }
    return 0f;
}


// Computes the user-based intensity component.
// Here, we assume an identity mapping for demonstration
↪    purposes.
float ComputeUserIntensity(float engagement)
{
    return engagement;
}
```

```
// Executes an action based on the computed interaction
↪  intensity.
// In this example, the object's color transitions from red (low
↪  intensity) to green (high intensity).
void PerformAction(float intensity)
{
    Renderer renderer = GetComponent<Renderer>();
    if (renderer != null)
    {
        Color targetColor = Color.Lerp(Color.red, Color.green,
        ↪  intensity);
        renderer.material.color = targetColor;
    }
    // Additional actions (animations, particle effects, etc.)
    ↪  can be incorporated here.
}
}
```

Summary: The above C# code implements a contextual interaction system for VR environments in Unity. It demonstrates the
core equations from the chapter—mapping the object state (S),
spatial context (C), and user state (U) to an interaction action
(A) using a weighted aggregation model. The code computes a
proximity-based intensity via a linear decay function and combines
it with a user state intensity, further modulated by environmental
semantics. This comprehensive implementation exemplifies how
to achieve adaptive and immersive interactive behaviors in virtual
reality applications.

Chapter 55

Designing VR Puzzle and Interaction Mechanics

Theoretical Foundations in Interactive Puzzle Design

A rigorous formulation of interactive puzzles within virtual reality necessitates the establishment of a robust theoretical framework. At its core, puzzle mechanics are an instantiation of stateful interactions, where each puzzle element is characterized by a state variable S and is subject to environmental influences denoted by a contextual parameter C. The mapping

$$P : S \times C \to E,$$

where E represents the ensemble of engagement responses, formalizes the transformational relationship between puzzle states and their corresponding outcomes. This abstraction encapsulates both deterministic and probabilistic transitions, serving as a foundation for the systematic exploration of challenge paradigms and the orchestration of interactive narratives. The framework thereby reconciles principles of human-computer interaction with computational models of dynamic state transitions, ensuring that puzzle mechanics remain both coherent and emergent.

Architectural Considerations for VR Puzzle Mechanics

The integration of puzzles into immersive virtual environments is predicated upon a modular design paradigm that emphasizes decoupled state management and event-driven architectures. Each interactive puzzle component is modeled as an autonomous entity within a larger system, permitting localized control of state transitions while maintaining global consistency. Formally, let E denote the set of puzzle elements, and assign to each element $e \in E$ a state transformation function

$$f_e : \mathcal{S} \to \mathcal{I},$$

where $\mathcal{S}$ is the state space and $\mathcal{I}$ is the interface domain capturing input and contextual indicators. Complementarily, an event mapping

$$g_e : \mathcal{I} \times \mathcal{C} \to \mathcal{O}$$

associates interactive inputs, in the presence of relevant contextual variables $\mathcal{C}$, to a set of outcomes $\mathcal{O}$. This architectural construct facilitates fine-grained control over puzzle dynamics and enables the dynamic reconfiguration of challenge parameters in response to both user actions and evolving environmental conditions.

Spatial-Temporal Dynamics in Puzzle Environments

Interactive puzzles in virtual reality are deeply rooted in spatial-temporal constructs, wherein the positioning and movement of both puzzle elements and users critically influence overall engagement. Time-dependent state changes can be modeled by a function $S(t)$, where $t \in \mathbb{R}^+$ represents the temporal continuum over which interactive dynamics unfold. Spatial constraints are quantitatively assessed through metrics such that, given a distance function $d : \mathcal{P} \times \mathcal{Q} \to \mathbb{R}$, the proximity condition

$$d(p, e) < \delta$$

ensures that puzzle triggers are activated when a user position p approaches an element e within a threshold δ. The interplay between spatial proximity and temporal evolution engenders a system in which puzzle challenges can adapt dynamically, thereby permitting the calibration of difficulty and the orchestration of sequential puzzle events in a coherent manner.

Enhancing Engagement through Intuitive Interaction Mechanics

A central objective in the design of VR puzzles is the orchestration of mechanisms that foster deep cognitive engagement and facilitate intuitive problem solving. Emphasis is placed on the deliberate calibration of affordances and feedback loops that enable users to discern the underlying logic of interactive puzzles. By incorporating graded signal responses and a hierarchical feedback model, it becomes possible to modulate the challenge level in accordance with real-time user performance metrics. Critical to this approach is the integration of sensorimotor inputs, whereby subtle adjustments in user posture and motion are transduced into modulations of puzzle state. This coupling of physical interaction with digital feedback engenders an immersive milieu where the user's actions are met with proportional and contextually appropriate responses, reinforcing a self-evident pathway toward puzzle resolution.

Multi-Modal Interactions and Adaptive Puzzle Dynamics

The inherent complexity of immersive puzzle experiences is amplified through the integration of multi-modal interaction paradigms. A comprehensive approach to puzzle design incorporates a diverse set of input modalities, formally denoted as

$$\mathcal{M} = \{m_1, m_2, \ldots, m_n\},$$

with each modality providing a distinctive channel for user engagement. The fusion of these channels is captured by a modality integration function

$$h : \mathcal{M} \times \mathcal{S} \to \mathcal{E},$$

where $\mathcal{E}$ corresponds to the enhanced engagement space. Adaptive mechanics leverage this function by dynamically weighting contributions from each modality based on contextual variables and user performance metrics. This orchestration ensures that interactive puzzles remain responsive to variations in user behavior while simultaneously offering a layered complexity that supports both incremental challenge escalation and immediate, intuitive responsiveness. Through such a multi-modal and adaptive strategy, puzzle mechanics achieve a synthesis of precision and adaptability, thereby establishing a robust environment for immersive and intellectually stimulating interaction.

C# Code Snippet

```csharp
using System;
using System.Collections.Generic;
using UnityEngine;

namespace VRPuzzleMechanics
{
    // Enumeration representing discrete puzzle states.
    public enum PuzzleState
    {
        Inactive,
        Active,
        Solved,
        Failed
    }

    // Represents the contextual parameters (C) influencing a puzzle
    ↪   element.
    public class PuzzleContext
    {
        public float DifficultyMultiplier;    // Environmental or
        ↪   difficulty factor.
        public Vector3 UserPosition;          // Position of the user
        ↪   in the scene.
        public Vector3 PuzzlePosition;        // Position of the
        ↪   puzzle element.
        public float TimeSinceActivation;     // Time since the
        ↪   puzzle became active.

        public PuzzleContext(float difficulty, Vector3 userPos,
        ↪   Vector3 puzzlePos, float time)
        {
            DifficultyMultiplier = difficulty;
            UserPosition = userPos;
            PuzzlePosition = puzzlePos;
            TimeSinceActivation = time;
        }
    }

    // Represents the outcome (E) produced by a puzzle interaction.
```

```csharp
public class PuzzleOutcome
{
    public string ResultMessage;
    public bool Success;

    public PuzzleOutcome(string message, bool success)
    {
        ResultMessage = message;
        Success = success;
    }
}


// Represents the interface domain (I) for state transformation.
public class PuzzleInterface
{
    public string InteractionHint;

    public PuzzleInterface(string hint)
    {
        InteractionHint = hint;
    }
}


// Puzzle element class encapsulating state (S) and providing
//    key mappings.
public class PuzzleElement
{
    public PuzzleState State;      // Current state of the puzzle.
    public float StateValue;       // Numeric representation of
    //    state (S).

    // Constructor initializes the puzzle element state.
    public PuzzleElement(PuzzleState initialState, float
    //    initialStateValue)
    {
        State = initialState;
        StateValue = initialStateValue;
    }

    // Mapping P: S x C -> E
    // Computes an engagement outcome based on the current state
    //    and given context.
    public PuzzleOutcome ComputeEngagementOutcome(PuzzleContext
    //    ctx)
    {
        // Calculate spatial proximity: d: P x Q ->
        float distance = Vector3.Distance(ctx.UserPosition,
        //    ctx.PuzzlePosition);
        const float delta = 5.0f; // Activation threshold

        bool isClose = distance < delta;
        bool success = false;
        string message = "";
```

418

```csharp
        if (State == PuzzleState.Active)
        {
            // Example condition: enhanced state value over a
            ↪    threshold triggers a success.
            if (isClose && (StateValue *
            ↪    ctx.DifficultyMultiplier) > 10.0f)
            {
                success = true;
                message = "Puzzle Solved!";
                State = PuzzleState.Solved;
            }
            else
            {
                success = false;
                message = "Puzzle in Progress...";
            }
        }
        else
        {
            message = "Puzzle is not active.";
        }
        return new PuzzleOutcome(message, success);
}

// State transformation function f_e: S -> I
// Returns a PuzzleInterface containing interaction hints
↪    based on the puzzle state.
public PuzzleInterface TransformState()
{
    string hint = "";
    switch (State)
    {
        case PuzzleState.Inactive:
            hint = "Explore the area to activate the
            ↪    puzzle.";
            break;
        case PuzzleState.Active:
            hint = "Interact with available elements to
            ↪    progress.";
            break;
        case PuzzleState.Solved:
            hint = "Well done! Proceed to the next
            ↪    challenge.";
            break;
        case PuzzleState.Failed:
            hint = "Try again or adjust your strategy.";
            break;
    }
    return new PuzzleInterface(hint);
}

// Event mapping function g_e: I x C -> O
```

```
    // Integrates the interface hint with contextual input to
    ↪   determine the outcome.
    public PuzzleOutcome ProcessEvent(PuzzleInterface
    ↪   pInterface, PuzzleContext ctx)
    {
        string outcomeMessage = pInterface.InteractionHint +
        " | Difficulty: " + ctx.
        DifficultyMultiplier.ToString("F2");
        // Arbitrary condition based on context for
        ↪   demonstration.
        bool outcomeSuccess = ctx.DifficultyMultiplier < 2.0f;
        return new PuzzleOutcome(outcomeMessage,
        ↪   outcomeSuccess);
    }
}


// Represents a single input modality (m_i) for multi-modal
↪   interactions.
public class MultiModalInput
{
    public string ModalityName;
    public float InputStrength; // Represents the strength or
    ↪   activation level for this modality.

    public MultiModalInput(string name, float strength)
    {
        ModalityName = name;
        InputStrength = strength;
    }
}


// Manages the integration of multiple input modalities.
public class PuzzleMultiModalManager
{
    public List<MultiModalInput> Inputs;
    public PuzzleElement PuzzleElement;

    public PuzzleMultiModalManager(PuzzleElement element)
    {
        PuzzleElement = element;
        Inputs = new List<MultiModalInput>();
    }

    // Modality integration function h: M x S -> E
    // Aggregates modality inputs to modify the puzzle state and
    ↪   computes the outcome.
    public PuzzleOutcome
    ↪   IntegrateModalitiesAndComputeOutcome(float
    ↪   baseStateValue)
    {
        float totalInput = 0.0f;
        foreach (var input in Inputs)
        {
```

420

```
            totalInput += input.InputStrength;
        }
        // Update state by integrating input modalities.
        float enhancedState = baseStateValue + totalInput;
        PuzzleElement.StateValue = enhancedState;

        // Simulate context creation for the multi-modal
        ↪   outcome.
        PuzzleContext ctx = new PuzzleContext(
            difficulty: 1.5f,
            userPos: new Vector3(0, 0, 0),
            puzzlePos: new Vector3(3, 0, 4),
            time: Time.time
        );

        return PuzzleElement.ComputeEngagementOutcome(ctx);
    }
}

// Main manager class to integrate and control VR puzzle
↪   mechanics within Unity.
public class VRPuzzleManager : MonoBehaviour
{
    public PuzzleElement PuzzleElement;
    public PuzzleMultiModalManager MultiModalManager;

    // Initialization of the puzzle element and multi-modal
    ↪   inputs.
    void Start()
    {
        // Start with an active puzzle element with an initial
        ↪   state value.
        PuzzleElement = new PuzzleElement(PuzzleState.Active,
        ↪   5.0f);
        MultiModalManager = new
        ↪   PuzzleMultiModalManager(PuzzleElement);

        // Register multiple interaction modalities (e.g., hand
        ↪   gestures and voice commands).
        MultiModalManager.Inputs.Add(new
        ↪   MultiModalInput("HandGesture", 2.5f));
        MultiModalManager.Inputs.Add(new
        ↪   MultiModalInput("VoiceCommand", 1.0f));
    }

    // Update is called once per frame to evaluate puzzle
    ↪   mechanics.
    void Update()
    {
        // Create dynamic context based on player's current
        ↪   position.
        PuzzleContext ctx = new PuzzleContext(
            difficulty: 1.0f,
```

```
        userPos: transform.position,
        puzzlePos: new Vector3(2, 0, 3),
        time: Time.time
    );

    // Compute engagement outcome using the core mapping P:
    ↪   S x C -> E.
    PuzzleOutcome outcome =
    ↪   PuzzleElement.ComputeEngagementOutcome(ctx);
    Debug.Log("Engagement Outcome: " +
    ↪   outcome.ResultMessage);

    // Process the puzzle event using state transformation
    ↪   f_e and event mapping g_e.
    PuzzleInterface pInterface =
    ↪   PuzzleElement.TransformState();
    PuzzleOutcome eventOutcome =
    ↪   PuzzleElement.ProcessEvent(pInterface, ctx);
    Debug.Log("Event Outcome: " +
    ↪   eventOutcome.ResultMessage);

    // Demonstrate multi-modal integration h: M x S -> E to
    ↪   adapt puzzle dynamics.
    PuzzleOutcome modalOutcome = MultiModalManager.
    IntegrateModalitiesAndComputeOutcome(
    PuzzleElement.StateValue);
    Debug.Log("Multi-Modal Outcome: " +
    ↪   modalOutcome.ResultMessage);
    }
  }
}
```

Summary: This C# code snippet demonstrates a comprehensive implementation of VR puzzle mechanics in Unity. It integrates key equations and mappings discussed in the chapter: - Mapping P: $S \times C \to E$ is implemented in ComputeEngagementOutcome to determine puzzle outcomes based on state and context. - The state transformation function f ($S \to I$) is realized in TransformState, offering context-sensitive interaction hints. - The event mapping function g ($I \times C \to O$) is used in ProcessEvent for further engage outcome derivation. - Spatial and temporal dynamics are captured via distance checks and context parameters. - Multi-modal integration (h: $M \times S \to E$) is achieved in PuzzleMultiModalManager, aggregating diverse user inputs to adapt the puzzle state dynamically. Together, these elements form a modular and adaptive framework for designing interactive VR puzzles.

Chapter 56

Scripting Interactive Narratives in Immersive Environments

Theoretical Foundations of Interactive Narratives

The architectural underpinning of interactive narratives in immersive environments is established through a rigorous formalization of narrative state spaces and transition mappings. Narrative states, represented by the set $\mathcal{N}$, encapsulate multifaceted parameters that define both the intrinsic narrative content and the extrinsic contextual influences. This formalism permits the abstraction of narrative progression as a function

$$\Phi \colon \mathcal{N} \times \mathcal{U} \to \mathcal{D},$$

where $\mathcal{U}$ denotes the set of user interactions and environmental stimuli, and $\mathcal{D}$ signifies the domain of narrative developments. The function Φ synthesizes both deterministic transitions and probabilistic branching, allowing for emergent storytelling that evolves naturally in response to a continuously changing user context.

Architectural Paradigms for Narrative Integration

Integrating narrative elements into virtual reality systems requires a modular architecture that decouples narrative content management from low-level interactive event processing. In this paradigm, narrative engines operate as autonomous modules that interface with context analyzers and event dispatchers. Let $\mathcal{T}$ denote the collection of narrative triggers, and define the narrative response mapping as

$$\Psi : \mathcal{T} \times \mathcal{S} \to \mathcal{N},$$

with $\mathcal{S}$ representing the state space of interactive variables. Such a configuration enables each narrative module to react to localized triggers while still maintaining overall coherence across the immersive environment. The modular integration facilitates concurrent narrative threads and non-linear progression, ensuring that the narrative adapts fluidly in alignment with the dynamic interplay of user actions and environmental contexts.

Stateful Narrative Modeling and Dynamic Scripting

Stateful modeling constitutes a critical aspect of scripting narratives that are both adaptive and rooted in the dynamics of user interaction. Narrative progression is envisaged as a sequence of state transitions governed by a transition function

$$T : \mathcal{N} \times \mathcal{E} \to \mathcal{N},$$

where $\mathcal{E}$ is the set of interactive events. Complementary to this, a probabilistic function

$$P : \mathcal{N} \times \mathcal{E} \to [0, 1]$$

assigns likelihoods to various transitions, thereby accommodating non-deterministic narrative branches. The confluence of deterministic state updates with stochastic dynamics enables a narrative script to evolve in a manner that reflects both explicit user inputs and implicit contextual cues. This dynamic scripting approach ensures that the narrative remains fluid and responsive while preserving the internal logic of story progression.

Temporal-Spatial Narrative Synchronization

Synchronization of narrative elements with temporal and spatial dimensions is essential to achieve an immersive storytelling experience within a virtual reality context. Let $t \in \mathbb{R}^+$ represent time and $p \in \mathbb{R}^3$ represent the user position within the three-dimensional environment. Narrative triggers are contingent upon satisfying both temporal and spatial constraints. Formally, consider a narrative activation function defined by

$$A(t, p, \ell) = \begin{cases} 1, & \text{if } d(p, \ell) < \delta \text{ and } t - t_0 > \tau, \\ 0, & \text{otherwise,} \end{cases}$$

where $\ell \in \mathbb{R}^3$ designates the spatial location associated with a narrative cue, $d(p, \ell)$ computes the Euclidean distance between the user position and the narrative locus, δ is a spatial threshold, and τ is the temporal threshold governing activation delay. The function $A(t, p, \ell)$ captures the precise conditions necessary for the timely and context-sensitive initiation of narrative events, ensuring that storytelling elements are introduced only when the spatial and temporal criteria are adequately satisfied.

User Engagement and Adaptive Narrative Evolution

Adaptive narrative evolution lies at the intersection of user engagement measurement and dynamic state transition. User engagement is quantified by a vector $\mathbf{u} \in \mathbb{R}^n$ that may encapsulate metrics such as gaze direction, proximity, and interaction frequency. The evolution of narrative states in response to user behavior can be modeled by an adaptive update function

$$N_{\text{next}} = F(N_{\text{current}}, \mathbf{u}),$$

where $N_{\text{current}} \in \mathcal{N}$ represents the prevailing narrative state and F is a function that synthesizes user input with the current narrative context to yield a subsequent state N_{next}. This formulation permits continuous recalibration of narrative arcs, thereby enabling the system to respond in real time to shifts in user behavior. Iterative evaluations of the interactive metrics, alongside feedback from narrative triggers, drive the convergence of user behavior and narrative evolution into an emergent and non-linear storytelling process, where narrative progression is both adaptive and deeply imbued with the dynamics of the immersive environment.

C# Code Snippet

```csharp
using System;
using System.Linq;

namespace VRNarrative
{
    // A simple 3D vector struct to represent spatial positions.
    public struct Vector3
    {
        public double X, Y, Z;
        public Vector3(double x, double y, double z)
        {
            X = x;
            Y = y;
            Z = z;
        }
        public double DistanceTo(Vector3 other)
        {
            return Math.Sqrt(Math.Pow(X - other.X, 2) + Math.Pow(Y -
            ↪ other.Y, 2) + Math.Pow(Z - other.Z, 2));
        }
        public override string ToString()
        {
            return $"({X:0.00}, {Y:0.00}, {Z:0.00})";
        }
    }

    // Represents the current state of the narrative.
    public class NarrativeState
    {
        public int StateId { get; set; }
        public string Description { get; set; }
        public NarrativeState(int id, string description)
        {
            StateId = id;
            Description = description;
        }
        public override string ToString()
        {
            return $"State {StateId}: {Description}";
        }
    }
```

```csharp
// Encapsulates user interaction data such as engagement
↪    metrics.
public class UserInteraction
{
    public double[] EngagementValues { get; private set; }
    public UserInteraction(double[] engagement)
    {
        EngagementValues = engagement;
    }
}


// Represents an interactive event (e.g., a click action) that
↪    may affect narrative flow.
public class InteractionEvent
{
    public string EventType { get; set; }
    public double Intensity { get; set; }
    public InteractionEvent(string eventType, double intensity)
    {
        EventType = eventType;
        Intensity = intensity;
    }
}


// The NarrativeEngine integrates various algorithms
↪    corresponding to the chapter's key equations.
public class NarrativeEngine
{
    private Random random = new Random();

    // Phi: Represents the narrative progression mapping:
    //      :  x  →
    // Computes narrative development by combining narrative
    ↪    state with user interaction metrics.
    public string ComputeNarrativeDevelopment(NarrativeState
    ↪    state, UserInteraction interaction)
    {
        double score = interaction.EngagementValues.Sum();
        return $"{state.Description} with engagement score
        ↪    {score:0.00}";
    }

    // Psi: Implements narrative response mapping:
    //      :  x  →
    // Maps a narrative trigger to an updated narrative state.
    public NarrativeState GetNarrativeResponse(string trigger,
    ↪    NarrativeState currentState)
    {
        if (trigger == "advance")
        {
            return new NarrativeState(currentState.StateId + 1,
            ↪    $"Narrative advanced from state
            ↪    {currentState.StateId}");
```

```
    }
    return currentState;
}


// T: Deterministic state transition function:
//    T :  ×  →
// Updates narrative state based on an interaction event.
public NarrativeState TransitionState(NarrativeState
↪   currentState, InteractionEvent e)
{
    if (e.Intensity > 0.5)
    {
        return new NarrativeState(currentState.StateId + 1,
        ↪   $"Transitioned due to event {e.EventType}");
    }
    return currentState;
}


// P: Probabilistic transition function:
//    P :  ×  → [0,1]
// Computes the likelihood for a state transition given
↪   event intensity and current state.
public double GetTransitionProbability(NarrativeState state,
↪   InteractionEvent e)
{
    double baseProbability = e.Intensity;
    double adjustment = (state.StateId > 0) ? 1.0 /
    ↪   state.StateId : 1.0;
    return Math.Min(baseProbability * adjustment, 1.0);
}


// Activation function A(t, p, ) defined as:
//    A(t, p, ) = 1 if d(p, ) <  and t - t0 > , otherwise 0.
// Checks if temporal and spatial conditions are met to
↪   trigger narrative events.
public bool ActivationFunction(double currentTime, double
↪   startTime, Vector3 userPosition, Vector3
↪   narrativeLocation, double spatialThreshold, double
↪   timeThreshold)
{
    double distance =
    ↪   userPosition.DistanceTo(narrativeLocation);
    return (distance < spatialThreshold) && ((currentTime -
    ↪   startTime) > timeThreshold);
}


// F: Adaptive narrative update function.
//    N_next = F(N_current, u)
// Updates narrative state based on current state and user
↪   engagement metrics.
public NarrativeState UpdateNarrativeState(NarrativeState
↪   currentState, UserInteraction interaction)
{
```

```
        double engagementScore =
        ↪   interaction.EngagementValues.Sum();
        if (engagementScore > 1.5)
        {
            return new NarrativeState(currentState.StateId + 1,
            ↪   $"Adaptive update due to high engagement
            ↪   ({engagementScore:0.00})");
        }
        return currentState;
    }
}

// Main program demonstrating the integration of the narrative
↪   equations and adaptation algorithms.
public class Program
{
    public static void Main()
    {
        // Initialize starting narrative state and the narrative
        ↪   engine.
        NarrativeState initialState = new NarrativeState(1,
        ↪   "Beginning of the story.");
        NarrativeEngine engine = new NarrativeEngine();

        // Simulate user interaction with a set of engagement
        ↪   metrics.
        UserInteraction interaction = new UserInteraction(new
        ↪   double[] { 0.8, 0.7, 0.9 });

        // Compute narrative development using the Phi function:
        ↪   (N, U) → D.
        string narrativeDevelopment =
        ↪   engine.ComputeNarrativeDevelopment(initialState,
        ↪   interaction);
        Console.WriteLine("Narrative Development: " +
        ↪   narrativeDevelopment);

        // Apply a narrative trigger using the Psi mapping: (T,
        ↪   S) → N.
        NarrativeState advancedState =
        ↪   engine.GetNarrativeResponse("advance",
        ↪   initialState);
        Console.WriteLine("After Trigger Response: " +
        ↪   advancedState);

        // Perform a deterministic state transition using the T
        ↪   function: T(N, E) → N.
        InteractionEvent clickEvent = new
        ↪   InteractionEvent("click", 0.6);
        NarrativeState transitionedState =
        ↪   engine.TransitionState(advancedState, clickEvent);
        Console.WriteLine("After Transition Event: " +
        ↪   transitionedState);
```

```csharp
            // Calculate the probabilistic transition using the P
            ↪ function: P(N, E) → [0,1].
            double probability =
            ↪ engine.GetTransitionProbability(advancedState,
            ↪ clickEvent);
            Console.WriteLine("Transition Probability: " +
            ↪ probability.ToString("0.00"));

            // Evaluate the temporal-spatial activation function
            ↪ A(t, p, ).
            double currentTime = 10.0;
            double startTime = 5.0;
            Vector3 userPos = new Vector3(1.0, 1.0, 1.0);
            Vector3 narrativeLoc = new Vector3(1.5, 1.5, 1.0);
            bool activated = engine.ActivationFunction(currentTime,
            ↪ startTime, userPos, narrativeLoc, spatialThreshold:
            ↪ 1.0, timeThreshold: 3.0);
            Console.WriteLine("Activation Function Result: " +
            ↪ activated);

            // Update the narrative state adaptively based on user
            ↪ engagement via the F function.
            NarrativeState updatedState =
            ↪ engine.UpdateNarrativeState(transitionedState,
            ↪ interaction);
            Console.WriteLine("Adaptive Narrative Update: " +
            ↪ updatedState);
        }
    }
}
```

Summary: This C# code snippet encapsulates the core algorithms discussed in the chapter. It demonstrates narrative progression using a mapping from narrative states and user interactions (), handling of narrative triggers (), deterministic and probabilistic state transitions (T and P), a temporal-spatial activation function (A), and an adaptive update mechanism (F). These components collectively integrate to form an immersive, dynamic narrative engine suitable for VR environments.

Chapter 57

Implementing Physics-Based Puzzles for VR

Modeling Physical Interactions in Immersive Puzzles

The construction of physics-based puzzles necessitates the precise modeling of physical interactions within a virtual environment. Puzzle elements are conceptualized as entities obeying the principles of classical mechanics, described by equations such as

$$\mathbf{F} = m\mathbf{a},$$

where m represents mass, $\mathbf{a}$ denotes acceleration, and $\mathbf{F}$ embodies the net force acting on an object. In the context of virtual reality, interactive objects are treated as rigid bodies subject to collision detection, frictional forces, and restitution coefficients. The mathematical abstraction of these interactions provides a framework whereby forces, torques, and impulse responses are computed accurately. Such modeling incorporates both continuous dynamics and discrete event handling, ensuring that physical responses are simulated with high fidelity. Emphasis is placed on ensuring that energy dissipation and momentum transfer conform to established mechanical laws, thereby sustaining the believability of the puzzle mechanics.

Integration of Rigid Body Dynamics with Puzzle Elements

The integration of rigid body dynamics into puzzle design is achieved by embedding the physics simulation as a core component of the virtual environment. Each puzzle element is assigned a set of dynamic properties, such as position, velocity, and angular momentum, which evolve over time according to numerical integration methods. The system operates under the constraint that state updates adhere to

$$\mathbf{x}(t + \Delta t) = \mathbf{x}(t) + \mathbf{v}(t)\Delta t + \frac{1}{2}\mathbf{a}(t)\Delta t^2,$$

and similarly for rotational dynamics, ensuring that translational and angular motions are computed within an integrated framework. Collision resolution and constraint enforcement between adjacent elements are treated using impulse-based algorithms that maintain system stability. The synthesis of user interactions with the underlying physics is formalized by mapping discrete events to modifications in the state vector of the puzzle elements, thus allowing for a seamless union between dynamic simulation and interactive control.

Designing Interactive Mechanisms and Logical Puzzle Constraints

A critical aspect of implementing physics-based puzzles lies in the design of interactive mechanisms that compel the engagement of environmental elements and logical progression. Each puzzle is structured such that the activation of physical interactions triggers state transitions within an abstract puzzle state machine. The interdependency between physical actions and logical conditions is modeled by functions of the form

$$\Gamma \colon \mathcal{P} \times \mathcal{E} \to \mathcal{S},$$

where $\mathcal{P}$ denotes the physical state space, $\mathcal{E}$ represents the set of user-induced events, and $\mathcal{S}$ corresponds to discrete puzzle states. This formulation permits the explicit encoding of dependency relationships, such that solutions require both manipulation of physical properties and the resolution of logical conditions. Logical constraints are imposed to dictate permissible state transitions, ensuring that the evolution of the puzzle reflects coherent problem-solving sequences. The underlying structure establishes a deterministic mapping between user actions and puzzle outcomes while also accommodating non-linearities introduced by physical perturbations.

Constraint-Based Modeling in Environmental Puzzle Layouts

The spatial and temporal organization of puzzle elements is rooted in constraint-based modeling, which prescribes boundary conditions and interaction domains for the virtual objects. In such settings, the dynamics of movable components are regulated by constraints that maintain structural integrity and define interaction zones. These conditions are mathematically characterized by equations of the form

$$M\ddot{\mathbf{q}} + C\dot{\mathbf{q}} + K\mathbf{q} = \mathbf{f},$$

where M, C, and K denote the mass, damping, and stiffness matrices, respectively, $\mathbf{q}$ represents the generalized coordinates, and $\mathbf{f}$ is the external force vector. The imposition of kinematic constraints and boundary conditions ensures that puzzle elements interact within predefined limits, thereby orchestrating a controlled yet dynamic environment. These constraints are critical in dictating the allowable motion paths and in enforcing consistency with the virtual world's geometry. The simultaneous enforcement of multiple constraints leads to emergent behaviors that challenge users to exploit environmental configurations for puzzle resolution.

Analysis of Dynamic Puzzle Responses and Logical Progression

A comprehensive analysis of puzzle dynamics is achieved through a synthesis of physics simulation output and logical state evolution. The interplay between deterministic physical responses and user-initiated actions is captured through energy-based methods and state transition analysis. The conservation of mechanical energy, quantified by the relation

$$E = K + U,$$

where K is the kinetic energy and U is the potential energy, is monitored to ensure that the simulated dynamics adhere to theoretical expectations. Furthermore, the logical progression of puzzles is evaluated using state transition matrices that correlate physical interactions with changes in puzzle status. The probabilistic aspects of user interaction are incorporated via functions that assign transition probabilities, integrating stochastic elements with the deterministic simulation. Detailed mathematical proofs and stability analyses underpin the integration of dynamic responses into the overall puzzle architecture, highlighting the balance between controlled constraint enforcement and emergent gameplay complexity.

C# Code Snippet

```csharp
using System;
using UnityEngine;

public enum PuzzleState
{
    Inactive,
    Active,
    Complete
}

public class PuzzleElement : MonoBehaviour
{
    // Physical properties
    public float mass = 1.0f;
    public float restitution = 0.8f; // Coefficient for collision
    ↪    response
    public Vector3 velocity = Vector3.zero;
    public Vector3 acceleration = Vector3.zero;

    // Gravity constant
    private Vector3 gravity = new Vector3(0, -9.81f, 0);

    // Variables for constraint (spring-damper) modeling based on:
    // M * q'' + C * q' + K * q = f
    public Vector3 anchorPosition; // Initial (or fixed) position
    ↪    for constraint
    public float springStiffness = 10.0f;   // K: stiffness constant
    public float springDamping = 2.0f;      // C: damping coefficient
```

```
// Accumulator for external forces
private Vector3 netForce = Vector3.zero;

void Start()
{
    // Initialize the anchor position with the starting position
    anchorPosition = transform.position;
}

void FixedUpdate()
{
    // Reset net force at the start of each physics step
    netForce = Vector3.zero;

    // Apply gravity force: F = m * g
    netForce += mass * gravity;

    // Here any external forces (e.g., from user interactions)
    ↪    could be added via ApplyForce()

    // Compute spring-damper constraint force:
    // F_constraint = -springStiffness*(displacement) -
    ↪    springDamping*(velocity)
    Vector3 displacement = transform.position - anchorPosition;
    Vector3 constraintForce = -springStiffness * displacement -
    ↪    springDamping * velocity;
    netForce += constraintForce;

    // Compute acceleration using Newton's second law (F = m *
    ↪    a)
    acceleration = netForce / mass;

    // Time step for simulation
    float dt = Time.fixedDeltaTime;

    // Update position using kinematic integration:
    // x(t + dt) = x(t) + v(t)*dt + 0.5*a(t)*dt^2
    Vector3 newPosition = transform.position + velocity * dt +
    ↪    0.5f * acceleration * dt * dt;

    // Update velocity:
    // v(t + dt) = v(t) + a(t)*dt
    Vector3 newVelocity = velocity + acceleration * dt;

    // Simple collision detection with the "floor" (y = 0) and
    ↪    apply restitution:
    if (newPosition.y < 0)
    {
        newPosition.y = 0;
        newVelocity.y = -newVelocity.y * restitution;
    }
```

```csharp
        // Update the transform and velocity for the next cycle
        transform.position = newPosition;
        velocity = newVelocity;
    }

    // Method to add external forces to the puzzle element (e.g.,
    ↪   user interaction)
    public void ApplyForce(Vector3 force)
    {
        netForce += force;
    }

    // Compute kinetic energy using E_k = 1/2 * m * |v|^2
    public float ComputeKineticEnergy()
    {
        return 0.5f * mass * velocity.sqrMagnitude;
    }

    // Compute potential energy relative to the floor using E_p = m
    ↪   * g * h
    public float ComputePotentialEnergy()
    {
        // Using absolute value of gravity in the y-direction and
        ↪   current height
        return mass * Mathf.Abs(gravity.y) * transform.position.y;
    }
}

public class PuzzleManager : MonoBehaviour
{
    public PuzzleState CurrentState = PuzzleState.Inactive;
    public PuzzleElement[] puzzleElements;

    // Threshold to decide when the system is at rest (puzzle
    ↪   solved)
    public float energyThreshold = 0.1f;

    void Start()
    {
        // Automatically find all PuzzleElement instances if not
        ↪   assigned via the Inspector
        if (puzzleElements == null || puzzleElements.Length == 0)
        {
            puzzleElements = FindObjectsOfType<PuzzleElement>();
        }
        // Activate the puzzle upon starting
        CurrentState = PuzzleState.Active;
    }

    void FixedUpdate()
    {
        // Evaluate the overall energy in the puzzle by summing
        ↪   kinetic and potential energies
```

436

```
float totalEnergy = 0f;
foreach (PuzzleElement element in puzzleElements)
{
    totalEnergy += element.ComputeKineticEnergy() +
        element.ComputePotentialEnergy();
}

// If total energy is below a set threshold, consider the
    puzzle complete
if (CurrentState == PuzzleState.Active && totalEnergy <
    energyThreshold)
{
    CurrentState = PuzzleState.Complete;
    Debug.Log("Puzzle Completed! Total Energy: " +
        totalEnergy);
}
}

// Example method mapping a physical event to a logical state
    transition.
// This simulates the Gamma function: :    ×    → , where    is
    physical state,
//    represents user-induced events, and    corresponds to puzzle
    states.
public void HandlePuzzleEvent(GameObject triggeringObject)
{
    if (CurrentState == PuzzleState.Inactive)
    {
        CurrentState = PuzzleState.Active;
        Debug.Log("Puzzle Activated by event from: " +
            triggeringObject.name);
    }
}
}
```

Summary: This comprehensive C# code snippet demonstrates the integration of physics-based equations and algorithms used in VR puzzle implementations. It covers the simulation of rigid body dynamics using Newton's second law ($F = m*a$) and kinematic integration ($x(t+t) = x(t) + v(t)t + 0.5*a(t)t^2$), constrained by a spring-damper model. The code also computes kinetic and potential energy for assessing system stability and implements a simple puzzle state machine that transitions based on energy thresholds and external events.

Chapter 58

Scripting Object-Based Storytelling in VR

Object-Centric Narrative Constructs

Within immersive virtual environments, objects are endowed with narrative significance by serving as both repositories and transmitters of story elements. Each interactive object is assigned a set of intrinsic properties that encode narrative cues, enabling the object to function as an autonomous narrative agent. The design of these objects requires a synthesis of physical simulation and symbolic representation. In this paradigm, objects are not merely passive elements but are instead imbued with state information that evolves according to the interplay of physics and scripted narrative logic. The assignment of narrative significance to discrete entities facilitates a distributed storytelling framework, wherein the serendipitous interactions between objects yield emergent narrative sequences.

Environmental Cue Integration

The confluence of physical interactions and ambient environmental cues establishes a multidimensional narrative space that extends beyond isolated objects. Environmental cues such as lighting gradients, acoustic modulations, and dynamic spatial textures are orchestrated to reinforce the narrative state encoded by interactive objects. Mathematically, this relationship can be conceptualized by defining a mapping function

$$\phi : \mathcal{O} \to \mathcal{E},$$

where $\mathcal{O}$ represents the space of interactive objects and $\mathcal{E}$ denotes the corresponding environmental cue domain. The integration of these two informational streams cultivates a layered narrative experience in which the environment serves as an active participant, dynamically reacting to changes in object states and, in turn, exerting an influence on the narrative trajectory.

Mechanisms of Dynamic Narrative Propagation

Narrative propagation within virtual reality is driven by a set of mechanisms that govern the progression from one narrative state to another. Central to this approach is the establishment of a state-based model that captures both the deterministic aspects of physical interactions and the discretionary narrative transitions induced by those interactions. In this context, a finite state machine is employed where the state transition function

$$\delta : \mathcal{S} \times \mathcal{I} \to \mathcal{S}$$

maps the current narrative state $\mathcal{S}$ and a set of interaction events $\mathcal{I}$ to a subsequent narrative state. The execution of narrative scripts is thus synchronized with the evolution of the physical simulation, ensuring that each object interaction triggers a corresponding update in the narrative framework. This mechanism necessitates the concurrent management of both continuous physical processes and discrete narrative transitions.

Formal Modeling of Narrative Dynamics

The formalization of narrative dynamics involves the construction of mathematical models that capture the evolution of story elements as a function of interactive inputs. Let $\mathcal{N}$ denote the narrative state space and $\mathcal{I}$ represent the set of interaction events generated by both user actions and environmental perturbations. The narrative progress is then described by a function

$$\Gamma : \mathcal{N} \times \mathcal{I} \to \mathcal{N},$$

which encapsulates the transition rules governing narrative evolution. This formulation permits a rigorous analysis of narrative coherence, where the integration of physical simulation with logical state progression is scrutinized through energy conservation principles and temporal evolution equations. For example, the modulation of narrative intensity over time may be expressed as

$$T(\tau) = \int_{\tau_0}^{\tau} \eta(t)\, dt,$$

with $\eta(t)$ representing a temporal modulation function that adjusts the pacing of narrative delivery according to dynamic environmental and interaction-based triggers. Such formal models provide a foundation for achieving a harmonious blend of story and interactivity, ensuring that the emergence of narrative threads is both systematic and responsive.

Interaction Semantics and Contextual Modifiers

A critical aspect of object-based storytelling lies in the semantic enrichment of interactive events through contextual modifiers. Each object within the narrative framework is associated with modifiers that are sensitive to the contextual parameters of the virtual environment. These modifiers, mathematically characterized by the function

$$\Lambda : \mathcal{C} \times \mathcal{O} \to \mathcal{N},$$

where $\mathcal{C}$ signifies a structured set of contextual states and $\mathcal{O}$ the space of interactive objects, serve to recalibrate narrative outcomes based on prevailing situational dynamics. The nuanced interplay between object states and their ambient context fosters an adaptive narrative structure, one that evolves continuously as environmental variables shift. In this respect, the semantics of each interaction are not static but are instead modulated by a confluence of physical states, contextual awareness, and predetermined narrative logic, resulting in a rich tapestry of narrative progression that is both coherent and multifaceted.

C# Code Snippet

```csharp
using System;
using System.Collections.Generic;

namespace VRNarrative
{
    // Enumerations representing narrative states and interaction
    //   events.
    public enum NarrativeState
    {
        Initial,
        RisingAction,
        Climax,
        FallingAction,
        Conclusion
    }

    public enum InteractionEvent
    {
        None,
        Touch,
        Grab,
        Release,
        Trigger
    }

    // Class representing interactive objects that carry narrative
    //   significance.
    public class InteractiveObject
    {
        public int Id { get; set; }
        public string Name { get; set; }
        public double NarrativeIntensity { get; set; } // Intrinsic
        //   intensity factor

        public InteractiveObject(int id, string name, double
        //   intensity)
        {
            Id = id;
            Name = name;
            NarrativeIntensity = intensity;
        }
    }

    // Class representing environmental cues resulting from object
    //   properties.
    public class EnvironmentCue
    {
        public double Lighting { get; set; }
        public double SoundLevel { get; set; }
        public double SpatialTexture { get; set; }
```

```csharp
    public EnvironmentCue(double lighting, double sound, double
    ↪   texture)
    {
        Lighting = lighting;
        SoundLevel = sound;
        SpatialTexture = texture;
    }
}

// Class representing the structured context for mapping
↪   interaction semantics.
public class Context
{
    public double AmbientNoise { get; set; }
    public double Brightness { get; set; }

    public Context(double ambientNoise, double brightness)
    {
        AmbientNoise = ambientNoise;
        Brightness = brightness;
    }
}

// Static class encapsulating the narrative modeling functions.
public static class NarrativeModel
{
    // Mapping function :   →  , converts an interactive object
    ↪   into an environment cue.
    public static EnvironmentCue Phi(InteractiveObject obj)
    {
        // Example: derive environmental lighting, sound level,
        ↪   and spatial texture based
        // on the object's narrative intensity.
        double lighting = Math.Min(1.0, obj.NarrativeIntensity +
        ↪   0.3);
        double soundLevel = Math.Max(0.0, obj.NarrativeIntensity
        ↪   - 0.2);
        double spatialTexture = 0.5 * obj.NarrativeIntensity;
        return new EnvironmentCue(lighting, soundLevel,
        ↪   spatialTexture);
    }

    // Finite state machine transition function : S × I → S.
    public static NarrativeState Delta(NarrativeState
    ↪   currentState, InteractionEvent evt)
    {
        switch (currentState)
        {
            case NarrativeState.Initial:
                if (evt == InteractionEvent.Touch)
                    return NarrativeState.RisingAction;
                break;
```

442

```
            case NarrativeState.RisingAction:
                if (evt == InteractionEvent.Grab)
                    return NarrativeState.Climax;
                break;
            case NarrativeState.Climax:
                if (evt == InteractionEvent.Release)
                    return NarrativeState.FallingAction;
                break;
            case NarrativeState.FallingAction:
                if (evt == InteractionEvent.Trigger)
                    return NarrativeState.Conclusion;
                break;
            default:
                break;
        }
        // No state change if conditions are not met.
        return currentState;
}

// Narrative progression function :  × I → .
// Here it leverages the deterministic state transition
↪   defined in Delta.
public static NarrativeState Gamma(NarrativeState
↪   currentNarrative, InteractionEvent evt)
{
    return Delta(currentNarrative, evt);
}

// Temporal modulation function T() = [,] (t) dt.
// Uses numerical integration (trapezoidal rule) to simulate
↪   temporal evolution.
public static double TemporalModulation(double tau0, double
↪   tau, Func<double, double> eta)
{
    int steps = 100;
    double dt = (tau - tau0) / steps;
    double integral = 0.0;
    for (int i = 0; i < steps; i++)
    {
        double t = tau0 + i * dt;
        double tNext = t + dt;
        integral += 0.5 * (eta(t) + eta(tNext)) * dt;
    }
    return integral;
}

// Interaction semantics function :  ×  → .
// Maps contextual parameters and object properties to a
↪   narrative outcome.
public static string Lambda(Context ctx, InteractiveObject
↪   obj)
{
```

```csharp
        double modifier = (ctx.Brightness + (1.0 -
        ↪   ctx.AmbientNoise)) / 2.0;
        double adjustedIntensity = obj.NarrativeIntensity *
        ↪   modifier;
        if (adjustedIntensity < 0.3)
            return "Subdued narrative";
        else if (adjustedIntensity < 0.7)
            return "Moderate narrative";
        else
            return "Intense narrative";
    }
}

// A sample driver class to demonstrate the integration of these
↪   narrative systems.
public class NarrativeDriver
{
    public static void Main(string[] args)
    {
        // Create an interactive object with assigned narrative
        ↪   intensity.
        InteractiveObject obj = new InteractiveObject(1,
        ↪   "Ancient Relic", 0.6);

        // Map the interactive object to its corresponding
        ↪   environmental cues using .
        EnvironmentCue envCue = NarrativeModel.Phi(obj);
        Console.WriteLine("Environmental Cue => Lighting:
        ↪   {0:F2}, Sound Level: {1:F2}, Spatial Texture:
        ↪   {2:F2}",
                        envCue.Lighting, envCue.SoundLevel,
                        ↪   envCue.SpatialTexture);

        // Initialize the narrative state.
        NarrativeState currentState = NarrativeState.Initial;
        Console.WriteLine("Initial Narrative State: " +
        ↪   currentState);

        // Simulate a sequence of user/environment interaction
        ↪   events.
        List<InteractionEvent> events = new
        ↪   List<InteractionEvent>
        {
            InteractionEvent.Touch,
            InteractionEvent.Grab,
            InteractionEvent.Release,
            InteractionEvent.Trigger
        };

        foreach (var evt in events)
        {
            NarrativeState newState =
            ↪   NarrativeModel.Gamma(currentState, evt);
```

444

```
            Console.WriteLine("Event: {0} transitions narrative
            ↪  from {1} to {2}", evt, currentState, newState);
            currentState = newState;
        }

        // Compute the temporal modulation T() over the interval
        ↪  [0, 10]
        // using a sample temporal modulation function (t) = 0.1
        ↪  + 0.05 * sin(t).
        double tau0 = 0.0;
        double tau = 10.0;
        double narrativePacing =
        ↪  NarrativeModel.TemporalModulation(tau0, tau, t =>
        ↪  0.1 + 0.05 * Math.Sin(t));
        Console.WriteLine("Narrative pacing (integrated
        ↪  intensity) over time: {0:F2}", narrativePacing);

        // Compute the narrative outcome based on contextual
        ↪  modifiers .
        Context ctx = new Context(0.4, 0.8);
        string narrativeOutcome = NarrativeModel.Lambda(ctx,
        ↪  obj);
        Console.WriteLine("Narrative Outcome based on context
        ↪  and object: " + narrativeOutcome);
    }
  }
}
```

Chapter 59

Creating Interactive Tutorials within VR Environments

Architectural Constructs for In-VR Tutorials

In immersive virtual reality systems, the design of tutorial constructs is integrated into the core architecture of the environment. The system architecture is conceived as a tightly coupled network of interactive modules, wherein tutorial components are embedded as first-class entities. This integration obviates the need for extrinsic instructional overlays by fostering an environment in which guidance is inherent to the spatial and interactive design. The architecture is predicated on a modular design philosophy where each tutorial element is instantiated as a dynamic stateful object. These objects interface with the underlying simulation pipeline through well-defined data buses, ensuring that tutorial prompts are contextually synchronized with the unfolding scene dynamics. The intrinsic modularity permits the decentralized activation of tutorial segments, whereby the activation function $\psi : \mathcal{M} \to \mathcal{T}$ maps scene modules $\mathcal{M}$ to specific tutorial states $\mathcal{T}$.

446

Mechanisms of Engagement in Tutorial Interactions

The efficacy of in-VR tutorials rests on the deployment of engagement-driven mechanisms that leverage the spatial and sensory affordances of the virtual environment. Engagement is typically elicited through well-placed trigger zones, haptic feedback, and dynamic auditory cues that correspond to user interactions. The design framework formulates these mechanisms as part of a stimulus-response system, where the mapping function $\phi : \mathcal{I} \to \mathcal{E}$ associates discrete user interactions $\mathcal{I}$ with multisensory feedback events $\mathcal{E}$. This function is calibrated to ensure that each interactive action not only serves as a learning opportunity but also reinforces the tutorial narrative. By embedding these mechanisms directly within the 3D space, the tutorial system transforms passive instruction into an active learning process, thereby enhancing cognitive absorption through multi-modal sensory integration.

Contextual Prompting and Adaptive Cue Integration

The delivery of tutorial content is inherently dependent on the contextual state of the virtual environment. Contextual prompting is achieved by continuously monitoring environmental parameters such as lighting variations, spatial dimensions, and ambient acoustics. These parameters form a multidimensional contextual vector $\mathbf{c} \in \mathbb{R}^n$, which is used to modulate the presentation of prompts. The adaptive cue integration function $\Lambda : \mathcal{C} \times \mathcal{U} \to \mathcal{P}$ dynamically translates the current contextual state $\mathcal{C}$ and user interaction profile $\mathcal{U}$ into a set of instructional prompts $\mathcal{P}$. This function ensures that the timing, intensity, and modality of tutorial messages correspond with the evolving state of the environment and the user's immediate actions. The mathematical formalism provides a robust mechanism for maintaining instructional relevance and consistency throughout the tutorial experience.

Dynamic State Transitions in Tutorial Flow

The progression of an in-VR tutorial is governed by a dynamic state-transition model that encapsulates both deterministic processes and user-induced variability. Each tutorial segment is defined as a discrete state within a finite state machine, where the state space $\mathcal{S}$ evolves based on external events and internal triggers. The state transition function $\delta : \mathcal{S} \times \mathcal{E} \rightarrow \mathcal{S}$ formalizes the conditions under which the tutorial system transitions from one state to the next. This model accommodates the inherent nonlinearity and unpredictability of user behavior, ensuring that the tutorial adapts its course in a manner that is both context-sensitive and temporally coherent. The interplay between pre-defined scripted transitions and real-time interaction events fosters a fluid instructional progression, wherein the tutorial narrative evolves synchronously with the dynamics of the virtual environment.

Quantitative Analysis and Theoretical Modeling of Tutorial Dynamics

A rigorous quantitative framework underpins the theoretical modeling of interactive tutorial systems within VR environments. The evolution of tutorial dynamics can be represented by a continuous-time model, wherein the tutorial intensity function $P(t)$ is formulated as an integral of a time-dependent modulation function $\eta(t)$. Specifically, the accumulated tutorial prompt intensity over a time interval $[t_0, t]$ is expressed as

$$P(t) = \int_{t_0}^{t} \eta(\tau) \, d\tau.$$

This formulation facilitates the analysis of temporal pacing and instructional density, enabling the calibration of tutorial flow based on user engagement metrics. Additionally, perturbative analysis of the state-transition dynamics, described by the function δ, allows for the precise quantification of state stability and the responsiveness of tutorial prompts. By employing this mathematical apparatus, the tutorial system achieves a high degree of fidelity in the synchronization between environmental stimuli, user actions, and the instructional narrative.

C# Code Snippet

```csharp
using System;
using System.Collections.Generic;

namespace VRTutorial
{
    // Enumeration representing discrete tutorial states.
    public enum TutorialState
    {
        NotStarted,
        Intro,
        Intermediate,
        Completed
    }

    // Enumeration for types of user interactions.
    public enum InteractionType
    {
        Move,
        Grab,
        Look,
        Touch
    }

    // Enumeration for types of feedback events.
    public enum FeedbackEvent
    {
        Visual,
        Audio,
        Haptic
    }

    // Class representing a module within the VR scene.
    public class SceneModule
    {
        public string ModuleName { get; set; }

        public SceneModule(string name)
        {
            ModuleName = name;
        }
    }

    // Class representing user profile data.
    public class UserProfile
    {
        public string UserID { get; set; }
        // Additional user parameters can be added here.
    }

    // Class representing the environmental context.
```

```csharp
public class ContextState
{
    public float Lighting { get; set; }
    public float AmbientNoise { get; set; }

    public ContextState(float lighting, float ambientNoise)
    {
        Lighting = lighting;
        AmbientNoise = ambientNoise;
    }
}

// The main TutorialManager that integrates the core tutorial
↪   algorithms.
public class TutorialManager
{
    // Current state of the tutorial.
    private TutorialState currentState;
    // Starting time of the tutorial session.
    private DateTime startTime;
    // Accumulated tutorial prompt intensity P(t) from t0 to t.
    private double promptIntensity;

    public TutorialManager()
    {
        currentState = TutorialState.NotStarted;
        startTime = DateTime.Now;
        promptIntensity = 0.0;
    }

    // Activation function :  →
    // Maps a scene module to a corresponding tutorial state.
    public TutorialState ActivateModule(SceneModule module)
    {
        if (module.ModuleName.Contains("Intro"))
            currentState = TutorialState.Intro;
        else if (module.ModuleName.Contains("Intermediate"))
            currentState = TutorialState.Intermediate;
        else
            currentState = TutorialState.Completed;

        return currentState;
    }

    // Engagement mapping function :  →
    // Maps a user interaction () to a feedback event ().
    public FeedbackEvent
    ↪   MapInteractionToFeedback(InteractionType interaction)
    {
        switch (interaction)
        {
            case InteractionType.Move:
                return FeedbackEvent.Audio;
```

```
        case InteractionType.Grab:
            return FeedbackEvent.Haptic;
        case InteractionType.Look:
            return FeedbackEvent.Visual;
        case InteractionType.Touch:
            return FeedbackEvent.Haptic;
        default:
            return FeedbackEvent.Visual;
    }
}

// Adaptive cue integration function :   ×   →
// Generates an instructional prompt based on the context ()
↪   and user profile ().
public string AdaptiveCueIntegration(ContextState context,
↪   UserProfile user)
{
    if (context.Lighting < 0.5f)
        return "Environment is dim. Increase light for
        ↪   better visibility.";
    else if (context.AmbientNoise > 0.7f)
        return "High ambient noise detected. Consider using
        ↪   noise-cancelling headphones.";
    else
        return "Environment is optimal for the tutorial.";
}

// State transition function :   ×   →
// Updates the tutorial state based on the current state and
↪   feedback event.
public TutorialState UpdateState(FeedbackEvent feedback)
{
    if (currentState == TutorialState.Intro && feedback ==
    ↪   FeedbackEvent.Audio)
        currentState = TutorialState.Intermediate;
    else if (currentState == TutorialState.Intermediate &&
    ↪   feedback == FeedbackEvent.Haptic)
        currentState = TutorialState.Completed;

    return currentState;
}

// Updates the tutorial prompt intensity.
// P(t) = [t0 to t] () d
// Here, we simulate integration using a simple discrete
↪   summation.
public void UpdatePromptIntensity(double eta, double
↪   deltaTime)
{
    promptIntensity += eta * deltaTime;
}

public double GetPromptIntensity()
```

```csharp
{
    return promptIntensity;
}

// Simulates the in-VR tutorial workflow.
public void SimulateTutorial()
{
    Console.WriteLine("Initial Tutorial State: " +
    ↪  currentState);

    // Activate a module using the activation function .
    SceneModule module = new SceneModule("IntroModule");
    ActivateModule(module);
    Console.WriteLine("Module Activated. Current State: " +
    ↪  currentState);

    // Simulate a user interaction and map it to
    ↪  corresponding feedback ().
    FeedbackEvent feedback =
    ↪  MapInteractionToFeedback(InteractionType.Move);
    Console.WriteLine("Feedback Event from Interaction: " +
    ↪  feedback);

    // Update state based on the feedback ().
    UpdateState(feedback);
    Console.WriteLine("State after Feedback: " +
    ↪  currentState);

    // Demonstrate adaptive cue integration () with current
    ↪  context and user profile.
    ContextState context = new ContextState(0.3f, 0.2f);
    UserProfile user = new UserProfile { UserID =
    ↪  "VRUser001" };
    string prompt = AdaptiveCueIntegration(context, user);
    Console.WriteLine("Adaptive Prompt: " + prompt);

    // Simulate integration of tutorial prompt intensity
    ↪  over time,
    // using time-dependent modulation function (t) = 0.5 +
    ↪  0.1*t.
    double simulationTime = 5.0; // Total simulation time in
    ↪  seconds.
    double timeStep = 0.5;        // Time step in seconds.
    for (double current = 0.0; current < simulationTime;
    ↪  current += timeStep)
    {
        double eta = 0.5 + current * 0.1; // Modulation
        ↪  function (t)
        UpdatePromptIntensity(eta, timeStep);
    }
    Console.WriteLine("Accumulated Tutorial Prompt
    ↪  Intensity: " + GetPromptIntensity());
}
```

```
    }

    // Program entry point for simulation.
    class Program
    {
        static void Main(string[] args)
        {
            TutorialManager tutorialManager = new TutorialManager();
            tutorialManager.SimulateTutorial();
        }
    }
}
```

Summary: This comprehensive C# code snippet demonstrates a
modular VR tutorial system by implementing core equations and
algorithms from the chapter. It includes functions for mapping
scene modules to tutorial states (), converting user interactions
to feedback events (), integrating adaptive cues based on context
and user profile (), performing state transitions (), and simulating
the prompt intensity integration $P(t)$ over time. The code effectively mirrors the theoretical models and algorithms discussed in
the chapter.

Chapter 60

Scripting Gesture-Based Commands and Shortcuts

Foundational Concepts in Gesture Recognition Systems

The implementation of gesture recognition systems in interactive environments is based on the systematic interpretation of human motion data. Various input modalities, typically acquired from optical sensors and inertial measurement devices, provide continuous data streams that are processed and converted into abstract representations. Formally, a mapping function

$$\Gamma : \mathcal{D} \to \mathcal{G}$$

is defined, where $\mathcal{D}$ denotes the space of raw sensor data and $\mathcal{G}$ represents the set of gesture classes. This function is central to translating physical movements into discrete commands, enabling the activation of shortcuts and procedural triggers in a computational system.

Mathematical Formulation and Signal Pre-processing

The fidelity of gesture recognition is highly dependent on the pre-processing of acquired signals. Sensor data, recorded as a temporal sequence

$$\{\mathbf{x}(t)\}_{t=t_0}^{t_f},$$

is subjected to noise reduction, normalization, and smoothing operations. These procedures are encapsulated in a transformation operator

$$\Psi : \mathcal{X} \to \mathcal{X}',$$

with $\mathcal{X}$ representing the original data space and $\mathcal{X}'$ the denoised and normalized signal space. Such preprocessing is requisite to attenuate extrinsic disturbances and to enhance the signal characteristics that are pertinent to gesture dynamics.

Feature Extraction and Temporal Analysis

Critical to the gesture recognition pipeline is the extraction of discriminative features from preprocessed signals. This process maps each segment of the signal to a high-dimensional feature vector within

$$\mathcal{F} \subseteq \mathbb{R}^n.$$

The extraction function

$$\Phi : \mathcal{X}' \to \mathcal{F}$$

incorporates statistical, spectral, and temporal attributes such as velocity, acceleration, and orientation differentials. Temporal segmentation further refines this process, isolating contiguous intervals that correspond to complete gesture events. The precision of feature extraction contributes significantly to the overall system accuracy by capturing the nuances of gestural motion.

Classification Algorithms and Command Binding

Following feature extraction, classification algorithms are employed to map feature vectors to specific gesture labels. This mapping is formalized by a classification function

$$\Theta : \mathcal{F} \to \mathcal{C},$$

where $\mathcal{C}$ constitutes the set of commands and shortcuts. The classification process leverages supervised learning techniques, involving the training of models on labeled data sets to differentiate between subtle variations in gesture execution. Robust classifiers, whether based on kernel methods, decision boundaries, or deep learning architectures, enable the system to reliably distinguish among a wide range of gestures. Each recognized gesture is thereby bound to a corresponding command, facilitating an intuitive control mechanism for triggering shortcuts in the interactive environment.

System Integration and Interaction Latency Optimization

The integration of a gesture recognition subsystem into a broader interactive framework necessitates careful design to minimize latency in command activation. The overall response time

$$T_{\text{response}} = T_{\text{acquisition}} + T_{\text{processing}} + T_{\text{command}}$$

comprises the sensor data acquisition, the computational processing, and the final command execution phases. Optimization strategies involve parallel signal processing, hardware acceleration, and streamlined scheduler architectures. Such methodologies ensure that gesture-induced commands are executed with temporal precision, thereby maintaining the seamless interaction experience demanded by real-time systems.

Robustness and Adaptability in Gesture-Based Interaction

Robust interaction systems must accommodate the inherent variability in human motion and environmental conditions. To address this, adaptive mechanisms are integrated into the gesture recognition framework. The iterative refinement of the mapping function is represented by the update equation

$$\Gamma_{\text{new}} = \Gamma_{\text{prev}} + \alpha \cdot \Delta\Gamma,$$

where α is an adaptation coefficient and $\Delta\Gamma$ quantifies the error correction between predicted and observed gestural patterns. This adaptive process, which may incorporate probabilistic confidence measures and threshold-based decision criteria, enhances the system's ability to operate reliably under diverse conditions. As a result, the gesture recognition framework achieves a high degree of robustness, ensuring that intuitive commands and shortcuts are activated accurately and efficiently.

C# Code Snippet

```csharp
using System;
using System.Collections.Generic;

namespace VRGestureRecognition
{
    // Gesture classes are mapped as follows:
    //    SwipeLeft   --> -1
    //    Tap         -->  0
    //    SwipeRight  -->  1
    public enum GestureClass
    {
        SwipeLeft = -1,
        Tap = 0,
        SwipeRight = 1
    }

    public enum Command
    {
        None,
        Shortcut_OpenMenu,
        Shortcut_CloseMenu,
        Shortcut_Select
    }

    // Represents a single sensor data sample.
    public class SensorData
    {
        public double TimeStamp { get; set; }
        public double Acceleration { get; set; }
        public double Velocity { get; set; }
        public double Orientation { get; set; }
```

457

```csharp
}

// GestureRecognizer encapsulates the entire processing
↪   pipeline.
// It implements:
//   - Transformation operator (): PreprocessData converts raw
↪   data () to preprocessed signals (')
//   - Feature extraction (): ExtractFeatures maps preprocessed
↪   data (') to feature space (  )
//   - Classification (): ClassifyGesture maps feature vectors
↪   () to gesture classes ()
//   - Adaptive update for the mapping function (_new = _prev +
↪   ·)
//   - Response time computation: T_response = T_acquisition +
↪   T_processing + T_command
public class GestureRecognizer
{
    // Represents the parameters of the mapping function .
    // For illustrative purposes, we model  as a weight vector.
    private double[] gamma;
    private double adaptationCoefficient = 0.1;

    public GestureRecognizer(int featureLength)
    {
        gamma = new double[featureLength];
        // Initialize gamma parameters (for demo, starting at
        ↪   zero).
        for (int i = 0; i < gamma.Length; i++)
        {
            gamma[i] = 0.0;
        }
    }

    // Transformation operator : Preprocess raw sensor data.
    public List<SensorData> PreprocessData(List<SensorData>
    ↪   rawSensorData)
    {
        var processedData = new List<SensorData>();
        foreach (var data in rawSensorData)
        {
            processedData.Add(new SensorData
            {
                TimeStamp = data.TimeStamp,
                Acceleration = Normalize(data.Acceleration),
                Velocity = Normalize(data.Velocity),
                Orientation = Normalize(data.Orientation)
            });
        }
        return processedData;
    }

    // Simple normalization function (dummy implementation).
    private double Normalize(double value)
```

458

```csharp
{
    // Assuming a known range [0, 10] for normalization.
    return Math.Min(1.0, Math.Max(0.0, value / 10.0));
}

// Feature extraction operator : Compute a feature vector
↪   from preprocessed data.
// Here we calculate the average acceleration, velocity, and
↪   orientation.
public double[] ExtractFeatures(List<SensorData>
↪   processedData)
{
    double sumAcc = 0.0, sumVel = 0.0, sumOrient = 0.0;
    int count = processedData.Count;
    if (count == 0) return new double[] { 0, 0, 0 };

    foreach (var data in processedData)
    {
        sumAcc += data.Acceleration;
        sumVel += data.Velocity;
        sumOrient += data.Orientation;
    }
    return new double[] { sumAcc / count, sumVel / count,
    ↪   sumOrient / count };
}

// Classification function : Map features to a gesture
↪   class.
// This simple linear classifier uses a dot product between
↪   gamma () and the feature vector.
public GestureClass ClassifyGesture(double[] features)
{
    double score = 0.0;
    for (int i = 0; i < features.Length && i < gamma.Length;
    ↪   i++)
    {
        score += gamma[i] * features[i];
    }

    // Threshold-based classification logic.
    if (score > 1.5)
        return GestureClass.SwipeRight;
    if (score < -1.5)
        return GestureClass.SwipeLeft;
    return GestureClass.Tap;
}

// Bind each recognized gesture to a corresponding command.
public Command BindGestureToCommand(GestureClass gesture)
{
    switch (gesture)
    {
        case GestureClass.SwipeRight:
```

```
                return Command.Shortcut_OpenMenu;
            case GestureClass.SwipeLeft:
                return Command.Shortcut_CloseMenu;
            case GestureClass.Tap:
                return Command.Shortcut_Select;
            default:
                return Command.None;
        }
    }


    // Adaptive update implements:
    //   _new = _prev +  *  ,
    // where  is computed from the error between predicted and
    // ↪  actual gestures.
    public void AdaptiveUpdate(double[] features, GestureClass
    ↪  predictedGesture, GestureClass actualGesture)
    {
        double[] deltaGamma = new double[features.Length];
        // Compute error (difference between integer
        // ↪  representations).
        int error = (int)actualGesture - (int)predictedGesture;

        // Adjust gamma parameters proportionally to the feature
        // ↪  values and error.
        for (int i = 0; i < features.Length; i++)
        {
            deltaGamma[i] = error * features[i];
            gamma[i] = gamma[i] + adaptationCoefficient *
            ↪  deltaGamma[i];
        }
    }


    // Calculates the overall response time:
    //   T_response = T_acquisition + T_processing + T_command
    public double CalculateResponseTime(double acquisitionTime,
    ↪  double processingTime, double commandTime)
    {
        return acquisitionTime + processingTime + commandTime;
    }
}

// Program demonstrates the end-to-end gesture recognition
// ↪  pipeline.
public class Program
{
    public static void Main()
    {
        // Simulate sensor data acquisition with dummy values.
        List<SensorData> rawData = new List<SensorData>
        {
            new SensorData { TimeStamp = 0.0, Acceleration =
            ↪  2.0, Velocity = 3.0, Orientation = 5.0 },
```

460

```
                        new SensorData { TimeStamp = 0.1, Acceleration =
                        ↪   2.2, Velocity = 3.1, Orientation = 5.1 },
                        new SensorData { TimeStamp = 0.2, Acceleration =
                        ↪   1.9, Velocity = 2.9, Orientation = 4.9 }
                };

                // Initialize the recognizer with a feature vector of
                ↪   length 3.
                GestureRecognizer recognizer = new
                ↪   GestureRecognizer(featureLength: 3);

                // Preprocess raw sensor data (:  → ').
                List<SensorData> processedData =
                ↪   recognizer.PreprocessData(rawData);

                // Extract features from the processed data (: ' →   ).
                double[] features =
                ↪   recognizer.ExtractFeatures(processedData);

                // Classify the gesture (:  → ).
                GestureClass recognizedGesture =
                ↪   recognizer.ClassifyGesture(features);

                // Bind the gesture to an interactive command.
                Command command =
                ↪   recognizer.BindGestureToCommand(recognizedGesture);

                // Output the recognized gesture and bound command.
                Console.WriteLine("Recognized Gesture: " +
                ↪   recognizedGesture);
                Console.WriteLine("Bound Command: " + command);

                // Simulate a scenario in which the actual gesture is
                ↪   SwipeRight.
                GestureClass actualGesture = GestureClass.SwipeRight;
                recognizer.AdaptiveUpdate(features, recognizedGesture,
                ↪   actualGesture);

                // Measure overall response time.
                double t_acquisition = 0.05;  // seconds
                double t_processing = 0.1;    // seconds
                double t_command = 0.02;      // seconds
                double responseTime =
                ↪   recognizer.CalculateResponseTime(t_acquisition,
                ↪   t_processing, t_command);
                Console.WriteLine("Response Time: " + responseTime + "
                ↪   seconds");
        }
    }
}
```

Chapter 61

Implementing VR Spatial Awareness Systems

Theoretical Foundations of Spatial Awareness in Virtual Environments

Spatial awareness in virtual reality is underpinned by the formalization of spatial relationships and perceptual cues within a mathematically defined three-dimensional space, denoted by $\mathcal{V} \subseteq \mathbb{R}^3$. A transformation function, $T : \mathbb{R}^3 \to \mathbb{R}^3$, is employed to map real-world coordinates into this virtual environment. The function T typically amalgamates affine transformations with nonlinear adjustments to maintain consistent relationships between depth, scale, and orientation. The representation of spatial cues relies on the integration of multiple sensory modalities into a unified coordinate framework, thereby facilitating the perception of congruent virtual surroundings.

Visual Cue Integration for Enhanced Perception

Visual cues are the primary conduit for conveying spatial information and are synthesized through a series of mathematical operations that simulate natural viewing conditions. The view projection matrix, $P \in \mathbb{R}^{4 \times 4}$, transforms three-dimensional coordinates into two-dimensional screen space while preserving depth and perspective. Stereo disparity is computed as

$$d = \frac{Bf}{z},$$

where B represents the interocular baseline, f the focal length, and z the depth of an object. This computation enhances the perception of depth by providing differential images to each eye.

Further refinement of visual spatial cues is achieved through dynamic lighting and shading algorithms. Light attenuation is modeled by functions such as

$$F(z) = e^{-\beta z},$$

where β is a tunable parameter that modulates light decay as a function of distance, z. The simulation of shadows and occlusion effects employs depth-based blending, ensuring that rendered objects exhibit realistic interactions with ambient light sources. These operations collectively generate high-fidelity visual representations that anchor the user's perception of virtual space.

Auditory Signal Processing for Spatial Localization

Auditory processing contributes a critical layer to spatial awareness by enabling the localization of sound sources through directional and temporal cues. The computation of interaural time differences (ITD) is central to this process and is mathematically given by

$$\Delta t = \frac{d}{c},$$

where d is the path length difference between the ears and c denotes the speed of sound. This measure provides a precise estimate of the azimuthal position of sound sources.

Complementing ITD, interaural level differences (ILD) are used to capture variations in sound pressure, thus reinforcing spatial differentiation of auditory stimuli. The application of head-related transfer functions (HRTFs) further refines this process by modeling the frequency-dependent filtering imposed by the head, torso, and outer ear. The convolution of incoming signals with HRTF profiles adjusts both amplitude and spectral content, thereby simulating the natural localization cues experienced in real environments. Together, these auditory signal processing techniques generate a robust three-dimensional audio landscape that aligns closely with the visual rendering of virtual spaces.

Sensor Fusion and Calibration Methodologies

The integration of visual and auditory cues into a coherent spatial framework necessitates the application of sensor fusion techniques. Multimodal data streams from cameras, audio sensors, and inertial measurement units (IMUs) are combined using probabilistic models to yield a consistent state estimate of the virtual environment. This fusion process is encapsulated by the recursive estimation equation

$$X_k = f(X_{k-1}, Z_k),$$

where X_k is the state estimate at time k, and Z_k represents the composite measurement vector.

The calibration of individual sensors is performed iteratively to mitigate inherent biases and measurement noise. Such calibration protocols commonly adopt robust statistical methods that adjust sensor outputs based on cumulative error analyses. The iterative refinement ensures that discrepancies among sensor modalities are minimized, thereby enhancing the accuracy of spatial representations. The resulting fusion framework produces a deterministic mapping of multimodal inputs to a spatial awareness model that supports real-time interaction.

Evaluation of Spatial Awareness Metrics

Quantitative assessment of spatial awareness systems is achieved through the formulation of metrics that compare rendered spatial cues against predetermined reference standards. One commonly employed measure is the Euclidean distance error, defined as

$$\delta = \sqrt{(x_r - x_e)^2 + (y_r - y_e)^2 + (z_r - z_e)^2},$$

where (x_r, y_r, z_r) are the coordinates produced by the VR system and (x_e, y_e, z_e) represent the expected positions derived from controlled spatial models.

In addition to positional accuracy, temporal response differentials and variance analyses of auditory localization are computed to evaluate the robustness of the spatial awareness framework. These statistical evaluations, carried out over large datasets, facilitate the optimization of rendering pipelines and calibration procedures. The integration of these quantitative metrics ensures that the spatial cues provided by the system are both precise and consistent across a diverse range of virtual scenarios.

C# Code Snippet

```csharp
using System;
using System.Numerics;

namespace VRProgramming
{
    public class VRSpatialAwarenessSystem
    {
        // Applies an affine transformation to a 3D point using a
        //  4x4 transformation matrix.
        // This corresponds to the transformation function T: R^3 ->
        //  R^3.
        public static Vector3 ApplyTransformation(Vector3 point,
            Matrix4x4 transform)
        {
            Vector4 homogeneousPoint = new Vector4(point, 1.0f);
            Vector4 transformed =
                Vector4.Transform(homogeneousPoint, transform);
            if (Math.Abs(transformed.W) > 1e-5)
                return new Vector3(transformed.X, transformed.Y,
                    transformed.Z) / transformed.W;
            return new Vector3(transformed.X, transformed.Y,
                transformed.Z);
        }

        // Projects a 3D point into 2D screen space using a given
        //  view projection matrix.
        // This simulates the view projection operation: P in
        //  R^(4x4).
        public static Vector2 ProjectToScreen(Vector3 point,
            Matrix4x4 projectionMatrix)
        {
            Vector4 homogeneousPoint = new Vector4(point, 1.0f);
            Vector4 projected = Vector4.Transform(homogeneousPoint,
                projectionMatrix);
```

```csharp
    if (Math.Abs(projected.W) > 1e-5)
    {
        return new Vector2(projected.X / projected.W,
        ↪  projected.Y / projected.W);
    }
    return new Vector2(projected.X, projected.Y);
}


// Computes stereo disparity using the equation: d = (B * f)
↪  / z.
// B : interocular baseline, f : focal length, z : depth.
public static double ComputeStereoDisparity(double baseline,
↪  double focalLength, double depth)
{
    if (Math.Abs(depth) < 1e-5)
        throw new ArgumentException("Depth must be non-zero
        ↪  for stereo disparity calculation.");
    return (baseline * focalLength) / depth;
}


// Models light attenuation using the formula: F(z) =
↪  exp(-beta * z).
public static double LightAttenuation(double beta, double z)
{
    return Math.Exp(-beta * z);
}


// Computes the interaural time difference (ITD) using the
↪  equation: t = d / c.
// d : path length difference between ears, c : speed of
↪  sound.
public static double ComputeITD(double pathDifference,
↪  double speedOfSound)
{
    if (Math.Abs(speedOfSound) < 1e-5)
        throw new ArgumentException("Speed of sound must be
        ↪  non-zero for ITD calculation.");
    return pathDifference / speedOfSound;
}


// A simple sensor fusion update algorithm:
// X_k = X_{k-1} + alpha * (Z_k - X_{k-1}).
// Here, alpha is a blending factor that adjusts the weight
↪  of the new measurement.
public static Vector3 SensorFusionUpdate(Vector3
↪  previousState, Vector3 measurement, float alpha = 0.5f)
{
    return previousState + alpha * (measurement -
    ↪  previousState);
}


// Calculates the Euclidean distance error between rendered
↪  and expected positions.
```

466

```csharp
// = sqrt[(x_r - x_e)^2 + (y_r - y_e)^2 + (z_r - z_e)^2].
public static double ComputeEuclideanError(Vector3 rendered,
↪    Vector3 expected)
{
    return Vector3.Distance(rendered, expected);
}

// Main method demonstrating the computations.
public static void Main(string[] args)
{
    // Example parameters for stereo disparity.
    double baseline = 0.065;        // In meters (typical
    ↪    interocular distance)
    double focalLength = 1.2;       // Focal length in
    ↪    arbitrary units
    double depth = 2.0;             // Depth of the object in
    ↪    meters
    double stereoDisparity =
    ↪    ComputeStereoDisparity(baseline, focalLength,
    ↪    depth);
    Console.WriteLine("Stereo Disparity: " +
    ↪    stereoDisparity);

    // Example for light attenuation.
    double beta = 0.1;
    double attenuation = LightAttenuation(beta, depth);
    Console.WriteLine("Light Attenuation: " + attenuation);

    // Example for interaural time difference (ITD)
    ↪    calculation.
    double pathDifference = 0.1;    // In meters
    double speedOfSound = 343.0;    // Speed of sound in
    ↪    m/s
    double itd = ComputeITD(pathDifference, speedOfSound);
    Console.WriteLine("Interaural Time Difference (ITD): " +
    ↪    itd);

    // Sensor fusion update example.
    Vector3 previousState = new Vector3(1.0f, 2.0f, 3.0f);
    Vector3 measurement = new Vector3(1.5f, 2.5f, 3.5f);
    Vector3 fusedState = SensorFusionUpdate(previousState,
    ↪    measurement);
    Console.WriteLine("Fused State: " + fusedState);

    // Euclidean error calculation example.
    Vector3 renderedPosition = new Vector3(1.0f, 1.0f,
    ↪    1.0f);
    Vector3 expectedPosition = new Vector3(1.2f, 0.8f,
    ↪    1.1f);
    double error = ComputeEuclideanError(renderedPosition,
    ↪    expectedPosition);
    Console.WriteLine("Euclidean Distance Error: " + error);
```

```csharp
// Demonstrate coordinate transformation.
Matrix4x4 transformation =
    Matrix4x4.CreateTranslation(0.5f, 1.0f, 1.5f) *
    Matrix4x4.CreateFromYawPitchRoll(0.1f, 0.2f, 0.3f);
Vector3 originalPoint = new Vector3(2.0f, 3.0f, 4.0f);
Vector3 transformedPoint =
    ApplyTransformation(originalPoint, transformation);
Console.WriteLine("Transformed Point: " +
    transformedPoint);

// Demonstrate projecting a 3D point to 2D screen space.
Matrix4x4 projectionMatrix =
    Matrix4x4.CreatePerspectiveFieldOfView((float)Math.PI
    / 4, 16.0f / 9.0f, 0.1f, 100.0f);
Vector2 screenPoint = ProjectToScreen(originalPoint,
    projectionMatrix);
Console.WriteLine("Projected Screen Point: " +
    screenPoint);
        }
    }
}
```

Summary: The above C# code integrates key mathematical models and algorithms for VR spatial awareness. It includes functions for coordinate transformation, stereo disparity computation, light attenuation modeling, auditory localization via ITD, sensor fusion state updating, and Euclidean distance error computation for evaluating spatial cues. This modular implementation provides a clear reference for incorporating spatial cues within immersive VR environments.

Chapter 62

Scripting Environment-Based Feedback Mechanisms

Theoretical Foundations of Environmental Feedback

The formulation of environment-based feedback mechanisms is grounded in established principles of control theory and dynamic systems. In this context, a feedback system is conceptualized as a closed-loop structure where user actions, denoted by an input signal $u(t)$, are mapped to modifications in environmental cues, represented by a response function $r(t)$. The feedback loop is mathematically modeled by relationships of the form

$$r(t) = f\big(u(t), S(t)\big),$$

where $S(t)$ encapsulates the state of the virtual environment. The function f is typically non-linear, incorporating a range of control parameters that are tuned to ensure a reactive yet stable system. Such systems benefit from robustness provided by continuous monitoring and calibration of sensory signals, ensuring that variations in user behavior elicit highly contextualized visual or auditory responses.

Visual Feedback Mechanisms

Visual feedback is implemented by dynamically altering graphical properties within the virtual environment in response to external stimuli. The system modifies parameters such as brightness, contrast, hue, and saturation through a sequence of transformations that are applied in real time. For instance, the control variable $I(t)$ representing light intensity may be modeled by an attenuating exponential function of the form

$$I(t) = I_0 \, e^{-\gamma t},$$

where I_0 is the initial intensity and γ is a damping coefficient that reflects the speed of the intensity decay following a user action. Additional transformations incorporate spatial modulation by employing projection matrices that alter the perspective and shadowing effects. These matrices, denoted by $P \in \mathbb{R}^{4 \times 4}$, ensure that depth cues, occlusion effects, and reflective dynamics converge to simulate a realistic and responsive illumination model. This visual modulation mechanism is intricately linked with the rendering pipeline, demanding precise synchronization between scene graph updates and real-time user interaction.

Auditory Feedback Mechanisms

The auditory component of environmental feedback leverages spatial sound synthesis and dynamic sound cue modulation to reinforce immersive experiences. Sound cues are generated and processed using models that account for directionality, intensity, and temporal variation. A fundamental principle in auditory feedback design involves the computation of interaural time differences (ITD), formulated as

$$\Delta t = \frac{d}{c},$$

where d represents the differential path length to the ears and c is the speed of sound. This computation enables the system to spatialize sound sources effectively. In parallel, amplitude modulation follows an attenuation curve, typically modeled by

$$A(r) = A_0 \, e^{-\beta r},$$

with A_0 being the source amplitude, β the attenuation constant, and r the relative distance from the source. The integration of head-related transfer functions (HRTFs) further refines the auditory feedback by accounting for the spectral filtering effects imposed by the head and external ear geometry. These combined methods yield a dynamic audio landscape that is sensitive to both the spatial and temporal dimensions of user interactions.

Temporal Dynamics and Adaptive Calibration

Temporal dynamics are central to ensuring that environmental feedback appears immediate and contextually appropriate. Time-dependent activation functions, $a(t)$, modulate the strength and evolution of both visual and auditory cues. These functions are often derived from differential equations describing the decay or amplification of feedback signals. For example, an adaptive response may be defined by

$$\frac{da(t)}{dt} = -\lambda\,a(t) + g\big(u(t)\big),$$

where λ controls the rate of decay and $g(u(t))$ represents a function mapping instantaneous user actions to variations in feedback intensity. The calibration of such models is performed through iterative methods that minimize error deviations between intended feedback outputs and the actual responses observed in the environment. This recursive calibration process ensures that the system remains sensitive to changes in interface dynamics and user context, allowing for adaptive adjustments that maintain high levels of immersion.

Quantitative Metrics and Evaluation of Feedback Systems

Evaluation of environment-based feedback systems necessitates rigorous quantitative metrics that capture both the spatial and temporal accuracy of the responses. One widely utilized metric is the Euclidean error measurement, given by

$$\delta = \sqrt{(v_r - v_e)^2},$$

where v_r is the vector of rendered feedback parameters and v_e is the expected parameter vector derived from the theoretical model.

In addition, temporal performance is evaluated by measuring the latency τ between the occurrence of a user action and the onset of the feedback response. These evaluations are integrated into a composite performance index, defined as

$$\Phi = \omega_1\,\delta + \omega_2\,\tau,$$

where ω_1 and ω_2 are weight factors that balance spatial accuracy and temporal responsiveness. Such metrics allow for systematic analysis and optimization of the feedback mechanism, ensuring that environmental cues are finely tuned to reinforce the immersive qualities of the virtual environment.

C# Code Snippet

```csharp
using System;
using UnityEngine;

namespace VRProgramming
{
    // FeedbackSystem integrates visual and auditory
    ↪   environment-based feedback methods,
    // while also handling temporal dynamics and performance
    ↪   evaluation.
    public class FeedbackSystem : MonoBehaviour
    {
        // -----------------------
        // Visual Feedback Parameters
        // -----------------------
        // I0 in I(t) = I0 * exp(- * t)
        public float initialIntensity = 1.0f;
        //   is the damping coefficient
        public float visualDamping = 0.5f;
        private float currentIntensity;

        // -----------------------
        // Auditory Feedback Parameters
        // -----------------------
        // A0 in A(r) = A0 * exp(- * r)
        public float sourceAmplitude = 1.0f;
        //   is the attenuation constant for audio feedback
        public float attenuationConstant = 0.2f;
        // Speed of sound (c) in meters per second
        public float speedOfSound = 343.0f;

        // -----------------------
        // Temporal Dynamics Parameters
        // -----------------------
```

```
// Lambda in da/dt = - * a(t) + g(u(t)), where we assume
↪   g(u) = u(t)
public float lambdaDecay = 1.0f;
private float feedbackActivation = 0.0f;

// ----------------------
// Evaluation Metrics Parameters
// ----------------------
// Expected feedback value used for calculating the spatial
↪   error,
public float expectedFeedbackValue = 1.0f;
private float renderedFeedbackValue;
// Weight factors for spatial error (1) and latency (2)
public float omega1 = 0.7f;
public float omega2 = 0.3f;
// Feedback latency () measured in seconds
public float feedbackLatency = 0.0f;

// -------------------- ----
// Simulation Variables
// ----------------------
// Represents user actions, u(t)
private float userInput = 0.0f;
// Represents the state of the environment, S(t)
private float environmentState = 1.0f;

// ----------------------
// Unity Update Method
// ----------------------
void Update()
{
    float deltaTime = Time.deltaTime;

    // Simulate user input (for instance, u(t) = sin(t))
    userInput = Mathf.Sin(Time.time);

    // Update visual feedback based on the exponential decay
    ↪   model
    UpdateVisualFeedback(deltaTime);

    // Update auditory feedback (simulate interaural time
    ↪   difference and amplitude modulation)
    UpdateAuditoryFeedback();

    // Update temporal dynamics of the system using Euler
    ↪   integration of the differential equation
    UpdateTemporalDynamics(deltaTime);

    // Evaluate overall feedback performance based on
    ↪   spatial error and latency metrics
    float performanceIndex = EvaluateFeedback();
```

```csharp
        // Debug log the computed feedback parameters for
        ↪   monitoring purposes
        Debug.Log($"Visual Intensity: {currentIntensity:F3}, " +
                $"Auditory Amplitude:
                ↪   {ComputeAuditoryAmplitude(5.0f):F3}, " +
                $"Feedback Activation:
                ↪   {feedbackActivation:F3}, " +
                $"Performance Index: {performanceIndex:F3}");
    }

    // -----------------------
    // Visual Feedback: I(t) = I0 * exp(- * t)
    // -----------------------
    void UpdateVisualFeedback(float deltaTime)
    {
        // For demonstration, using deltaTime as the elapsed
        ↪   time since the last update.
        currentIntensity = initialIntensity *
        ↪   Mathf.Exp(-visualDamping * deltaTime);
    }

    // -----------------------
    // Auditory Feedback Methods
    // -----------------------
    // Update auditory feedback by computing interaural delay.
    ↪   Additional audio processing would use this value.
    void UpdateAuditoryFeedback()
    {
        // Simulate a distance difference for interaural time
        ↪   computation
        float simulatedDistanceDifference = 0.3f; // in meters
        float interauralDelay = ComputeInterauralTimeDifference(
        simulatedDistanceDifference);
        // In a full implementation, interauralDelay would
        ↪   influence audio spatialization.
    }

    // Computes auditory amplitude based on distance:
    // A(r) = A0 * exp(- * r)
    float ComputeAuditoryAmplitude(float distance)
    {
        return sourceAmplitude * Mathf.Exp(-attenuationConstant
        ↪   * distance);
    }

    // Computes interaural time difference:
    // t = d / c, where d is the distance difference and c is
    ↪   the speed of sound.
    float ComputeInterauralTimeDifference(float
    ↪   distanceDifference)
    {
        return distanceDifference / speedOfSound;
    }
```

```
// ------------------------
// Temporal Dynamics: Feedback Activation
// ------------------------
// Implements: da/dt = - * a(t) + g(u(t))
// Using Euler integration with g(u(t)) assumed to be a
// ↪  direct mapping of u(t).
void UpdateTemporalDynamics(float deltaTime)
{
    float derivative = -lambdaDecay * feedbackActivation +
    ↪  userInput;
    feedbackActivation += derivative * deltaTime;
}


// ------------------------
// Performance Evaluation Metric
// ------------------------
// Evaluates overall system performance:
// = 1 *  + 2 * , where  = |renderedFeedback -
// ↪  expectedFeedback|
float EvaluateFeedback()
{
    renderedFeedbackValue = feedbackActivation;
    float spatialError = Mathf.Abs(renderedFeedbackValue -
    ↪  expectedFeedbackValue);
    float performanceIndex = omega1 * spatialError + omega2
    ↪  * feedbackLatency;
    return performanceIndex;
}


// ------------------------
// Projection Matrix Modifier (Example for Visual
// ↪  Transformations)
// ------------------------
// Applies rotation and scaling to a projection matrix to
// ↪  simulate spatial modulations.
Matrix4x4 GetProjectionMatrixModifier(Matrix4x4
↪  originalMatrix)
{
    Matrix4x4 rotation =
    ↪  Matrix4x4.Rotate(Quaternion.Euler(10f, 20f, 30f));
    Matrix4x4 scaling = Matrix4x4.Scale(new Vector3(1.1f,
    ↪  1.1f, 1.1f));
    return originalMatrix * rotation * scaling;
}
}
}
```

Chapter 63

Integrating Real-Time Data into VR Scenes

Overview of Real-Time Data Streams in Virtual Reality

Real-time data integration into virtual reality environments constitutes a paradigm in which continuously updated external signals influence the state of a virtual scene. In such systems, temporal data streams denoted by $D(t)$ are injected into the state space $S(t)$ of the virtual environment. This injection is governed by a mapping function $\phi : D(t) \to S(t)$ that encapsulates domain-specific transformation rules. The process supports dynamic scene updates by enabling modifications in visual, auditory, and interaction modalities as a function of live input. This approach creates a continuously evolving virtual experience that mirrors real-world data variabilities through rigorous mathematical and computational models.

Data Acquisition and Preprocessing

The integration begins with the systematic collection of live data from heterogeneous sources such as sensor networks, user input devices, and external service APIs. Data acquired via these means can be represented as a time-dependent signal $x(t)$, often subject to noise and variable sampling frequencies. Preprocessing techniques are applied to obtain a refined estimate $\hat{x}(t)$ from the raw input, expressed mathematically as

$$\hat{x}(t) = F\big(x(t)\big),$$

where F is a filtering operator designed to mitigate noise and interpolate missing data points. This stage ensures that the incoming data maintains a sufficient level of fidelity, thereby providing reliable inputs for subsequent scene integration processes.

Dynamic Scene Updating and Data-Driven Interactions

Subsequent to preprocessing, the refined data stream triggers modifications within the virtual scene. The process of dynamic scene updating is characterized by a state transition function

$$T : S(t) \times \hat{x}(t) \rightarrow S(t + \Delta t),$$

where Δt represents a discrete time increment. This function facilitates modifications to environmental attributes—such as object positioning, lighting intensities, and interaction parameters—by systematically mapping data values to visual and auditory adjustments. The design of T is aimed at ensuring that transitions appear smooth and are coherent with the pre-existing scene, thereby preserving immersive properties while adapting to live data inputs.

Architectural Considerations for Data-Driven VR Systems

A robust framework for real-time data integration necessitates a modular architecture that partitions responsibilities across distinct functional layers. At the foundational layer, a data acquisition module continuously retrieves and preprocesses live inputs. An intermediate processing layer then computes the transformation function T, decoupling raw data from scene manipulation. Finally, a rendering engine consumes the updated scene state $S(t + \Delta t)$, ensuring that visual and auditory outputs reflect the integrated data. This layered architecture may be formally represented by the composition

$$S(t + \Delta t) = R \circ T \circ F\big(x(t)\big),$$

where R denotes the rendering operation. Such a modular design not only accommodates scalability but also permits independent optimization of each component to maintain system performance even under fluctuating data loads.

Synchronization and Latency Management

The fidelity of real-time data integration is critically dependent on the synchronization of data acquisition and scene updates. Latency τ, defined as

$$\tau = t_r - t_d,$$

with t_d representing the timestamp of data acquisition and t_r the time at which the scene is updated, must be minimized to sustain responsiveness. Techniques for latency reduction include implementing efficient buffering mechanisms, asynchronous processing pipelines, and optimized network protocols for data transmission. Ensuring temporal coherence between data input and scene updates safeguards the integrity of the virtual experience, thereby aligning rapid environmental changes with the intrinsic dynamics of the incoming data.

Mathematical Models for Adaptive Data Integration

The adaptive integration of real-time data within VR scenes can be modeled mathematically by differential equations that describe the evolution of the scene state. A representative model is given by

$$\frac{dS}{dt} = F\big(D(t), S(t)\big),$$

where the operator F encapsulates the combined influence of live data inputs and the internal dynamics of the environment. Linearization of this model around equilibrium points allows for stability analysis via the eigenvalues of the Jacobian matrix associated with F. Advanced methods, including adaptive control strategies and predictive algorithms, can be incorporated to continuously refine F, thereby compensating for data inconsistencies and fluctuations. These mathematical frameworks provide a rigorous foundation for the design of VR systems that are capable of dynamic, data-driven scene transformations.

C# Code Snippet

```csharp
using System;
using System.Diagnostics;
using System.Threading;

namespace VRRealTimeDataIntegration
{
    // Represents the state of the VR scene, encapsulating
    // ↪  parameters such as object position and lighting intensity.
    public class SceneState
    {
        public float ObjectPosition { get; set; }
        public float LightingIntensity { get; set; }

        public SceneState(float objectPosition = 0f, float
        ↪  lightingIntensity = 1f)
        {
            ObjectPosition = objectPosition;
            LightingIntensity = lightingIntensity;
        }

        public override string ToString()
        {
            return $"Position: {ObjectPosition:F2}, Lighting:
            ↪  {LightingIntensity:F2}";
        }
    }

    // Simulates real-time data acquisition from external sources.
    public class DataAcquisition
    {
        private Random rand = new Random();

        // Simulates a time-dependent sensor reading (x(t)).
        public float AcquireData()
        {
            // Generate a random sensor value in the range [0, 10].
            return (float)(rand.NextDouble() * 10.0);
        }
    }

    // Applies a filtering operator F on raw data x(t) to produce a
    // ↪  refined signal ^x(t).
    public class DataFilter
    {
        private float previousFilteredValue = 0f;
        private readonly float alpha; // Low-pass filter
        ↪  coefficient.

        public DataFilter(float alpha = 0.5f)
        {
```

```
        this.alpha = alpha;
    }

    // Implements: ~x(t) = F(x(t)) = alpha*x(t) +
    ↪  (1-alpha)*previousFilteredValue
    public float FilterData(float rawData)
    {
        float filtered = alpha * rawData + (1 - alpha) *
        ↪  previousFilteredValue;
        previousFilteredValue = filtered;
        return filtered;
    }
}


// Responsible for computing the scene transition.
// Implements the state transition function T : S(t) x ~x(t) ->
↪  S(t + t)
public class SceneTransition
{
    // Updates the current scene state based on the filtered
    ↪  data and elapsed time (t).
    public SceneState UpdateScene(SceneState currentState, float
    ↪  filteredData, float deltaTime)
    {
        // For demonstration: integrate position and adjust
        ↪  lighting.
        float newPosition = currentState.ObjectPosition +
        ↪  filteredData * deltaTime;
        // Example transformation: lighting intensity is
        ↪  modulated based on the data value.
        float newLighting = 1.0f + 0.1f * filteredData;
        // Clamp the lighting intensity between 0.5 and 2.0.
        newLighting = Math.Max(0.5f, Math.Min(newLighting,
        ↪  2.0f));

        return new SceneState(newPosition, newLighting);
    }
}

// Simulated rendering engine which acts as the rendering
↪  operation R.
public class Renderer
{
    public void Render(SceneState state)
    {
        // In a real VR system, this would update the visual
        ↪  scene.
        Console.WriteLine("Rendering Scene State: " +
        ↪  state.ToString());
    }
}
```

```
// Integrates all components to perform data-driven scene
↪  updates.
// The overall process is represented by: S(t+t) = R  T  F(x(t))
public class VRSystem
{
    private DataAcquisition dataAcquisition = new
    ↪  DataAcquisition();
    private DataFilter dataFilter = new DataFilter(alpha: 0.6f);
    private SceneTransition sceneTransition = new
    ↪  SceneTransition();
    private Renderer renderer = new Renderer();
    private SceneState currentState = new SceneState();
    private Stopwatch stopwatch = new Stopwatch();

    // Runs the VR system simulation for a specified number of
    ↪  iterations.
    public void Run(int iterations, float deltaTime)
    {
        Console.WriteLine("Starting VR Real-Time Data
        ↪  Integration...\n");
        stopwatch.Start();

        for (int i = 0; i < iterations; i++)
        {
            // Acquire timestamp of data capture (t_d)
            long acquisitionTime =
            ↪  stopwatch.ElapsedMilliseconds;

            // Acquire raw data x(t) from sensor
            float rawData = dataAcquisition.AcquireData();

            // Filter raw data to obtain refined signal ~x(t)
            float filteredData = dataFilter.FilterData(rawData);

            // Update the scene using the transition function T
            ↪  and integrate differential equation dS/dt =
            ↪  F(D(t), S(t))
            currentState =
            ↪  sceneTransition.UpdateScene(currentState,
            ↪  filteredData, deltaTime);

            // Capture timestamp after scene update (t_r)
            long renderTime = stopwatch.ElapsedMilliseconds;
            long latency = renderTime - acquisitionTime; //  =
            ↪  t_r - t_d

            // Render the scene with the updated state.
            renderer.Render(currentState);
            Console.WriteLine($"Raw Data: {rawData:F2}, Filtered
            ↪  Data: {filteredData:F2}, Latency (ms):
            ↪  {latency}\n");

            // Pause to simulate frame time based on deltaTime.
```

```
        Thread.Sleep((int)(deltaTime * 1000));
    }

    stopwatch.Stop();
    Console.WriteLine("VR Real-Time Data Integration
    ↪  Completed.");
  }
}

// Program entry point.
class Program
{
    static void Main(string[] args)
    {
        // Create a VR system instance and run the simulation.
        VRSystem vrSystem = new VRSystem();
        // Example: Run for 10 iterations with a time step t =
        ↪  0.1 seconds.
        vrSystem.Run(iterations: 10, deltaTime: 0.1f);
    }
  }
}
```

Summary: The above C# code implements a comprehensive simulation of a data-driven VR scene update system. It models the process of real-time data acquisition, signal filtering ($F(x(t)) = \hat{x}(t)$), scene state transition ($T: S(t) \times \hat{x}(t) \rightarrow S(t+t)$), and rendering ($R$), while also accounting for latency management. This code demonstrates how mathematical models and real-time algorithms can be integrated into a VR environment, fulfilling the key equations and strategies outlined in the chapter.

Chapter 64

Scripting Adaptive User Interfaces in VR

Theoretical Foundations of Adaptive User Interfaces

Within immersive virtual reality systems, adaptive user interfaces are construed as dynamic constructs that recalibrate in response to variations in user behavior and environmental context. The operational premise of such interfaces is predicated on a mapping from observable user interactions and context-dependent variables to a continuously evolving interface state. Let $U(t)$ denote a vector that encapsulates user behavioral metrics at time t, and let $C(t)$ represent the concurrent contextual parameters extracted from the virtual environment. The adaptive mapping function, defined as

$$A : (U(t), C(t)) \rightarrow I(t),$$

embodies the transformative operator which modulates interface elements to align with user needs and situational demands. This formalism establishes a theoretical framework that underpins the design and implementation of adaptive interfaces, ensuring that interface adjustments remain both perceptible and functional within a continuously changing spatial context.

User Behavior and Contextual Modeling

1 Behavioral Dynamics in Immersive Environments

The quantification of user behavior within virtual reality necessitates a rigorous model wherein interaction metrics are continuously acquired and analyzed. The state vector $U(t)$ is constructed from a variety of measurable parameters, including but not limited to gaze tracking, gesture recognition, and locomotion patterns. These components are mathematically modeled as time-varying signals, allowing for a comprehensive assessment of user engagement and intent. Such measurements facilitate the identification of patterns that drive the adaptive mechanisms inherent to the interface, thereby enabling the system to anticipate user actions and alter the perceptual layout in real time.

2 Contextual Cues and Environmental Dynamics

The term $C(t)$ constitutes an aggregate of contextual cues that are instrumental in shaping the adaptive user interface. These cues comprise environmental factors such as spatial orientation, ambient lighting, and the positional attributes of interactive elements within the virtual scene. A formal representation of the composite context is achieved by aggregating these distinct signals into a coherent vector that informs the adaptive mapping process. The integration of $C(t)$ with $U(t)$ permits a nuanced modulation of interface parameters, which in turn facilitates an adaptive behavior that is sensitive to both the situational context and the intricacies of user interaction dynamics.

Algorithmic Frameworks for Adaptive UI Scripting

1 Mathematical Formalization of Adaptive Mappings

Algorithmic approaches to adaptive user interfaces are rigorously defined through mathematical mappings that translate user and contextual data into an interface configuration. The functional relationship

$$I(t) = A\left(U(t), C(t)\right),$$

may be decomposed into constituent sub-functions, each addressing linear or non-linear characteristics of the adaptive process. Linear models often serve as an initial approximation due to their computational efficiency, whereas non-linear components incorporate higher-order interactions that capture the complex dependencies between $U(t)$ and $C(t)$. Such compositions are iteratively refined through feedback mechanisms that monitor discrepancies between intended and actual interface behaviors, thereby optimizing the function A over successive iterations.

2 Optimization Strategies and Adaptive Algorithmic Design

Optimization within adaptive UI systems is achieved through the deployment of iterative refinement techniques and adaptive algorithms designed to converge upon an optimal interface state. Strategies such as gradient descent, adaptive filtering, and reinforcement learning are employed to systematically adjust parameters within the mapping function A. These methods aim to minimize the error in the predicted versus desired interface outcomes, thereby enhancing system responsiveness and user satisfaction. The seamless integration of these algorithmic approaches is vital for achieving a balance between computational tractability and the fidelity of adaptive responses within immersive environments.

Architectural Integration and Modular Design Considerations

1 Component-Based Architecture for Dynamic UI Elements

The implementation of adaptive user interfaces within a virtual reality framework benefits significantly from a component-based architectural paradigm. This modular design approach segregates the responsibilities of data acquisition, adaptive computation, and rendering into distinct yet interrelated subsystems. Each component operates autonomously, processing inputs from $U(t)$ and $C(t)$

to generate an intermediate interface state before forwarding the result to the rendering module. This decoupling not only enhances system scalability but also permits targeted optimization of individual components, leading to a robust and flexible design capable of accommodating complex adaptive behaviors.

2 Data Flow Pipelines and Interface Update Mechanisms

The seamless operation of adaptive user interfaces is contingent upon the efficient flow of data through a series of well-defined pipeline stages. Initially, real-time inputs corresponding to $U(t)$ and $C(t)$ are subjected to preprocessing and normalization, thereby ensuring consistency in the adaptive computations that follow. The subsequent stage involves the application of the mapping function A, with the interface state being iteratively updated to reflect the latest input data. This process can be formally expressed as

$$I(t + \Delta t) = R\left(A\left(U(t), C(t)\right)\right),$$

where R denotes the rendering operation and Δt represents the discrete update interval. The hierarchical structure of the data flow pipeline is instrumental in achieving a high degree of responsiveness, while simultaneously maintaining the spatial coherence and usability of the interface.

Performance Considerations in Adaptive User Interfaces

1 Temporal Responsiveness and Latency Minimization

The efficacy of adaptive user interfaces in virtual reality is critically dependent upon the minimization of system latency. The temporal delay τ, defined as

$$\tau = t_{\text{update}} - t_{\text{acquisition}},$$

must be constrained to ensure that user interface adjustments occur in synchrony with real-time behavioral and contextual changes.

Techniques for latency reduction include the optimization of adaptive algorithms and the implementation of parallel processing strategies within the rendering pipeline, ensuring that adaptation remains both timely and perceptually seamless.

2 Scalability and Resource Optimization in Adaptive Systems

Scalability within adaptive user interface systems hinges on the judicious management of computational resources, particularly as the complexity of user behavior and environmental dynamics increases. Resource optimization strategies typically involve simplifying the adaptive mapping function A through the use of approximative models and prioritization of critical user interface elements. By dynamically adjusting the granularity of adaptive responses based on real-time performance metrics, the system is able to maintain an optimal balance between computational load and the quality of user interaction, thereby preserving the inherent benefits of adaptivity in immersive virtual environments.

C# Code Snippet

```csharp
using UnityEngine;

public class AdaptiveUIController : MonoBehaviour
{
    // Dimension for user and context vectors
    private const int vectorLength = 3;

    // User behavior metrics U(t)
    private float[] userMetrics;
    // Contextual parameters C(t)
    private float[] contextParameters;
    // Computed interface state I(t)
    private float[] interfaceState;

    // Weights for the mapping function A: I(t)= userWeights * U(t)
    //    + contextWeights * C(t)
    private float[] userWeights;
    private float[] contextWeights;

    // Learning rate for gradient descent optimization
    public float learningRate = 0.01f;

    // Desired interface state for optimization target
    private float[] targetInterfaceState;
```

```
void Start()
{
    userMetrics = new float[vectorLength];
    contextParameters = new float[vectorLength];
    interfaceState = new float[vectorLength];
    userWeights = new float[vectorLength];
    contextWeights = new float[vectorLength];
    targetInterfaceState = new float[vectorLength];

    // Initialize arrays with default values
    for (int i = 0; i < vectorLength; i++)
    {
        userMetrics[i] = Random.Range(0f, 1f);
        contextParameters[i] = Random.Range(0f, 1f);
        userWeights[i] = 0.5f;
        contextWeights[i] = 0.5f;
        targetInterfaceState[i] = 1.0f; // Desired target state
    }
}

void Update()
{
    // Update dynamic input data
    UpdateUserMetrics();
    UpdateContextParameters();

    // Compute interface state I(t) using mapping function:
    // I(t) = A(U(t), C(t)) = userWeights * U(t) +
    ↪    contextWeights * C(t)
    ComputeInterfaceState();

    // Render the updated interface state (R operation)
    RenderInterface();

    // Optimize adaptive mapping using gradient descent to
    ↪    reduce error
    OptimizeAdaptiveMapping();
}

// Simulate obtaining real-time user behavior metrics U(t)
void UpdateUserMetrics()
{
    for (int i = 0; i < vectorLength; i++)
    {
        // Using PingPong to simulate oscillating user behavior
        ↪    values with time
        userMetrics[i] = Mathf.PingPong(Time.time * 0.1f + i,
        ↪    1.0f);
    }
}
```

```
// Simulate obtaining real-time environmental context parameters
↪   C(t)
void UpdateContextParameters()
{
    for (int i = 0; i < vectorLength; i++)
    {
        // Using sine function to simulate smoothly changing
        ↪   environmental factors
        contextParameters[i] = Mathf.Abs(Mathf.Sin(Time.time *
        ↪   0.1f + i));
    }
}

// Compute interface state I(t) based on the adaptive mapping A:
// I(t) = A(U(t), C(t)) = (userWeights * U(t)) + (contextWeights
↪   * C(t))
void ComputeInterfaceState()
{
    for (int i = 0; i < vectorLength; i++)
    {
        interfaceState[i] = userWeights[i] * userMetrics[i] +
        ↪   contextWeights[i] * contextParameters[i];
    }
}

// Render the interface state (simulating the R operation from
↪   I(t + t) = R(A(U(t), C(t))))
void RenderInterface()
{
    // For demonstration, log the interface state values.
    Debug.Log("Updated Interface State: " +
            interfaceState[0].ToString("F2") + ", " +
            interfaceState[1].ToString("F2") + ", " +
            interfaceState[2].ToString("F2"));
    // In a production system, UI elements would be updated
    ↪   accordingly.
}

// Optimize weights using a gradient descent approach to
↪   minimize the error between
// the computed interface state I(t) and a desired target state.
void OptimizeAdaptiveMapping()
{
    for (int i = 0; i < vectorLength; i++)
    {
        // Calculate error: E = I(t) - targetInterfaceState
        float error = interfaceState[i] -
        ↪   targetInterfaceState[i];
        // Update rule for weights based on gradient descent:
        // weight = -learningRate * error * (partial derivative
        ↪   with respect to the weight)
        // For userWeights, the derivative is proportional to
        ↪   userMetrics[i]
```

```
        userWeights[i] -= learningRate * error * userMetrics[i];
        // For contextWeights, the derivative is proportional to
        ↪   contextParameters[i]
        contextWeights[i] -= learningRate * error *
        ↪   contextParameters[i];
      }
    }
}
```

Summary: This C# code snippet demonstrates an adaptive user interface system within a VR environment. It models user behavior (U(t)) and context parameters (C(t)), computes an interface state (I(t)) using the mapping function A(U(t), C(t)), and updates the UI accordingly. Additionally, the code incorporates a gradient descent optimization method to iteratively refine the mapping weights, ensuring that the adaptive interface aligns with the desired state in a dynamically changing immersive context.

Chapter 65

Implementing Custom VR Animation Transitions

Fundamental Principles in Custom VR Animation Transitions

The design of custom animation transitions for virtual reality interfaces is underpinned by the necessity to achieve seamless and context-sensitive movement between discrete animation states. In the virtual environment, the animation state at any given time is represented by a multidimensional vector, denoted as $A(t)$, which encapsulates parameters such as position, orientation, scale, and potentially more complex attributes. The transition from one state $A(t_0)$ to another state $A(t_1)$ is conceptualized as a mapping governed by an interpolation function that guarantees both temporal continuity and spatial coherence. The primary objective is to ensure that transitions occur in a manner that preserves the visual fluidity and realism required in immersive environments, minimizing perceptible discontinuities that could detract from user experience.

Mathematical Formalization of Transition Mappings

A rigorous formulation of the transition process involves the definition of a transition mapping function $T : [t_0, t_1] \rightarrow \mathbb{R}^n$, where n corresponds to the number of animation parameters. An often-employed formulation is based on interpolation, in which the animation state is computed as

$$A(t) = (1 - \sigma(t)) \, A(t_0) + \sigma(t) \, A(t_1),$$

where $\sigma(t)$ is an easing function satisfying $\sigma(t_0) = 0$ and $\sigma(t_1) = 1$. This function may be linear or adopt non-linear characteristics to introduce acceleration and deceleration effects. The utilization of such easing functions is critical when delineating transitions that must appear natural and responsive, thereby reducing mechanical artifacts in rapid state changes. In this context, the precise formulation of $\sigma(t)$ is tailored to the expected dynamics of the corresponding virtual interaction.

Temporal Interpolation Techniques and Easing Functions

Temporal interpolation techniques play a pivotal role in modulating the rate of change between key animation states. Linear interpolation provides a straightforward approach, yet non-linear methods such as cubic interpolation, Hermite splines, or S-curve functions are preferable in scenarios necessitating a more nuanced representation of motion. Consider, for instance, a parameterized version of the transition function expressed as

$$S(t) = (1 - \tau(t)) \, S_0 + \tau(t) \, S_1,$$

with the normalized time parameter defined by

$$\tau(t) = \frac{t - t_0}{t_1 - t_0}.$$

When $\tau(t)$ is substituted with a non-linear easing variant, such as

$$\tau_{\text{eased}}(t) = 3\tau(t)^2 - 2\tau(t)^3,$$

the resulting animation trajectory exhibits a gradual acceleration followed by deceleration. Such transitions are particularly effective in maintaining visual consistency when the motion involves perceptibly variable speeds. A thoughtful selection of the easing function contributes substantially to the minimization of abrupt transitions, ensuring that changes in the visual display conform to principles of natural movement.

Context-Sensitive Modulation of Animation Transitions

In virtual reality, adaptation to the ambient context is essential for achieving a dynamic and responsive user experience. The introduction of contextual data into the transition mapping is realized by extending the easing function to account for external parameters, typically encapsulated within a vector $C(t)$. The adaptive transition may be expressed as

$$A(t) = (1 - \sigma'(t, C(t)))\, A(t_0) + \sigma'(t, C(t))\, A(t_1),$$

where $\sigma'(t, C(t))$ is a modified easing function that incorporates context-sensitive modulations. Elements of $C(t)$ may include metrics such as user gaze direction, velocity, and the spatial distribution of interactive objects. By allowing $\sigma'(t, C(t))$ to vary in accordance with these parameters, it becomes possible to adjust the timing and curvature of the interpolation dynamically. This consequently enables a form of feedback modulation that responds to variations in user behavior and environmental complexity, thereby ensuring that transitions are not only smooth but also appropriately calibrated to the immediate interactive context.

Integrative Approaches to Visual Fluidity and Naturalism

The synthesis of temporal interpolation and context-sensitive modulation culminates in animation transitions that enhance the overall realism and visual fluidity in virtual reality applications. Extensive attention has been devoted to the formulation of mapping functions that reconcile the inherent discrepancies between computational approximations and perceptual expectations. The ability to blend animation layers—each characterized by distinct dynamics and contextual dependencies—can be mathematically modeled through weighted summation techniques. For instance, when multiple factors influence a given transition, the overall state may be represented as a superposition of independently computed states, each modulated by its respective weight factor. These weight factors are determined by context-dependent criteria that ensure the prominence of certain animation characteristics over others, as dictated by real-time environmental feedback. The resulting composite animation trajectory exhibits a robustness that is crucial for maintaining both the temporal coherence and the aesthetic naturalism central to immersive virtual reality experiences.

C# Code Snippet

```csharp
using System;
using UnityEngine;

/// <summary>
/// Represents the state of an animation at a given moment.
/// Contains fundamental parameters such as position, rotation, and
↪   scale.
/// </summary>
public class AnimationState
{
    public Vector3 Position;
    public Quaternion Rotation;
    public Vector3 Scale;

    public AnimationState(Vector3 position, Quaternion rotation,
↪       Vector3 scale)
    {
        Position = position;
        Rotation = rotation;
        Scale = scale;
    }

    /// <summary>
    /// Linearly interpolates between two AnimationState instances.
    /// </summary>
    /// <param name="from">Starting state.</param>
    /// <param name="to">Ending state.</param>
    /// <param name="t">Interpolation factor between 0 and
↪       1.</param>
    /// <returns>The interpolated AnimationState.</returns>
    public static AnimationState Lerp(AnimationState from,
↪       AnimationState to, float t)
    {
```

```csharp
        Vector3 position = Vector3.Lerp(from.Position, to.Position,
        ↪  t);
        Quaternion rotation = Quaternion.Slerp(from.Rotation,
        ↪  to.Rotation, t);
        Vector3 scale = Vector3.Lerp(from.Scale, to.Scale, t);
        return new AnimationState(position, rotation, scale);
    }
}

/// <summary>
/// Contains easing functions to smooth the animation transitions.
/// </summary>
public static class EasingFunctions
{
    /// <summary>
    /// Linear easing function.
    /// </summary>
    public static float Linear(float t)
    {
        return t;
    }

    /// <summary>
    /// Cubic ease-in-out function: 3t^2 - 2t^3.
    /// Provides a smooth acceleration and deceleration.
    /// </summary>
    public static float CubicEaseInOut(float t)
    {
        return 3f * t * t - 2f * t * t * t;
    }
}

/// <summary>
/// Implements the interpolation algorithm for transitioning between
/// ↪  two animation states.
/// This class encapsulates the evaluation of a transition based on
/// ↪  time,
/// applying an easing function and optionally incorporating
/// ↪  context-sensitive factors.
/// </summary>
public class AnimationTransition
{
    public AnimationState StartState { get; private set; }
    public AnimationState EndState { get; private set; }
    public float StartTime { get; private set; }
    public float EndTime { get; private set; }

    // When enabled, context-sensitive modulation is applied to the
    // ↪  easing function.
    public bool UseContext { get; set; }

    /// <summary>
```

```csharp
/// Initializes the transition with given start and end states
↪    and the associated time frame.
/// </summary>
/// <param name="startState">Initial animation state
↪    A(t0).</param>
/// <param name="endState">Final animation state A(t1).</param>
/// <param name="startTime">Start time t0.</param>
/// <param name="endTime">End time t1.</param>
public AnimationTransition(AnimationState startState,
↪    AnimationState endState, float startTime, float endTime)
{
    StartState = startState;
    EndState = endState;
    StartTime = startTime;
    EndTime = endTime;
    UseContext = false;
}


/// <summary>
/// Evaluates the current animation state A(t) based on the
↪    linear interpolation formula:
/// A(t) = (1 - (t)) * A(t0) + (t) * A(t1),
/// where (t) is the easing function (here, CubicEaseInOut) that
↪    can be modulated by context.
/// </summary>
/// <param name="t">Current time.</param>
/// <param name="contextFactor">
/// An optional factor representing contextual data (e.g., user
↪    gaze, speed).
/// When UseContext is enabled, the easing value is multiplied
↪    by contextFactor.
/// </param>
/// <returns>The interpolated AnimationState at time
↪    t.</returns>
public AnimationState Evaluate(float t, float contextFactor =
↪    1.0f)
{
    if (t <= StartTime)
        return StartState;
    if (t >= EndTime)
        return EndState;

    // Normalize time parameter (t) = (t - t0) / (t1 - t0)
    float normalizedTime = (t - StartTime) / (EndTime -
↪    StartTime);

    // Apply the easing function: (t) = 3~2 - 2~3
    float easedT =
↪    EasingFunctions.CubicEaseInOut(normalizedTime);

    // If context sensitivity is enabled, modify the easing
↪    value dynamically.
    if (UseContext)
```

496

```csharp
        {
            // Clamp contextFactor to ensure reasonable modulation.
            contextFactor = Mathf.Clamp(contextFactor, 0.5f, 1.5f);
            easedT = Mathf.Clamp01(easedT * contextFactor);
        }

        // Compute the animation state A(t) by interpolating between
        ↪   A(t0) and A(t1)
        return AnimationState.Lerp(StartState, EndState, easedT);
    }
}

/// <summary>
/// Demonstrates the blending of multiple animation states through
↪   weighted summation,
/// which is a more advanced technique to combine separate animation
↪   layers.
/// </summary>
public class CompositeAnimationTransition
{
    /// <summary>
    /// Blends multiple AnimationState objects based on
    ↪   corresponding weight factors.
    /// The resulting state is a weighted sum of positions and
    ↪   scales, and a sequential blend of rotations.
    /// </summary>
    /// <param name="states">Array of animation states.</param>
    /// <param name="weights">Array of corresponding
    ↪   weights.</param>
    /// <returns>The composite blended AnimationState.</returns>
    public static AnimationState Blend(AnimationState[] states,
    ↪   float[] weights)
    {
        if (states == null || weights == null || states.Length !=
        ↪   weights.Length)
            throw new ArgumentException("States and weights must be
            ↪   non-null and have the same length.");

        Vector3 blendedPosition = Vector3.zero;
        Vector3 blendedScale = Vector3.zero;
        Quaternion blendedRotation = states[0].Rotation;

        // Sum of all weights to normalize.
        float totalWeight = 0f;
        for (int i = 0; i < weights.Length; i++)
        {
            totalWeight += weights[i];
        }
        if (totalWeight == 0f) totalWeight = 1f;

        // Normalize weights.
        for (int i = 0; i < weights.Length; i++)
        {
```

497

```
            weights[i] /= totalWeight;
        }

        // Blend positions and scales using weighted summation.
        for (int i = 0; i < states.Length; i++)
        {
            blendedPosition += states[i].Position * weights[i];
            blendedScale += states[i].Scale * weights[i];
        }

        // For rotations, perform sequential spherical linear
        ↪   interpolation.
        for (int i = 1; i < states.Length; i++)
        {
            blendedRotation = Quaternion.Slerp(blendedRotation,
            ↪   states[i].Rotation, weights[i]);
        }

        return new AnimationState(blendedPosition, blendedRotation,
        ↪   blendedScale);
    }
}

/// <summary>
/// A sample MonoBehaviour to demonstrate the use of custom VR
↪   animation transitions within a Unity scene.
/// This controller applies smooth and context-sensitive animation
↪   transitions to a target GameObject.
/// </summary>
public class VRAnimationController : MonoBehaviour
{
    // The object whose transform will be animated.
    public Transform target;

    private AnimationTransition transition;
    private float animationDuration = 2.0f;
    private float startTime;

    void Start()
    {
        // Record the current state as the starting state.
        AnimationState startState = new AnimationState(
            target.position,
            target.rotation,
            target.localScale
        );

        // Define an ending state with modified position, rotation,
        ↪   and scale.
        AnimationState endState = new AnimationState(
            target.position + new Vector3(0, 2, 0),
            Quaternion.Euler(target.rotation.eulerAngles + new
            ↪   Vector3(0, 90, 0)),
```

498

```
        target.localScale * 1.5f
    );

    startTime = Time.time;
    transition = new AnimationTransition(startState, endState,
    ↪    startTime, startTime + animationDuration);

    // Enable context-sensitive adjustment for the easing
    ↪    function.
    transition.UseContext = true;
}

void Update()
{
    float currentTime = Time.time;

    // Simulate a context factor for demonstration purposes
    ↪    (e.g., responding to user dynamics).
    float contextFactor = 1.0f + 0.5f * Mathf.Sin(Time.time);

    // Evaluate the current animation state using the defined
    ↪    transition.
    AnimationState currentState =
    ↪    transition.Evaluate(currentTime, contextFactor);

    // Apply the interpolated state to the target's transform.
    target.position = currentState.Position;
    target.rotation = currentState.Rotation;
    target.localScale = currentState.Scale;
}
}
```

Chapter 66

Integrating Core Systems to Build Immersive VR Environments

Architectural Integration Framework

The construction of a cohesive virtual reality environment mandates an architectural framework that rigorously integrates diverse core systems. A modular design paradigm is employed, wherein each component—ranging from animation and physics simulation to input handling and audio spatialization—is instantiated as an autonomous unit. The inter-component interactions are governed by clearly delineated interfaces and standardized data exchange protocols, facilitating interoperability while preserving the encapsulation of subsystem functionalities. The resulting architecture is characterized by its ability to dynamically converge discrete scripted systems and design elements into a unified operational schema, thereby ensuring that state transitions, user interactions, and environmental feedback coalesce without perceptible discontinuities.

Temporal and Spatial Synchronization Mechanisms

Central to the operation of integrated virtual environments is the synchronization of subsystems that frequently operate on disparate temporal and spatial scales. Temporal alignment is achieved by interpolating between discrete animation keyframes and state updates. For example, a generic state interpolation may be expressed mathematically as

$$S(t) = (1 - \alpha(t)) S_0 + \alpha(t) S_1,$$

where S_0 and S_1 denote the foundational and target states, respectively, and the easing parameter $\alpha(t)$ evolves continuously over the interval $t \in [t_0, t_1]$. Spatial coherence is maintained by ensuring that positional, rotational, and scaling transformations are computed within a common coordinate framework. This process demands precise calibration of update cycles across subsystems, such that the aggregate behavior of the environment adheres to deterministic and synchronously derived dynamics.

Dynamic Adaptation of Scripted Systems and Contextual Modulation

Scripted systems in immersive virtual environments are designed to be highly responsive to dynamic contextual data. The integration process incorporates feedback loops wherein environmental and user-specific parameters, represented as vectors $C(t) \in \mathbb{R}^m$, exert modulatory influence on interpolation functions. A modified transition mapping may be articulated in the form

$$A(t) = (1 - \sigma'(t, C(t))) A(t_0) + \sigma'(t, C(t)) A(t_1),$$

where $\sigma'(t, C(t))$ is a context-sensitive easing function. The modulation of transitions by external data streams ensures that the dynamic behavior of the virtual world is continuously recalibrated in response to changes in user inputs, sensor feedback, and ambient conditions. This dynamic adaptation fortifies the immersive quality of the experience by permitting real-time variation in the behavior of individual subsystems.

Interoperability of Multimedia and Interaction Subsystems

A multilayered integration of audiovisual and interactive subsystems underpins the operational realism of full-scale virtual reality environments. The audiovisual domain, encompassing both high-fidelity rendering and spatially coherent audio, is interwoven with interaction subsystems responsible for gesture recognition, object manipulation, and input event processing. Such integration is achieved through a middleware communication layer that standardizes data formats and synchronizes event propagation. The inter-system data flow is meticulously managed to prevent latency-induced inconsistencies and to preserve the perceptual continuity of sensory stimuli. This interoperability permits the simultaneous deployment of heterogeneous subsystems without the sacrifice of individual performance metrics, thereby contributing to the robustness and fidelity of the overall environment.

Optimization and Scalability in Multi-Modal System Integration

Performance optimization occupies a pivotal role in the successful integration of core virtual reality systems. The synthesized architecture must cater to the computational demands of simultaneous rendering, physics simulation, audio processing, and input handling. Techniques such as adaptive level-of-detail management, asynchronous event scheduling, and distributed processing architectures are adopted to minimize computational overhead and latency. The application of these methods is mathematically modeled by allocating discrete weight factors to each subsystem, ensuring that resource allocation is dynamically balanced during peak operational loads. The continuous monitoring of performance metrics facilitates real-time adjustments, whereby inter-component dependencies are decoupled and prioritized based on current computational bandwidth. This assiduous optimization enables the scalable deployment of immersive virtual environments while maintaining a high degree of responsiveness and operational stability.

C# Code Snippet

```csharp
using System;
using UnityEngine;

namespace VRIntegration
{
    // Utility class containing interpolation methods based on
    //     dynamic easing functions.
    public static class VRInterpolation
    {
        /// <summary>
        /// Smooth easing function using smoothstep (3t^2 - 2t^3)
        ///     for temporal interpolation.
        /// Implements: alpha(t) = 3t^2 - 2t^3.
        /// </summary>
        public static float EaseFunction(float t)
        {
            return t * t * (3f - 2f * t);
        }

        /// <summary>
        /// Interpolates between two float states using the generic
        ///     easing function.
        /// Implements: S(t) = (1 - alpha(t)) * S0 + alpha(t) * S1.
        /// </summary>
        public static float InterpolateFloat(float start, float end,
            float t)
        {
            float alpha = EaseFunction(t);
            return (1f - alpha) * start + alpha * end;
        }

        /// <summary>
        /// Computes a context-sensitive easing value.
        /// The context parameter (C(t)) modulates the transition
        ///     scale.
        /// This function simulates: sigma'(t, C(t)) =
        ///     EaseFunction(t * (1 + average(C))).
        /// </summary>
        public static float ContextualEasing(float t, float[]
            context)
        {
            float avg = 0f;
            if (context != null && context.Length > 0)
            {
                foreach (float c in context)
                {
                    avg += c;
                }
                avg /= context.Length;
            }
```

```csharp
        // Modulate t based on the average context and ensure it
        ↪  stays in [0,1]
        float modulatedT = Mathf.Clamp01(t * (1f + avg));
        return EaseFunction(modulatedT);
    }


    /// <summary>
    /// Performs interpolation with contextual modulation.
    /// Implements: A(t) = (1 - sigma'(t, C(t))) * A0 +
    ↪  sigma'(t, C(t)) * A1.
    /// </summary>
    public static float InterpolateWithContext(float start,
    ↪  float end, float t, float[] context)
    {
        float sigma = ContextualEasing(t, context);
        return (1f - sigma) * start + sigma * end;
    }


    /// <summary>
    /// Performs spatial interpolation between two Vector3
    ↪  positions using Unity's Lerp and easing.
    /// </summary>
    public static Vector3 InterpolateVector3(Vector3 start,
    ↪  Vector3 end, float t)
    {
        float alpha = EaseFunction(t);
        return Vector3.Lerp(start, end, alpha);
    }
}

// Class to simulate the integration and synchronization of
↪  diverse VR subsystems.
public class VRSystemIntegrator
{
    /// <summary>
    /// Simulates state transitions over time using both generic
    ↪  and contextual interpolation.
    /// Demonstrates temporal and spatial synchronization
    ↪  mechanisms.
    /// </summary>
    public void SimulateStateTransition()
    {
        float initialState = 0f;
        float targetState = 10f;
        float duration = 2f; // Transition duration in seconds
        float elapsed = 0f;
        // Sample context simulating sensor or user input
        ↪  values.
        float[] context = new float[] { 0.2f, 0.4f };

        // Simulation loop (in an actual Unity project, this
        ↪  would be in Update())
        while (elapsed < duration)
```

```csharp
        {
            float t = elapsed / duration; // Normalize time
            ↪  [0,1]

            // Generic state interpolation using the easing
            ↪  function.
            float currentState =
            ↪  VRInterpolation.InterpolateFloat(initialState,
            ↪  targetState, t);
            // Contextual interpolation adapting to
            ↪  environmental parameters.
            float contextualState =
            ↪  VRInterpolation.InterpolateWithContext(initialState,
            ↪  targetState, t, context);

            // Output the interpolated states (simulation of
            ↪  real-time feedback)
            Debug.Log($"Time: {elapsed:F2}s | Generic State:
            ↪  {currentState:F2} | Contextual State:
            ↪  {contextualState:F2}");

            // Simulate time progression (in production code,
            ↪  use Time.deltaTime)
            elapsed += 0.1f;
        }
    }
}

// MonoBehaviour class to demonstrate VR system integration
↪  within a Unity environment.
public class VRIntegrationDemo : MonoBehaviour
{
    private VRSystemIntegrator integrator;

    // Initialize and start the simulation.
    void Start()
    {
        integrator = new VRSystemIntegrator();
        integrator.SimulateStateTransition();
    }
}
```

www.ingramcontent.com/pod-product-compliance
Lightning Source LLC
LaVergne TN
LVHW051349050326
832903LV00030B/2900